INDIGENOUS PEOPLES INSPIRING SUSTAINABLE DEVELOPMENT

Based on nearly a decade of collaboration by leading Indigenous and non-Indigenous legal experts and researchers, *Indigenous Peoples Inspiring Sustainable Development* amplifies the guidance and wisdom of Indigenous knowledge and law, as reflected in First Nations treaties with countries. It explores the potential of these covenants to guide sustainable development opportunities in the context of evolving international and domestic legal regimes. Through comparative legal research and contextualized examples across diverse communities' and countries' accords, the volume uncovers whether and how the principles, provisions, and practices of Indigenous treaties can strengthen efforts to address pressing social, environmental, and economic challenges. Through cutting-edge insights and stories, the authors analyse how the implementation of these treaties could foster, rather than frustrate, efforts to advance the global Sustainable Development Goals (SDGs) by upholding the United Nations Declaration on the Rights of Indigenous Peoples.

Marie-Claire Cordonier Segger holds the Chair in Sustainable Development Law and Policy and is Law Fellow/Director of Studies, Lucy Cavendish College, at the University of Cambridge. She serves as Senior Director of the Centre for International Sustainable Development Law (CISDL), Vice-Chair of the UNESCO Voices of Future Generations Children's Initiative, Vice-President of the International Law Association of Canada, President of the Sustainable Development Law and Governance Association, and Adjunct Professor of Law at the University of Victoria, Canada, and is a laureate of the Weeramantry International Justice Award and a Fellow of the Royal Society of Canada.

Wayne Garnons-Williams is the Chair of the International Intertribal Trade and Investment Organization (IITIO); Chair of the National Sixties Scoop Healing Foundation of Canada; Senior Lawyer and Principal Director of Garwill Law Professional Corporation; Principal Director of the Indigenous Sovereign Trade Consultancy Ltd; Lecturer, Indigenous Entrepreneurship Program, United College, University of Waterloo; International Fellow in Comparative and Federal Indian Law (University of Oklahoma); and a Senior Legal Fellow of the CISDL.

TREATY IMPLEMENTATION FOR SUSTAINABLE DEVELOPMENT

Over the past decades, a series of international treaties have entered into force to address pressing global concerns of social and economic development and environmental protection. On climate change, biodiversity and biosafety, desertification, agriculture and seeds, and trade and investment liberalisation, regimes have been established which align with global commitments related to sustainable development, many with nearly universal membership. Successful domestic implementation of these international treaty regimes is one of the most significant challenges facing international law today. Although much has been written on the content and form of treaty law, there is relatively little that examines the transition from international legal theory and treaty texts to domestic regulation and practice.

This series of books addresses this need and provides a serious contribution to ongoing global debates by conducting a detailed analysis of how myriad new treaty regimes that cover the future's most pressing concerns can be made to work in practice.

Series Editors:

Marie-Claire Cordonier Segger

Markus Wilhelm Gehring

Volumes in the Series:

Indigenous Peoples Inspiring Sustainable Development: Implementing UNDRIP through International Law and Covenants, Marie-Claire Cordonier Segger and Wayne Garnons-Williams (2026)

CITES as a Tool for Sustainable Development, edited by Marie-Claire Cordonier Segger, Andrew Wardell, and Alexandra Harrington (2023)

Local Content and Sustainable Development in Global Energy Markets, edited by Damilola S. Olawuyi (2020)

Intergenerational Justice in Sustainable Development Treaty Implementation, edited by Marie-Claire Cordonier Segger, Marcel Szabo, and Alexandra R. Harrington (2020)

Children's Rights and Sustainable Development, Claire Fenton-Glynn (2019)

Sustainable Development, International Aviation, and Treaty Implementation, edited by Armand de Mestral, Paul Fitzgerald, and Tanveer Ahmad (2018)

NAFTA and Sustainable Development, edited by Hoi L. Kong and L. Kinvin Wroth (2018)

Sustainable Development, International Criminal Justice, and Treaty Implementation, edited by Sébastien Jodoin and Marie-Claire Cordonier Segger (2015)

Legal Aspects of Implementing the Cartagena Protocol on Biosafety, edited by Marie-Claire Cordonier Segger, Frederic Perron-Welch, and Christine Frison (2014)

Indigenous Peoples Inspiring Sustainable Development

IMPLEMENTING UNDRIP THROUGH INTERNATIONAL LAW AND COVENANTS

MARIE-CLAIRE CORDONIER SEGGER

WAYNE GARNONS-WILLIAMS

CAMBRIDGE
UNIVERSITY PRESS

CAMBRIDGE UNIVERSITY PRESS

Shaftesbury Road, Cambridge CB2 8EA, United Kingdom

One Liberty Plaza, 20th Floor, New York, NY 10006, USA

477 Williamstown Road, Port Melbourne, VIC 3207, Australia

314–321, 3rd Floor, Plot 3, Splendor Forum, Jasola District Centre, New Delhi – 110025, India

103 Penang Road, #05-06/07, Visioncrest Commercial, Singapore 238467

Cambridge University Press is part of Cambridge University Press & Assessment, a department of the University of Cambridge.

We share the University's mission to contribute to society through the pursuit of education, learning and research at the highest international levels of excellence.

www.cambridge.org
Information on this title: www.cambridge.org/9781108428965

DOI: 10.1017/9781108553889

When citing this work, please include a reference to the DOI 10.1017/9781108553889

First published 2026

A catalogue record for this publication is available from the British Library

Library of Congress Cataloging-in-Publication Data
NAMES: Cordonier Segger, Marie-Claire, 1973- author. | Garnons-Williams, Wayne, author.
TITLE: Indigenous peoples inspiring sustainable development : implementing UNDRIP through international law and covenants / Marie-Claire Cordonier Segger, University of Montreal; Wayne Garnons-Williams.
DESCRIPTION: Cambridge, United Kingdom ; New York, NY : Cambridge University Press, 2025. | Includes bibliographical references and index.
IDENTIFIERS: LCCN 2025000119 (print) | LCCN 2025000120 (ebook) | ISBN 9781108428965 (hardback) | ISBN 9781108451758 (paperback) | ISBN 9781108553889 (epub)
SUBJECTS: LCSH: Indigenous peoples (International law) | United Nations. General Assembly. Declaration on the Rights of Indigenous Peoples. | Indigenous peoples–Legal status, laws, etc. | Sustainable development–Law and legislation.
CLASSIFICATION: LCC KI30 2007 .C67 2025 (print) | LCC KI30 2007 (ebook) | DDC 341.4/852–dc23/eng/20250114
LC record available at https://lccn.loc.gov/2025000119
LC ebook record available at https://lccn.loc.gov/2025000120

ISBN 978-1-108-42896-5 Hardback

Contents

Tables

Notes on Contributors

EDITORS

Professor Dr Marie-Claire Cordonier Segger, FRSC FRSA WIJA, PhD (Cantab), DPhil (Oxon), MEM (Yale), BCL & LLB (McGill), BA Hons (UVic/Carl) is a renowned professor and jurist in international and sustainable development law. She holds the Chair in Sustainable Development Law and Policy, as law fellow in Lucy Cavendish College at the University of Cambridge. As senior director of the CISDL, she also serves as executive secretary to the United Nations Framework Convention on Climate Change (UNFCCC) Climate Law and Governance Initiative, chairs the Convention on Biological Diversity (CBD) Biodiversity Law and Governance Initiative, and vice-chairs the UNESCO Voices of Future Generations Children's Rights Initiative. At the University of Cambridge, she is a fellow of the Centre for Environment, Energy and Natural Resources Governance (CEENRG), the Lauterpacht Centre for International Law (LCIL), and the Bennett School for Public Policy. She is also vice-president of the International Law Association (ILA) of Canada and chairs the ILA Committee on International Law for the SDGs; and serves as adjunct professor of international law at the University of Victoria and the University of Waterloo, where she holds a fellowship in the Balsillie School of International Affairs (BSIA). She has published over 26 books in 4 languages; authored over 160 articles and reports; edits the Cambridge University Press book series on Implementing Treaties for Sustainable Development; and serves on the editorial boards of five law journals. Through the UN and for key Nations, she advises the negotiation and implementation of sustainable development treaties on biodiversity, climate change, natural resources, human rights and trade and investment, having served as senior legal expert to the International

Development Law Organisation (IDLO), the UNFCCC Presidency, the CBD and the Ramsar Convention on Wetlands, among other roles. She is an elected fellow of the Royal Society of Canada and the Royal Society of the Arts in the UK, and a laureate of the international Justitia Regnorum Fundamentum Award, the H.E. Judge C. G. Weeramantry International Justice Award, the Climate Law and Governance Global Leadership Award, and other honours.

Adv Wayne Garnons-Williams, BA (Windsor), LLB (Queen's), MPA (Dalhousie), LLM (Oklahoma), is the CEO of the not-for-profit registered charity, the National Sixties Scoop Healing Foundation of Canada. Adv Garnons-Williams is a lecturer at the University of Waterloo, United College, bachelor of Indigenous entrepreneurialism program. He is also the Senior Lawyer and Principal Director of the law firm Garwill Law Professional Corporation. Further, he leads an international business entitled Indigenous Sovereign Trade Consultancy Ltd. and is the founding President of the International Inter-tribal Trade and Investment Organization (IITIO), a 501 (c)(3) educational charity incorporated in Oklahoma with international representation from Australia, New Zealand, Taiwan and Canada. He is past board secretary of the Council of the Great Lakes Region, past Chair of the Federation of Saskatchewan Indian Nations Appeal Tribunal, past Chair of the National Council of Federal Aboriginal Employees and is currently on the board of directors of the International Law Association and is one of the founding members of the Working Group on Indigenous International Trade. Adv Garnons-Williams was instrumental in advising on the development of Indigenous trade policy for Canada as well as being appointed lead Canadian Indigenous negotiator for the Indigenous Peoples Economic Trade and Cooperation Arrangement (IPETCA).

Adv Garnons-Williams is also a Research Fellow specializing in International Comparative Indigenous law at the University of Oklahoma, College of Law as well as a Senior Legal Fellow for the CISDL. He is appointed by Order in Council to the NAFTA Chapter 19 Trade Remedies roster and the CUSMA Advisory Committee Member on Private Commercial Disputes, Article 31.22.

He holds the United States-Canada Law Institute Sidney J. Picker Award, the H.R.S. Ryan Law Alumni Award of Distinction from Queen's University, Faculty of Law and the Oklahoma Supreme Court Sovereignty Symposium medallion among others honours. Adv Garnons-Williams is from the Moosomin First Nation, Treaty 6.

ASSISTANT EDITOR

Adv Eva Wu, BCL & JD (McGill), Hon BSc Environment (McGill), is an Associate Fellow of the CISDL and a participant of the thirty-first Willem C. Vis International Commercial Arbitration moot, receiving an Honourable Mention for the team's Respondent Memorandum. She practices with Woods LLP, a boutique litigation and arbitration firm in Montreal. Her work prior to law has largely involved leading and advising organizations spanning the high Arctic to Antarctica. She was the 2017 Parks Canada Youth Ambassador, named Top 25 Under 25 Environmentalist by The Starfish Canada, and an Arctic Inspiration Prize laureate for North in Focus, an NGO she co-founded with Indigenous partners addressing youth suicide. Adv Wu served on the Board of Directors for the Sierra Club Canada Foundation and the Arctic Youth Network, which she co-founded. She worked with the Myko Social Score platform in developing an app to reduce personal carbon footprints, followed by a brief career in corporate consulting with Deloitte LLP, where she helped businesses launch operations in the digital world, largely in relation to global trade, taxation, and sustainability.

EXPERTS

Amb Francisco Calí Tzay is Maya Kaqchikel from Guatemala and the first Indigenous member of a United Nations Treaty Body, having served for sixteen years on the Committee on the Elimination of Racial Discrimination (CERD). He held the Presidency of CERD from 2014 to 2016 and later served as Chairman of CERD's Early Warning/Urgent Action Procedure through December 2019. He has represented Indigenous Peoples at the United Nations since the early 1980s, bringing attention to human rights violations against Indigenous communities in Guatemala and worldwide. Amb Tzay was also an active participant in the Intersessional Working Group that led to the adoption of the UN Declaration on the Rights of Indigenous Peoples, engaging both as a representative of the International Indian Treaty Council and as a delegate of the Government of Guatemala.

Beyond his UN roles, Amb Tzay served as Guatemala's Ambassador to the Federal Republic of Germany and was Director of Human Rights at the Ministry of Foreign Affairs of Guatemala. He was a founder and member of several Indigenous organizations in his home country and worked with the

Presidential Commission against Discrimination and Racism against Indigenous Peoples in Guatemala (CODISRA). He also presided over the National Reparation Program for Victims of the Internal Armed Conflict in Guatemala. Through each of these positions, Amb Tzay has continually championed the rights, well-being, and recognition of Indigenous Peoples at national and international levels.

Professor Robert Joseph, PhD (Waikato), LLM (Waikato), LLB (Waikato), is Iwi Māori (Tainui, Tuwharetoa, Ngāti Kahungunu, Ngāi Tahu) and an Associate Professor of Law at the Te Piringa Faculty of Law with the University of Waikato. He is an enrolled Barrister and Solicitor with the High Court of New Zealand, Director with the Te Mata Hautū Taketake – The Māori and Indigenous Governance Centre at the University of Waikato, Director with the Te Taumata, Ministry for Foreign Affairs and Trade of New Zealand Government, and Director for the Hohonu Ltd Research Company. He was a Fulbright Scholar at Harvard University and the University of Arizona in 2017. He is also the New Zealand Representative of IITIO and the Common Roots, Common Futures International Indigenous Pathways to Self-Determination and Governance Consortium. He is furthermore Pūkenga with the High Court of New Zealand on the Marine and Coastal Area (Takutai Moana) Act 2011 and a Licenced Researcher and Legal Historian for the Waitangi Tribunal and Crown Forestry Rental Trust. He also sits on the board of the Battle of Orākau Heritage Society Inc. and the Te Hunga Roia Māori o Aotearoa Inc., which is the Māori Law Society.

RESEARCHERS

Dr Tara Dawn Atleo, PhD (Waterloo), MA (London), BSc (VIU), is assistant professor in the University of British Columbia, former CEO of the Maaqutusiis Hahoulthee Stewardship Society and a member of the Ahousaht First Nation, whose territory in coastal British Columbia is part of the Emerald Edge, the world's largest intact coastal temperate rainforest. Dr Atleo holds a Governor General's Medal and won the Gold Award in the UNFCCC COP23 Climate Law & Governance International Essay Competition for her paper 'The Importance of Locally Developed Indigenous Planning Tools and Policy for Climate Change Action in Ahousaht Traditional Territories'. Her research focuses on environmental economics, specifically how to use non-market valuation techniques for culturally significant areas in Ahousaht traditional territories and across British Columbia.

Dr. Cecilia Campero, PhD (Pontificia Chile), MS (Pontificia Chile), is an adjunct professor in the School of Humanitarian studies and an Associate Faculty in the School of Business at Royal Roads University. Her research focuses on the political economy/ecology of natural resource extraction and development. Her primary interests are in water politics, local and regional development, gender equality, Indigenous rights, impact assessments and equity dimensions of resource management. Professor Campero's geographic focus is on Canada, and Latin America, with publications appearing in such high-ranking journals as *The Extractive Industries and Society*, *Environmental Science and Policy*, and *Marine Policy*. Professor Campero served as the principal investigator on a SSHRC-IDG funded project on Indigenous Knowledge, the SDGs and Impact Assessments (2024–2026).

Kiana Cardinal-Arcand, JD & JID (UVic), BA (Alberta), is a Nehiyâw Iskwew (Cree woman) from Alexander First Nation in Treaty Six Territory. She holds a Bachelor of Arts in Native Studies and a Certificate in Aboriginal Governance & Partnerships from the University of Alberta.

She has held key leadership roles within the Confederacy of Treaty Six First Nations, beginning as a Youth Engagement Officer and advancing to Youth Council Coordinator and Youth Jr. Policy Analyst. She was elected Co-Chair of the Assembly of First Nations National Youth Council, serving two terms as an Executive Board Member and representing Alberta First Nations youth at the national and international levels. A dedicated advocate and lobbyist for First Nations youth, Adv Cardinal-Arcand was a recipient of the 2018 Aboriginal Youth Role Model of Alberta Award.

Elaina Cox, MSc (Waterloo), BSc Env (Guelph), is a Top 25 Environmentalist Under 25 award winner equipped with several years of experience in environmental, climate, and sustainability work through affiliations with governments, academic institutions, national and international organizations and non-profits. She is employed with the Sustainable Forestry Initiative to support diverse community interests within the forestry sector of Canada and the United States. She sits on a variety of boards and councils to which she has made significant contributions to their evolving projects and successes. Her areas of expertise encompass national and international biodiversity, reconciliation, and climate instruments and agreements; the incorporation of traditional knowledge and practices; and, advocating for the inclusion of women, youth and Indigenous Peoples and their perspectives in decision-making processes.

Adv Hannibal El-Mohtar, LLM (Peking), BCL & LLB (McGill), BSc (uOttawa), is an international trade and investment lawyer and Associate Fellow with the CISDL. He advises on Asia-Pacific trade, cross-border, and economic security matters. He also represents clients before the Canadian International Trade Tribunal. Adv El-Mohtar has worked at national law firms in Canada and China, and prior to joining the CISDL, was Editor-in-Chief of the *McGill Journal of Sustainable Development Law* (vol 13), and a participant in the UNFCCC Conference of the Parties 22. Adv El-Mohtar is also a Director with the Hong Kong Canada Business Association (Ottawa Chapter).

Adv Hafijul Islam Khan, PhD Cand (Waterloo), LLM (Dhaka), LLM (CEU), is an environmental lawyer affiliated with the Supreme Court of Bangladesh, working to promote climate justice. He is leading the Centre for Climate Justice-Bangladesh (CCJ-B) as Director (on Leave). He is one of the lead climate negotiators and acting as co-coordinator, Loss and Damage Team, LDCs Climate Group at UNFCCC. He is currently serving as Member of the Executive Committee of Warsaw International Mechanism for loss and damage at UNFCCC. He also acted as Advisor and Member (short time), to the Transitional Committee for Loss and Damage Fund at UNFCCC. He is currently involved with New York University Law School as a research fellow. He is a PhD candidate at Waterloo University.

Dr Odette Lara-Morales, PhD (ARU-UK), MA (ARU-UK), B.Com (UAT-MX), is a Lecturer in Indigenous Entrepreneurship at United College, University of Waterloo. She is also an Associate Fellow at the CISDL and a Project Officer with the United Nations Association in Canada. She holds a PhD in Marketing, Enterprise, and Sustainable Tourism and has extensive experience in higher education and international research. She has taught management courses at the Faculty of Business and Law at Anglia Ruskin University in Cambridge, UK, and has designed and delivered courses such as Indigenous Rights in Global Context at United College, University of Waterloo. Her academic work intersects sustainability, business, and Indigenous governance, with a strong emphasis on ethical and community-driven approaches to economic and environmental resilience. As a Nahua Indigenous descendant from Mexico, Dr Lara-Morales is deeply committed to advancing the SDGs, particularly in the areas of ecological and cultural preservation, gender equality, and poverty reduction in Indigenous communities. She actively contributes to initiatives that promote sustainable development through policy engagement, capacity-building programmes, and interdisciplinary collaboration. Beyond her academic and professional roles, Dr Lara-Morales is a dedicated mentor and advocate for youth leadership. She works closely with young people, equipping and inspiring them with the skills needed to drive social change. Passionate about fostering the next generation of leaders, she strives to create opportunities that empower youth to build sustainable, inclusive, and resilient communities.

Yasmin Mosellhy, LLM (Cambridge), LLB (German University in Cairo) is a qualified Egyptian lawyer and researcher at the University of Antwerp studying the normative legal implication of the Agenda Accelerator 2030 on Partnerships on local norms. She has also worked with grassroots human organizations with a specific focus on human rights defenders in Libya, Bahrain, and Palestine.

Smriti Pokhrel, PhD Cand (UVic), LLM (Lucknow) is a CISDL Associate Fellow researching Indigenous rights, constitutional law, and environmental justice, with notable publications in academic journals. As a dedicated advocate for Indigenous communities, she co- founded 'Educating Nepal', supporting the Majhi Indigenous Community. Recent honours include Silver Medallist in the Judge CG and Mrs Rosemary Global Fellowship for International Law on Sustainable Development, and nomination for the prestigious Vanier Scholarship. Her expertise bridges legal practice, academic research, and community advocacy across South Asia.

Christopher Wieczorek, BCL & JD Candidate (McGill), MSc (Oxford), BA (Dalhousie), is Researcher at the CISDL. Before starting law school, he held advisory and policy roles with the Government of British Columbia. He has also worked for NGOs in the environmental conservation and energy transition sectors. Christopher Wieczorek's graduate research focused on the opportunities and challenges of Canada's renewable energy transition.

Kelly Weiling Zou, JD & JID (UVic), BComm (Queen's), is an experienced grassroots organizer dedicated to supporting historically and politically ostracized communities. Adv Weiling Zou combines her academic and lived experiences to advocate for racial, environmental, disability, and queer justice. As a CISDL Researcher, she has participated in several round tables, and UN conferences learning and sharing knowledge on the SDGs ad UNDRIP.

Foreword

This book explores various Indigenous treaty clauses and their sustainability and Indigenous interpretation with a greater understanding of how Indigenous Peoples have lived, and continue to live, in a relationship with their ecosystems while maintaining a sustainable Indigenous economy. All this is in the context of Indigenous Peoples being minority voices in larger, constitution-driven Nation-States. Constitutional recognition of Indigenous Peoples' rights in certain countries has been pivotal to safeguarding Indigenous Peoples' collective rights. Across the globe, we have witnessed exemplary cases, each illustrating the unique context of its respective country.

Greenland enjoys extensive self-governance that is an inspiring example of the implementation of Indigenous self-determination for many Indigenous Peoples worldwide. The 2023 draft constitution asserts that 'Inuit are the Indigenous People of our land.' Further draft provisions underline that Greenland is governed based on collective rights and that the principle of common ownership of all land, sea, and resources is inalienable. The draft constitution's progressive language sets out the right to live in a clean and healthy environment that is protected on a sustainable basis, putting forth the principle that sustainable use entails caring for nature, for the economy, and for social and cultural sustainability.

The application of the right to Indigenous land and territory requires that States recognize the titles issued to Indigenous Peoples by the Crown, or when these do not exist, respect the provisions of international law according to which Indigenous Peoples possess communal property rights over the lands and resources that they have historically used and occupied by virtue of their customary land tenure systems.

Governments have prioritized extractive industries and agricultural development in the ancestral territories of Indigenous Peoples as a method of economic recovery from the pandemic. States have labelled as strategic and then accelerated projects that have substantial impact on both the environment and human rights and have too often used the COVID-19 health emergency as an excuse to approve projects and policies lacking good faith consultation, and lacking the free, prior, and informed consent of Indigenous Peoples. In addition, States have reduced penalties for environmental violations, criminalized human rights defenders, and weakened or eliminated environmental impact assessment and public participation requirements.

I commend the efforts of the writers of this book to link the United Nations Declaration on the Rights of Indigenous Peoples and the SDGs through Indigenous treaty law in the hopes that the recent developments will provide a focus on the obligations of Nation-States and their assisting international organizations to respect, protect, and promote the rights and perspectives of Indigenous Peoples.

Ambassador Francisco Calí Tzay
UN Special Rapporteur – Rights of Indigenous Peoples

Acknowledgements

The editors especially thank and acknowledge the kind guidance and support of leaders, elders, and researchers involved in treaty instruments who helped inform this volume.

Further, this volume would not have been possible without a dedicated team of brilliant and hardworking Indigenous and non-Indigenous researchers, including Dr Tara Dawn Atleo of the University of British Columbia, Prof Cecilia Campero, Adv Kiana Cardinal-Arcand of the University of Victoria, Ms Elaina Cox of the University of Waterloo, Adv Yasmin Mosellhy, Adv Hannibal El-Mohtar, Prof Robert Joseph, Dr Hafijul Islam Khan, Dr Odette Lara-Morales of the University of Waterloo, Adv Smriti Pokhrel of the University of Victoria, Amb Francisco Calí Tzay, Mr Christopher Wieczorek of McGill University, Adv Eva Wu of McGill University, Adv Kelly Weiling Zou of the University of Victoria, and others. Most importantly, we are grateful to Dr Jackie Grant, Dr John Berger, Dr Finola O'Sullivan, and their team at Cambridge University Press including Auropradeepa Rajapriyan of Straive for their excellent engagement and encouragement.

The completion of this volume was generously supported by a competitively awarded grant from the Canadian Social Sciences and Humanities Research Council (SSHRC), and the New Frontiers Research Fund of Canada.

Abbreviations and Acronyms

IACA	Indian Arts and Crafts Act
ANZTEC	Agreement between New Zealand and the Separate Customs Territory of Taiwan, Penghu, Kinmen, and Matsu on Economic Cooperation
APEC	Asia-Pacific Economic Cooperation
BCAFN	British Columbia Assembly of First Nations of Canada
C/TMC	Carcross/Tagish Management Corporation
CANDO	Canadian Economic Development Officers Association
CBD	Convention on Biological Diversity
CER	Canadian Energy Regulator Act
CERD	Committee on the Elimination of Racial Discrimination
CESD	Canadian Commissioner of the Environment and Sustainable Development
CHN	Council of the Haida Nation
CIGI	Centre for International Governance Innovation
CISDL	Centre for International Sustainable Development Law
CITES	Convention on International Trade in Endangered Species of Wild Fauna and Flora
CLCA	Comprehensive Land Claims Agreements
CNI	Chickasaw Nation Industries
CONADI'	Chilean National Corporation for Indigenous Development
COP	Conference of the Parties
CPN	Citizen Potawatomi Nation of Oklahoma
CUFTA	Canada-Ukraine Free Trade Agreement
CUSMA	Canada–United States–Mexico Agreement
CWB	Community Well-Being Index
DFO	Department of Fisheries and Oceans

EEZ	Exclusive economic zone
EIA	Environmental impact assessment
EU-NZ-FTA	European Union-New Zealand Free Trade Agreement
EZLN	Ejército Zapatista de Liberación Nacional
FAO	Food and Agriculture Organization
FCA	Federal Court of Appeal
FPIC	Free, Prior, and Informed Consent
FTA	Free Trade Agreement
FTZ	Free/Foreign Trade Zone
GBF	Kunming-Montreal Global Biodiversity Framework
GDP	Gross Domestic Product
GHG	Greenhouse Gases
GRATK	Genetic Resources and Associated Traditional Knowledge
IACB	Indian Arts and Crafts Board
IBA	Impact and Benefit Agreement
ICH Convention	Convention for the Safeguarding of the Intangible Cultural Heritage
ICOMOS	International Council on Monuments and Sites
IEAC	Independent Expert Advisory Committee
IIPFCC	International Indigenous Peoples' Forum on Climate Change
IITIO	International Inter-tribal Trade and Investment Organization
ILA	International Law Association
ILO 169	International Labor Organization, Indigenous and Tribal Peoples Convention, 1989
IP	Intellectual Property
IPETCA	Indigenous Peoples Economic and Trade Cooperation Arrangement
ITAG	Inclusive Trade Action Group
ITK	Indigenous traditional knowledge
IUCN	International Union for the Conservation of Nature
IWG	Global Affairs Canada Indigenous Working Group
JBNQA	James Bay and Northern Quebec Agreement
KFNA	Kluane First Nation Agreement
LILCA	Labrador Inuit Land Claims Agreement
LSF	Living Standards Framework
MDGs	Millennium Development Goals
Mercosur	Southern Common Market
MFAT	New Zealand Ministry of Foreign Affairs and Trade

MOU	Memorandum of Understanding
NAFO	Northwest Atlantic Fisheries Organization
NAFTA	North American Free Trade Agreement
NGOs	Non-Governmental Organizations
NZ-UK	New Zealand–United Kingdom Trade Agreement
OECD	Organisation for Economic Co-operation and Development
RCAP	Report of the Royal Commission on Aboriginal People
RFMOs	Regional Fisheries Management Organizations
SDGs	Sustainable Development Goals
SFF	Canadian Sustainable Fisheries Framework
SME	Small and Medium Enterprise
TAC	Total Allowable Catch
TFN	Tsawwassen First Nation
Tipnis	Isiboro Sécure Indigenous Territory and National Park
TK	Traditional Knowledge
TRC	Truth and Reconciliation Commission
UFA	Umbrella Final Agreement
UK-AUS FTA	United Kingdom-Australia Free Trade Agreement
UK-NZ FTA	United Kingdom-New Zealand Trade Agreement
UN	United Nations
UNCCD	United Nations Convention to Combat Desertification and Drought
UNCED	United Nations Conference on the Environment and Development
UNCLOS	United Nations Convention on the Law of Sea
UNDRIP	United Nations Declaration on the Rights of Indigenous Peoples
UNEP	United Nations Environment Programme/ UN Environment
UNESCO	United Nations Educational, Scientific and Cultural Organization
UNFCCC	United Nations Framework Convention on Climate Change
UNGA	United Nations General Assembly
UNSFA	United Nations Agreement on Straddling and Highly Migratory Fish Stocks
UNTS	United Nations Treaty System
USC	United States Code
USD	United States Dollars

USMCA	United States–Mexico–Canada Agreement
VNR	Voluntary National Review
WCED	World Commission on Environment and Development
WGIP	Working Group on Indigenous Populations
WIPO	World Intellectual Property Organization
WTO	World Trade Organization

PART I

Introduction

1

Introduction

1.1 IMPLEMENTING UNDRIP THROUGH INTERNATIONAL LAW AND COVENANTS

> The Three Sisters offer us a new metaphor for an emerging relationship between [I]ndigenous knowledge and Western science, both of which are rooted in the earth. I think of the corn as traditional ecological knowledge, the physical and spiritual framework that can guide the curious bean of science, which twines like a double helix. The squash creates the ethical habitat for coexistence and mutual flourishing. I envision a time when the intellectual monoculture of science will be replaced with a polyculture of complementary knowledges. And so all may be fed.
>
> The traditional ecological knowledge of [I]ndigenous harvesters is rich in prescriptions for sustainability. They are found in Native science and philosophy, in lifeways and practices, but most of all in stories, the ones that are told to help restore balance, to locate ourselves once again in the circle....[1]

For thousands of years, Indigenous Peoples have been living with and learning from Mother Earth, preserving knowledge of traditional sustainability sciences, practices, laws, and stories that foster respect for the interdependent and gift–reciprocity relationships found among living beings and the environments they inhabit.[2] Now, after centuries of diminishing

[1] Robin Wall Kimmerer, *Braiding Sweetgrass* (Milkweed Editions 2013) 139 and 179.

[2] See E Richard Atleo (Umeek), *Tsawalk: A Nuu-chah-nulth Worldview* (UBC Press 2004); John Borrows, *Earth-Bound: Indigenous Resurgence and Environmental Reconciliation* (Resurgence and Reconciliation 2018); John Borrows, *Canada's Indigenous Constitution* (University of Toronto Press 2010); Aaron Mills, 'Miinigowiziwin: All That Has Been Given for Living Well Together: One Vision of Anishinaabe Constitutionalism' (Dissertation, University of Victoria

Indigenous ways of life while enabling unsustainable dominance and exploitation, in some countries education, science and political will may be slowly turning to accept the Indigenous ways of being as an interdependent and symbiotic way for humans and other living beings to continue flourishing on this planet. Through a convergence of Indigenous knowledge and legal traditions with the necessary sustainable development agendas and commitments being adopted worldwide, important new pathways become possible.[3]

Such transformations were foreseen by writers, philosophers, naturalists, scientists, and ecologists who have argued that current economies need to evolve past the desire to be conquerors and controllers of nature so as to respect the laws of, and become part of, living (biotic) communities.[4] This contrast between destructive approaches to development and Indigenous reciprocity and gratitude is pertinently detailed by Robin Wall Kimmerer, whose words of wisdom open this chapter. Kimmerer is both a member of the Potawatomi Nation and a distinguished Professor of Environmental and Forest Biology at the State University of New York College of Environmental Science and Forestry. Her works bring together her two identities – her Indigenous heritage and its culture, and her scientific method and knowledge harnessed through her role in academia – to explain how traditional wisdom has equal value to science, and can be twined to form a more holistic understanding of the world.[5]

This harmonization of worldviews is especially critical as the world faces record-breaking natural disasters, global food and resource shortages, and human rights violations globally. In the age of the Anthropocene, far-reaching economic, technological, societal, and environmental change requires collaborative and coordinated efforts to foster sustainability, for a good quality of life for future generations. Particularly as the impacts, and advancements, from the recent COVID-19 pandemic become more apparent, the vitality of the economy, society, and environment is even more contingent on expanding current knowledge and legal systems to learn from Indigenous ways of

2019); Val Napoleon, 'Ayook: Gitksan Legal Order, Law, and Legal Theory' (PhD Dissertation, University of Victoria 2009); James Tully, 'Sustainable Democratic Constitutionalism and Climate Crisis' (2020) 65 McGill Law Journal 545.

3 Nancy J Turner, *The Earth's Blanket: Traditional Teachings for Sustainable Living* (University of Washington Press 2005) 232; Kimmerer (n 1).

4 Aldo Leopold, *A Sand County Almanac with Essays on Conservation from Round River* (Oxford University Press 1966) 217, 220.

5 Kimmerer (n 1) generally.

knowing that have stewarded global ecosystems for millennia.[6] Widely ratified agendas, such as the 2015 United Nations Sustainable Development Goals (SDGs) for 2030[7] and the United Nations Declaration on the Rights of Indigenous Peoples (UNDRIP),[8] help provide the framework necessary for tackling these complex, inter-dependent problems, to create wide-ranging, deep-rooted solutions. Countries and Nations adopting these declarations have solemnly committed to undertake crucial domestic actions to advance sustainability, development, Indigenous rights and justice, and to prioritize international cooperation and assistance to fulfil their commitments. However, when the genuine efforts of many continue to fall short of delivering the desired results, treaties that engage Indigenous Parties may help to secure the systems that are needed, complementing and augmenting such principles and commitments.

Are collaborations, or even amalgamations of Indigenous and non-Indigenous worlds of knowledge necessary to secure a sustainable future for all living beings? This volume represents one endeavour to provide answers in the affirmative. Specifically, the guidance and wisdom of Indigenous knowledge found in treaties is given prominence, by demonstrating that these negotiated covenants have the potential to provide the foundation for sustainable development to expand on present international and domestic legal regimes. This analysis is anchored within the principles and guidance of the

6 Inter-American Court of Human Rights, *Advisory Opinion AO-32/25 (Climate Emergency and Human Rights, Requested by Chile and Colombia, 29 May 2025)*, para 302 (noting that the collective dimension of the right to a healthy climate "protects the collective interest of present and future generations of humans and other species in maintaining a climate system fit to ensure their well-being") and International Court of Justice, *Obligations of States in respect of Climate Change (Advisory Opinion, 23 July 2025, General List No. 187)*, para 457 (finding that "States have obligations under international human rights law to respect and ensure the effective enjoyment of human rights by taking necessary measures to protect the climate system and other parts of the environment"). Recognizing 'the important roles and contributions of [I]ndigenous Peoples and local communities as custodians of biodiversity and as partners in its conservation, restoration and sustainable use'. COP CBD, 'Kunming-Montreal Global Biodiversity Framework' (18 December 2022) UN Doc CBD/COP/15/L25 art 7(a).

7 The 17 SDGs that were codified address key sectors of social, economic and environmental policy and action, with specific time-bound targets to end poverty and hunger, secure health, education, gender equality, clean energy, fresh water and sanitation, employment, innovation, sustainable consumption and production, climate change, biodiversity and land conservation, marine ecosystems and fisheries, and foster and enshrine justice. United Nations General Assembly, 'Transforming Our World: The 2030 Agenda for Sustainable Development' (21 October 2015) UN Doc A/RES/70/1.

8 United Nations General Assembly, 'United Nations Declaration on the Rights of Indigenous Peoples' (2 October 2007) UN Doc A/RES/61/295.United Nations General Assembly, 'United Nations Declaration on the Rights of Indigenous Peoples' (2 October 2007) UN Doc A/RES/61/295.

17 SDGs and the UNDRIP, alongside context and examples from countries of the opportunities world on how Indigenous knowledge and treaties are already creating to inform, sustainable futures for all. Comparative legal research methods uncover whether and how these accords respond to sustainable development objectives across key social, environmental, and economic challenges, in this book.

1.2 OUTLINE

This volume is structured in five parts, each discussing different aspects of understanding and implementing the various international, trans-national, and Nation-to-Nation treaties in a manner that can advance sustainable development and affirm Indigenous knowledge and rights in selected legal systems.

Following this introductory note in Part I, the foundations are laid for the rest of the volume in Part II, which explores international conventions enshrining basic tenets of international Indigenous policy, rights, and law. Notably, this includes the principles and commitments reflected in the UNDRIP and the UN SDGs, as well as the rights, duties, and obligations reflected in the Indigenous and Tribal Peoples Convention, 1989 (ILO 169) and in Nation-to-Nation and Nation-to-State trade as the prerequisite for Indigenous Nation-building. The theoretical elements of leveraging treaty and international law for sustainable development, together with its implications, are also defined and provided in this part.

Chapter 2 provides analysis of the international legal framework governing Indigenous Peoples' rights, focusing on treaty obligations from ILO 169, and the principles reflected in the UNDRIP. It explores the fundamental principle of free, prior, and informed consent (FPIC) as reflected in these instruments and its crucial role in sustainable development. Examining ILO 169, the chapter discusses guidelines related to self-determination, land rights, cultural preservation, and State obligations to consult and cooperate with Indigenous Peoples, providing selected examples in the context of Indigenous communities in Canada. Analysing the UNDRIP, the chapter offers an exploration of self-determination, land rights, cultural heritage, and States' duties to obtain FPIC. Emphasizing the significance of consent as a cornerstone of efforts to link Indigenous rights and sustainable development, the chapter concludes by acknowledging the complexities involved in its practical application. By delving into substantive and procedural aspects of international law, this chapter discusses the role of international legal norms in promoting Indigenous rights and facilitating sustainable development.

Chapter 3 explores the journey from principles to the practical implementation of sustainable development, in the context of advancing the global SDGs. It begins by examining the foundational principles of international public policy and law that guide sustainable development efforts by examining the history and motivation behind adopting a global set of goals and targets for sustainable development by 2030. Then, the chapter focuses on Indigenous Peoples roles in advancing the SDGs, acknowledging the historical disparities faced by these communities and how treaties have the potential to foster or frustrate the achievement of these goals and targets. Canadian experiences are explored, with a focus on whether and how the modern treaty system can provide a tangible improvement in furthering sustainable development. The chapter then delves into guidelines for sustainable resource management and Indigenous development within the SDG framework, emphasizing inclusive approaches and participatory decision-making. By bridging principles with practical strategies, this chapter underscores the importance of integrating Indigenous knowledge, fostering partnerships, and implementing the SDGs to achieve sustainable development which respects Indigenous rights and aspirations.

Chapter 4 details the vital potential for Indigenous trade and investment to help, rather than hinder, sustainable development efforts. Firstly, it discusses the prerequisites for Indigenous trade, emphasizing a Nation-building approaches centred on the significance of robust Tribal infrastructure. The chapter then addresses the barriers hindering Indigenous inter-Tribal trade, including state or provincial level interference in Tribal jurisdiction, poor Tribal governance, the lack of Indigenous foreign trade zones, the exclusion of Indigenous Traditional Knowledge (TK) from intellectual property (IP) regimes, and historical challenges in trade financing, as well as other factors such as Canada's failure to honour its Jay Treaty obligations. Additionally, the chapter explores Indigenous trade and commerce engagements with non-Indigenous enterprises, both with and without federal permission, highlighting the implications, challenges, and opportunities involved. By examining these aspects, the chapter highlights the need to empower Indigenous Nations through trade and investment, fostering economic opportunities while respecting cultural heritage, and working towards sustainable development.

In Part III, there is an exploration of ways in which treaty implementation can address sustainable development, by targeting key sectors and bodies of legal discourse. This section spans contexts and examples that encompass TK within IP regimes, the intersection of treaty law and renewable resource management and extraction, the intricate relationships and importance of protecting Indigenous cultural heritage, and the role of consent, law, and regulation in the context of extractive, non-renewable industries.

In Chapter 5, the complex relationship between TK and IP concerning genetic resources is explored. First, with an examination into the challenges of distinguishing TK from IP and a presentation of the Munzer Model as a potential compromise for addressing TK within the IP framework. The chapter then delves into national efforts to protect and recognize TK, with examples from United States and Canadian cases, including the Cowichan Sweater example from the 2010 Vancouver Olympic Winter Games. Furthermore, the evolving landscape of TK in international trade agreements is detailed, highlighting the increasing recognition of TK, and respect for TK as a 'new norm'. By analysing historic and current developments in TK recognition, this chapter emphasizes the need for a balanced approach that respects the unique nature of TK while navigating the complexities of IP frameworks. It underscores the importance of preserving and utilizing TK and genetic resources for the benefit of Indigenous communities and for advancing sustainable development.

Chapter 6 then considers the complexities of the intersection between renewable resources, sustainable development, and Indigenous treaty law. It begins by examining international guidance for renewable energy sources and their role in achieving sustainability objectives. This chapter then delves into the principles and rules governing sustainable forestry practices, fisheries management, and energy development. It highlights the importance of international agreements, protocols, and treaties in promoting responsible resource management, conservation, and the recognition of Indigenous rights and knowledge. By considering these principles and rules within the context of Indigenous treaty law, it highlights the need for harmonious and inclusive approaches to renewable resource use in the age of sustainable development. It underlines the significance of collaboration, respect for Indigenous knowledge, and the integration of sustainability principles to ensure a balanced and equitable relationship between renewable resources, Indigenous rights, and sustainable development.

Subsequently, in Chapter 7, the intricate relationship between Indigenous cultural heritage and Indigenous rights is discussed, not only in the context of advancing sustainable development but especially with a focus on enabling the well-being of Indigenous communities. It begins by analysing the guidance provided by the UNDRIP and ILO 169 regarding the preservation and protection of cultural heritage, particularly in the context of the triple planetary crises: climate change, biodiversity loss, and degradation of natural systems. Additionally, it emphasizes the importance of resilient and vibrant cultural heritage for achieving sustainable development. The chapter highlights the challenges posed by this triple planetary crises to Indigenous cultural heritage and emphasizes the need for resilience and safeguarding measures. It further examines the treatment of cultural heritage in Indigenous treaties, delving into legal and historical perspectives in the United States' jurisprudence and political landscape, then addresses the ability of Canadian modern treaties to foster or frustrate the ability to safeguard cultural heritage. By considering these aspects, the chapter underscores the significance of recognizing and preserving Indigenous cultural heritage, highlighting the need for enhanced legal frameworks, collaborative approaches, and the integration of Indigenous rights and knowledge to ensure the continuity and vitality of cultural heritage for present and future generations.

Chapter 8 concludes Part III with an exploration of the complex relationship between extractive industries, sustainable development, and Indigenous treaty law. It begins by examining the international law guidance available for extractive industries, analysing frameworks and principles that promote responsible and sustainable practices in resource extraction while considering the social, economic, and environmental dimensions. This chapter focuses on the specific challenges of oil and gas exploration, highlighting the impacts on Indigenous communities and emphasizing the importance of meaningful consultation, consent, and fair benefit-sharing in alignment with Indigenous treaty rights, including Indigenous decisions to withhold consent and focus on development of alternatives to fossil fuels. Furthermore, it surveys the mining sector's implications for sustainable development, considering the social, economic, and environmental aspects and emphasizing the role of Indigenous treaty law in ensuring responsible practices, equitable resource distribution, and the protection of Indigenous rights and lands. In conclusion, the chapter emphasizes the need for a respect of Indigenous rights, integrated Indigenous perspectives and consent, and promotes sustainable practices to foster collaboration and achieve sustainable development that enables the well-being and self-determination of Indigenous Peoples.

Part IV presents case studies of treaty implementation to identify possible solutions that could advance sustainable development and Indigenous rights through treaties. This provides comparative insights from different domestic experiences and traditions, identifying areas of commonality and difference in efforts to activate domestic institutions in the interest of intergenerational equity. This section highlights histories, cases, and innovations from Canada, the United States, New Zealand, Chile, Bolivia, Bangladesh and Mexico to contextualize current regional trends and innovations.

First, a case study of Canada is presented in Chapter 9, examining the intricate relationship between Indigenous Peoples and the developments related to British, then Canadian, governance. It begins by exploring the historical and legal context of Indigenous Peoples in Canada, tracing the impact of colonization and the recognition of Indigenous rights. The potential for affirming these rights through treaties and trade agreements is then investigated, highlighting recognition and protection of Indigenous treaty rights, together with the opportunities and challenges presented by trade agreements for Indigenous economic development and self-determination. The Canadian government's efforts to domestically enforce the UNDRIP and the intersection of Canadian treaties with trade agreements are then analysed. This chapter emphasizes the importance of ongoing dialogue, collaboration, and the implementation of measures aligned with UNDRIP principles to foster the recognition, empowerment, and well-being of Indigenous Peoples within the Canadian context.

Chapter 10 delves into the United States' treatment of Indigenous Peoples, with a specific focus on Indigenous sovereignty and economic rights. It begins with a brief discussion of the historical context and treatment of Indigenous Peoples in the legal framework, with an emphasis on the series of cases dubbed the Marshall Trilogy. This includes the struggles and advancements in recognizing Tribal Nation sovereignty and economic rights. It examines the recognition and affirmation of Tribal Nation sovereignty within the United States, including legal developments and court decisions that have shaped Indigenous self-governance. Taking into account the landmark case of *McGirt v Oklahoma*, the chapter emphasizes the need to addressing past legal injustices, Tribal reservation boundaries, and Tribal jurisdiction. The discussion also considers Tribal sovereignty within the United States in the context of international Indigenous trade, showcasing the ways in which Indigenous communities engage in economic activities and exercise their sovereignty on the global stage. This chapter emphasizes the importance of recognizing and upholding the treaty right to economic sovereignty to protect and promote Indigenous economic rights within the United States.

Chapter 11 presents a New Zealand case study, examining the paradigm of giving nature legal standing within the country's judicial and legislative framework. It begins with an introduction that sets the stage for the discussion. The Māori philosophy of a relationship with nature, emphasizing the profound connection and inherent value Māori place on the environment, is then explored, as are the ways in which New Zealand law has affirmed this philosophy, particularly, through the roots of the country's environmental achievements as anchored in the Treaty of Waitangi. The chapter then considers two examples – the Te Urewera Land Legislation and the Whanganui River Legislation – showcasing the innovative approaches taken to grant legal personhood to natural entities. It further explores the incorporation of Māori Indigenous TK in sustainable development practices, highlighting Māori trade and the introduction of new measures of well-being and environmental protection. The chapter concludes by emphasizing the significance of giving nature legal standing and the implications for both Māori and New Zealand's approach to sustainable development.

Chapter 12 features examples of Indigenous peace agreements in the Andes region. It begins with an introduction that highlights the significance of understanding legal geography and its relevance to Indigenous Peoples. It then details the legal frameworks that protect Indigenous rights, focusing on international instruments such as declarations and conventions; and examines specific agreements in the Andes that enact these legal frameworks, with a spotlight on the National Agreement for Development and Peace in La Araucanía, 2018, in Chile, and the Agreement Between the Bolivian Government and the Confederation of Indigenous Peoples from the East, Chaco, and Amazonia in 2010. Focusing on the intersection of legal, social, and political dynamics in promoting Indigenous rights and fostering peace, and legal geographies of these agreements, the chapter considers the complex challenges and opportunities Indigenous communities face in achieving sustainable development and peace in the Andes region.

Part IV concludes with Chapter 13, which presents agreements between Indigenous Peoples and governments in Bangladesh and Mexico that focus on their roles in promoting sustainable development. The introduction sets the stage for subsequent discussions by emphasizing the importance of global legal and policy frameworks, like the UNDRIP and the SDGs, in shaping these agreements. The examples from Bangladesh and Mexico are analysed together with experts from these regions, shedding light on the unique characteristics, provisions, and outcomes of agreements between Indigenous Peoples and governments in these contexts. A comparative analysis is conducted to identify commonalities, differences, and lessons learned. Ultimately, the chapter concludes by highlighting the significance of ongoing dialogue, collaboration, and respect for Indigenous rights in achieving sustainable development goals globally. It underscores the importance of incorporating Indigenous perspectives and aspirations into the design and implementation of such agreements.

The last section, Part V, scopes future directions and options, distilling lessons learned from current practices for the reform of political and legal institutions at the national, regional, and global levels by drawing on a new treaty that provides innovations to address the complex problems presented throughout this volume.

Chapter 14 rounds out the volume by emphasizing the importance of incorporating the principles of the UNDRIP and sustainable development in newly negotiated Indigenous trade agreements. The introduction highlights the significance of UNDRIP in promoting the rights and aspirations of Indigenous Peoples. The chapter details the origins of the Indigenous Peoples Economic Trade and Cultural Agreement (IPETCA), focusing on its innovations that enabled trade negotiations that amplified Indigenous views and values while enabled by the States of New Zealand, Taiwan, Australia, and Canada. The chapter then delves into the sustainable development aspects of IPETCA, showcasing how it aligns with the principles of UNDRIP and seeks to foster economic growth while respecting Indigenous rights. It then discusses IPETCA's working mechanism and implementation, highlighting the role of the IPETCA Partnership Council and the Informal APEC Caucus in facilitating dialogue and collaboration. Finally, the chapter contemplates the viability of other States, like the United States joining IPETCA and the potential benefits it could bring. In conclusion, the chapter underscores the importance of innovative approaches like IPETCA in advancing Indigenous trade agreements that prioritize sustainable development and uphold the principles of UNDRIP.

This book concludes with insights for new directions that emphasize the critical importance of prioritizing Indigenous knowledge and treaties in efforts to advance sustainable development. This chapter summarizes the discussions brought forth throughout the volume and is centred on the wisdom and practices of Indigenous Peoples that promote respect, reciprocity, and harmony with the natural world. The convergence of Indigenous knowledge with global sustainable development agendas is now widely recognized as a crucial step towards a more balanced and resilient future. As the world faces unprecedented challenges such as natural disasters, resource scarcity, and human rights violations, the concluding chapter suggests, recognizing the strengths of diverse worldviews becomes essential. Through careful international legal analysis, respectful case studies of relationships, and comparative research, this volume explores the potential of treaties to foster sustainable futures that benefit all living beings.

PART II

Foundations of International Law for Indigenous Peoples and Sustainable Development

2

Indigenous Peoples Rights in ILO 169 and UNDRIP

2.1 INTRODUCTION

As Secretary-General of the UN, António Guterres, stated in the foreword to the Sustainable Development Goals Report 2022: 'We must deliver on our commitments to support the world's most vulnerable people, communities and nations.'[1] Such sentiment has long been the driver behind international accords and declarations that protect Indigenous Peoples, safeguarding cultures and Peoples that have faced colonization, human rights abuses, and natural resource degradation during the construction and expansion of the current global economy. At the centre of international laws respecting the rights of Indigenous Peoples, it is possible to highlight the Indigenous and Tribal Peoples Convention (ILO 169 or the Convention) and the customary international law principles enshrined in the United Nations Declaration on the Rights of Indigenous Peoples (UNDRIP). Drafted and implemented to safeguard Indigenous rights, these instruments especially recognize and reflect a cornerstone principle for Indigenous autonomy and sustainable development: the principle that development affecting Indigenous Peoples should only proceed with the free, prior, and informed consent (FPIC) of these Peoples, rather than being imposed.

This chapter presents an overview of the significance and supporting articles of ILO 169 and the UNDRIP that enable consent and Indigenous self-governance in the face of redefining Indigenous sustainable development, along with the evolution and impact of international law that has defined both

1 UN Department of Economic and Social Affairs, *Sustainable Development Goals Report 2022* (2022) 2 <https://digitallibrary.un.org/record/3980029?ln=en> accessed 27 January 2025.

the ILO 169 convention and the UNDRIP, shaping Indigenous treaty law seen today. Subsequently, examples from Canada are presented. Canadian policy has teetered between opposing and supporting instruments such as ILO 169 and the UNDRIP, specifically concerning recognition, reconciliation and resurgence of Indigenous Peoples through the enabling of consent. This initial explanation offers a foundation for the international juridical underpinnings of treaty law writ large found throughout the rest of this volume.

2.2 INDIGENOUS AND TRIBAL PEOPLES CONVENTION, 1989 (ILO 169)

ILO 169 is a legally binding treaty for ratifying countries that entered into force on 27 June 1989.[2] It was agreed through the International Labour Organization (ILO), a specialized agency of the United Nations that works with tripartite delegations of workers, business and government from 187 Member States to set labour standards and devise programmes and policies to promote decent work for all.[3] The ILO originally developed and ratified ILO 169's predecessor, ILO 107,[4] in 1957 to improve the living conditions of Indigenous Peoples, and this latter convention was later revised and renamed to recognize Indigenous Peoples' right to self-determination within a State and to set standards for governments regarding the political, economic, land, and cultural rights of Indigenous Peoples in their countries. Creating an updated ILO 107 was largely due to Indigenous groups, leaders, and other experts questioning the assimilationist and ethnocentric views reflected in ILO 107.[5] The updated Convention also provides greater recognition for the agency of Indigenous Peoples, calls for

[2] ILO, 'International Labour Organization Convention 169 Concerning Indigenous and Tribal Peoples in Independent Countries' (27 June 1989) 28 ILM 1382 (entered into force 5 September 1991) (hereafter 'ILO C169').

[3] ILO, '*Constitution of the International Labour Organization*' (adopted 1 April 1919, entered into force 28 June 1919).

[4] ILO, 'Convention (No 107) Concerning the Protection and Integration of Indigenous and Other Tribal and Semi-Tribal Populations in Independent Countries' (adopted 26 June 1957, entered into force 2 June 1959) ILO C107 (40th ILC Session 1957).

[5] ILO C169 departs from the assimilationist language of ILO C107 in its preamble: 'considering that the developments which have taken place in international law since 1957, as well as developments in the situation of indigenous and tribal peoples in all regions of the world, have made it appropriate to adopt new international standards on the subject with a view to removing the assimilationist orientation of the earlier standards ...', for more details on the context of ILO C107's development, see Mauro Barelli, 'The Role of Soft Law in the International Legal System: The Case of the United Nations Declaration on the Rights of Indigenous Peoples' (2009) 58 International and Comparative Law Quarterly 958, 965. See also Lee Swepston, 'A New Step in the International on Indigenous and Tribal Peoples: ILO Convention No 169 of 1989' (1990) 15 Oklahoma City University Law Review 677.

more direct participation in decision-making processes that affect their rights and livelihoods, includes a section on contact and cooperation across borders, and highlights the importance of FPIC.

However, not all of the weaknesses of ILO 107 were rectified through this updated agreement, in part due to the processes of adoption of Conventions of the ILO, which meant that final decisions on the commitments enshrined were still mainly taken by the non-Indigenous government and business representative signatories, even though Indigenous delegates were also present in the negotiation of ILO 169.[6] The Convention offers a compromise between Indigenous groups, businesses, and governments. Specifically related to consent, the terms for consultation and participation were left vague, which required judicial clarifications in jurisdictions like Canada. Ultimate control thus continued to remain with the State.

As of 2025, twenty-four countries had ratified ILO 169 and enabled the treaty to become law within their national borders, which is fewer than its predecessor ILO 107. Largely, this may be due to concerns raised by States about the meaning and implications of the self-determination powers conferred to Indigenous Peoples in the Convention, crucial but contested advances for ILO 169. As scholars have argued, countries such as Canada have hesitated, seeing these rights as threats to their sovereignty and governance in the face of growing Indigenous autonomy.[7] Further, many countries that have ratified ILO 169, mainly in Latin America, may not have the capacity to enforce the Convention fully.[8] Such obstacles to ratification and implementation of the Convention may influence other countries' decisions regarding non-ratification.

Despite various challenges and accomplishments of ILO 169, many Indigenous leaders still consider the Convention as an important international

6 For commonalities between the UNDRIP and ILO C169, see Mattias Åhrén, 'The Provisions on Lands, Territories and Natural Resources in the UN Declaration on the Rights of Indigenous Peoples: An Introduction' in Claire Charters and Rodolfo Stavenhagen (eds), *Making the Declaration Work: The United Nations Declaration on the Rights of Indigenous Peoples* (International Work Group for Indigenous Affairs 2009) 212. For details on the growing role of Indigenous delegations at the UN, see Rodolfo Stavenhagen, 'Making the Declaration Work' in Charters and Stavenhagen, ibid, 353.

7 In disputes over the text of ILO C169 and the UNDRIP, Canada was more associated with objections to the terms 'self-determination' and 'Peoples' than any other state, see Douglas Sanders, *Indigenous Peoples and Canada's Role on the International Stage* (Research Paper, Royal Commission on Aboriginal Peoples, December 1994) 20. For a more recent reflection on ILO C169, see Roberto Suárez Santos, 'Three Decades since the ILO's Convention 169: Reflections in Light of the Experience of the Private Sector with Prior Consultation' (2020) 24 (2–3) The International Journal of Human Rights 272–78.

8 ILO, '*Implementing the ILO Indigenous and Tribal Peoples Convention No. 169: Towards an Inclusive, Sustainable and Just Future*' (ILO 2019) 119.

instrument, which focuses on improving standards of living, self-determination, and advancing Indigenous human rights, and ultimately helped pave the way for the development of the UNDRIP adopted in 2007. It is a Convention that is largely representative of compromise, but a compromise that led to the inclusion of consent and consultation, as discussed in more detail below, in a legally binding mechanism that can be recognized for its landmark collaboration, even if ultimate adoption and enforcement may fall short of original expectations.

2.2.1 *Guidelines adopted in ILO 169*

ILO 169 is organized in ten parts, with forty-four articles. In the articles of ILO 169, States and other ILO drafters sought primarily to recognize the aspirations of Indigenous and Tribal Peoples to exercise agency and rights with regard to their own economic, social, environmental and political rights and development, including but not limited to their institutions, management styles, languages, religions, and identities.

Additionally, through these articles, the drafters of ILO 169 contributed to Indigenous self-determination by formally codifying the right to consultation, which later was incorporated as a right to FPIC in the UNDRIP, supporting the recognition of this legal principle internationally.[9] Within the ILO 169 context, consent is a process of consultation and participation in areas that affect Indigenous Peoples, allowing Indigenous Peoples to give or withhold consent that may affect their territories, education, economy, social, and cultural traditions and to do so without coercion, and allowing ongoing participation throughout decision-making processes. Under this framework, Indigenous Peoples and non-Indigenous counterparts or co-negotiators can have greater respect for Traditional Knowledge (TK) culture, and practices that pertain to Indigenous Peoples' own self-determination, sustainability, and equitable development.[10]

The concept of consultation is first presented in Articles 1–12 in Part I of the Convention with regard to general policy concerning governments' responsibility to protect the human rights and fundamental freedoms of Indigenous and Tribal Peoples in their countries. In Article 6, the Parties set out the basis of consent as it pertains to ILO 169, more specifically paragraphs

[9] The evolution and the unique qualities of FPIC are discussed in more detail in Section 2.3.

[10] Food and Agriculture Organization of the United Nations, 'Indigenous Peoples Free, Prior and Informed Consent' <https://perma.cc/KH4S-NDUL> accessed 23 January 2025.

6(1)(a), (b), and subsection 6(2). These clauses include important recognition of obligations related to consent, participation and representative institutions:

> Article 6
> (1) In applying the provisions of this Convention, governments shall:
> (a) consult the [P]eoples concerned, through appropriate procedures and in particular through their representative institutions, whenever consideration is being given to legislative or administrative measures which may affect them directly;
> (b) establish means by which these [P]eoples can *freely participate*, to at least the same extent as other sectors of the population, at all levels of decision-making in elective institutions and administrative and other bodies responsible for policies and programmes which concern them;
> (c) establish means for the *full development of these [P]eoples' own institutions and initiatives*, and in appropriate cases provide the resources necessary for this purpose.
> (2) The consultations carried out in application of this Convention shall be undertaken, in *good faith* and in a form appropriate to the circumstances, *with the objective of achieving agreement or consent to the proposed measures*.[11]

In Article 7, for its part, Parties set out a description of Indigenous Peoples' rights during the decision-making process.[12] Together, these articles oblige States which have ratified the Convention to give consideration to and consult with Indigenous groups in matters that affect them, such as education, land rights, political rights, and cultural rights, with the objective of receiving consent before moving forward. These articles are viewed by scholars and others as critical to advancing the rights of Indigenous Peoples, whereby obtaining consent may be necessary for effective participation in decision-making that affects Indigenous Peoples and their culture, communities, and

[11] ILO C169 (n 2) art 6 (emphasis added).

[12] Article 7 confers the right to make decisions on behalf of their social, economic, environmental, and political entitlements, specifically in paragraph 7(1) that Peoples 'shall *have the right to decide their own priorities* for the process of development as it affects their lives, beliefs, institutions and spiritual well-being and the lands they occupy or otherwise use, and to *exercise control*, to the extent possible, over their own economic, social, and cultural development' (emphasis added). Furthermore, 7(3) states that 'Governments shall ensure that, whenever appropriate, studies are carried out, in co-operation with the [P]eoples concerned', enabling Indigenous Peoples to co-generate knowledge that enables them to be more fulsomely aware of the data and results for which they base their decisions. ILO C169 (n 2) art 7.

territories.[13] It is likewise essential to note that in the concept of ILO 169, consultation is distinct from consent. Here, ILO 169 offers a process that *enables a pathway* to consent, with the '*objective* of achieving agreement or consent'. This does not require that consent is reached in every case which presents its issues, as discussed later in this chapter. Consent as a concept within FPIC is also further elaborated in discussions of UNDRIP below.

Subsequently, in Part II of the Convention, the Parties further reference and elaborate on consent. In Articles 13–19, the Parties outline the rights to land use and best practices: according to Article 16.2, consent is necessary for the relocation (as an exceptional measure) of Indigenous Peoples.[14] For its part, Article 15.2 safeguards the rights of Indigenous Peoples to participate in the use, management, and conservation of their resources.[15] FPIC has been interpreted to mean that decisions or activities affecting Indigenous Peoples must be preceded by meaningful consultation carried out in good faith, with

[13] For more on the debate surrounding the interpretation of FPIC, see Mauro Barelli, 'Free, Prior and Informed Consent in the Aftermath of the UN Declaration on the Rights of Indigenous Peoples: Developments and Challenges Ahead' (2012) 16 International Journal of Human Rights 2, 19–20. See also Adelfo Regino Montes and Gustavo Torres Cisneros, 'The United Nations Declaration on the Rights of Indigenous Peoples: The Foundation of a New Relationship between Indigenous Peoples, States and Societies' in Charters and Stavenhagen (n 6) 158 'In its explanation of why it voted against the Human Rights Council's approval of the declaration, Canada stated [...] that to recognise this right would be to give [I]ndigenous [P]eoples a right of veto over state decisions.'

[14] Relocation arising from exploration and exploitation of sub-surface resources. Article 16.2 contains the only provision in ILO C169 whereby consent, specifically 'free and informed consent', is required from Indigenous Peoples. The Parties agreed that 'Where the relocation of these [P]eoples is considered necessary as an exceptional measure, such relocation *shall take place only with their free and informed consent*', and that if consent cannot be obtained, then the relocation can only take place if appropriate procedures, including public inquiries, take place first. Additionally, relocation could require compensation and the right to return to the lands if possible. At face value, this is an achievement for Indigenous Peoples affirming their right to determine the status of any relocations. However, it leaves the door open, should consent not be provided, for possible forced extirpation. As a result, how this legally binding document ultimately divides powers between Indigenous and State interests remains a concern. ILO C169 (n 2) art 16. This is reflective of Schutling's argument that 'many Indigenous representatives feel that their lack of veto power allows governments too much freedom to do as they please'. Gerard Schutling, 'ILO Convention 169: Can It Help?' (1997) 10 Abya Yala News 4, 10.

[15] Article 15.2 is an additional acknowledgement of the powers that Indigenous Peoples can have for consultation relating to land-use, in this case in relation to State-owned lands, including rights to minerals and sub-surface resources. This article requires that 'governments shall establish or maintain procedures through which they shall consult these [P]eoples', and that 'The [P]eoples concerned shall wherever possible participate in the benefits of such activities and shall receive fair compensation for any damages which they may sustain as a result of such activities'. ILO C169 (n 2) art 15.

accurate and accessible information provided in a timely manner, free from coercion or manipulation, and respecting Indigenous Peoples rights to give or withhold consent according to their own decision-making processes.[16] This means, inter alia, that withholding consent could halt a policy or project that may affect Indigenous and Tribal Peoples. Consultation procedures, according to ILO 169, will also consider Indigenous and Tribal Peoples' traditional methods of decision-making, such as oral history and councils of elders, to provide effective consultation and dialogue that is motivated by mutual respect.[17]

Prior to ILO 169, international law had not fully recognized, especially not in such an extensive manner, the rights of Indigenous peoples.[18] Not only is the Convention viewed by many as providing unprecedented protections for Indigenous Peoples to come to decisions on their terms, which is especially crucial for projects such as development or extraction initiatives that historically and presently pose grave threats to Indigenous Peoples and often proceeded without their consent, but the Convention also empowers Indigenous Peoples to gain back a right to self-determination and cultural preservation within colonial frameworks.[19] However, this widespread recognition of Indigenous rights and powers has led many governments to be reluctant to ratify, ILO 169 (and similarly the UNDRIP), which may explain low rates of ratification and incorporation of this Convention as binding law.[20]

Nonetheless, ILO 169 offers an example of a binding legal advance for the rights of Indigenous Peoples, remains an active source of law internationally, and has been foundational in the drafting and adoption of the UNDRIP.

16 UN Economic and Social Council, 'International Workshop of Free, Prior and Informed Consent and Indigenous Peoples' (17–19 January 2005) PFII/2005/WS.2/4 <https://perma.cc/9QT6-WUZJ> accessed 22 January 2025.

17 ILO C169 (n 2); ILO, 'Indigenous Peoples: Consultation and Participation' <www.ilo.org/wcmsp5/groups/public/—asia/—ro-bangkok/documents/presentation/wcms_099187.pdf> accessed 27 January 2025.

18 See, on ILO C169's divergence from ILO C107's assimilationist approach and paternalistic assumptions, Athanasios Yupsanis, 'ILO Convention No 169 Concerning Indigenous and Tribal Peoples in Independent Countries 1989–2009: An Overview' (2010) 79 Nordic Journal of International Law 435; for an analysis of ILO C169's key dimensions see Swepston (n 5) 690.

19 S James Anaya, 'Indigenous Peoples' Participatory Rights in Relation to Decisions about Natural Resource Extraction: The More Fundamental Issue of What Rights Indigenous Peoples Have in Lands and Resources' (2005) 22(1) Arizona Journal of International and Comparative Law 7, 9.

20 supra (n18). ILO C169 (n 2).

To illustrate these intersections, a few selected Canadian examples of the role of ILO 169 in evolving public policy debates, and legal arguments can be provided. Canada's circumstances are crucial in this conversation, as a country that has not ratified ILO 169 and later adopted the UNDRIP but still imports consent requirements with varying degrees of success into consultation processes with Indigenous Peoples.

2.2.2 *ILO 169 in Relation to Canada's Indigenous Peoples*

Canada has a long history with the ILO, joining in 1919 as a founding member and since having ratified eight Fundamental Conventions, three Governance Conventions, and twenty-six Technical Conventions.[21] However, concerning ILO 169, Canada is not yet a ratifying country and thus does not implement the Convention as binding law: neither treaties with Indigenous Peoples nor development projects nor processes like sustainability impact assessments before legal developments related to the UNDRIP require consultation in the manner outlined through the ILO 169 articles.[22] Concerns raised include the implications of Indigenous self-governance as one of the country's main concerns for such types of clauses; namely, the country expresses concern about obligations that confer autonomy to Indigenous Peoples, which is perceived to take place at the expense of federal, provincial or even local authority over lands and resources.[23]

First, definitions for meaningful consultation arising in Canadian contexts may, however, still show semblance to, and are potentially influenced by, ILO 169. Second, there may be challenges arising from circumstances where a lack of clarity regarding meaningful consultations leads to conflicts between Indigenous and non-Indigenous interests. The former involves the integration of consultation procedures into modern land claims treaties signed between Canada's governments and Indigenous Peoples, and the latter is illustrated by

[21] 'Canada – ILO Cooperation' (ILO 2019) <www.ilo.org/pardev/donors/canada/lang–en/index.htm> accessed 10 February 2025.

[22] For a discussion on conventions, other than ILO C169, to which the UNDRIP may apply in Canada, see Brenda L Gunn, 'Overcoming Obstacles to Implementing the UN Declaration on the Rights of Indigenous Peoples in Canada' (2013) 31(2) Windsor Yearbook of Access to Justice 147, 166.

[23] Roberta Rice, 'The Internationalization of Indigenous Rights: UNDRIP in the Canadian Context' in Terry Mitchell, *UNDRIP and the 2009 Bolivian Constitution: Lessons for Canada* (Centre for International Governance Innovation 2014) 59–64.

courts' definition of meaningful consultation in the absence of ILO 169 through *Haida Nation v British Columbia (Minister of Forests)*.[24]

In Canada, modern treaties, also called Comprehensive Land Claims Agreements (CLCAs), are signed to provide jurisdiction and resolve ambiguities over land ownership and use that needed to be addressed under the previous Numbered Treaty regime.[25] In 2025, there were nearly thirty modern treaties between Indigenous communities and Canada, and more continue to be negotiated.[26] In general, these treaties elaborate how decisions are made regarding land and resources encompassed within the treaty territory. The Comprehensive Land Claim Agreement Between Her Majesty the Queen in Right of Canada and the Gwich'in as Represented by the Gwich'in Tribal Council of 1992 is no exception but nonetheless demonstrates an important discrepancy.[27] Like ILO 169, most modern treaties do not specifically require the word 'consent' but instead refer to 'consultation', which refers to sharing views on the matter but less clearly recognizing decision-making powers. In this modern treaty, the word 'consultation' is used only once in section 3.1.28 of the document, which lays out that consultation does not include consent for future and resource land use or the economic, social, or cultural rights and freedoms of the Gwich'in First Nations.[28]

> 3.1.28 Government *shall consult* with the Gwich'in Tribal Council in the planning of the institutions and the preparation of the settlement legislation and other legislation proposed to implement the provisions of this agreement.
>
> 'consultation' means:
>
> (a) the provision, to the Party to be consulted, of notice of a matter to be decided in sufficient form and detail to allow that Party to prepare its views on the matter;
> (b) the provision of a reasonable period of time in which the Party to be consulted may prepare its views on the matter, and provision of an opportunity to present such views to the Party obliged to consult; and
> (c) full and fair consideration by the Party obliged to consult of any views present.

[24] *Haida Nation v British Columbia (Minister of Forests)* [2004] 3 SCR 511.

[25] 'Treaties and Agreements' (Government of Canada 2020) <www.rcaanc-cirnac.gc.ca/eng/1100100028574/1529354437231> accessed 23 January 2025.

[26] ibid.

[27] Gwich'in Comprehensive Land Claim Agreement (Gwich'in Tribal Council–Government of Canada–Government of the Northwest Territories) (adopted 13 July 1991, entered into force 10 April 1992).

[28] ibid.

Moreover, in the absence of ILO 169, certain modern treaties weigh little on the matter of consultation. In the Land Claims and Self-Government Agreement Among the Tłįchǫ and the Government of the Northwest Territories and the Government of Canada, Section 20.3 on consent in the face of expropriation refers the decision-making authority of the Tłįchǫ lands to the Governor in Council rather than to the Tłįchǫ Government.[29] Such a provision appears to confer decision-making powers to the colonial authority rather than the Indigenous Peoples themselves, rather than providing the full breadth of powers to the Indigenous Party that underlie the principles of self-determination.[30]

Furthermore, even though as discussed elsewhere, in modern treaties Parties recognize a 'duty to consult',[31] differences may persist between the duty to consult and consent in its core sense in more practical terms. Referencing *Haida Nation v British Columbia (Minister of Forests)*,[32] leading legal scholars express concern that the duty to consult did not give Aboriginal groups a veto and elaborated that there is no legal assurance that consultation must lead to agreement.[33] In this view, the duty to consult propagates an unequal balance of power favouring the Crown, leading to lack of enablement

[29] Tłįchǫ Land Claims and Self-Government Agreement (The Tłįchǫ–Government of Canada–Government of the Northwest Territories) (adopted 25 August 2003, entered into force 4 August 2005) s 20.3, whereby the Parties agreed that 'Expropriation of Tłįchǫ lands *shall require the consent of the Governor in Council* where expropriation is under an Act of Parliament, or the Executive Council of the Government of the Northwest Territories where expropriation is under an Act of the Northwest Territories. The Governor in Council or the Executive Council, as the case may be, shall consider the principle in 20.1.1 and shall not give such consent unless the Governor in Council or the Executive Council, as the case may be, is satisfied that there is no other reasonable alternative to the expropriation. 20.3.2 *Notice* of the intention of an expropriating authority to seek the consent of the Governor in Council or the Executive Council, as the case may be, shall be given to the Tłįchǫ Government by the expropriating authority'.

[30] For more on the denial of Indigenous self-determination within Canada, against the backdrop of Indigenous self-government, see Gordon Christie, *Aboriginal Nationhood and the Inherent Right to Self-Government: Research Paper for the National Centre for First Nations Governance* (National Centre for First Nations Governance, May 2007).

[31] Marie-Claire Cordonier Segger, Wayne Garnons-Williams, and Eva Wu, 'Indigenous Treaties with Canada: Obstacles or Opportunities to Realizing the Sustainable Development Goals in Light of the United Nations Declaration on the Rights of Indigenous Peoples across Canada' (2023) 3(1) Inter Gentes <https://intergentes.com/wp-content/uploads/2023/09/indigenous-treaties-with-canada_ew-updates.pdf> accessed 18 March 2023.

[32] *Haida* (n 24).

[33] Sarah Morales, 'Braiding the Incommensurable: Indigenous Legal Traditions and the Duty to Consult' in John Borrows and others, *Braiding Legal Orders: Implementing the United Nations Declaration on the Rights of Indigenous Peoples* (Centre for International Governance Innovation 2019) 70.

of a more meaningful consultation process and contributing to reconciliation in Canada thus far.[34] As further leading scholars recommend, it is likely that 'a more comprehensive governance framework should include an interrelation of consultation and consent' to protect against any abuse of power due to the presumption of consent.[35]

2.3 THE UNITED NATIONS DECLARATION ON THE RIGHTS OF INDIGENOUS PEOPLES (UNDRIP)

The UNDRIP, an international declaration, was adopted after almost twenty-five years of deliberation between UN member States, Indigenous groups and others around the globe.[36] Deliberation began with a study released by the UN Economic and Social Council Special Rapporteur José R. Martinez Cobo in 1982 regarding the systemic discrimination faced by Indigenous Peoples worldwide.[37] The Declaration was created to protect the collective and individual rights of Indigenous Peoples internationally, consisting of forty-six articles, setting guidelines that 'constitute the minimum standards for the survival, dignity and well-being of the Indigenous Peoples of the world'.[38] When adopted in September 2007, a majority of 144 States were in favour of the UNDRIP with only four votes against (Australia, Canada, New Zealand, and the United States) and 11 abstentions (Azerbaijan, Bangladesh, Bhutan, Burundi, Colombia, Georgia, Kenya, Nigeria, Russian Federation, Samoa, and Ukraine).[39] The four countries against reversed their positions a few years later to support the Declaration.

[34] ibid 72.

[35] Gonzalo Bustamante and Thibault Martin, 'Benefit Sharing and the Mobilization of ILO Convention 169' in Mitchell (n 23) 57.

[36] UN Res 61/295, 'United Nations Declaration on the Rights of Indigenous Peoples' (2007) UN Doc A/RES/61/295 (UNDRIP). For more on the long process and history behind the UNDRIP, see Megan Davis, 'Indigenous Struggles in Standard-Setting: The United Nations Declaration on the Rights of Indigenous Peoples' (2008) 9(2) Melbourne Journal of International Law 439.

[37] José R Martinez Cobo, 'Study of the Problem of Discrimination against Indigenous Populations' (30 July 1981) UN Doc E/CN.4/Sub.2/476.

[38] See, for a discussion of how this minimum standard was initially interpreted within Australia, Canada, the United States, and New Zealand, Megan Davis, 'To Bind or Not to Bind: The United Nations Declaration on the Rights of Indigenous Peoples Five Years On' (2012) 19 Australian International Law Journal 17, 43.

[39] Erin Hanson, 'UN Declaration on the Rights of Indigenous Peoples' (Indigenous Foundations, UBC) <https://indigenousfoundations.arts.ubc.ca/un_declaration_on_the_rights_of_indigenous_peoples/> accessed 27 January 2025.

Though not legally binding in the same way as ILO 169, the UNDRIP sets out norms and expectations for the international community related to the rights of Indigenous Peoples. International, regional, and domestic courts and tribunals consider human rights instruments such as the UNDRIP to discern the principles upon which to base their legal interpretations, in some cases also finding that key principles found in UNDRIP also represent customary norms, as in other international human rights instruments. Some scholars suggest, 'the whole of the UNDRIP could be seen to codify customary international law, simply because many human rights treaty monitoring bodies have started to use the UNDRIP as a guide to interpreting their respective human rights instruments that are legally binding on most States of the world'.[40] In Canada, the UNDRIP opens a route through which Indigenous rights can be interpreted and affirmed through the courts.[41]

Additionally, the provisions of UNDRIP expanded on the concept of consultation and consent outlined in ILO 169 to clarify the principles behind FPIC. FPIC is integral to upholding the rights of Indigenous Peoples and ensuring effective participation in decision-making that affects Indigenous Peoples and their culture, communities, and territories. The concept describes processes free from manipulation and coercion, that are informed by sufficient and timely information and, most importantly, occur before a decision that affects Indigenous Peoples' rights and interests. Through FPIC, Indigenous Peoples can effectively be a part of the decision-making process in ways that, to many Indigenous Peoples, are more meaningful than what is found in ILO 169.[42] As enumerated in the UNDRIP's articles and as explained below, this Declaration recognizes and explains, in human and especially Indigenous rights terms, key duties and obligations, including FPIC.

[40] Aldo Chircop, Timo Koivurova, and Krittika Singh, 'Is There a Relationship between UNDRIP and UNCLOS?' (2019) 33 Ocean YB 1.

[41] For example, see *Thomas and Saik'uz First Nation v Rio Tinto Alcan Inc* [2022] B.C.S.C. 15 (CAN) [205]. Though in this case, the Supreme Court of British Columbia reached its decision without directly relying on the UNDRIP, the Court considered the potential implications of how the UNDRIP legislation can supplement, refine, and alter existing laws and jurisprudence to address Aboriginal rights.

[42] Tara Ward, 'The Right to Free, Prior, and Informed Consent: Indigenous Peoples' Participation Rights within International Law' (2011) 10(2) Journal of Human Rights 56; Ginger Gibson McDonald and Gaby Zezulka, 'Part I: Recent Development and Effective Roles for Government, Industry, and Indigenous Communities' in Boreal Leadership Council, *Understanding Successful Approaches to Free Prior and Informed Consent in Canada* (Boreal Leadership Council 2015) 8; Food and Agriculture Organization (n 10).

2.3.1 *Guidelines in the UNDRIP*

The UNDRIP's forty-six articles seek, according to scholars, to protect Indigenous Peoples' collective and individual rights internationally[43] to 'constitute the minimum standards for the survival, dignity, and well-being of the Indigenous Peoples of the world'.[44] The drafters of the UNDRIP expanded the concept of consent through FPIC, which appears throughout the Declaration, including references to relocation from lands, together with redress for losses of property rights related to culture, intellectual property, land, and resources.[45] FPIC is emphasized prior to the adoption of legislative and administrative measures[46] and prior to the approval of projects affecting their lands, territories, and resources.[47]

Other notable innovations stemming from the UNDRIP are related to Indigenous Peoples' rights to their own economic, political, social, and cultural development, including affirming that Indigenous Peoples are holders of all human rights and fundamental freedoms as recognized in the Charter of the United Nations,[48] have the right to self-government,[49] maintain institutional rights[50] and have rights to the land, territories, and resources that they have traditionally owned, occupied, or otherwise used or acquired.[51]

43 UNDRIP (n 36).
44 ibid.
45 ibid art 10, which recognizes free, prior, and informed consent of relocation: 'Indigenous [P]eoples shall not be forcibly removed from their lands or territories. No relocation shall take place without the free, prior and informed consent of the Indigenous [P]eoples concerned and after agreement on just and fair compensation and, where possible, with the option of return'. See also art 28.1, which recognizes redress and restitution for Indigenous Peoples: 'Indigenous [P]eoples have the right to redress, by means that can include restitution or, when this is not possible, just, fair and equitable compensation, for the lands, territories and resources which they have traditionally owned or otherwise occupied or used, and which have been confiscated, taken, occupied, used or damaged without their free, prior and informed consent'.
46 ibid art 19, which recognizes FPIC in legislature: 'States shall consult and cooperate in good faith with the Indigenous [P]eoples concerned through their own representative institutions in order to obtain their free, prior and informed consent before adopting and implementing legislative or ad- ministrative measures that may affect them'.
47 ibid art 32.2, which recognizes FPIC to land and resource use on their territory: 'States shall consult and cooperate in good faith with the [I]ndigenous [P]eoples concerned through their own representative institutions in order to obtain their free and informed consent prior to the approval of any project affecting their lands or territories and other resources, particularly in connection with the development, utilization or exploitation of mineral, water or other resources'.
48 ibid art 1.
49 ibid art 4.
50 ibid art 5.
51 ibid art 26.

2.3.2 UNDRIP Concerning Indigenous Peoples in Canada

For many Indigenous Peoples, the UNDRIP is a crucial step for reconciliation and advancement of rights in Canada. The UNDRIP is integrated throughout the 2015 Truth and Reconciliation Commission of Canada (TRC) Calls to Action[52] and, in particular, is invoked as central to both self-governance and land rights.[53] Similarly, the 2019 National Inquiry into Missing and Murdered Indigenous Women and Girls (MMIWG) endorses, in its Call for Justice, the 'immediate and full implementation of the United Nations Declaration on the Rights of Indigenous Peoples'.[54] For Indigenous Peoples demanding reconciliation and a future of sustainable development, the UNDRIP remains a central baseline for the country to achieve its promised goals.

However, Canada's relationship with the UNDRIP has been volatile. Since the discussions which led to UNDRIP were launched in 1985, Indigenous representatives from Canada have aided in its foundation and drafting.[55] The Canadian Government was involved in the development process as well through chairing intercessional consultations from 2000 to 2003 and working with Aboriginal Organizations to reach common ground.[56] However, Canada's goal throughout the consultations was perceived as seeking to advance concerns regarding maintaining State authority while developing the rights of the Indigenous population.[57] Canada actively participated in negotiations when the first draft was submitted in 1995 but subsequently withdrew from negotiations for the final draft.[58]

Regarding its adoption, Canada first voted against the UNDRIP as a United Nations resolution in 2007. In 2010, the Government of the time endorsed UNDRIP while qualifying it as 'aspirational', an approach adopted prior to

52 Truth and Reconciliation Commission of Canada, 'Honouring the Truth, Reconciling for the Future – Summary of the Final Report of the Truth and Reconciliation Commission of Canada' (2015) (TRC).

53 ibid 42, 45, 46, 47, 49, 50 and 92; Ward (n 42) 56.

54 National Inquiry into Missing and Murdered Indigenous Women and Girls, 'Calls for Justice' (3 June 2019) Call for Justice 1.2 (v).

55 Hanson (n 39).

56 'Canada's Position: United Nations Draft Declaration on the Rights of Indigenous Peoples' (Canada, Indian and Northern Affairs Canada) <https://perma.cc/YXW7-7D7M> accessed 23 January 2025.

57 UNGAOR, 'United Nations Declaration on the Rights of Indigenous Peoples' (13 September 2007) UN Doc A/RES/61/295 (2007).

58 Government of Canada, 'Forging New Paths of Collaboration: International Day of the World's Indigenous People, CIHR's IAPH and the Global Indigenous Health Research Projects' (Canadian Institute of Health Research) <https://perma.cc/ZWQ5-LFZD> accessed 23 January 2025.

reconciliation commitments.[59] All the while, many Canadian citizens, legal experts, Canadian grassroots organizations, Indigenous Peoples, and others supported the Declaration.[60] In 2016, Canada's newly elected government retracted the country's United Nations-defined 'objector' status to the UNDRIP, adopting a commitment to 'co-develop legislation to implement the Declaration by the end of 2020'.[61] Progress, however, was slow,[62] with the principles behind FPIC lying at the heart of many UNDRIP debates. The implications of Indigenous self-governance were underlined as one of the country's main concerns for FPIC,[63] one of the most widely challenged elements of the UNDRIP in a manner similar to the backlash faced by ILO 169 in relation to the term *consultation*.[64]

For Canada's Indigenous Peoples, the UNDRIP became an instrument in Canadian law following the 2021 *United Nations Declaration on the*

59 Sasha Boutilier, 'Free, Prior, and Informed Consent and Reconciliation in Canada: Proposals to Implement Articles 19 and 32 of the UN Declaration on the Rights of Indigenous Peoples' (2017) 7 Western Journal of Legal Studies 1, 4.

60 Hanson (n 39).

61 David Lametti, 'Speech: Assembly of First Nations: Special Chiefs Assembly' (Department of Justice Canada, 4 December 2019) <https://perma.cc/SEH5-PUUZ> accessed 23 January 2025.

62 Currently, there are only two pieces of legislation incorporating UNDRIP into law. The first, passed in 2019 in British Columbia, is an Act requiring the government to 'prepare and implement an action plan to achieve the objectives of the Declaration'. The second, passed in 2021 by the federal government, 'affirms the Declaration as a universal international human rights instrument with application in Canadian law'. *Declaration on the Rights of Indigenous Peoples Act*, S.B.C. 2019, c. 44 (CAN) s 4(1); *United Nations Declaration on the Rights of Indigenous Peoples Act*, S.C. 2021, c. 14 (CAN) s 6(1).

63 Rice (n 23) 59–64.

64 This was even specifically called out by Canadian UN Ambassador John McNee, who expressed that Canada had significant concerns especially regarding provisions on land territories and resources being 'overly broad, unclear and capable of a wide variety of interpretations'. Heidi Fraser-Kruck, *Canada's Failure to Support the United Nations Declaration on the Rights of Indigenous Peoples: An Intersectional Analysis of the Repercussions as Seen through the Inter-Woven Lenses of Women's Rights, Environmental Rights, and Poverty Alleviation* (University of Ottawa 2009); CBC News, 'Canada Votes "No" as UN Native Rights Declaration Passes' (CBC, 13 September 2007) <www.cbc.ca/news/canada/canada-votes-no-as-un-native-rights-declaration-passes-1.632160> accessed 16 March 2023. Minister of Indian Affairs at the time Chuck Strahl explained the government's reasoning to not support the Declaration as 'By signing on, you default to this document by saying that the only rights in play here are the rights of First Nations. And, of course, in Canada, that's inconsistent with our Constitution'. Steven Edwards, 'Tories Defend "No" in Native Rights Vote' (The Montreal Gazette, 2007) <www.pressreader.com/canada/montreal-gazette/20070914/281706905302273> accessed 23 January 2025.

Rights of Indigenous Peoples Act [*UNDRIP Act*].[65] This Act provides a framework for the Government of Canada to integrate and implement the Declaration. Enabling FPIC to become law transfers authority from government and industry interests to Indigenous Peoples, which has been affirmed through Canadian courts by enabling statute interpretation to be performed in ways that are more consistent with Canada's international obligations, informing courts' contextual approach, and identifying values and principles to inform legislative interpretation.[66] In this vein, as scholars have suggested, it is possible to define consent in the context of FPIC and in comparison to the duty to consult, whereby inherent in the definition of consent must be the right to 'say no' to a project for which consent is being sought.[67] Such conclusions imply that the gap between the rights that exist in Canada's modern treaties and section 35(1) of the *Charter of Rights and Freedoms*,[68] and the incremental rights that the UNDRIP enacts, is precisely the right of Indigenous Peoples to permit an activity to proceed or not, regardless of the prospect of compensation or redress. In Canada, it remains unclear whether the duty to consult that is already in place, or FPIC as included in the UNDRIP, or both, empower Indigenous Peoples to truly say 'no' in absolute terms to any project they deem to be harmful to their land or their livelihood.[69] This is of further importance, considering that the *UNDRIP Act* is an instrument of interpretation and requires alignment *with* the UNDRIP rather than the Declaration taking a direct legal effect.[70] As such, even though the UNDRIP is the foundation for calls to action demanded by Indigenous Peoples, concerns and interests in relation to land and resource exploitation may ultimately shape or even weaken political will and the effect of fully endorsing the UNDRIP.

2.4 CONCLUSION

In light of the accomplishments and shortfalls of both ILO 169 and the UNDRIP, these two agreements remain pivotal wins for addressing

[65] Sander Duncanson and others, 'Federal UNDRIP Bill Becomes Law' (Osler, 22 June 2021) <www.osler.com/en/resources/regulations/2021/federal-undrip-bill-becomes-law> accessed 23 January 2025.
[66] *Canada (Human Rights Commission) v Canada (Attorney General)*, 2012 F.C 445 (CAN) [350]–[354], aff'd 2013 FCA 75.
[67] Terry Mitchell, 'International Gaze Brings Critical Focus to Questions about Aboriginal Governance in Canada' in Mitchell (n 23) 43–48.
[68] Constitution Act 1982, Canadian Charter of Rights and Freedoms.
[69] Morales (n 33) 70.
[70] House of Commons Debates, 43-2, No. 60 (17 February 2021) 1810 (Hon David Lametti).

Indigenous rights internationally. Codifying and stipulating the requirements for consent, consultation, participation, and self-determination for Indigenous Peoples provides a foundation to build and stimulate sustainable and equitable economic development worldwide. In times of reconciliation and resurgence, the influence and outcomes of these legal instruments and the principles behind FPIC become ever more crucial to understanding how Indigenous Peoples determine their economic, social, and environmental implications.

3

Indigenous Peoples, Sustainable Development, and International Law

3.1 INTRODUCTION

For millennia, through rules and governance systems at all levels from community to country and beyond, humanity has sought ways to ensure their economic development, including stewardship of resources they depend on, can respect natural systems and the dignity of others. In public policy and law, this is often described as a commitment to advance more sustainable development.[1] Core to the concept is the need to advance, in a way that does not place one over the others, poverty eradication and improvements in quality of life for people, respect for human rights including cultural survival, and respect for nature, including environmental protection – development that can last for current and future generations. These priorities are paramount in sustainable development law, the norms, rules, and legal and governance instruments including treaties, which shape development pathways, advancing sustainability.[2] In the 2000 Millennium Development Goals (MDGs), countries emphasized the need 'to reduce extreme poverty and promote environmental sustainability by 2015,' and in the 2015 Sustainable Development Goals (SDGs), these priorities

[1] Marie-Claire Cordonier Segger and Damilola Olawuyi, *Sustainable Development Law: Principles, Practice and Prospects* (Oxford University Press 2025).

[2] ibid. See also Marie-Claire Cordonier Segger and Alexandra Harrington, 'Environment and Sustainable Development' in Simon Chesterman, David M Malone, and Santiago Villalpando (eds), *The Oxford Handbook of United Nations Treaties* (Oxford University Press 2019); Nico Schrijver, 'Advancements in the Principles of International Law on Sustainable Development' in Marie-Claire Cordonier Segger and Christopher Weeramantry (eds), *Sustainable Development Principles in the Decisions of International Courts and Tribunals 1992–2012* (Routledge 2017).

were further elaborated as specific goals and targets.[3] The United Nations (UN) adopted seventeen Sustainable Development Goals (SDGs) with 169 time-bound targets, as part of a global agenda for sustainable development towards 2030.[4] Since their inception, the SDGs, which are aspirational rather than legally binding in character, and their respective targets have provided public policy priorities and metrics to evaluate local, regional, and global progress towards more sustainable development. Progress towards achieving the seventeen goals is tracked by multiple indexes which reflect the multi-faceted nature of the SDGs, across many different areas of endeavour, including efforts to end poverty and hunger, to secure access to health, education, clean water, and energy, to incentivize sustainable infrastructure and communities, to protect life below water and on land, and to advance peace and justice.[5] But due in large part to their multi-layered, multi-actor, and multi-sector characteristics, approaches to achieving the SDGs have been slow to show success in achieving the 2030 targets.[6] In part, slow progress may also be due to weaknesses and gaps in the law, especially in implementation and enforcement, and in the financing required. An analysis of the important treaties that align with the SDGs and their targets, particularly those legally binding instruments involving Indigenous Parties, can provide insight into how multiple stakeholders can and should participate in addressing such diverse systemic interrelations, and advancing more sustainable development across Canada and beyond.

3 UN, 'Millennium Development Goals Background (2013)' <www.un.org/millenniumgoals/bkgd.shtml> accessed 24 January 2025.> accessed 24 January 2025.

4 UN General Assembly Res 70/1, 'Transforming Our World: The 2030 Agenda for Sustainable Development' (21 October 2015) UN Doc A/RES/70/1 (SDGs). The 17 SDGs that were codified address key sectors of social, economic, and environmental policy and action, with specific time-bound targets to end poverty and hunger, secure health, education, gender equality, clean energy, fresh water and sanitation, employment, innovation and infrastructure, equity, sustainable cities and communities, and consumption and production, also action on climate change, marine ecosystems and fisheries, biodiversity and land conservation, as well as to advance peace, justice and good governance, and partnerships. For more details, see also Winfried Huck, *Sustainable Development Goals: Article-by-Article Commentary* (Beck/Hart/Nomos 2022); Markus Kaltenborn, Markus Krajewski, and Heike Kuhn (eds), *Sustainable Development Goals and Human Rights* (Springer 2020); Jonas Ebbesson and Ellen Hey (eds), *The Cambridge Handbook of the Sustainable Development Goals and International Law* (Cambridge University Press 2020).

5 Jose Manuel Diaz-Sarachaga, Daniel Jato-Espino, and Daniel Castro-Fresno, 'Is the Sustainable Development Goals (SDG) Index an Adequate Framework to Measure the Progress of the 2030 Agenda?' (2018) 26(6) Sustainable Development 663.

6 René Kemp and Pim Martens, 'Sustainable Development: How to Manage Something That Is Subjective and Never Can Be Achieved?' (2007) 3(2) Sustainability: Science, Practice and Policy 5.

In this chapter, after a brief introduction to the principles and practices of international law on sustainable development, comparative legal research methods are employed to explore options for the SDGs and their targets to be advanced, addressing key social, environmental, and economic challenges, taking into account Indigenous legal principles. The importance and origins of the SDGs and their targets are first examined, followed by an analysis of their alignment with key priorities of Indigenous Peoples, particularly taking into account binding treaty commitments and obligations that address and potentially augment goals such as to end poverty and hunger, ensure access to health, education, clean water and energy, secure sustainable infrastructure and communities, or protect life below water and on land. Modern treaties between Indigenous Peoples and Canadian governments provide illustrative examples in the chapter, including highlights from the James Bay and Northern Quebec Agreement, the Kluane First Nation Agreement, and the Labrador Inuit Land Claims Agreement. This analysis seeks to provide a deeper, pluralistic understanding of the rights and obligations related to the United Nations Declaration of the Rights of Indigenous Peoples (UNDRIP) and the SDGs, while experimenting with new combined customary and treaty law analysis approaches. Finally, key challenges and guidelines guidelines and challenges related to managing resources, taking into account sustainable development obligations to Indigenous Peoples and marginalized groups, are introduced.

3.2 PRINCIPLES OF INTERNATIONAL LAW ON SUSTAINABLE DEVELOPMENT AND THE UN SDGS

While the central principles of sustainable development, including respect for the interests of current and future generations, have been understood by many civilizations throughout the ages, sustainable development concepts and commitments ere especially highlighted in worldwide consultations for Our Common Future, the influential 1987 report of the World Commission on Environment and Development (WCED), as featured in international law and policy debates at the United Nations Conference on the Environment and Development (UNCED) in 1992.[7] More than 178 countries adopted Agenda 21, a non-binding global action plan to build partnerships for

[7] WCED, *Our Common Future* (Oxford University Press 1987); United Nations Conference on Environment and Development, *Report of the United Nations Conference on Environment and Development* (12 August 1992) UN Doc A/CONF.151/26 (Vol I); Cordonier Segger and Olawuyi (n 1).

improving the sustainable development of both human lives and the environment.[8] Subsequently, over the next decades, commitments to sustainable development have been adopted as part of the object and purpose of many binding treaties and instruments in international law, supported by growing recognition of principles and norms that, identified in the International Law Association's (ILA) 2002 New Delhi Declaration of Principles of International Law Relating to Sustainable Development, are increasingly being deployed by international courts and tribunals worldwide.[9] In 2015, the UN SDGs were adopted as an annex to the 2030 Agenda for Sustainable Development, crystallizing international public policy consensus through an agenda for 2030 and beyond, and offering a succinct set of policy goals and time-bound targets of relevance worldwide to advance sustainable development, one that bridges international, national, regional, and sub-national governance domains[10] through 17 SDGs and 169 associated targets.[11] At their core, the SDGs are a tool for stakeholders to participate in enacting stronger commitments to improving quality of life across social, economic, and environmental spheres (see Figure 3.1).

However, while there has been progress in analysing and tracking efforts to achieve the SDGs at the international level, there remain very important gaps in ensuring that domestic governance systems learn to respect and support the achievement of the SDGs on the ground. This is a fundamental challenge, as without national and local regimes that recognize and support the achievement of the SDG commitments, there is no chance for promises of sustainable development to become a reality, especially for the poorest and most marginalized groups.[12] Additionally, as critiques of the SDGs highlight, the

8 United Nations Sustainable Development, 'United Nations Conference on Environment and Development Rio de Janeiro, Brazil – Agenda 21' (3–14 June 1992) <https://sustainabledevelopment.un.org/content/documents/Agenda21.pdf> accessed 24 January 2025.

9 ILA, 'New Delhi Declaration of Principles of International Law Relating to Sustainable Development' (adopted at the 70th Conference of the International Law Association, New Delhi, 2–6 April 2002), ILA, 'Sofia Guiding Statements on Sustainable Development and the Role of International Courts and Tribunals' (Report of the ILA Committee on International Law and Sustainable Development, adopted at the 75th ILA Conference, Sofia, 2012). Marie-Claire Cordonier Segger and CG Weeramantry (n 2), and Cordonier Segger and Olawuyi (n 1).

10 SDGs (n 4); Louis Meuleman and Ingeborg Niestroy, 'Common But Differentiated Governance: A Metagovernance Approach to Make the SDGs Work' (2015) 7(9) Sustainability 12295.

11 SDGs (n 4).

12 Martin Visbeck and others, 'A Sustainable Development Goal for the Ocean and Coasts: Global Ocean Challenges Benefit from Regional Initiatives Supporting Globally Coordinated Solutions' (2014) 49 Marine Policy 88.

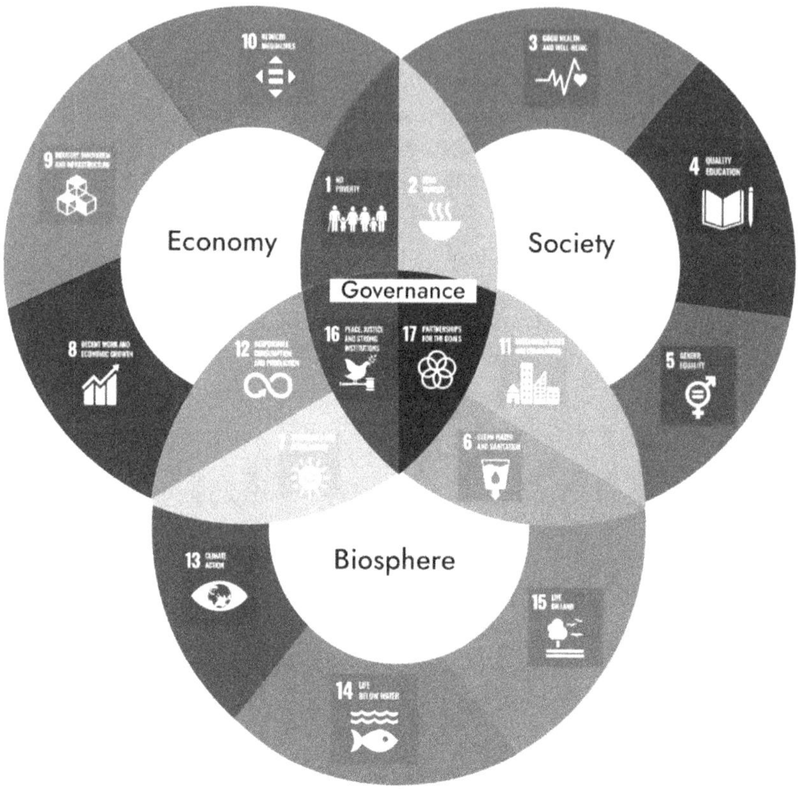

FIGURE 3.1 SDGs intersections.

goals themselves are far from perfect and many are either not ambitious enough, or risk perpetuating current inequalities.[13] For instance, while the goals celebrate the role of Indigenous Peoples in sustainable development, some commentators are concerned that they do not highlight, enough, the needs and rights of Indigenous Peoples,[14] or critique, enough, the role of

[13] Sara L Seck, 'Business, Human Rights, & the Triple Planetary Crisis: Confronting Overconsumption' (UConn Business & Human Rights Workshop, March 2022); see also Sumudu A Atapattu, Carmen G Gonzalez, and Sara L Seck, 'Intersections of Environmental Justice and Sustainable Development' in Sumudu A Atapattu, Carmen G Gonzalez, and Sara L Seck (eds), *The Cambridge Handbook of Environmental Justice and Sustainable Development* (Cambridge University Press 2021) 1.

[14] Dominic O'Sullivan, *Indigeneity, Culture and the UN Sustainable Development Goals* (Palgrave Macmillan 2023). See also Mandy Li-Ming Yap and Krushil Watene, 'The Sustainable Development Goals (SDGs) and Indigenous Peoples: Another Missed Opportunity?' (2019) 20(4) Journal of Human Development and Capabilities 451.

certain industries in causing climate change.[15] The link between climate change, human rights, and inequality was one of the points emphasized by the UN Special Rapporteur on Extreme Poverty in his 2019 report, which noted that the richest people are both 'responsible for and have benefited from the vast majority of [GHG] emissions' and 'have the greatest capacity to adapt'; meanwhile those most harmed are the poorest, 'who have contributed the least to emissions and have the least capacity to react'.[16] In this context, it becomes paramount to seek greater insight and highlight the views and contributions of Indigenous Peoples, including Indigenous wisdom and practices, to advancing the SDGs, and to focus not just on public policy, but also on binding law and governance which can remove existing barriers and incentivize more just and sustainable conduct. As discussed below, when carefully operationalized and respected, treaties – particularly those involving Indigenous Parties – can offer innovative approaches to advancing the SDGs.

3.3 INDIGENOUS PEOPLES AND THE SDGS

For Indigenous Peoples, the possible synergies between advancing sustainable development and realizing rights are subject to significant discussion in scholarly literature, including through public policy theories and practices.[17] Many leaders and an increasing body of scholarship are underlining that, historically, State-supported and enforced policies and regulations have alienated Indigenous groups by seizing control of resources which are of essential importance to Indigenous communities and, more often than not, mismanaging them.[18] As Indigenous groups seek to deploy laws and policies on sustainable development to improve well-being and achieve self-

[15] Seck (n 13).

[16] United Nations Human Rights Office of the High Commissioner, 'Report of the Special Rapporteur on Extreme Poverty and Human Rights: Climate Change and Poverty' (17 July 2019) UN Doc A/HRC/41/39 (17 July 2019) 14.

[17] Marcela Brugnach, Marc Craps, and Art Dewulf, 'Including Indigenous Peoples in Climate Change Mitigation: Addressing Issues of Scale, Knowledge and Power' (2014) 140(1) Climatic Change 19; Thomas F Thornton and Claudia Comberti, 'Synergies and Trade-offs between Adaptation, Mitigation and Development' (2013) 140(1) Climatic Change 5; Ameyali Ramos-Castillo, Edwin J Castellanos, and Kirsty Galloway McLean, 'Indigenous Peoples, Local Communities and Climate Change Mitigation' (2017) 140(1) Climatic Change 1; James Ford and others, 'Adaptation and Indigenous Peoples in the United Nations Framework Convention on Climate Change' (2016) 139(3–4) Climatic Change 429; Yolanda Terán Maigua and Cathy Gutierrez-Gomez, 'Responding to Cultural Loss: Providing an Integral Indigenous Perspective of a "Kichwa Child"' (2015) 92(1) Childhood Education 22.

[18] Christopher Nowlin, 'Indigenous Capitalism and Resource Development in an Age of Climate Change: A Timely Dance with the Devil?' (2020) 17(1) MJSDL 71, 75–76.

determination,[19] there may be new opportunity for improvement in how legislation and policy intersect with Indigenous rights.

Indigenous rights holders were among one of the major groups involved in consultations in the development of the SDGs.[20] Two targets and indicators reference Indigenous Peoples directly, articulated through SDG 2: Zero Hunger target 2.3.2 and SDG 4: Education target 4.5.1, and many others are directly relevant, including on poverty, access to clean water and energy, sustainable infrastructure and communities, climate change, life below water and on land, and justice.[21] However, although UNDRIP[22] is also monitored by the United Nations, its principles can still be more deeply reflected in the SDGs, and more can be done to highlight how sustainable development has the potential to not only advance the rights of Indigenous Peoples, but also to require the inclusion, participation, and consent of Indigenous Peoples globally. In such a sense, it can be argued, the textual content and implementation of many treaties with Indigenous Peoples have demonstrated legally binding obligations that are directly beneficial to the Indigenous Parties involved, and can also be directly linked to advancing specific SDGs and their respective targets. Below, selected examples from Canada demonstrate how, by fulfilling treaty obligations, these legal mechanisms have the potential to foster or frustrate progress towards attaining specific SDGs.

3.3.1 *Sustainable Development and Treaties in Relation to Indigenous Peoples in Canada*

Canada's treaties with Indigenous Peoples are constitutionally protected, mutually binding agreements.[23] However, the success of how treaties practically respect Indigenous rights and title within Canada largely depends on the implementation and respect for the legally binding obligations stipulated in the agreements. In Canada, the text within treaties with Indigenous

[19] S Prakash Sethi and others, 'Freeport-McMoRan Copper & Gold, Inc.: An Innovative Voluntary Code of Conduct to Protect Human Rights, Create Employment Opportunities, and Economic Development of the Indigenous People' (2011) 103(1) Journal of Business Ethics 1; Lily Gadamus and others, 'Building an Indigenous Evidence-Base for Tribally-Led Habitat Conservation Policies' (2015) 62 Marine Policy 116.

[20] United Nations Department of Economic and Social Affairs Indigenous Peoples, 'Indigenous Peoples and the Post-2015 Development Agenda' (United Nations, 2015) <www.un.org/development/desa/indigenouspeoples/focus-areas/post-2015-agenda/the-sustainable-development-goals-sdgs-and-indigenous/post2015.html> accessed 24 January 2025.

[21] United Nations Department of Economic and Social Affairs, 'The 17 Goals' (United Nations, 2018) <https://sdgs.un.org/goals> accessed 24 January 2025.

[22] More information on the UNDRIP can be found in Chapter 2, Section 2.3.

[23] Constitution Act 1982, Canadian Charter of Rights and Freedoms, ss 25, 35(1), which 'recognized and affirmed' both past and future treaty rights.

Peoples largely seeks to capture the spirit and intent of advancing growth across the three pillars of sustainability. However, the mixed observance of their terms on the part of the Government of Canada and the territorial or provincial governments at times leaves a heavily knotted legal tapestry for Indigenous rights and the relationship between Indigenous Peoples and the Crown. To best capture these histories of treaties and their impacts on development in Indigenous territories it is first necessary to distinguish their history in the context of Canadian constitutional law. Next, the disparities in sustainable development between Indigenous and broader Canadian populations are examined, along with examples of how implementing modern treaties can help address sustainable development gaps.

Canada has, broadly speaking, two types of treaties with Indigenous nations – historic treaties and modern treaties. From 1701 through 1923, seventy 'historic treaties', which included the eleven numbered treaties, were marked between the Crown and Indigenous groups,[24] most characterized as land-use agreements in exchange for relinquishing the right to land title.[25] These treaties were mainly unsigned but rather 'marked', reflecting the rich oral traditions and society of many Indigenous cultures that honour verbal commitments. Indigenous historians and others have noted that representatives of the Indigenous Peoples agreeing to the treaties negotiated in good faith for the survival of their communities and traditions in recognition of changing times due to colonial settlement as they were voluntarily or coercively transitioned from their formerly expansive self-determining and self-governing ways of living to one that was constrained by reserves colonial structures.[26] The Government of Canada, many scholars and others have underlined, could not have considered the best interests of Indigenous Peoples during the negotiation processes.[27] Many numbered treaties, for instance, were negotiated when the federal

[24] Government of Canada, 'Treaties and Agreements' (Government of Canada, 2022) <www.rcaanc-cirnac.gc.ca/eng/1100100028574/1529354437231#chp3> accessed 24 January 2025 (GoC Treaties). The numbered treaties were negotiated between 1871 and 1921. They promised Indigenous Peoples reserve lands, annuities, and the continued right to hunt and fish on unoccupied Crown lands in exchange for Aboriginal title.

[25] Ghislain Otis, 'Constitutional Recognition of Aboriginal and Treaty Rights: A New Framework for Managing Legal Pluralism in Canada?' (2014) 46(3) Journal of Legal Pluralism and Unofficial Law 320.

[26] Meno Boldt, *Surviving as Indians: the Challenge of Self-Government* (University of Toronto Press 1993) 4.

[27] Julie Jai, 'Bargains Made in Bad Times: How Principles from Modern Treaties Can Reinvigorate Historic Treaties' in John Borrows and Michael Coyle (eds), *The Right Relationship: Reimagining the Implementation of Historical Treaties* (University of Toronto Press 2017); on the Crown's evolving duty to negotiate, see Felix Hoehn, 'The Duty to Negotiate and the Ethos of Reconciliation' (2020) 83(1) Saskatchewan Law Review 1; for

government sought access to Indigenous lands for uses such as resource exploitation or railroad development.[28] In Treaty 6, it has been explained, First Nations felt pressure to sign an agreement with threats of starvation on the horizon, largely stemming from buffalo disappearing due to colonial settlement and increased non-Indigenous activities in the region.[29] Similarly, in Treaty 11, scholars have documented the way that government representatives offered false promises and forced the symbolic elections of chiefs to fulfil the minimum technical requirements of treaty negotiation, mainly in the interests of exploiting the oil-rich Mackenzie District and expanding control of lands and territory.[30]

Furthermore, despite many amendments and attempts at reform, many have underlined that the *Indian Act of 1876*, which was founded on the premise of assimilation and control of First Nations Peoples by the Crown, remains the principal vehicle for the exercise of federal jurisdiction over 'status Indians', and governs multiple aspects of Indigenous Peoples' lives.[31] The *Act* defined who is or is not an Indian and regulated band membership, government, taxation, lands, resources, and money management, among other matters.[32] The *Act*, as leaders and scholars have underlined, also created the residential school system, which was designed with the intention of legislating Indians out of existence, while specifically targeting Indian women and children to remove them from their First Nations and causing extensive harm (both physical and psychological), loss of life, and multigenerational trauma.[33] However, some also note that First Nations, specifically those with what was called 'Indian Status', also rely on the *Indian Act* as a legislative tool that held the federal government accountable for obligations towards First Nations, such as tax exemptions for property on reserves and protecting reserve land from seizure.[34] It meant to protect First Nations from

historical context, see also Jim Miller, *Compact, Contract, Covenant: Aboriginal Treaty-Making in Canada* (University of Toronto Press 2009).

28 See GoC Treaties (n 24).

29 *Letters from Charlie N. Bell to Morris, from the Laird Papers* (National Archives of Canada, 1874).

30 René Fumoleau and Arctic Institute of North America, *As Long as This Land Shall Last: A History of Treaty 8 and Treaty 11, 1870–1939* (University of Calgary Press 2004) 265–269.

31 Indian Act, RSC 1985, c I-5.

32 Mary C Hurley, *The Indian Act* (Library of Parliament 2009) Catalogue No PRB 09-12E. <http://publications.gc.ca/site/eng/361663/publication.html> 1 accessed 24 January 2025.

33 Frankie Young, 'A Trojan Horse: Can Indian Self-Government Be Promoted through the Indian Act?' (2019) 97(3) Canadian Bar Review 699.

34 *Mitchell v Peguis Indian Band* [1990] 2 SCR 85 226: 'ss. 87 and 89 of the Indian Act . . . constitute part of a legislative "package" which bears the impress of an obligation to native peoples which the Crown has recognized at least since the signing of the Royal Proclamation

interference by the provinces, and concerns were raised that should the *Indian Act* be abolished and no other legal protections be put in place, Indigenous lands and resources could be taken under provincial jurisdiction and be vulnerable to adverse political and economic interests.[35] Canadian courts have however begun to show willingness to recognize existing Aboriginal rights as a legal tenet, particularly in terms of natural resources access and land use interests.[36] Furthermore, constitutional protections through s 35(1) of the *Charter of Rights and Freedoms* help to clarify, for instance, legal recourse if an Aboriginal right is infringed,[37] if a right falls under s 35(1),[38] and what constitutes Aboriginal title.[39] In *R. v Sparrow*, the Court furthermore emphasized that there must be a generous and flexible interpretation of Aboriginal rights, and when in doubt, interpretation should favour the Indigenous Party.[40] Nonetheless, there remains a gap in the outcomes of efforts to realize these rights which still leave Indigenous Peoples disadvantaged within broader Canadian society.

These gaps were noted in the July 2018 Voluntary National Review (VNR), which Canada presented to the United Nations High-Level Political Forum on Sustainable Development, and which took stock of national actions, achievements, and challenges in implementing the 2030 Agenda.[41] It included key areas of focus such as the elimination of poverty, advancing gender equality and empowering women and girls, growing the economy and narrowing socio-economic gaps between different groups, advancing

of 1763. From that time on, the Crown has always acknowledged that it is honour-bound to shield Indians from any efforts by non-natives to dispossess Indians of the property which they hold qua Indians, i.e., their land base and the chattels on that land base.' Indian Act (n 31) ss 87, 89, which grant tax benefits and shield the real and personal property of certain First Nations members from charge or seizure. For a comparative analysis on the interaction between Canada's tax regime and Indian Act (n 31) s 87, see Fiona Martin, 'The Taxation Exemption of Canadian Indians as Governments and Individuals: How Does This Compare with Australia and New Zealand?' (2011) 40(2) Common Law World Review 132. For more on the challenges of reforming ibid s 89, see Adrian Pel, 'Reforming Section 89 of the Indian Act: Tinker, Waiver, Soldier (On), Sigh?' (2020) 4(1) Lakehead Law Journal 65.

35 Young (n 33) 700.

36 Kirk N. Lambrecht, *Aboriginal Consultation, Environmental Assessment, and Regulatory Review in Canada* (University of Regina Press 2013); Dwight G. Newman and Ibironke T. Odumosu-Ayanu (eds), *Indigenous-Industry Agreements, Natural Resources and the Law* (Routledge 2020).

37 *R. v Sparrow* [1990] 1 SCR 1075 (SCC).

38 *R. v Van der Peet* [1996] 2 SCR 507 (SCC).

39 *Tsilhqot'in Nation v British Columbia* [2014] 2 SCR 257 (SCC).

40 *Sparrow* (n 37) [1093].

41 Global Affairs Canada, 'Canada's Implementation of the 2030 Agenda for Sustainable Development – Voluntary National Review' (Government of Canada, 2018) (VNR).

self-determination and improving relations with Indigenous Peoples, fostering inclusion, advancing action on climate change and clean growth.[42] In the report, Canada articulated detailed and specific gaps in the progress of Indigenous Peoples towards achieving the SDGs, acknowledging that 'for Indigenous Peoples, the Canadian reality is not, and never has been, equitable or fair',[43] pledging to 'better align Canada's laws and policies with the UNDRIP'.[44] This is reflective of comments made by the United Nations Special Rapporteur on the Rights of Indigenous Peoples in his 2013 visit to Canada, when he remarked that 'Canada consistently ranks near the top among countries concerning human development standards, and yet amidst this wealth and prosperity, Aboriginal People live in conditions akin to those in countries that rank much lower and in which poverty abounds'.[45] Table 3.1 captures some of these disparities in the status of Indigenous Peoples in Canada across selected SDGs, including data from the 2018 VNR, compared to the non-Indigenous population.

Due to colonization, neglected government responsibilities, systemic discrimination, and side-lined treaty obligations, Indigenous Peoples have been mainly left with limited opportunities for sustainable development and adequate care in comparison to the broader Canadian population.[46] It is in the context of these disparities, which have been known and recognized by Indigenous Peoples throughout Canada prior to the release of the VNR, that modern treaties arose to help mitigate the systemic disadvantage imposed on communities across the country.

Modern treaties, also referred to as Comprehensive Land Claims Agreements (CLCAs), unlike historic treaties, are agreements negotiated through a common language with Indigenous negotiators including legal representation, which was

[42] ibid.

[43] ibid 4.

[44] See Section 3.3, Indigenous Rights, United Nations Declaration on the Rights of Indigenous Peoples & Canada.

[45] James Anaya, 'Statement upon Conclusion of the Visit to Canada by the United Nations Special Rapporteur on the Rights of Indigenous Peoples, James Anaya' (United Nations Human Rights Office of the High Commissioner, 2013) <www.ohchr.org/en/statements/2013/10/statement-upon-conclusion-visit-canada-united-nations-special-rapporteur-rights> accessed 24 January 2025.

[46] The stark reality of these disparities has been further brought into focus by the COVID-19 pandemic in which Indigenous communities became more vulnerable given their already reduced rates of access to quality health care systems in many communities. Diane Selkirk, 'Why Indigenous Communities Are Uninviting Visitors' (BBC, 2020) <www.bbc.com/travel/article/20200525-why-first-nations-communities-are-uninviting-visitors> accessed 24 January 2025.

TABLE 3.1 *Disparities in access to sustainable development for Indigenous Peoples across Canada*[a]

SDG	Conditions faced by Indigenous Peoples in Canada[b]	Status of non-Indigenous Canadians
SDG 1: End Poverty	There is disproportionately high representation of Indigenous Peoples in low-income groups from 2002 to 2016: estimated to be at least twice the rate of representation compared to Canada overall.[c] Indigenous Peoples are considered to be 'over-represented' across the populations of Canadians identified as homeless.	Child poverty rates for status First Nations living on-reserve increased to 60% in 2010 compared to 13% of non-Indigenous, non-racialized, and non-immigrant Canadian children.[d]
SDG 2: End Hunger	First Nations living on-reserve experiencing food insecurity between 2008 and 2010: 44.9% of children aged 0–11 years experienced any type of food insecurity, and between 40.1% and 14.1% of adults aged 18 and over experienced moderate and severe food insecurity respectively. 66% of Inuit adults aged 25 and older live with food insecurity.	Between 2011 and 2012, only 8% of non-Indigenous Canadians were food insecure.[e]
SDG 4: Education	Only 11% of the Indigenous population held university degrees in 2016,[f] and as of 2011, only 48% of Indigenous Peoples aged 25–64 held post-secondary degrees in general.[g] Indigenous Peoples are also more likely than non-Indigenous graduates to complete programmes below a bachelor's level (i.e. trades or college programmes).[h]	Similarly in 2016, 29% of the total Canadian population held university degrees. As of 2011, 65% of Canadians aged 25–64 held post-secondary degrees in general.[i]
SDG 5: Gender Equality	220 Indigenous women per 1,000, aged 15 years and older, experienced violent incidents in 2014.[j]	81 non-Indigenous women per 1,000 from the same period experienced violent victimization, nearly three times the rate of non-Indigenous women.[k]
SDG 6: Water and Sanitation	In 2018, 76 long-term drinking water advisories remained in effect for 12 months or longer on First Nations reserves.[l] These advisories do not include those not on reserve, for instance in communities across Inuit Nunangat, where water and sanitation concerns remain critical.	Similar data is hard to find for non-Indigenous Canadians, which generally reflects the fact that most non-Indigenous Canadians have access to safe and clean water.
SDG 11: Human Settlements	In 2016, 37% of persons identified as registered Indians living on-reserve lived in dwellings deemed unsuitable.[m] Even more	8% of non-Indigenous Canadians overall lived in dwellings deemed

(*continued*)

TABLE 3.1 (*continued*)

SDG	Conditions faced by Indigenous Peoples in Canada[b]	Status of non-Indigenous Canadians
	drastically, 52% of Inuit living in Inuit Nunangat and 11% of Inuit living outside Inuit Nunangat lived in unsuitable housing.[n]	unsuitable in the same period.[o]

[a] Data is an essential element of the SDGs and is equally necessary for assessing the achievement of the modern treaties in Canada. Data that collects qualitative insights relating to Indigenous rights is also needed. This is of particular importance in the context of Indigenous communities that have experienced a sustained lack of rights-based equality throughout history. Jérémie Gilbert and Corinne Lennox, 'Towards New Development Paradigms: The United Nations Declaration on the Rights of Indigenous Peoples as a Tool to Support Self-determined Development' (2019) 23(1–2) The International Journal of Human Rights 104.

[b] VNR (n 41) 4.

[c] The VNR provided actual rates of representation in low-income groups for Indigenous peoples living 'off-reserve', illustrated as approximately twice that of the Canadian population overall, and qualitatively described the rates for those living on-reserve as being 'higher', hence the summary description in Table 3.1 of 'estimated to be at least twice the rate'. ibid 22–23.

[d] David Macdonald and Daniel Wilson, 'Shameful Neglect: Indigenous Child Poverty in Canada' (Canadian Centre for Policy Alternatives, 2016) 24.

[e] VNR (n 41).

[f] Poverty and inequality are closely tied to education. Increasing access to quality education equitably across Canada is key to address other connected SDGs and to break the cycles of inequality. Elaine Unterhalter and Amy North, *Education, Poverty and Global Goals for Gender Equality: How People Make Policy Happen* (Routledge 2018).

[g] Karen Kelly-Scott and Kristina Smith, 'Aboriginal Peoples Fact Sheet for Canada' (Statistics Canada, 2015) 6.

[h] ibid.

[i] ibid.

[j] Several reports, such as the *National Inquiry into Missing and Murdered Indigenous Women and Girls* and the Truth and Reconciliation Report, document the violence and discrimination against Indigenous peoples, particularly women and girls, that is rooted in the impacts of colonization. See National Inquiry into Missing and Murdered Indigenous Women and Girls, 'Reclaiming Power and Place: Executive Summary of the Final Report' (National Inquiry into Missing and Murdered Indigenous Women and Girls, June 2019) 53; Truth and Reconciliation Commission of Canada, 'Honouring the Truth, Reconciling for the Future – Summary of the Final Report of the Truth and Reconciliation Commission of Canada' (Truth and Reconciliation Commission of Canada, 2015) (TRC).

[k] VNR (n 41) 50.

[l] A drinking water advisory is considered long term when it has been in place for more than a year. While a drinking water advisory is in effect residents must either purchase water, boil water, or otherwise ensure their drinking water is purified. Although the Government of Canada has pledged to end long-term drinking water advisories on-reserve by March 2021 and has lifted eighty-eight advisories since 2015, sixty-one advisories remain in effect and new advisories continue to be added since this pledge was made. This lack of access to clean water and sanitation further contributes to health issues related to the lack of access to adequate infrastructure and services which are further addressed in other SDGs. Government of Canada, 'Water in First Nations Communities – Ending Long-Term Drinking Water Advisories' (Government of Canada, 2022) <www.sac-isc.gc.ca/eng/1506514143353/1533317130660> accessed 24 January 2025.

[m] It should be emphasized that the impacts of growing up in a disadvantaged home constitute not only a public health issue but can have intergenerational effects that contribute to a cycle of poverty. Diane M Purvin, 'Weaving a Tangled Safety Net: The Intergenerational Legacy of Domestic Violence and Poverty' (2003) 9 Violence against Women 1263–1264.

[n] VNR (n 41) 85.

[o] ibid.

previously prohibited under the *Indian Act*.[47] In 2025, twenty-six modern treaties had been agreed, and more were under negotiation.[48] These agreements, spurred by *Calder et al v Attorney-General of British Columbia* [*Calder*][49] in 1973, first recognized Aboriginal rights and Indigenous title to land in Canada, and beginning with the James Bay and Northern Quebec Agreement of 1975 (JBNQA),[50] provide jurisdiction and seek to resolve ambiguities over land ownership and use that were not addressed under the previous Numbered Treaty regime. The claims are based on the traditional use and occupancy of land by Peoples who have signed no prior treaties. Some of these treaties relate to self-governance, some to land rights, and, most often, both issues are combined into one comprehensive treaty system.[51] Settlements under land claims agreements generally also include terms for financial arrangements, land, local governance, management of land and resources, and rights to wildlife, language, and culture. This enables Indigenous signatories to own and manage land and resources, and have a share in any revenue generated through resource development.[52] Modern treaties also have a greater emphasis on the well-being of the Peoples governed through these treaties. The Community Well-Being (CWB) index, for example, showed that well-being under modern treaties First Nations was not only on average higher than historic treaty First Nations, but also improved at twice the pace.[53] The CWB results clearly demonstrate that implementing modern treaties can help address certain sustainable development gaps in certain instances. The following three examples, the JBNQA, the Kluane First Nation Agreement (KFNA), and the Labrador Inuit Land Claims Agreement (LILCA), help highlight how modern

[47] Government of Canada, 'Treaties and Agreements' (Government of Canada, 2020) <www.rcaanc-cirnac.gc.ca/eng/1100100028574/1529354437231> accessed 24 January 2025.

[48] ibid.

[49] [1973] SCR 313 (SCC).

[50] James Bay and Northern Québec Agreement and Complementary Agreements (Cree Nation of Eeyou Istchee–Inuit of Nunavik–Government of Canada–Government of Quebec–Hydro-Quebec) (adopted 11 November 1975) (JBNQA). This agreement was first enacted through An Act Approving the Agreement Concerning James Bay and Northern Québec, SQ 1976, c 46, RSQ c C-67, and the James Bay and Northern Québec Native Claims Settlement Act, SC 1976–77, c 32, RS c J-03.

[51] ibid.

[52] ibid.

[53] The Community Well-Being index measures socio-economic well-being primarily through education, labour force activity, income, and housing for Indigenous communities across Canada over time. Based on census data from 1981 to 2016, the CWB index offers a summary measure of well-being that can be compared across First Nations and Inuit communities. Indigenous Services Canada, *National Overview of the Community Well-Being Index, 1981 to 2016* (Government of Canada, 2019) <www.sac-isc.gc.ca/eng/1419864229405/1557324163264> accessed 24 January 2025.

treaties and their resulting obligations can help foster or frustrate sustainable development progress.

The JBNQA is a treaty seen as 'an epic achievement in the ongoing effort to reconcile the rights and interests of Aboriginal [P]eoples and those of non-Aboriginal [P]eoples in Northern Québec'.[54] It was the first modern treaty to be negotiated following the *Calder* decision and set out a series of land category definitions while documenting rules of administration for economic, social services, and land development that were hard fought for by the Cree and Inuit rights holders and their negotiators.[55] In addition to adopting important innovations as the first modern treaty, in the agreement the Parties also stipulate three categories of land that allocate specific resource rights to the Indigenous People and non-treaty beneficiaries who wish to access the treaty lands.

- *Category I lands* (approximately 1% of the total land area) are those allocated exclusively for the use of Indigenous Peoples, set aside for 'self-administration'.[56] Inuit and Cree beneficiaries possess the exclusive right to hunt, fish and trap, while non-beneficiaries may obtain permission to hunt and fish from Cree, Inuit, or Naskapi authorities but do not have the right to trap. Natural resource rights remain the property of the Quebec Government in Category I lands.[57] Environmental protection of Category I lands is the stated responsibility of the Aboriginal Peoples.[58]
- *Category II lands* (approximately 14% of the total land area) entail land-use rights for Aboriginal Peoples, however, mining exploration and other related activities are permitted to occur without any requirement of consent, as authorized by the Government of Quebec. Inuit and Cree beneficiaries, and non-beneficiaries, follow the same rights to hunt, fish, and trap as for Category 1 lands.[59]
- *Category III lands* (approximately 85% of the total land area) cover the largest geographical area, where no exclusive rights avail for Inuit and Cree Peoples to hunt and fish, though they do enjoy the exclusive right to trap. Category III are public lands.[60]

[54] *Quebec (Attorney General) v Moses* [2010] 1 SCR 557 (SCC) [14].
[55] Christa Scholtz and Maryna Polataiko, 'Transgressing the Division of Powers: The Case of the James Bay and Northern Quebec Agreement' (2019) 34(3) Canadian Journal of Law and Society 393.
[56] JBNQA (n 65) 8, s 5.1.
[57] ibid 7.
[58] ibid s 5.1.
[59] ibid s 5.2.
[60] ibid s 5.3.

With Cree and Inuit being Indigenous Peoples whose cultures stem from subsistence hunting and gathering on the land, be it through trap lines or through marine harvesting, access to land is vital for self-reliance, cultural survival, and economic prosperity post-JBNQA.[61] As well, industries such as the seal skin fur trade are direct by-products of subsistence lifestyles and provide crucial income for hunters and trappers in the JBNQA settlement area and beyond.[62] In this context, the JBNQA can be seen as furthering SDG targets in relation to reducing hunger, including targets 2.1[63] and SDG 2.2,[64] while having an indirect but equally crucial method of using income generated from subsistence lifestyles to reduce poverty in SDG 1 through targets 1.2[65] and 1.4.[66] Additionally, the provisions of the JBNQA provide for the transfer of approximately $150 million to the James Bay Cree and the Inuit of Quebec to serve as compensation from the Canadian and provincial governments for hydroelectric developments.[67] This amount, according to authorities, was meant to serve as a method of providing economic resources to these communities, recognizing that these payments were the result of the transfer of ownership rights to natural resources,[68] which is also noted in SDG 1.4.

To ensure that all members of these communities are included in the economic benefits generated from compensation, the JBNQA administered the settlements for Cree beneficiaries through the Cree Regional Authority and Inuit by creating the non-profit Makivik Corporation.[69] The Corporation

[61] ibid s 30.
[62] Fisheries and Oceans Canada, 'The Importance of the Seal Harvest' <www.dfo-mpo.gc.ca/fisheries-peches/seals-phoques/harvest-importance-chasse-eng.html> accessed January 24 2025. See also Alethea Arnaquq-Baril, 'Angry Inuk' (National Film Board, 2016) <www.nfb.ca/film/angry_inuk/> accessed 24 January 2025.
[63] Target 2.1 states, 'By 2030, end hunger and ensure access by all people, in particular the poor and people in vulnerable situations, including infants, to safe, nutritious and sufficient food all year round'. SDGs (n 4) 19.
[64] Target 2.2 states, 'By 2030, end all forms of malnutrition, including achieving, by 2025, the internationally agreed targets on stunting and wasting in children under 5 years of age, and address the nutritional needs of adolescent girls, pregnant and lactating women and older persons'. SDGs (n 4) 19.
[65] Target 1.2 states, 'By 2030, reduce at least by half the proportion of men, women and children of all ages living in poverty in all its dimensions according to national definitions'. SDGs (n 4) 19.
[66] Target 1.4 states, 'By 2030, ensure that all men and women, in particular the poor and the vulnerable, have equal rights to economic resources, as well as access to basic services, ownership and control over land and other forms of property, inheritance, natural resources, appropriate new technology and financial services, including microfinance'. SDGs (n 4) 19.
[67] JBNQA (n 65) s 25.2.
[68] Martin Papillon, 'Aboriginal Quality of Life under a Modern Treaty: Lessons from the Experience of the Cree Nation of Eeyou Istchee and the Inuit of Nunavik' (2008) Institute for Research on Public Policy 8. For details on the legal context of the JBNQA, see Scholtz and Polataiko (n 70) 393 pt 5.
[69] JBNQA (n 65) ss 26, 27.

is unique in being a hybrid entity: a private body with a public mission.[70] Makivik in such a sense has a direct impact on SDG 1 for poverty reduction, both from its inception in the JBNQA to its execution and operations today and by ensuring entire communities receive economic benefits from the land claims agreement. It also helped pave the way for other land claims corporations, such as Nunavut Tunngavik Inc. for the Nunavut Land Claims Agreement, the Inuvialuit Regional Corporation for the Inuvialuit Final Agreement, the Carcross/Tagish Management Corporation (C/TMC) for Carcross/Tagish First Nation Final Agreement and many others.

The second treaty example, the Kluane First Nation Agreement or KFNA, was signed between the Kluane First Nation and the Government of Canada and the Government of Yukon in 2003, and contains a detailed focus on land rights similar to the JBNQA.[71] Much like the JBNQA, this treaty can be seen to foster SDG 2 through targets 2.1, 2.2, and 2.4 by allowing for food sovereignty and autonomy when it comes to harvesting from and maintaining traditional practices on the land.[72] The KFNA as a treaty also created a new standard for Indigenous rights and title related to land management and co-governance. Specifically, this concerns the designation of Special Management Areas as stipulated in the agreement, where protections are implemented to preserve and protect natural resources and associated areas of environmental and cultural significance.[73] A direct outcome of these negotiations is Kluane National Park and Reserve.[74] Though established in 1943 for game hunting, this park is under the joint responsibility of Kluane First Nation, the Champagne and Aishihik First Nations which are Party to the Champagne and Aishihik First Nations Final Agreement of 1992,[75] and Parks Canada, the government agency responsible for managing national parks and historic sites across the country. When established, the Kluane Game Sanctuary, as it was once called, denied the First Nations their right to hunt, fish, and trap in a significant portion of the Southern Tutchone

70 Richard Janda, 'Why Does Form Matter – The Hybrid Governance Structure of Makivik Corporation' (2006) 30(3) Vermont Law Review 788.

71 Kluane First Nation Final Agreement (Kluane First Nation–Government of Canada–Government of the Yukon) (adopted 18 October 2003) (KFNA).

72 Target 2.4 states, 'By 2030, ensure sustainable food production systems and implement resilient agricultural practices that increase productivity and production, that help maintain ecosystems, that strengthen capacity for adaptation to climate change, extreme weather, drought, flooding and other disasters and that progressively improve land and soil quality'. SDGs (n 4) 19.

73 KFNA (n 86) ch 10 – Special Management Areas.

74 Ibid.

75 Champagne and Aishihik First Nations Final Agreement (Champagne and Aishihik First Nations–Government of Canada–Government of the Yukon) (adopted 19 June 1992).

traditional territory.[76] As leaders and scholars have noted, not only did this affect food security and access to land and prevented the First Nations from managing life on said land, but it also inflicted great cultural and personal losses that have affected five generations. The land claims agreement that helped establish Kluane National Park sought to return the ability of these First Nations to assert right to carry out traditional activities in the national park.[77] Renewing this connection to the land and enabling the First Nations, who have a vast knowledge of the ways of life in this territory, to set management priorities for the natural resources in Kluane National Park and Reserve fosters strong outcomes for conserving the region and thus far may represent a successful collaboration between Indigenous and Canadian governments.[78] Parties in the KFNA, and by extension the Champagne and Aishihik First Nations Final Agreement, have strong records of fostering SDG 15: Sustainable Development through targets 15.2,[79] 15.6,[80] and 15.9.[81] To some extent, as leaders and scholars also note, efforts to advance this SDG may also offer points of concern. Though few issues and disagreements have been presented officially to date, there may be FPIC concerns for commitments addressing land expropriation for development.[82] As stipulated in the treaty, the Government of Yukon or any other entity deemed an 'authority' by virtue of legislation is legally bound to consult[83] with the affected First Nation for the purpose of reaching an agreement.[84] However, there is no

76 Parks Canada, 'Harvesting – First Nations Rights and Responsibilities, Kluane National Park and Reserve' (Parks Canada) <https://parks.canada.ca/pn-np/yt/kluane/activ/tradition/ii> accessed 11 February 2025; see also Guy Charlton, 'The Law of Native American Hunting, Fishing and Gathering Rights Outside of Reservation Boundaries in the United States and Canada' (2015) 39 Canada-United States Law Journal 68.

77 Parks Canada, 'Kluane National Park and Reserve – Dän Keyi (Our People's Land)' (Parks Canada, 2019) <www.pc.gc.ca/en/pn-np/yt/kluane/culture/autochtone-indigenous> accessed 24 January 2025.

78 Kluane National Park Management Board, 'Cooperative Management' *Kluane National Park Management Board* <https://kluanenpmb.ca/> accessed 11 February 2025.

79 Target 15.2 states, 'By 2020, promote the implementation of sustainable management of all types of forests, halt deforestation, restore degraded forests and substantially increase afforestation and reforestation globally'. SDGs (n 4) 29.

80 Target 15.6 states, 'Promote fair and equitable sharing of the benefits arising from the utilization of genetic resources and promote appropriate access to such resources, as internationally agreed'. SDGs (n 4) 29.

81 Target 15.9 states, 'By 2020, integrate ecosystem and biodiversity values into national and local planning, development processes, poverty reduction strategies and accounts'. SDGs (n 4) 29.

82 For more information about free, prior, and informed consent, please see Chapter 2, ILO 169, UNDRIP and the Matter of Consent.

83 Refer to the contentions around 'duty to consult' and FPIC that is raised in Chapter 2 for more context.

84 KFNA (n 86) ch 7 – Expropriation.

explicit provision for a First Nation to stop development under the terms of the KFNA, rather the agreement only requires that consultation occur and comply with the outlined procedures.[85] This in the future, according to researchers, may open a door for industry and/or the Governments of Canada and Yukon to potentially override the nature of recognizing the ownership rights and interests of the Kluane First Nations community if natural resources found on their lands are deemed more valuable than obtaining true FPIC as outlined in UNDRIP.[86]

A further example from a treaty involves the Labrador Inuit Land Claims Agreement (LILCA) which was signed between the Inuit of Labrador, the Government of Canada, and the Government of Newfoundland and Labrador in 2005 and created the autonomous region now known as Nunatsiavut.[87] With concerns about future extractive activities in mind, the Labrador Inuit included terms in the LILCA explicitly recognizing the Indigenous body's authority to require an Environmental Assessment, as under the *Canadian Environmental Assessment Act*,[88] and approvals by the Crown Authority and the Nunatsiavut Government,[89] before a resource use project may commence in Labrador Inuit lands.[90] The Environmental Assessment includes the consideration of cumulative effects on the environment (e.g. short- and long-term effects on natural resources and the integrity of ecosystems), impacts on Labrador Inuit communities (e.g. noise and other forms of pollution or habitat destruction that can negatively impact harvesting), measures to mitigate significant adverse environmental effects (e.g. choice of different sites or conducting additional research for mitigation measures prior to starting the project) and alternative approaches to achieving project goals.[91] The Crown Authority and Nunatsiavut Government are required to consult each other on how the Environmental Assessment process is to be applied and harmonized

85 ibid.

86 Martin Papillon and Thierry Rodon, 'Indigenous Consent and Natural Resource Extraction: Foundations for a Made-in-Canada Approach' (Institute for Research on Public Policy, 4 July 2017) <https://irpp.org/research-studies/insight-no16/> accessed 11 February 2025.

87 Labrador Inuit Land Claims Agreement (Inuit of Labrador–Government of Newfoundland and Labrador–Government of Canada) (adopted 22 January 2005) (LILCA).

88 S.C. 1992, c 37 (CEAA); LILCA (n 102) s 11.3.2 *Chapter 11 Environmental Assessment* stating, 'The Nunatsiavut Government may require an assessment of the Environmental Effects of an undertaking, project, work or activity related to Exploration in Labrador Inuit Lands under Inuit Laws only if the undertaking, project, work or activity is subject to Environmental Assessment under the *Canadian Environmental Assessment Act* or the *Environmental Protection Act*'.

89 This is the self-government body created through the self-government clauses for the Nunatsiavut region.

90 LILCA (n 102) s 11.2.1.

91 LILCA (n 102) s 11.2.10.

between Canadian law and Labrador Inuit rights.[92] At face value, these provisions could promote SDG 13 Climate Action and SDG 15 Life on Land generally by assessing the environmental impacts of proposed projects while considering measures that reduce land degradation.[93] The important role of biodiversity in climate change mitigation and adaptation is highlighted in the Environmental Assessment for the protection of adverse environmental impacts and increases the resilience of Labrador Inuit communities, with the potential to promote SDG 13.1.[94] The provisions also integrate a national climate change policy (i.e. the *Canadian Environmental Assessment Act*[95]) to guide planning and decision-making,[96] thereby promoting SDG 13.2.[97]

Some leaders and scholars offer a different understanding of how government commitments are fulfilling the legal obligation of this binding treaty. Concerns have been raised with regards to the Muskrat Falls hydroelectric project, for which the Labrador Inuit argue the Government of Canada, as represented by the Department of Fisheries and Oceans (DFO), did not carry out their duty to consult with the Labrador Inuit.[98] Located on the Grand River flowing into the Lake Melville ecosystem,[99] the project could cause catastrophic downstream impacts[100] not only affecting the Inuit in the region,

92 ibid s 11.2.9. It is important to note that Inuit law follows a very different regime and accountability structure compared to First Nations conception of Indigenous law. Law, in an Inuit sense, is closer to community values than regimented rules. As such, harmony should be sought between the Canadian perception of law and Inuit values and law, in making decisions on resource projects that can affect Inuit. See generally Jarich Oosten, Frederic Laugrand, and Willem Rasing, *Inuit Laws – Tirigusuusiit, Piqujait, and Maligait* (2nd edn, Nunavut Arctic College 2017); Natalia Loukacheva, 'Indigenous Inuit Law, "Western" Law and Northern Issues' (2012) 3(2) Arctic Review on Law and Politics 200.

93 Katherine Lofts and others, 'Feature – Brief on Sustainable Development Goal 13 on Taking Action on Climate Change and Its Impacts: Contributions of International Law, Policy and Governance' (2017) 13(1) MJSDL 183.

94 Target 13.1 stating, 'Strengthen resilience and adaptive capacity to climate-related hazards and natural disasters in all countries'. SDGs (n 4) 27.

95 CEAA (n 103).

96 LILCA (n 102) s 11.2.9.

97 Target 13.2 stating, 'Integrate climate change measures into national policies, strategies and planning'. SDGs (n 4) 27.

98 *Nunatsiavut v Canada (Attorney General)*, 2015 FC 492 (CAN).

99 Also known as Churchill River, the Grand River or Mishtashipu is spiritually, culturally and socio-economically important to Indigenous peoples through fishing, trapping, ceremony, and travel. Jessica Penney and Patricia Johnson-Castle, 'Not So Grand Plans: The Continued Erasure of Indigenous Rights in Newfoundland and Labrador's Hydroelectric "Development"' (Yellowhead Institute, 2021) <https://yellowheadinstitute.org/2021/06/10/not-so-grand-plans-hydro/> accessed 24 January 2025.

100 Methylmercury is one of the primary concerns stemming from this project. Exposure long-term to methylmercury can cause a host of different neurocognitive delays in children and impact cardiovascular health in adults. Residents in this area already face more exposure to

but also the Innu, Natuashish, and NunatuKavut communities in the area more broadly.[101] Concerns have been highlighted that land claim rights were not respected and FPIC was not obtained for the project.[102] Critics further assert that Nalcor,[103] the provincial Crown corporation developing Muskrat Falls, did not study Lake Melville during its Environmental Impact Assessment because 'it predicted that the Muskrat Falls dam would have no measurable impacts on the estuary, a traditional Inuit hunting and fishing ground', a decision which was based on assumptions and not science.[104]

An inquiry conducted for the project ultimately found that the Government failed to safeguard the best interests of the province's population, noting the failures to adequately research alternatives, investigate negative impacts, and inform the public about the risks of the project, further validating Labrador Inuit perspectives.[105] Even then, the Nunatsiavut Government was unsuccessful in

methylmercury compared to the average Canadian, and will only be further impacted once the contamination reaches critical country food sources, such as seals, salmon, char, mussels, clams, and bird eggs, that subsidize diets amidst the food insecurity crisis in northern Inuit communities. ibid; Ryan S Calder and others, 'Future Impacts of Hydroelectric Power Development on Methylmercury Exposures of Canadian Indigenous Communities' (2016) 50 (23) Environmental Science & Technology 49–50.

101 *Nunatsiavut* (n 113).

102 Penney and Johnson-Castle (n 114).

103 Muskrat Falls is also not the first time that Nalcor did not properly consult Indigenous Peoples and generate public outcry. In the 1960s and 1970s, the Churchill Falls project, also on the Grand River, included no consultation with Innu Nation, who traditionally travelled and trapped along the river which was flooded by the project. The Upper Churchill Redress Agreement now retroactively compensates the Innu by paying out $2 million dollars a year from Nalcor. Government of Newfoundland and Labrador, 'Lower Churchill Project' (Government of Newfoundland and Labrador, 2018) <www.gov.nl.ca/lowerchurchillproject/default.htm> accessed 24 January 2025. These incredibly damaging environmental projects are partly due to the Government of Newfoundland and Labrador's mismanagement of public contracts, the price of which are being shifted to the Indigenous peoples of the province. The Government is now incentivized to push forward with contentious projects despite outcry because it negotiated an unfavourable power purchasing agreement with Hydro Quebec, which sells electricity to Quebec at a rate that is 'barely distinguishable from being free', until 2041. This is costing the Government of Newfoundland and Labrador losses of billions of dollars of revenue each year, which they are desperately trying to recoup through any means necessary. *Churchill Falls (Labrador) Corp. v Hydro-Québec* [2018] 3 SCR 101 (SCC); James P Feehan and Melvin Baker, 'The Origins of a Coming Crisis: Renewal of the Churchill Falls Contract' (2007) 30(1) Dalhousie Law Journal 209.

104 Sarah Cox, 'Mercury Rising: How the Muskrat Falls Dam Threatens Inuit Way of Life' (The Narwhal, 2019) <https://thenarwhal.ca/mercury-rising-muskrat-falls-dam-threatens-inuit-way-of-life/> accessed 24 January 2025; Michelle Kamula and Zou Zou Kuzyk, 'Sediment and Organic Carbon' in Nunatsiavut Government, *Lake Melville: Avativut, Kanuittailinnivut (Our Environment, Our Health) Scientific Report* (Nunatsiavut Government 2016) 41–47.

105 The Honourable Richard D LeBlanc, *Muskrat Falls: A Misguided Project – Volume 1: Executive Summary, Key Findings and Recommendations* (Commission of Inquiry Respecting the Muskrat Falls Project, Queen's Printer for Newfoundland and Labrador 2020) <www.gov

both the Newfoundland Supreme Court and the Federal Court of Canada when challenging the Government of Newfoundland and Labrador's duty to consult, since the Nunatsiavut Government focused on the downstream effects of the project, including increased methylmercury levels.[106] This argument was not accepted as a legally binding requirement to consult Labrador Inuit through *Nunatsiavut v Canada (Attorney General)*.[107] However, many Indigenous leaders in Labrador have emphasized that the Government should have operated in good faith and respected the fundamental principles behind the rights they were promised through the LILCA.[108] At time of publication, all Parties had agreed to establish an Independent Expert Advisory Committee (IEAC) that includes the Nunatsiavut Government, Innu Nation, the NunatuKavut Community Council and federal, provincial, and municipal governments to mitigate concerns where possible.[109]

From an SDG perspective, the poor execution of fulfilling treaty obligations in the case of Muskrat Falls would weaken efforts to advance SDG 13 and its targets. Leaders and scholars raise concerns of significant climate change impacts based on the environmental degradation caused by this project, and that any renewable energy generated, which also applies to production from the Churchill Falls project,[110] is not destined to assist Nunatsiavut communities.[111] Subsequently, Indigenous Peoples also pay the price in terms of gaps in accessing SDGs 6 Clean Water and Sanitation, 7 Affordable and Clean Energy, 11 Sustainable Cities and Communities, 14 Life Below Water, and 15 Life on Land. Overall, it has been observed, the case of Muskrat Falls offers an example of decision-making which not only frustrated progress on sustainable development, but also disregarded Indigenous rights won by the Nunatsiavut Peoples through the LILCA.[112]

.nl.ca/iet/files/Volume-1-Executive-Summary-Key-Findings-and-Recommendations.pdf> accessed 24 January 2025.

106 *Nunatsiavut* (n 113).

107 ibid para 29.

108 Bill Flowers, 'Inadequate Consultation on the Muskrat Falls Project' (Institut de recherche en politiques publiques, 13 December 2016) <https://policyoptions.irpp.org/fr/magazines/decembre-2016/inadequate-consultation-on-the-muskrat-falls-project/> accessed 24 January 2025.

109 Nunatsiavut Government, 'Update to Beneficiaries – Make Muskrat Right' (Nunatsiavut Government, 2017) <https://perma.cc/8RAT-RGYJ> accessed 24 January 2025.

110 *Churchill Falls* (n 103).

111 These six fly-in-only communities on Labrador's North Coast remain reliant on carbon-heavy diesel generators for electricity and heating, which is counter-intuitive in an era that so desperately requires decarbonization. Penney and Johnson-Castle (n 114).

112 Cole Atlin and Mark CJ Stoddart, *Governance in Times of Crisis: The Muskrat Falls Case*, Harris Centre of Regional Policy and Development (April 2021) 28.

Though JBNQA and KFNA commitments demonstrate the potential for success in supporting the SDGs, LILCA experience contextualizes the nuances of balancing Indigenous rights in the era of sustainable transitions. These three examples show that SDGs can not only be fostered, but can also be frustrated, depending not only on the commitments in the treaties themselves, but also on how treaty obligations are fulfilled. Additionally, there remain limitations on the ability of the modern treaties to be used in a full and holistic manner to achieve the SDGs, in addition to the inherent issues of political and social support for their achievement. One limitation, observed in both the JBNQA and the KFNA, is the emphasis on procedural compliance that tends to characterize the modern treaties overall.[113] Concerns remain as to the efficacy of the modern treaties in enabling Indigenous rights, given this focus, and some suggest the emphasis on procedural compliance has instead served to reinforce a subordinate Indigenous–Crown relationship.[114]

Contentious decisions have also arisen in disputes related to land title, particularly regarding land development by Crown or private interests. For example, in *Delgamuukw v British Columbia*[115] and *Tsilhqot'in Nation v British Columbia* the Court clarified Aboriginal title as a vehicle to achieve the 'goal of faithfully translating pre-sovereignty Aboriginal interests into equivalent modern legal rights.'[116] However, leaders and scholars have noted, the benefits and limitations on title remain uncertain. Justified infringement poses a conflict for the practical application of rights to land title, whereby the Government retains the ability to limit title in cases of 'compelling and substantial public purpose'[117] and is not inconsistent with the Crown's fiduciary duty to the Aboriginal group and their future generations. This is of special concern during a period of national and international transition, with many critical natural resources in high demand for clean transitions, which may pit state and economic interests against the rights conferred to Indigenous Peoples. The ability for pluralism to flourish in the Canadian legal framework is a second Indigenous rights area that many suggest is challenged by the threat of a subordinate Indigenous-Crown relationship. Legal pluralism can

[113] Otis (n 25) 330.

[114] Terry Mitchell, 'International Gaze Brings Critical Focus to Questions about Aboriginal Governance in Canada' in Terry Mitchell, *UNDRIP and the 2009 Bolivian Constitution: Lessons for Canada* (Centre for International Governance Innovation 2014) 46.

[115] [1997] 3 SCR 1010 (SCC).

[116] *Tsilhqot'in* (n 39) [32].

[117] Though infringements cannot be 'inconsistent with the Crown's fiduciary duty to the Aboriginal group', the power held by governments still poses a systemic concern for the limits on Indigenous self-government. *Tsilhqot'in* (n 39) [88].

be characterized by the acknowledgement and empowerment of Indigenous systems of law for Indigenous Peoples which is supported and applied inside the Canadian legal system.[118] It can be seen as foundational to self-governance, a key pathway to agency in a rights-based approach to development. The expression and fulfilment of legal pluralism in Canada have been the subject of much dispute between the Crown and Indigenous Peoples, as evidenced in a particularly paradoxical case relating to the Nisga'a of British Columbia Final Agreement with the Crown.[119] During the negotiation of this agreement, the Nisga'a took steps to explicitly limit the State-acknowledged effect of their own Indigenous laws with specific treaty language, to 'insulate their traditional laws and institutions from direct interference by state institutions, including non-Indigenous judges'.[120]

These examples of treaties and their implementation demonstrate the potential for success in advancing sustainable development through Indigenous rights and well-being. Such types of agreements exist in other jurisdictions as well, although as established, they may foster but also frustrate progress towards achieving the SDGs. Further examples of treaties which deeply sustainable development in practice are discussed in Part IV, Indigenous Treaty Implementation for Sustainable Development in Key Countries.

3.4 GUIDELINES FOR SUSTAINABLE RESOURCE MANAGEMENT AND INDIGENOUS DEVELOPMENT

Outside the specific principles and treaties between Indigenous Peoples and States, international law has the potential to shape principles, regulatory frameworks, institutions, and standards for sustainable development.[121] In the 2020 International Law Association (ILA) Guidelines for Sustainable Natural Resources Management for Development, experts specifically consider natural

[118] Law Commission of Canada, *Justice Within: Indigenous Legal Traditions* (Discussion Paper, Law Commission of Canada 2006) <https://publications.gc.ca/pub?id=9.667883&sl=0> accessed 11 February 2025.

[119] *Campbell et al v AG BC/AG Cda & Nisga'a Nation et al*, 2000 BCSC 1123 (CAN). This case affirms that the self-government provisions and provisions giving the Nisga'a Nation the authority to make laws under the Nisga'a Final Agreement (Nisga'a of British Columbia Final Agreement (Nisga'a Nation–Government of Canada–Government of British Columbia) (adopted 27 April 1999, entered into force 11 May 2000)) are constitutionally valid under section 35(1) of the *Charter of Rights and Freedoms*.

[120] Otis (n 25) 330.

[121] Marie-Claire Cordonier Segger, Ilaria Espa and Nico Schrijver (eds), *Sustainable Development in International Law on Natural Resources* (Wolters Kluwer, in production for 2025). Marie-Claire Cordonier Segger and Nico J Schrijver, 'ILA Guidelines for Sustainable Natural Resources Management for Development' (2021) 68 Netherlands International Law Review 317.

resource management, and how international law offers increasingly detailed and local, national, regional, and global guidelines in transforming sustainable development.[122] Global concerns arising from increasing degradation of natural resources worldwide have led to many new advances in the field of international law on sustainable development. The experts of the ILA Committee considered instances in which commitments to the sustainable management of natural resources for development have been enshrined in international treaty law, reflected in the practices of States and international organizations, recognized in the decisions of international courts and tribunals, and increasingly operationalized through international 'soft law' goals, standards and guidelines in relation to different resources. As the ILA Committee's expert rapporteur explains, "the ILA Committee's work has demonstrated that the world's natural resources, once seen as national and subject to permanent sovereignty, are now increasingly recognized as eliciting common global, regional, transboundary and national ILA Sustainable Natural Resources Guidelines concerns, thereby challenging international law to provide more coherent and effective cooperative regimes for sustainable management. Tensions can exist with regard to certain nationally-based resources, however myriad rules and standards now define, guide and direct State practice, providing a roadmap for the progressive development of international law on the sustainable management of natural resources for development."

The 2020 ILA Guidelines on the Role of International Law in Sustainable Natural Resources Management for Development are organized in three parts, as noted in the ILA Resolution and related publications. Part I presents, sector by sector in a non-exhaustive survey, certain guidelines for the sustainable management of global, regional, trans-boundary and national natural resources, covering: (1) global natural resources such as celestial bodies, the atmosphere and a stable climate system, biological diversity and ecological systems, and the ocean and its mineral and living resources; (2) regional and trans-boundary natural resources of global importance such as forests and landscapes, rivers and freshwater ecosystems, and migratory species; and (3) national natural resources of global relevance such as forests and landscapes, land and soil, mineral commodities, including precious minerals, and sustainable energy. Part II addresses trends and innovations in international legal instruments and approaches in sustainable natural resources management for development, with a non-exhaustive selection covering trends from: (1) human rights approaches; (2) economic instruments; (3) environment and sustainable development cooperation including scientific collaboration,

[122] International Law Association, 'The Role of International Law in Sustainable Natural Resources Management for Development' (2020) Kyoto Conference Resolution No. 4/2020.

financing mechanisms, monitoring, reporting and verification, and public participation and access to information and justice; and (4) peace-building and post-conflict instruments, including secure land and water access. In this section, the Guidelines also explore (5) innovative techniques and requirements in international instruments on the sustainable management of natural resources for development, with special attention to: (a) sustainable resources management through transparency and stakeholder engagement, (b) equitable benefitsharing from sustainable natural resources management, (c) legal indicators of effectiveness for sustainable natural resources management, and (d) control of illicit flows for sustainable natural resources management. They also provide a brief, nonexhaustive update on (6) sustainable natural resources management in international dispute settlement. Finally, in Part III, explanatory notes are provided for the interpretation and application of the Guidelines.

In the view of the ILA Committee, international law has the potential to shape the principles, regulatory frameworks, institutions, standards and incentives for natural resource management on multiple local, national, regional and global levels. The ILA Committee's findings suggest that "international law both reflects and also serves as a critical catalyst for the design, adoption, and implementation of sustainable natural resource management and resolution of disputes in relation to the use of natural resources. Global natural resources which have been recognized as common concerns or the common heritage of humankind crucially require increased collective commitment and compliance with the international law and practices reflected in the ILA Sustainable Natural Resources Guidelines. Regional and trans-boundary natural resources of global importance are also greatly at risk, and their sustainability depends on the crafting, implementation and enforcement of effective and collaborative international legal regimes. Further, the sustainable management of national natural resources of global relevance can be greatly facilitated by international law. Indeed, international law and non-binding international and national instruments such as standards and guidelines function as a baseline for States and other actors involved in natural resource management, shaping operating environments in which sustainable development will either be fostered, or frustrated."[123] As the Committee concluded, in assessing the role of international law in this context, "it is crucial to take into account how concepts of sovereignty and territory are evolving to accommodate new scientific understanding of interrelated ecological systems and conditions, whereby notions of custodial sovereignty may offer useful insights. The Committee's work has established that sovereignty, of key

[123] ibid.

importance to international law from its inception, is becoming both more fluid and more qualified in the face of shared responsibilities for the sustainable use of trans-boundary, regional, and global international natural resources, and collaborative regimes for management." Experts, through the committee process, identified tensions in the context of nationally-based natural resources, and as the rapporteur and chair noted, "considered how international legal regimes may offer options to reconcile key concerns, avoiding or reducing the potential for conflict between and within States over resource use, as well as defusing potential clashes between resource conservation and exploitation goals." Crucially, they recognize, "natural resources are also essential to advance nearly all 17 Sustainable Development Goals, and many of their 169 targets, from poverty elimination, to ending hunger, to access to water and energy, to combating climate change and promoting peace, justice and security." [124]

3.5 CONCLUSION

As the world faces an era of change, where public demand for reconciliation and de-marginalization of vulnerable populations continues to grow, evaluating the fulfilment of obligations towards treaties and fostering progress to achieving SDG targets is critical. There remains a need to critically assess whether governments party to their sustainable development and treaty-related agreements respect the associated obligations to implement and enforce the spirit and intent of these documents. In this way, important insights and lessons can be translated into frameworks at national and international levels to uplift and ensure commitments to sustainable development are attained.

[124] ibid.

4

Indigenous Trade and Investment for Sustainability

4.1 INTRODUCTION

Commitments in international accords such as ILO 169 and the United Nations Declaration on the Rights of Indigenous Peoples UNDRIP are agreed in a context of injustice, characterized by social and economic exclusion. As analysts note, Indigenous Peoples comprise 6 per cent of the global population, with life expectancy twenty years lower than non-Indigenous populations worldwide.[1] In the face of these poor conditions, there remain important prospects for the development of global inter-Tribal trade and investment to revitalize Indigenous economies and foster sustainable development. International trade agreements, for example, the application of Canada's Indigenous Trade Chapter, New Zealand's Waitangi clauses, and the latter's leadership in the Indigenous Peoples Economic and Trade Cooperation Arrangement (IPETCA),[2] hold potential to help raise the quality of life, health, and overall life expectancy of Indigenous Peoples. As leaders and scholars emphasize, more sustainable development that benefits Indigenous Peoples benefits the Earth, including all humanity. Indigenous Peoples hold Traditional Knowledge (TK) and insights crucial for realizing the right to a clean, healthy, and sustainable environment, fostering sound stewardship of natural resources, mitigating and reversing biodiversity loss, and tackling climate change.[3]

1 'Indigenous Peoples – Understanding Poverty' (World Bank, 2022) <https://perma.cc/4CP9-HMNM> accessed 24 January 2025.

2 The IPETCA will be discussed in greater detail as a unique advancement for Indigenous trade in Chapter 14, 'Innovative Approaches to the UNDRIP Principles in Indigenous Trade Agreements'.

3 John G Hansen and Rose Antsanen, 'What Can Traditional Indigenous Knowledge Teach Us About Changing Our Approach to Human Activity and Environmental Stewardship in

The beginnings of this shift are already occurring in jurisdictions around the world. In Canada, there are already over 50,000 Aboriginal businesses – and the vast majority are Small and Medium Enterprises (SMEs). They contributed over $31 billion to Canada's GDP, with about $12 billion of that from Indigenous entrepreneurs.[4] In the United States, the Tribal economy includes thirty-nine trade-ready US Tribes located in Oklahoma alone,[5] which have over $12.9 billion in cumulative economic impact, with combined gross annual revenue of almost $2 billion and well over 15,000 US jobs in various Tribal industries. In Washington State,[6] twenty-nine Tribes have a total economic impact of $2.4 billion, and in Minnesota,[7] eleven Tribes have a $2.6 billion economic impact.

As Canada-US inter-Tribal trade and investment grows and is revitalized, and other countries like New Zealand and Australia likewise adopt trade and investment policies and legal innovations to advance Indigenous participation, the need for insights to understand Indigenous participation in the world's sustainable economic development is vital. This chapter considers historical and modern foundations of Indigenous trade and investment for sustainable development, with a focus on the principles and priorities set out in ILO 169 and the UNDRIP, and a view to fostering economies that place the principles and rules relating to sustainable development at the forefront. An examination of the prerequisites for Indigenous trade and investment also features in this chapter, namely: nation-building; remedying five key barriers to Indigenous inter-Tribal trade; and understanding how Indigenous trade and commerce can engage with non-Indigenous enterprise. Throughout, Canadian and US examples are provided to illustrate the importance of trade solutions for addressing sustainability and their downstream impacts for reconciliation and healthy futures for Indigenous Peoples worldwide.

Order to Reduce the Severity of Climate Change?' (2018) 9(3) International Indigenous Policy Journal 2 <https://ojs.lib.uwo.ca/index.php/iipj/article/view/7553/6197> accessed 24 January 2025.

4 Canadian Council of Aboriginal Business, 'The Future of Canada's Economy Is Indigenous' (2020) <www.ccab.com/wp-content/uploads/2019/10/CCAB_OpportunityPackage2020_AA_WebFinal.pdf> accessed 24 January 2025.

5 Kyle D Dean, 'Oklahoma: The Economic Impact of Tribal Nations in Oklahoma Fiscal Year 2017' (Minders School of Business, 2019) <www.oknativeimpact.com/wp-content/uploads/2022/03/All-Tribe-Impact-Report-2022-Final.pdf> accessed 24 January 2025.

6 National Congress of American Indians, 'Securing Our Future – Policy Paper' (2013) 9.

7 ibid.

4.2 PREREQUISITE FOR INDIGENOUS TRADE: NATION-BUILDING APPROACH FOR TRIBAL INFRASTRUCTURE

To first understand the importance of Indigenous-focused trade and investment to advance Indigenous interests, it is helpful to examine why many leaders and experts argue that Indigenous self-government is an essential pathway in the face of current unsuccessful governance that has pervaded Indigenous communities since colonization.[8]

As leading scholars explain, for Indigenous economic development the relationship between federal governments and Indigenous Nations, particularly in Canada or the United States, has mostly been based on a failed paternalistic model of federal control over Tribal implementation. This was the *standard approach* to Indigenous economic development, but it is long outdated due to five principal characteristics; it is 'short-term and non-strategic; it lets persons or organizations other than the Indigenous People set the development agenda; it views development as primarily an economic problem; it views Indigenous culture as an obstacle to development; and it encourages narrowly defined and often self-serving leadership'.[9]

The results of the failed model have been, as many studies demonstrate, appalling. Typically, as scholars note, this manifests as failed enterprises, a politics of spoils, an economy dependent on federal dollars and decision-making, brain drain, impressions of incompetence and chaos undermining Tribal sovereignty, and continued poverty,[10] all of which likely contribute to Indigenous Peoples being so severely disadvantaged compared to the rest of the self-governing world.[11] This has also led to the demise of previous 'best intentions' when attempting to develop domestic inter-Tribal trade accords, which some describe as 'doomed from the start' due to having followed the ossified *standard approach* to economic growth. Even though various Tribal Nations agreed to such accords, many note, the achievement of any meaningful implementation and outcomes was likely to fail and did.

8 For more on the failed model of paternalistic governance, see Taiaiake Alfred, *Peace, Power, Righteousness: An Indigenous Manifesto* (2nd edn, Oxford University Press 2009); Kiera L Ladner and Myra J Tait (eds), *Surviving Canada: Indigenous Peoples Celebrate 150 Years of Betrayal* (ARP Books 2017).

9 Stephen Cornell and Joseph Kalt, 'Two Approaches to Economic Development on American Indian Reservations: One Works, the Other Doesn't' in Miriam Jorgensen (ed), *Rebuilding Native Nations: Strategies for Governance and Development* (University of Arizona Press 2006) 4, ch 1.

10 ibid 11.

11 World Bank (n 1).

The alternative to the *standard approach*, as proposed by leaders and experts, is the *nation-building approach*, which moves away from a dependency relationship with a federal government and instead asserts Tribal economic sovereignty, focusing on strengthening the Tribal institutional capacity to 'exercise sovereignty effectively, thereby providing a positive environment for sustained economic development'.[12] This approach combines five key factors, namely practical sovereignty, effective governing institutions, institutions that match Indigenous political cultures, strategic orientation for decision-making, and nation-building leadership.[13] As explained below, each factor contributes to effective self-governance and autonomy for Indigenous institutions to thrive within trade networks.

Firstly, practical sovereignty is the comprehensive assertion of sovereignty or self-rule. The Tribal Nation moves from dependency on federal decision-making to claiming responsibility for the Tribal Nation's own business and political decisions. The importance of practical sovereignty comes from putting the development agenda in Indigenous hands. As leading experts explain, 'When decisions move into Tribal hands, agendas begin to reflect Tribal interests, perceptions, and concerns. Self-governance marries decisions and their consequences, leading to better decisions ... if outsiders make bad decisions, they seldom pay the price. Instead, the Indian community pays the price'.[14] The absence of any success where Indigenous Nations are not making significant decisions clearly shows that practical sovereignty is a necessary condition for sustainable economic development,[15] and draws a parallel to the rationales underlying free, prior, and informed consent (FPIC) for decision-making under the UNDRIP.

Secondly, effective governing institutions provide stability, predictability, transparency, and accountability – an economic environment in which Indigenous business owners enjoy the comfort and confidence necessary for setting up shop and attracting business into the territory.[16] Good governance, in such a sense, needs to incorporate stability, arm's length management, fair dispute resolution, and government focused on results for its constituents.[17] The application of good Tribal Nation governance attracts and keeps business, allowing for inter-Tribal trade.

[12] Cornell and Kalt (n 9) 11.
[13] ibid 11–12.
[14] ibid 13–14.
[15] ibid 14.
[16] ibid.
[17] ibid 15.

Institutions that can be political and cultural matches between the expressed Indigenous political mandate and a proposed economic project are also vital to the *nation-building approach*. An Indigenous government would probably not support a large scale open pit mining project on Indigenous sacred lands, for instance, as the degree of the cultural match would be nil. To maintain their legitimacy, Tribal institutions can both govern and be seen to be governing for the good of the people.[18] These institutions can be both effective and culturally appropriate. On the road to sustainable economic development, Indigenous governments can innovate and create institutions that resonate with community beliefs but remain flexible to modern times.[19]

The fourth factor, strategic orientation for decision-making, is the opposite of reactionary decision-making, which simply responds ad hoc to outside influences, and which has no vision of an ideal end-state that would constitute long-term economic development success for the Tribal Nation. The alternative is to think, 'what kind of society are we trying to build?'[20] This requires determining long-term objectives, identifying priorities and concerns, and taking a hard-nosed look at the assets the governing institution has to work with and the constraints it has to deal with.[21]

Finally, dedicated leadership is underpinned by the quality of both the elected political leadership and appointed business leadership. They focus on the same project with mutual understanding from two different perspectives. The elected political leadership focuses on developing government and regulatory infrastructure to attract and keep businesses within the Tribal jurisdiction. The appointed business leadership focuses on creating viable businesses that can thrive within the Indigenous community.[22] A corollary of this fifth factor is that non-Indigenous governments have a role to play in Tribal sustainable economic development. Federal leadership in the area of Indigenous sustainable economic development needs to consist of the steadfast support of, rather than dictatorship over, the efforts of the Tribal Nations to develop their own economic and political sovereignty.[23]

There is, of course a direct relationship between the exercise of an inherent Indigenous economic right of inter-Tribal trade and the practical ability of that same Tribe to sustain the exercise of this inter-Tribal trading capacity.

[18] ibid 17.
[19] ibid.
[20] ibid 18.
[21] ibid.
[22] ibid.
[23] ibid 19.

The better a Tribe can align its internal governance approach to a sustainable nation-building model, it can be suggested, the more likely that the Tribal Nation will be able to sustain its economic development through, among other enterprises, inter-Tribal trade and investment.

4.3 BARRIERS TO INDIGENOUS INTER-TRIBAL TRADE

For all the economic promise of Indigenous business embedded in good Indigenous governance, entrepreneurial trade and future prosperity, it has been noted that the United States and other States have historically denied Indigenous Peoples an equal opportunity for sustainable economic prosperity. The colonial-Indigenous dichotomy has shifted over time, starting as a Nation-to-Nation treaty relationship of equals,[24] and gradually turning into a present relationship best described in studies as paternalistic oversight by Nation-States that break treaty obligations and that systematically seek to overrule, dominate, or destroy long-standing Indigenous trade jurisdiction.[25] In Canada, the economic destruction of Indigenous Peoples is well documented, taking place as it has on all fronts, through Canada's Indian Act,[26] which removed or blocked long-held inherent economic rights to land, resources, and inter-Tribal trade. Additionally, the impacts of language denial and destruction of Indigenous Peoples' cultures using Canada's Residential School system and its the Sixties Scoop, as well as disproportionately low and unequal funding for Indigenous education, health care, and infrastructure, described by some as 'starvation-level' support must be underlined.[27]

As a result of this policy of exclusion, Indigenous People were not in the room for, or even consulted in the development of, the post-World War II global trade systems. In more recent times, improvements may be identified, and many of Canada's Indigenous Peoples are beginning to play a central role in sustainably developing their own economies. The federal government has

[24] James S Frideres, *Native People in Canada: Contemporary Conflicts* (Prentice-Hall Canada Inc. 1983) 14; Royal Commission on Aboriginal Peoples, 'Volume 1 – Looking Forward Looking Back' (1996) 39.

[25] Royal Commission on Aboriginal Peoples, 'Volume 2 – Restructuring the Relationship' (1996) 454; *R v Sioui* [1990] 1 SCR 1025 (CAN) [1057] where, per Lamer J., 'Great Britain and France felt that the Indian nations had sufficient independence and played a large enough role in North America for it to be good policy to maintain relations with them very close to those maintained between sovereign nations'.

[26] Indian Act 1876 SC 1876 ss 18, 39.

[27] Truth and Reconciliation Commission of Canada, 'Honouring the Truth, Reconciling for the Future – Summary of the Final Report of the Truth and Reconciliation Commission of Canada' (2015).

additionally begun to recognize its fiduciary obligation to consult Indigenous Peoples on international economic commitments, otherwise risking intrusions on Aboriginal rights as dictated by section 35 of the *Charter of Rights and Freedoms*.[28] However, such steps have yet to overcome many barriers to the expression of the inherent Indigenous economic right to inter-Tribal trade.

Five barriers to Indigenous trade have been identified in Canada and the United States, and may be equally relevant to other jurisdictions like Australia and New Zealand. These include poor Indigenous governance, state interference with Indigenous jurisdiction, failures to honour Jay Treaty obligations, the requirement of Indigenous foreign trade zones, and the modern intellectual property regime's failure to accommodate Indigenous Traditional Knowledge (TK). These barriers hinder the exercise of the inherent Indigenous economic right to inter-Tribal trade, but to remove each complex obstacle, collaboration between Indigenous, federal, and provincial or state jurisdiction is required.

4.3.1 *Barrier to Trade #1: Poor Tribal Governance*

As the authors of the Harvard Project on American Indian Economic Development [Harvard Project] argue, successful international inter-Tribal trade can only start with proper governance, which needs to be designed and built by the Indigenous communities and Nations undertaking the trade. In this view, bedrock of successful economic development ensures that the Indigenous governance of the jurisdiction in which an Indigenous business operates is optimally set for these businesses to achieve long-term economic success, and largely reflects the issues and principles outlined in the previous *nation-building approach* section.[29] At its core, overcoming poor Tribal governance boils down to identifying good governance for Indigenous businesses, and keeping Indigenous-owned and operated ventures separate from Indigenous government.

First, a good governance regime for Indigenous entities means that it can support and attract small and medium Indigenous enterprises and allow them to expand. Good governance, for any small business, means a government that is stable, predictable, accountable, transparent, and at arm's length from

[28] *Hupacasath First Nation v Canada (Minister of Foreign Affairs)*, 2015 F.C.A. 4, 379 D.L.R. (4th) 737 (CAN).

[29] Harvard Project on American Indian Economic Development, 'About' (Harvard Kennedy School, 2023) <https://indigenousgov.hks.harvard.edu/about> accessed 24 January 2025.

'for-profit' ventures. Additionally, they suggest, rules are more important than resources.[30] Indigenous Nations with few resources but effective institutions, that is, good rules, generally do better in the long term, because they maintain frugal governance systems and are accountable for even modest expenses.[31] Without good rules, resources will be wasted and may even be entirely lost. In sum, good governance brings prosperity.[32]

The challenge for Indigenous governments is to create an environment that invites and attracts talented people to participate in sustainable development by building their own businesses in their community, serving their own people, and trading with other Indigenous Nations locally and across borders. This infrastructure creation is unmistakably the task of the local Indigenous government.

As scholars have argued, Indigenous Nation-owned enterprises that are insulated from political interference are nearly five times as likely to be profitable as those that are not.[33] Thus, secondly, a fundamental rule of good governance for Indigenous trade is that Indigenous-owned and operated business activities should remain independent from Indigenous government. Businesses should be transparent to their community, and accountable to both community and government for ethical results.[34]

4.3.2 *Barrier to Trade #2: State or Provincial Interference in Tribal Jurisdiction*

Government interference in Indigenous affairs constitutes a prime barrier to trade. Overcoming this interference is crucial to regaining autonomy, developing good governance, and addressing other barriers to trade. To fully comprehend the origin and extent of this obstacle, it is useful to consider two North American situations: first, the state of affairs for Indigenous Nations prior to the existence of the United States and Canada, second, the autonomy

30 Cornell and Kalt (n 9); Harvard Project on American Indian Economic Development, 'Determinants of Development Success in the Native Nations of the United States' (Harvard University, University of Arizona, 2008).

31 Steven Cornell, 'What Makes First Nations Enterprises Successful? Lessons from the Harvard Project' (Harvard Project on American Indian Economic Development, Native Nations Institute for Leadership, Management, and Policy, 2006) JOPNA No 2006-01 9–12 and 43.

32 ibid.

33 Miriam Jorgensen and Jonathon Taylor, 'What Determines Indian Economic Success? Evidence from Tribal and Individual Indian Enterprises' (Harvard Project on American Indian Economic Development, 2000) PRS 00-3 4–5.

34 ibid.

that existed within Canada's post-colonial, provincial-Tribal experience alongside the post-Revolution state-Tribal experience in the US.

First, scholars explain before colonization, Indigenous Nations in what are now the two States of Canada and the United States had their own Tribal territories, covering the entire continent of North America. Indigenous Nations exercised their own sovereign powers to engage in inter-Tribal trade and develop strategic multi-national alliances with other Tribes, with few hierarchical distinctions in the level of authority, autonomy, or sovereignty exercised even after separating territory into the Dominion of Canada and the United States. Even during the American colonial period, the British Crown-owned American Colonies (the original thirteen US colonies) were perceived as treating the Indigenous Tribes in the same way as the northern British American colonies (Upper-Canada, Lower Canada, and Maritime colonies of Nova Scotia, New Brunswick, and Prince Edward Island). With the arrival of a newly formed United States of America, independent of the British Crown, however, some historians underline real differences in treatment.[35] While the British colonies of what became the United States removed themselves from British rule, certain North American British colonies never rebelled nor declared independence.[36] Having remained 'loyal' to the British Crown while their neighbours directly to the south rebelled, historians suggest, these colonies were consolidated within the British Dominion of Canada as provinces in 1867, when the British parliament had passed the *British North America Act* [*BNA*],[37] establishing the Dominion of Canada and converting the 'loyal' colonies into provinces.[38]

The treatment meted out to the Indigenous People under the BNA was very different from the treatment of American Indigenous People placed under the US Constitution. The United States treated Indigenous People as existing in their own right, that is outside the US Constitution. In what became Canada in 1876, Parliament passed the first *Indian Act*, which did not recognize

[35] Harold Cardinal, *The Unjust Society: The Tragedy of Canada's Indians* (Douglas & McIntyre 1999); For a critical reflection on Indigenous-settler relations in North America, see Thomas King, *The Inconvenient Indian: A Curious Account of Native People in North America* (Doubleday Canada 2012).

[36] The Seven Years War (1756–1763) would see the British end French influence in Canada (in the United States, the conflict is known as the 'French and Indian War'). Daniel Baugh, *The Global Seven Years War 1754–1763* (Routledge 2014).

[37] British North America Act 1867 (UK).

[38] The Paramountcy Doctrine in Canadian constitutional law establishes that where there is a conflict between valid provincial and federal laws, the federal law will prevail, and the provincial law will be inoperative to the extent that it conflicts with the federal law. *Smith v The Queen* [1960] SCR 776 (CAN).

Tribal sovereignty except, many historians suggest, in its continuance of the British tradition of treaty negotiation as a means of subjugation of Indigenous Tribes.[39] This tacit acknowledgement of sovereignty was quite real: otherwise, there would be no need to negotiate these treaties, and mere application of brute force by the (British) Army and the Royal Mounted Police would suffice to enforce the *Indian Act*.

Furthermore, scholars argue, merely relegating Indigenous Peoples to the status of wards of a British Dominion and through its implementation through the *Indian Act* was, and remains, a repugnant act of repression of the basic human rights of the Indigenous Peoples of Canada.[40] By failing to replace the *Indian Act* with legislation that would at least nod to the human rights of the Indigenous Peoples whose territories it has seized, they suggest, the Canadian Government appears to be perceiving Indigenous Peoples as somehow constituting an 'Indian Problem' that must be addressed, rather than honouring the spirit and intent of the treaties with Indigenous Peoples that are foundational to the existence of the country.[41]

On the other hand, the framers of the US Constitution chose not to include Indigenous Peoples except as a passing reference, to 'Indians' in three references, with that in relation to the federal power of trade and commerce being of most importance to this analysis.[42] At the time of formation, various Tribes had developed extensive trading relationships with the colonial governments. The relatively good relations between the trading Tribes east of the Mississippi River and the newly formed states allowed relative peace, some historians suggest. The Tribes that maintained peaceful trading relationships also maintained the ability to retain and instruct legal representation, as well as the standing to lobby federal decision-makers on areas affecting the exercise of their Tribal sovereignty.

The new unity of states created a hierarchical level of power where, historians suggest, a set of state governors anxiously sought to exploit all new opportunities afforded them by their newly created status.[43] Most turned their

39 British sovereignty has been described as a legal fiction concocted to facilitate political subjection, see Douglas Moodie, reviewing John Borrows, '*Recovering Canada: The Resurgence of Indigenous Law*' (2004) 49(2) McGill Law Journal. See also John Borrows, *Recovering Canada: The Resurgence of Indigenous Law* (University of Toronto Press 2002).

40 Borrows (n 39).

41 Cardinal (n 35); King (n 35).

42 United States Constitution, art 1, s 8 Commerce Clause, which states that the United States Congress shall have power '[t]o regulate commerce with foreign nations, and among the several states, and with the Indian tribes'.

43 For an overview of early legal battles over US Indigenous sovereignty, see David E Wilkins, *American Indian Sovereignty and the US Supreme Court: The Masking of Justice* (University of

immediate attention to the Tribes whose lands had, in the gubernatorial imagination if not in fact, just fallen into their hands. The various Tribes east of the Mississippi River were still incontestably occupying (i.e. residing, travelling, and trading within) the entire extent of their original territories when the original coastal thirteen American colonies were formed. As one documented example, the Cherokee Nation (one of the five 'trading Tribes') Indigenous Tribal government found itself surrounded, first by a newly formed colony, then by an independent state.[44] As noted in historical records, the governor of the newly created state of Georgia desired to tax the Cherokee People and seize the Cherokee land for its riches.[45]

Tribes like the Cherokee Nation thus found their relations with the former colonies to be destabilized. In an important jurisdictional fight between the Cherokee Tribe and the state of Georgia, the US Supreme Court determined that Tribes possess a specific level of sovereignty, that of 'domestic dependent nations'.[46] This decision recognizes Indigenous sovereignty in relation to a state government's interest. Thus, according to this early US Supreme Court decision, a state cannot legislate or tax within a Tribal Nation's jurisdiction, but as experts have explained, supreme power over the Tribal Nations is retained by the Congress of the United States.[47] In essence, the Tribes aspiring to exercise their sovereignty may do so with limited state interference and limited federal support.

US-based Tribes are thus characterized by some as relatively more free and able to govern themselves and their domestic affairs.[48] US-based Tribes can pass their own domestic laws, which typically translate into the promotion of the well-being of their members and governance of their Tribal affairs. The governance authority for US Tribes has included areas that state governments claim. Scholars have underlined an unmistakable pattern of economic success

Texas Press 1997) For a more recent survey of government attempts to regulate and profit from American Indian activities in the 1980s in the US, see David E Wilkins and K Tsianina Lomawaima, *Uneven Ground: American Indian Sovereignty and Federal Law* (University of Oklahoma Press 2002).

44 For more on Cherokee history, see Duane King (ed), *The Cherokee Indian Nation: A Troubled History* (University of Tennessee Press 1979).

45 *Worcester v Georgia*, 31 US (6 Pet.) 515 (1832) [559]; *Cherokee Nation v Georgia*, 30 US (5 Pet.) 1 (1831) [18].

46 ibid.

47 The concept of 'Congressional Plenary Power' provides no limitation and is very much akin to the British and Canadian common law concept of Parliamentary Supremacy regarding the deference the Supreme Court must provide to the democratic will of the people as expressed through Congressional action. *United States v Kagama*, 118 US 375 (1886) [379], [380]; *Lone Wolf v Hitchcock*, 187 US 553 (1903) [565].

48 David E Wilkins and Heidi K Stark, *American Indian Politics and the American Political System* (4th ed, Rowman & Littlefield 2017).

for Tribes that embrace and exercise their sovereignty and exercise good governance on their lands. Additionally, US recognition of and support for Tribal sovereignty has made it possible for US Indigenous Peoples to develop solid Tribal economies, particularly in the State of Oklahoma, where the experience of four Tribes, the Choctaw Nation, Citizen Potawatomi Nation, Chickasaw Nation, and the Cheyanne and Arapaho Nation, illustrate the degree of Tribal sustainable business success attainable.

4.3.3 *Barrier to Trade #3: Canada's Failure to Honour Its Jay Treaty Obligations*

Studies suggest that while the US Government has attempted to honour its responsibilities to uphold the Jay Treaty principles, the Canadian Government may not yet acknowledge that it has any responsibility to uphold the Jay Treaty on behalf of the Indigenous Peoples.[49] Such a failure, in light of the legal situation, suggests that the Canadian Government has not yet succeeded in reforming structures which undermine Indigenous sovereignty and autonomy, and creates yet another systemic barrier for Indigenous Peoples participating in trade.

Reference to the inherent Indigenous economic right of inter-Tribal trade is found in the wording of the 1793–1794 *Treaty of Amity, Commerce and Navigation between His Britannick Majesty and the United States of America and Britain* [Jay Treaty],[50] in Article III, which includes a protection clause for inter-Tribal trade:

> Indian[s] dwelling on either side of said boundary line *freely to pass and re-pass* by land, or inland navigation, *into the respective territories and countries of the two parties on the continent of America* and to navigate all the lakes, rivers and waters thereof, and *freely to carry on trade and commerce with each other* [...].[51]

Various cases in the United States have weighed and found wanting the notion that the Jay Treaty was negated by the War of 1812.[52] As a result, the

49 ibid.

50 The British Parliament ratified the Jay Treaty in 1793, but the US Congress tarried, ratifying only after much debate and when it became clear that war would ensue unless the Treaty was signed. The ratification dates for the two sides are thus a year apart: 1793 and 1794. Treaty of Amity, Commerce, and Navigation (His Britannic Majesty–United States of America) (adopted 24 June 1795) (Jay Treaty); Denise Evans, 'Superimposed Nations: The Jay Treaty and Aboriginal Rights' (1995) 4 Dalhousie Journal of Legal Studies 215.

51 Jay Treaty (n 50) art III (emphasis added).

52 *Karnuth v U.S.*, 279 US 231(1929) 240–241; *McCandless v US ex rel. Diabo*, 25 F.2d 71 (1928); *Akins v United States*, 407 F. Supp. 748 (1978) [759]; *United States v Dion*, 476 US 734 (1986) [739–740].

US federal government requires that the Indigenous rights conferred in these principles can be removed only if Congress expressly legislates the abrogation.[53] That Congress must expressly abrogate an Indigenous treaty right is consistent with the Indian case law rules of interpretation requiring Congress to treat Indian rights under the treaty as standing unless Congress has expressly extinguished those rights.[54] In contrast, the Canadian federal government claims – many suggest falsely – that the treaty between Great Britain and the United States was negated by the War of 1812.[55]

This Canadian policy position also fails to take into account Canada's continuing obligation under the Treaty of Ghent,[56] where the rights of Tribes and Tribal members set forth in the Jay Treaty are re-established in Article IX.[57] Article IX of the Treaty of Ghent commanded the Crown's representatives in Canada to 'restore to the [T]ribes or nations respectively, all the possessions, rights, and privileges which they enjoyed' as of 1811, before the outbreak of the War of 1812.[58]

Canada's failure to comply with these obligations can be described as yet another example of a colonial Nation subverting the sovereignty of Indigenous Nations in matters of trade and investment.[59] Some scholars have recommended that power needs to be handed back to the Indigenous Peoples in such cases in order to have the possibility of enabling sustainable economic development.

4.3.4 *Barrier to Trade #4: Lack of Indigenous Foreign Trade Zones*

In contrast to nineteenth-century trade barriers, a tax-free trade zone, commonly called a free trade zone or foreign trade zone (henceforth FTZ)[60] is a

53 ibid [767], 'Congress' intention to abrogate Indian treaty rights must be clear and plain'.

54 *Lone Wolf* (n 47) [566]–[568], applied by *McGirt v Oklahoma*, 591 US (2020) 7.

55 The Hon. Lillian Dyck, 'Border Crossing Issues and the Jay Treaty Report' (Standing Committee on Aboriginal Peoples, Senate of Canada, 2016) <https://sencanada.ca/content/sen/committee/421/APPA/Reports/APPA-JayTreatyReport_e.pdf> accessed 24 January 2025.

56 ibid. The Government of Canada has never formally rejected, nor has it withdrawn from its obligations under the Treaty of Ghent. Thus, while it has never been enforced by the Nation-State of Canada, the Treaty of Ghent nonetheless remains in effect and enforceable as a treaty that must be respected under Canadian law.

57 Treaty of Ghent (His Britannic Majesty–United States of America) (adopted 16 February 1815) art IX. At the time of signing, 'His Britannic Majesty' was, for the purposes of law, what is now Canada, and His Majesty's obligation is today Canada's treaty obligation.

58 ibid.

59 See Borrows (n 39). For more on the complicated relationship between Indigenous freedom and Canadian constitutionalism, see John Borrows, *Freedom and Indigenous Constitutionalism* (University of Toronto Press 2016) pt 3.

60 The World Customs Organization refers to these as 'Free Zones'. 'Free Zones' (World Customs Organization, 2022) <www.wcoomd.org/en/topics/facilitation/activities-and-programmes/free-zone.aspx> accessed 24 January 2025.

distinct geographic area in which goods can be 'landed, handled, manufactured or reconfigured, and re-exported without the intervention of customs authorities'.[61] FTZs are designed to attract foreign business, investment, and jobs to the host territory through FTZ-specific incentives, including lower or exempt value-added taxes, lower (sometimes free) duties, especially for target sectors or industries, duty deferral (paying import duties only upon re-export), income tax exemption, reduced storage fees, and overall reduced supply chain costs.[62] These mechanisms also do not constitute a loss of sovereignty or jurisdiction for the host territory. Bringing the benefits of FTZs to Indigenous lands and businesses, some suggest, could enable Indigenous ventures to access these same benefits.[63] However, the manifestations of this potential vary between the United States and Canada.

In the United States, the Department of the Interior has offered American Indigenous Tribes the opportunity to host their own FTZs.[64] The programme was taken up by five US Tribal Nations; currently, the Citizen Potawatomi Nation of Oklahoma (CPN) has its own fully operational FTZ.[65] The CPN has successfully pioneered the development of an Indigenous FTZ embedded in its Tribal lands,[66] which gives businesses, particularly Indigenous-owned and Tribal businesses, a distinct competitive advantage offered by the FTZ mechanism.

With proper planning, an Indigenous-owned or Tribal corporation might not only take advantage of corporate tax-free status, but also qualify for various incentives that create economic opportunity within US 'Indian

61 ibid; Susan Tiefenbrun, 'U.S. Foreign Trade Zones of the United States, Free Trade Zones of the World, and Their Impact on the Economy' (2013) 12(2) Journal of International Business and Law 152–153.

62 Tiefenbrun (n 61) 154.

63 Bureau of Indian Affairs, *Indian Affairs Manual Part 90 Free Trade Zones* (Bureau of Indian Affairs) <www.bia.gov/as-ia/ieed/division-economic-development/indian-affairs-manual-part-90-free-trade-zones accessed> 12 February 2025; for discussion of Indigenous participation in international agreements, see Government of Canada, *The Comprehensive and Progressive Agreement for Trans-Pacific Partnership and Indigenous Rights* (Government of Canada) <www.asiapacific.ca/publication/international-trade-inclusivity-cptpp-and-indigenous> accessed 12 February 2025.

64 In much of the earlier US and Canada legal text cited here, including for reserves, trust lands and so on, the old terms 'Indian' and 'Native American' are preserved verbatim.

65 Tribal Economic Development Principles-at-Glance Series, 'Native American Foreign Trade Zones' (U.S. Department of the Interior, 2020).

66 Jacob Laughlin, 'Foreign-Trade Zones in Indian County: Is a Foreign-Trade Zone Right for Your Tribe?' (2017) 42(1) American Indian Law Review 185; Chip Minty, 'Iron Horse Industrial Park Revs as Economic Engine East of Shawnee' *The Journal Record* (Oklahoma City, 21 July 2023) <https://journalrecord.com/2023/07/21/iron-horse-industrial-park-revs-as-economic-engine-east-of-shawnee/> accessed 24 January 2025.

Country'.[67] It is possible that regional economic incentives for Tribal businesses can help foster more sustainable economic development for US Tribal Nations, providing an added incentive to establish a portion of the Indigenous business in an FTZ that is located within Tribal jurisdiction. Additionally, Tribal corporations are exempted from federal and state income tax, sales tax, property tax, personal property tax, and also benefit from 'HUBZone' contracting conditions. With US Native American Free Trade Zones, Indian Tribal enterprises are treated as states and are therefore treated as tax-exempt for charitable contributions and gifts, are not subject to certain excise taxes and can access various other tax credits and incentives.[68]

Canadian structures, on the other hand, present a different story. The Canadian federal government, analysts explain, seeks to position Canada as a desirable destination for foreign investment. The Government of Canada claims to be the first country in the G-20 to offer a 'tariff-free zone' for industrial manufacturers, with some describing the country as one large FTZ.[69] In practice, however, Canada does not operate physically distinct, duty-free enclaves like traditional foreign-trade zones in the United States; rather, it offers a range of 'FTZ-type programs' that confer some of the same tariff and tax benefits, but with important differences. Among these FTZ-type programs, the duty deferral program (DDP) – encompassing the duties relief program, the duty drawback program, and the customs bonded warehouse program – is the principal mechanism by which firms may defer, or later be refunded, customs duties on imported goods that are eventually exported. Two additional programs, the Export Distribution Centre Program (EDCP) and

67 'Indian Country', a legislated US legal term found at 18 US Code §1151, meaning (a) all land within the limits of any Indian reservation under the jurisdiction of the United States Government; (b) all dependent Indian communities within the borders of the United States whether within the original or subsequently acquired territory thereof, and whether within or without the limits of a state; and (c) all Indian allotments, the Indian titles to which have not been extinguished, including rights-of-way running through the same.

68 Dr James Collard, 'Iron Horse Industrial Park' (2019) Presentation at the International Intertribal Trade and Investment Organization (IITIO) Conference and Trade Mission, University of Oklahoma College of Law.

69 'Foreign Trade Zone' (Government of Canada: Department of Finance, Canada, 2013) <www.canada.ca/en/department-finance/programs/international-trade-finance-policy/foreign-trade-zone.html> accessed 24 January 2025. Duty-free Manufacturing Tariff Regime, which states that 'In recent years, Canada has implemented a major new initiative that will eliminate tariffs on all manufacturing inputs by 2015 – the first country in the G-20 to offer a tariff-free zone for industrial manufacturers. Canada's initiative applies across the entire country, making Canada one large FTZ for firms importing manufacturing inputs'.

the Exporters of Processing Services Program (EOPS), provide relief from Canada's Goods and Services Tax (GST) or Harmonized Sales Tax (HST) for export-oriented businesses. Unlike US FTZs (which are legally treated as outside US customs territory, allowing duty deferral indefinitely until they reach the US market), goods brought into any Canadian FTZ-type program still undergo Canadian customs clearance and must be exported within a set timeframe – typically four years – to avoid incurring import duties.

While Canada's approach emphasizes country-wide access to deferral, exemption, and drawback programmes anywhere a firm operates, this unorthodox approach has drawbacks. Since the entire country has been declared part of this initiative, distinct zones with the economic incentives and competitive advantages typically expected of a FTZ are comparatively absent. In contrast, nearly all other FTZs are located in specific geographic areas.[70] Canada's approach may, accordingly, frustrate the intended boost to job creation and foreign investment. For a clear comparison of FTZs in the US and Canada, see Table 4.1 from the US International Trade Commission.[71]

Establishing exclusive Indigenous Free Trade Zones (ITZs) on Indigenous lands could allow for intensive and focused economic development in Canada, some suggest.[72] Developing ITZs may offer an option for Canada. The Canadian federal government can amend its *Indian Act* to expressly permit ITZs dedicated exclusively to inter-Tribal trade. This approach could fulfil the economic mandate of the Government of Canada to execute its fiduciary obligation toward Canada's Indigenous Peoples while providing Canada with a way out of its vicious cycle of paternalistic imposed economic solutions. Designated ITZs could empower Canada's First Nations, Métis, and Inuit governments, allowing Indigenous Peoples to pass resolutions to activate their own ITZs within their own territories, sustainably developing their ITZs as they see fit.

70 As implied in the word 'zone', common to many of the names for this type of initiative around the world. A true FTZ is a fiscal limbo, a geographic area set aside for tax minimization, and in which the usual tariffs are deferred. Canada cannot yet be said to have established such a place within its borders.

71 US International Trade Commission, 'Free Trade Zones: Impact on Trade and Public Policy Implications' (2023) 31 <www.usitc.gov/publications/332/pub5423.pdf> accessed 12 February 2025.

72 This is especially important considering that international inter-Tribal trade is *prima facie* an inherent economic right. Constitution Act 1982, Canadian Charter of Rights and Freedoms s 35; UN Res 61/295, 'United Nations Declaration on the Rights of Indigenous Peoples' (2007) UN Doc A/RES/61/295 (UNDRIP) arts 20(1) and 36(1).

TABLE 4.1 *Selected features of FTZ, FTZ-type, and related programs in the United States, Canada, and Mexico*

Program	Country	Duty deferral	Duty exemption	Duty reduction	Duty drawback	Tax relief	Geographic restriction	Time restriction
FTZ program	United States	✓	✓	✓	X	✓	✓	X
Drawback program	United States	X	X	X	✓	✓	X	✓
Customs bonded warehouse	United States	✓	✓	X	X	✓	✓	✓
Duties relief program	Canada	✓	✓	X	X	✓	X	✓
Duty drawback program	Canada	X	X	X	✓	✓	X	✓
Customs bonded warehouse	Canada	✓	✓	X	X	✓	✓	✓
EDCP/EOPS	Canada	X	X	X	X	✓	X	✓

✓ = Yes, it is a central feature of the program; X = No, it is not a central feature of the program.
FTZ, Foreign Trade Zone; EDCP, the Export Distribution Centre Program; EOPS, the Exporters of Processing Services Program.

4.3.5 *Barrier to Trade #5: Indigenous Traditional Knowledge Excluded from Intellectual Property Regimes*

Although some argue that it has not received the attention deserved in the establishment of global IP regimes, Indigenous TK nevertheless exists.[73] In Chapter 5, further detail is provided on the history and context that underscore the importance of protecting TK within broader legal regimes. Here, it suffices to note that TK refers to the knowledge or skills Indigenous Peoples possess regarding their culture and folklore, their technologies, and their use of native plants for medicinal purposes.[74] This knowledge functions as a collective construct, embodying a community and a history that extends beyond the scope of individual legal entities. This is compared to the intellectual property regime, which some commentators suggest protects individual and corporate interests, and is fixed over a specific period.[75]

Strong cases have been made but failed to include TK in trade agreements, such as for the former North American Free Trade Agreement (NAFTA), and its successor, the Canada US Mexico Agreement (CUSMA).[76] Incorporating TK into trade agreements would provide measures that appropriately credit and respect TK in keeping with customary/traditional Indigenous law; some suggest that these would be designed not to confer economic benefits on individual creators but for use and licensing by Indigenous Peoples collectively.[77] Exercising economic sovereignty, supporting Indigenous entrepreneurialism and prosperity, and exercising traditional sustainable development practices in a modern trade regime, hold potential to enhance Indigenous Peoples' ability to protect, regulate, and make use of their own TK without fear of piracy and theft, and without fear that users will fail to properly compensate TK holders.[78]

[73] For more on this subject, see Daniel F Robinson, *Confronting Biopiracy: Challenges, Cases and International Debates* (Routledge 2010); Christoph B Graber and Martin A Girsberger, 'Traditional Knowledge at the International Level: Current Approaches and Proposals for a Bigger Picture that Include Cultural Diversity' in Hansjörg Seiler and Jörg Schmid (eds), *Recht des Ländlichen Raums: Festgabe der Universität Luzern für Paul Richli zum 60. Geburtstag* (Schulthess 2006); Christoph B Graber, 'Stimulating Trade and Development of Indigenous Cultural Heritage by Means of International Law: Issues of Legitimacy and Method' (I-Call Working Paper No 2012/01, January 2012).

[74] Megan Davis, 'International Trade Rules and Indigenous Knowledge: A Basic Introduction' (2006) 6(20) Indigenous Law Bulletin 10. See also Robinson (n 73).

[75] Pierre-Emmanuel Moyse, 'Report of the Workshop on Indigenous Traditional Knowledge, Traditional Cultural Expressions, and Intellectual Property – ISED/CIPP Practical Workshop on Indigenous Knowledge and Cultural Expressions and Intellectual Property' (Centre for Intellectual Property Policy, 2020) 5.

[76] Canada-United States-Mexico Agreement (Mexico–Canada–United States) (adopted 30 November 2018, entered into force 1 July 2020) (CUSMA).

[77] Davis (n 74).

[78] Moyse (n 75) 27.

Indigenous Nations around the world face the need to engage in the active protection of their TK in their governance, economic development, industries, and businesses. Elsewise, some suggest, this gap in TK trade protections at the international level neglects Indigenous ways of knowing as a valid source of research and intellectual property that should be owned by the Indigenous communities themselves.[79] The current situation is also seen as exposing TK to exploitation and competition from outside, non-Indigenous interests. These competitive interests may compound the other four barriers already faced by Indigenous entrepreneurs and ventures, and need to be addressed to not only give power and property back to Indigenous Peoples, but also to warrant respect and acknowledgement for Indigenous knowledge and innovation.

4.3.6 *Trade Financing: A Historical Sixth Barrier*

Ten years ago, trade financing would have been identified as a sixth barrier. In the past decade however, the financing of trade has begun to be addressed by the private sector and the public sector in both Canada and the United States. Initial challenges centred on the inability of Tribal Nations to obtain significant large-scale financing, as the Tribal Nations of Canada and the United States had very little collateral to pledge against the loans.[80] The land that First Nations occupy in Canada, typically recognized by treaty, has been treated as lands belonging to the Canadian federal government but reserved (presumably not permanently but at the pleasure of the government) for Indigenous Nations. As such, reserve land held in trust could not be pledged or leveraged as collateral to guarantee loans. Likewise, in the United States, 'Indian lands' were also deemed to be held in trust by the federal government and cannot be pledged or leveraged as a form of loan guarantee.

With the advent of increased economic wealth of Tribes through Tribal business ventures ranging from a game of chance operations (such as bingo halls and casinos) to profitable agricultural, livestock, and manufacturing, various US Tribes have been able to develop their own Tribal banking institutions.[81]

[79] Robinson (n 73); Davis (n 74).

[80] On barriers to collateral and financing under the *Indian Act*, see Chapter 3.

[81] There are twenty Native American (Indigenous)-owned banks and credit unions; more than half are based primarily in Oklahoma: All Nations Bank (owner – Absentee Shawnee Tribe); Bank of Cherokee County (owned by the Cherokee Nation); Bay Bank (owned by Oneida Nation); Chickasaw Community Bank (owned by the Chickasaw Nation); Choctaw Federal Credit Union (owned by the Choctaw Nation); Eagle Bank (owned by Confederated Salish and Kootenai Tribes); First American Credit Union (owned by Navajo Land Credit Union); Sovereign Bank, formerly First National Bank and Trust Co. (owned by the Citizen Potawatomi Tribe); Four Corners Federal Credit Union (owned by Navajo Nation); Gateway First Bank (largest Native American-owned bank in terms of total assets); Lac Courte Oreilles

In Canada, too, there have been advances in creating Indigenous-friendly financial institutions.[82] While a few Indigenous-owned and operated banking institutions have opened, such as the First Nations Bank of Canada, the Me-Dian Credit Union, and the Assiniboine Credit Union, Canada has mainly seen cooperative business relationships develop between the central chartered banks in Canada and reputable Aboriginal financial and economic development organizations.[83] Each of Canada's 'Big Five' banks[84] now has a section of their services devoted to personal and corporate Indigenous banking and investment.

In such a way, accommodation and recognition of the barriers to entry for Indigenous business-people were recognized, and allied institutions were able to work in a collaborative manner to dismantle this barrier, offering a potential example of collective and cooperative action in enabling Indigenous enterprises to succeed. Indeed, it may be suggested that recent progress in Indigenous finance makes it all the more vital to recognize and overcome the other five barriers still extant to foster Indigenous participation in trade and contribute to the advancement of sustainable development.

Federal Credit Union (owned by Lac Courte Oreilles Tribal members); Lakota Federal Credit Union (owned by Oglala Lakota Oyate People); Lumbee Guaranty Bank (the second-largest Native American-owned bank by total assets); Native American Bank (owned by twenty Tribal Nations and Alaska Native Corporations); People's Bank of Seneca (for which the Eastern Shawnee Tribe is the current majority shareholder); Pinnacle Sisseton-Wahpeton Federal Credit Union (owned by the Sisseton-Wahpeton Sioux Tribe); Turtle Mountain State Bank (first privately owned Native American bank on a federally recognized Indian Reservation); White Earth Reservation Federal Credit Union (owned by the White Earth Band of Chippewa Indians); Woodlands National Bank (owned by the Mille Lacs Band of Ojibwe). Ward Williams, 'Native American-Owned Banks by State' (Investopedia, 2023) <www.investopedia.com/native-american-owned-banks-by-state-5085713> accessed 24 January 2025.

82 For helpful reference on this subject, see Momentus, *Addressing Gaps in Indigenous Access to Finance Pre-Scoping Report* (16 October 2023) submitted to First Nations Financial Management Board, 21.

83 Aboriginal Financial Institutions are defined by the NACCA as being 'Indigenous-controlled, community-based financial organizations. AFIs provide developmental lending, business financing and support services to First Nations, Métis, and Inuit businesses in all provinces and territories. Support includes business loans, non-repayable contributions, financial and management consulting, and business start-up and aftercare services'. 'Indigenous Financial Institutions' (National Aboriginal Capital Corporations Association, 2022) <https://nacca.ca/aboriginal-financial-institutions/> accessed 24 January 2025.

84 'Indigenous Markets' (CIBC, 2023) <www.cibc.com/en/commercial/areas-of-specialization/indigenous-banking.html> accessed 24 January 2025; 'Indigenous Peoples and RBC' (RBC, 2023) <www.rbc.com/indigenous/> accessed 24 January 2025; 'Indigenous Financial Services' (Scotiabank, 2023) <www.scotiabank.com/ca/en/commercial-banking/industries/indigenous.html> accessed 24 January 2025; 'Indigenous Banking at BMO' (BMO, 2023) <www.bmo.com/main/personal/indigenous-banking/> accessed 24 January 2025; 'TD and Indigenous Peoples in Canada' (TD, 2023) <www.td.com/ca/en/about-td/diversity-and-inclusion/indigenous-peoples> accessed 24 January 2025.

4.4 INDIGENOUS TRADE AND COMMERCE: ENGAGING WITH NON-INDIGENOUS ENTERPRISE

There is now, as there has been since contact, a great deal of commerce among Indigenous and non-Indigenous populations. Indigenous individuals own and operate sole proprietorships, partnerships, and consortiums. Tribal Nations have majority-owned and majority-controlled businesses on all scales, with many enterprises doing business with their non-Indigenous counterparts. For Indigenous trade with (non-Indigenous) States outside the borders now confining the Indigenous Nation, a State may or may not require the Indigenous business to obtain federal permission. It is possible to examine each condition: trade without, and trade with, federal permission to consider how Indigenous trade and commerce can and should engage with non-Indigenous enterprise.

4.4.1 *Tribal Nations Trading with Foreign States without Federal Permission*

In North America, Indigenous Tribes have been trading with other Tribes since time immemorial. When Europeans arrived, historians explain, various European representatives made attempts to secure exclusive trading rights with Indigenous Peoples.[85] Although these attempts were likely motivated more by rivalries over their various kingdoms' colonial territorial expansion than by respect for Nation-to-Nation trade agreements, they nonetheless had the effect of acknowledging the Indigenous sovereignty.[86] However, most Tribal Nations in Canada and the United States eventually found themselves enclosed entirely within the boundaries of the modern State, which placed limitations on the Tribal Nations' exercise of their rights of inter-Tribal trade as domestic-dependent Nations. Where the State considers the inter-Tribal trade to be 'foreign', Indigenous and other jurists explain, their sovereignty is curtailed because the constitutions of Canada and the United States reserve the power of trade and commerce with other States to the federal sphere of jurisdiction.[87]

The US Supreme Court in the decision of *United States v Wheeler*, 435 US 313, 326 (1978), has determined that US Tribes 'cannot enter into direct

[85] See, eg, John Borrows, 'Wampum at Niagara: The Royal Proclamation, Canadian Legal History, and Self-Government' in Michael Asch (ed), *Aboriginal and Treaty Rights in Canada: Essays on Law, Equality, and Respect for Difference* (UBC Press 1997) 157; see also Neal Salisbury, 'The Indians' Old World: Native Americans and the Coming of Europeans' (1996) 53 The William and Mary Quarterly 435.

[86] ibid.

[87] ibid.

commercial or governmental relations with foreign powers',[88] and cannot enter into commercial or government relations with States such as Canada without the prior approval of the US federal government. What is left unresolved is whether a US Tribe can enter into a commercial or governmental agreement with a Tribe outside of the United States. In Canada, the right of an Indigenous individual to conduct cross-border trade, as per *R. v Mitchell*,[89] never came into existence, and the right of an Aboriginal group to inter-Tribal trade with another Tribal Nation is still very much open to judicial recognition.

Inter-Tribal trade beyond State borders has been recognized in Article 3 of the Jay Treaty, as jurists note, and some of these principles are embodied in US legislation allowing Canadian Indigenous Peoples specific opportunities for entry and treatment as domestic and not foreign individuals.[90] Applying the US jurisprudence, Canadian Tribes would not be characterized States and are remarkably similar to the US domestic-dependent Indigenous Nations. Canadian First Nations[91] members entering into commercial relationships with US Tribes and Tribal members should, it has been recommended, therefore not be treated as 'foreigners' to the United States in the strict sense. Applying the Jay Treaty principles as found in the US legislation, there may well be space to accommodate unhindered inter-Tribal trade and commerce.

4.4.2 *Tribes Trading with Foreign States with Federal Permission*

Some Tribal Nations in Canada and the United States since the 2000s have embraced the notion of selling their products via international markets without exercising their inherent Indigenous economic right of inter-Tribal trade.[92] Such Tribal Nations may, for instance, be home to successful businesses that have achieved domestic market saturation and chose to seek new international markets through the regular international trade mechanisms available to all businesses within a modern State. For example, the Chickasaw Nation holding company, Chickasaw Nation Industries (CNI), in the United States serves significant corporate clients internationally.[93] In Canada, some leaders and analysts underline that various First Nations industrial parks have been

[88] *United States v Wheeler*, 435 US 313 (1978) [326].

[89] *R. v Mitchell* [2001] 1 SCR 911 (CAN).

[90] Immigration and Nationality Act of the United States 1952 (amended 1965) s 289.

[91] Probably, although not as clearly, also Métis and Inuit.

[92] For more generally on business and Indigenous law, see Dwight Newman (ed), *Business Implications of Aboriginal Law* (LexisNexis Canada 2018).

[93] CNI is a federally chartered corporation wholly owned by the Chickasaw Nation and headquartered in Norman, Oklahoma. 'Chickasaw National Industries' (2023) <www.chickasaw.com/> accessed 24 January 2025.

established to develop and welcome international trade of all kinds, such as the Oneida Industrial Park of the Six Nations[94] and the large multidimensional projects such as the industrial, residential, and commercial projects of the TFN Economic Development Corporation owned by the Tsawwassen First Nation.[95]

One notable example of Indigenous trade afforded by the conventional, non-rights-evoking trade mechanisms while fully exercising a Tribal Nation's inherent right to international inter-Tribal trade is the billion-dollar partnership between the Mi'kmaq Nation in Canada with Clearwater Seafoods Inc., a Canadian fish processing company, in 2020 and 2021. As recorded, historic turmoil existed across the vast Mi'kmaq territory along the Atlantic coast between colonists and the Mi'kmaq regardless of peace treaties, including the Halifax Treaties, guaranteeing uninhibited hunting and harvesting, and exclusive trade with the British at posts known as 'truck houses' to obtain 'necessary goods' to earn a moderate livelihood.[96] However, subsequent conflict over the right to hunt, fish, and gather over two centuries later led to judicial recourse. According to the Supreme Court of Canada to conclude that the clause in the 1760 treaty regarding securing necessities does not extend to the 'open-ended accumulation of wealth'.[97] According to jurists, this interpretation hastened to limit, but also acknowledged the existence of, a protected Indigenous commercial right to fisheries harvest.[98]

As scholars note, while questioning the assumption that Indigenous Nations somehow have less right of trade than the descendants of relatively newly arrived settled foreigners, the Mi'kmaq Nation also restarted modest commercial lobster operations in 2020. Non-Indigenous Nova Scotia commercial lobster fishers objected to the competition, suggesting that the Mi'kmaq would overfish lobster stocks in the off season, and ultimately this led to vandalization and destruction of Mi'kmaq property.[99]

94 'Oneida Industrial Park of the Six Nations' (Six Nations of the Grand River Development Corporation, 2023) <https://sndevcorp.ca/nation-enterprise/> accessed 24 January 2025.

95 'TFN Development Corporation of the Tsawwassen First Nation' (TFN Economic Development Corporation, 2023) <https://tfnedc.com/> accessed 24 January 2025.

96 'Treaties and Agreements' (Government of Canada 2020) <www.rcaanc-cirnac.gc.ca/eng/1100100028574/1529354437231> accessed 24 January 2025.

97 *R. v Marshall* [1999] 3 SCR 456 (CAN) 470.

98 Shelley Kirsten Denny, 'Ankukamkua'tu, "Doing Treaty": An Alternative Fisheries Governance Model for Mi'kmaq Aboriginal and Treaty Rights to Fish in Nova Scotia' (PhD thesis, Dalhousie University 2022) 350.

99 Professor Megan Bailey, Associate Professor at Dalhousie University and Canada Research Chair in Integrated Ocean and Coastal Governance, noted that scientists considered the Mi'kmaq harvest to have no statistical significance. Mi'kmaq lobster fishers set only some 500 traps, compared to hundreds of thousands of lobster traps set by non-Indigenous commercial fishers in the Atlantic. Gabriel Friedman, '"No Science" behind Lobster Dispute: Unpacking the Ugly Conflict Exploding in Nova Scotia' (Financial Post, 2020) <https://financialpost.com/commodities/agriculture/no-science-behind-lobster-dispute-unpacking-the-ugly-conflict-exploding-in-nova-scotia> accessed 24 January 2025; Leyland Cecco, 'Why Were Indigenous

Into this breach stepped a global seafood investor, Clearwater Seafoods Inc., with a $1 billion deal with the Mi'kmaq Nation, wherein Clearwater Seafoods Inc. shares a 50 per cent ownership in the Indigenous commercial lobster fishery.[100] Critically, Clearwater is also co-owned by US Tribal Nations. The deal ended the most overt violence since Clearwater, now co-owned by the Mi'kmaq Nation, also purchases the non-Indigenous commercial lobster catch.[101] In January 2021, shareholders of Clearwater overwhelmingly approved the new partnership.[102]

The Mi'kmaq Nation was viewed by many as opening their door to international markets and trade through this partnership, while still exercising their treaty-bound rights, offering insights into future opportunities.[103] Modern inter-Tribal trade agreements like this might encourage US Tribal Nations to engage in trade with Canadian Indigenous communities, encompassing new markets and new ways to bring Indigenous trade to market.

4.5 CONCLUSION

Preserving possibilities for the future – of individuals, groups, and the planet itself – is an important reason for Indigenous Peoples and modern States to be interested in the global establishment and revival of inter-Tribal trade. From the discussion of treaty rights, the necessity to build Indigenous business as a *Nation*, and current international barriers to and opportunities for Indigenous and inter-Tribal trade, it is possible to look forward to the cutting edge of Indigenous trade and TK.

Crews in Canada Shot at with Flare for Fishing' (The Guardian, 2020) <www.theguardian.com/environment/2020/sep/23/why-indigenous-crews-in-canada-were-shot-at-with-flares-for-fishing> accessed 24 January 2025.

[100] ibid.

[101] Geoffrey Morgan, 'Clearwater Seafoods Sold in $1 Billion Deal that Will See Mi'kmaq Communities Own 50 Per Cent' (Financial Post, 2020) <https://financialpost.com/commodities/clearwater-seafoods-sold-in-1-billion-deal-that-will-see-mikmaq-communities-own-50-per-cent> accessed 24 January 2025.

[102] Ironically, a purchase agreement here accomplishes what colonial treaties and governments have not managed. Clearwater Foods Incorporated, 'Clearwater Seafoods Incorporated, Premium Brands Holdings Corporation and Mi'kmaq First Nations' Coalition Celebrate Completion of Historic Transaction' (2021) Press Release <www.clearwater.ca/news/clearwater-seafoods-incorporated-premium-brands-holdings-corporation-and-mikmaq-first-nations-coalition-celebrate-completion-of-historic-transaction/> accessed 24 January 2025.

[103] See, eg, Denny (n 98) 306.

PART III

Indigenous Treaty Law Innovations on Sustainable Development

5

Traditional Knowledge, Genetic Resources, and Indigenous Treaty Law

5.1 INTRODUCTION

The modern global Intellectual Property (IP) regime was developed only after World War II as part of a plan for the post-war revitalization of the world economy and was largely spearheaded by only a few countries.[1] The project of developing a truly global IP regime required input via the United Nations (UN) from member States, particularly given concerns of many UN member States on how to access a global market for their goods and services. In the establishment of the regime, many scholars note that there was little interest or concern for the views of Indigenous Peoples, and it is unclear if Indigenous Traditional Knowledge (TK) was even considered. Few States were able to champion the interests of Indigenous Peoples, and in the debates, regimes for TK and property rights to Indigenous knowledge related to materials, medicines, plants, or animals may not have been considered a priority, or even well-understood.[2]

TK nevertheless exists. TK embraces the content of knowledge itself as well as traditional cultural expressions, including distinctive signs and symbols associated with TK. According to leaders and jurists, TK can also include agricultural, scientific, technical, ecological, and medicinal knowledge as well

[1] Paul Kuruk, 'Protecting Folklore under Modern Intellectual Property Regimes: A Reappraisal of the Tensions between Individual and Communal Rights in Africa and the United States' (1999) 48(4) American University Law Review 769.

[2] ibid; For further reference, see Rebecca C Fan, 'Evolution of Indigenous People's Rights and Indigenous Knowledge Debate' in Damien Short and Corinne Lennox (eds), *Handbook of Indigenous Peoples' Rights* (Routledge 2016).

as biodiversity-related knowledge.[3] Understood this way, TK is the property of Indigenous communities that can nurture communities and ecosystems. Like property that is both physical and intellectual for non-Indigenous regimes, TK creates a foundation for trade, livelihoods, and pride that can uplift and sustain Indigenous Peoples in the modern world. However, the various IP regimes of States are not always able to offer adequate protection for Indigenous TK, and existing structures can perpetuate barriers and prejudices for Indigenous trade and the creation of Indigenous-based enterprise.[4]

Efforts to improve the protection of TK have been informed largely by a recognition of the need to counter adverse effects on Indigenous communities arising from the widespread theft and unauthorized commercial exploitation of TK, especially in the pharmaceutical, agricultural, cosmetic, artistic design, and entertainment industries, with the retail market sectors being particular offenders.[5] As experts note, Indigenous groups have long been vocal in complaints about the lack of adequate compensation, loss of community rights, misrepresentations of products and practices as Indigenous, and the unauthorized public disclosure and use of secret knowledge, images, and other sensitive information pertaining to Indigenous communities.[6]

The lack of protectionary measures in the IP context can further expose Indigenous businesses and communities to exploitation and competition from other interests. Ensuring that authority and property over TK remain with the Indigenous Peoples who developed the knowledge is an important step to ensure respect and acknowledgement for Indigenous knowledge and innovation. This chapter first explores the fundamentals of TK and IP to distinguish the two concepts. Examples are then provided of how TK is currently

[3] For the purposes of this examination, general TK definitions will be used, however subsets involving medical and biological TK as well as the subset of traditional cultural expression can be examined separately. Further information on traditional cultural expression, and medical and biological TK and some examination into its subsets is provided by the World Intellectual Property Organization (WIPO). See WIPO, 'Intellectual Property and Genetic Resources, Traditional Knowledge and Traditional Cultural Expressions: An Overview' (WIPO Publication No 933, 2020) (WIPO IP & TK).

[4] See Chapter 4 for a discussion of current IP rules as barriers to advancing Indigenous trade and business. This specific barrier receives further attention in this chapter, which expands on possible paths forward for integrating TK into global knowledge regimes. See also Ruth Okediji, 'Traditional Knowledge and the Public Domain' (26 June 2018) Centre for International Governance Innovation Papers No 176.

[5] Earl W Kintner and Jack L Lahr, *An Intellectual Property Law Primer: A Survey of the Law of Patents, Trade Secrets, Trademarks, Franchises, Copyrights, and Personality and Entertainment Rights* (C. Boardman Company 1982) 61, 117, 119, 125, 273.

[6] Darrell A Posey and Graham Dutfield, *Beyond Intellectual Property: Toward Resource Rights for Indigenous Peoples and Local Communities* (International Development Research Centre 1996) 27.

addressed in the economies of Canada and the United States, including through an illustrative case study from Canada, before analysing the inclusion of provisions on TK in international treaties.

5.2 DISTINGUISHING INTELLECTUAL PROPERTY AND TRADITIONAL KNOWLEDGE

IP and TK have important conceptual differences. The World Intellectual Property Organization (WIPO) defines IP as 'creations of the mind, such as inventions; literary and artistic works; designs; and symbols, names and images used in commerce'.[7] Building on this characterization, IP is often protected in law through internationally recognized legal instruments, specifically patents, copyright, and trademarks, which enable people or corporations to temporarily be recognized as having an exclusive claim over the item reserved and as such be able to financially benefit from the use of this idea, product, concept, or image, for instance through royalties or licenses.

Patents can be defined in their simplest terms as 'an agreement between an inventor and the public, represented by the federal government: in return for a full public disclosure of the invention the inventor is granted the right for a fixed period of time ... It is a limited monopoly, designed not primarily to reward the inventor ... but to encourage public disclosure of inventions.'[8] Patents generally cover innovative products or processes, giving the patent holder the right to exclude others from manufacturing, implementing, advertising, direct selling, or importing the patented invention for a specific limited time.

Copyright, on the other hand, does not protect ideas in themselves but rather their expression, which must be original and fixed in a tangible medium. A copyright is essentially the right to copy or disseminate, that is, 'giving the holder the exclusive right to reproduce, adapt, distribute, perform, and display the work.'[9] The central premise underlying the law of copyright and patents is economic as the intention is to promote and protect innovation and originality by rewarding the inventor, author, or owner (including

7 World Intellectual Property Organization, 'About IP – What Is Intellectual Property' (World Intellectual Property Organization (WIPO), n.d.) <www.wipo.int/about-ip/en/> accessed 4 February 2025; see Oluwatobiloba Moody, 'Trade-Related Aspects of Traditional Knowledge Protection' in John Borrows and Risa Schwartz (eds), *Indigenous Peoples and International Trade* (2020).

8 Kintner and Lahr (n 5) 127.

9 *Black's Law Dictionary* (5th pocket ed, Thomson Reuters West 2016) 304.

enterprises which support and own the innovation) with a significant grouping of often exclusive, individual economic rights.[10]

Finally, trademark, in effect, can be described as a commercial substitute for one's signature. It is a 'word, phrase, logo, or other graphic symbol used by a manufacturer or seller to distinguish its product or products from those of others'.[11] Its main purpose is to designate the sources of specific goods and services.[12]

Turning to TK, it is much older and is roughly the understanding or skill of Indigenous Peoples pertaining to culture and practices, science, technological or ecological insights, and stewardship or use of native plants for medicinal purposes. Most definitions of TK are comprehensive. According to the WIPO, which has spearheaded serious discussions at the international level, TK includes:

> ... all tradition-based literary, artistic or scientific works; performances; inventions; scientific discoveries; designs; marks, names and symbols; undisclosed information; and all other tradition-based innovations and creations resulting from intellectual activity in the industrial, scientific, literary, or artistic fields.... Categories of TK could include among others: agricultural knowledge; scientific knowledge; technical knowledge; ecological knowledge; medicinal knowledge, including related medicines and remedies; biodiversity-related knowledge; 'expressions of folklore' in the form of music, dance, song, handicrafts, designs, stories and artwork; elements of languages, such as names, geographical indications and symbols; and, movable cultural properties.[13]

TK thus includes and extends beyond the subject matter of IP in the 'modern' sense. What sets TK apart from ordinary IP is the requirement that the knowledge must be 'tradition-based', 'generally regarded as pertaining to a particular people or its territory, and constantly evolving in response to a changing environment.'[14] The Government of Panama, as an example, has

[10] Mohsen al Attar, Nicole Aylwin, and Rosemary J Coombe, 'Indigenous Cultural Heritage Rights in International Human Rights Law' in Catherine Bell and Robert Patterson (eds), *Protection of First Nations' Cultural Heritage: Laws, Policy and Reform* (University of British Columbia Press 2009) 320.

[11] *Black's Law Dictionary* (n 9) 338.

[12] ibid.

[13] WIPO, 'Intellectual Property Needs and Expectations of Traditional Knowledge Holders: Report on Fact-finding Missions on Intellectual Property and Traditional Knowledge 1998–1999' (WIPO, 2001) 25; for more see Tobias Stoll, 'Intellectual Property and Technologies – Article 31' in Jessie Hohmann and Marc Weller (eds), *The UN Declaration on the Rights of Indigenous Peoples: A Commentary* (Oxford University Press 2018).

[14] ibid.

separately defined TK, using terms such as 'collective Indigenous Rights', in their domestic legislation, with an important emphasis. For them, collective Indigenous rights '*have no known author or owner and no date of origin* and constitute the heritage of an entire Indigenous [P]eople'.[15]

5.2.1 *Traditional Knowledge in Relation to Intellectual Property*

An essential distinction between TK and IP is that TK is not fixed in time, going back to 'time immemorial' and forward indefinitely, while IP fixes intellectual property to a specific time period. TK is also assigned to a collective entity and is cultured and handed down. It is part of the recipient's identity but not restricted to the recipient.[16] This can be contrasted with IP, which is assigned to a specific owner, be they an individual or corporation. Because of these differences, TK does not typically meet the criteria of novelty or originality as found in the requirement for IP tools such as found in patents or copyrights[17] and is widely held by members of the community as a collective right, not an individual right. In such ways, TK both includes and surpasses the subject matter of IP in the 'modern' sense.

Supporters of TK rights often argue that the existing IP regime, which favours discrete innovation and creation over more gradual and incremental processes, appears inherently inadequate and indeed, unfair to Indigenous Peoples.[18] The argument for protecting TK via the implementation of a TK regime often starts with a recognition that due to its very nature, TK has tremendous cultural significance. TK can also be desirable and of high value for use by non-Indigenous Peoples who have nothing to do with Indigenous values and heritage and who are outside Indigenous culture. For example, many non-Indigenous Peoples and companies have benefitted from

[15] Panama Legislative Assembly, Law No. 20 (26 June 2000) ch 1, art 2(v) (emphasis added) <https://perma.cc/FLS5-M48K> accessed 4 February 2025.

[16] Graham Dutfield, 'TRIPS-Related Aspects of Traditional Knowledge' (2001) 33(2) Case Western Reserve Journal of International Law 240.

[17] Simon Brascoupé and Karin Endemann, 'Intellectual Property and Aboriginal People: A Working Paper' (Minister of Indian Affairs and Northern Development, 1999) No R32–204/1999IE, 9 <https://perma.cc/R4WQ-4S9C> accessed 4 February 2025.

[18] ibid. For more on the debates surrounding TK protection, see Graham Dutfield, 'TK Unlimited: The Emerging but Incoherent International Law of Traditional Knowledge Protection' (2017) 20(5–6) Journal of World Intellectual Property 167. On the unfairness of the existing IP regime towards TK holders, see Stephen R Munzer and Kal Raustiala, 'The Uneasy Case for Intellectual Property Rights in Traditional Knowledge' (2009) 27 Cardozo Arts & Entertainment LJ 37, 40.

Indigenous healing methods. Yet, in most situations, a Tribe has limited legal recourse against entities who use and benefit from its Tribal knowledge.[19]

IP laws, which may be the most obvious basis for protection of TK would, unless radically overhauled, ordinarily prove unavailable to Indigenous Peoples who are collective holders of TK. This is in large part due to spiritual and cosmological reasons – most Indigenous theories of existence and ethics hesitate to attach exclusive economic rights to TK, or other aspects of cultural heritage. As Indigenous scholars and leaders often underline, knowledge is not a commodity that can be purchased, sold, and exploited at will for personal profit.[20] Indigenous ethics and spirituality generally emphasize the development and preservation of group rights and group identity rather than focusing on pursuit of individual and personal economic gains.[21]

Exercising economic sovereignty, supporting Indigenous entrepreneurialism and prosperity, and exercising traditional sustainable development practices in a modern trade regime are underpinned by Indigenous Peoples' ability to protect, regulate, and use their own TK. It is important for this to be done without fear of piracy and theft, and without fear that users will fail to properly recognize, respect, or compensate the holders or owners of the TK for its use.[22]

A possible solution for the inclusion and equal acceptance of TK in IP could be the acceptance, support, and protection of TK in international trade agreements by the inclusion of an Indigenous trade chapter or side letter that would leave intact existing IP regimes while making its protections available to Indigenous holders of TK. This can be done by adding parallel TK provisions, similar to those recommended by expert jurists, to acknowledge and protect Indigenous rights.[23]

5.2.2 *An Alternative Compromise for Traditional Knowledge*

Using terms that could serve well as a starting point for the inclusion of a subheading 'Traditional Knowledge' in an 'Aboriginal' chapter of the North

[19] An example of TK exploitation is the Cowichan Sweater Case, as presented later in this chapter.

[20] Marlene Brant Castellano, 'Ethics of Aboriginal Research' (2004) 1(1) Journal of Aboriginal Health 104; for more, see Mindy Li-Ming Yap and K Watene, 'The Sustainable Development Goals (SDGs) and Indigenous Peoples Another Missed Opportunity?' 20(4) (2019) Journal of Human Development and Capabilities 451.

[21] Tonina Simeone, 'Indigenous Traditional Knowledge and Intellectual Property Rights' (Library of Parliament of Canada 2004) No PRB 03-38E 5.

[22] Ibid; see also WIPO IP & TK (n 3) 20.

[23] Munzer and Raustiala (n 18).

American Free Trade Agreement (NAFTA, its successor known as the Canada US Mexico Agreement or CUSMA and USMCA), leading scholars have recommended a 'robust package of legal protection for TK.'[24] One mechanism, known as the Munzer Model, recommends domestic State enforcement of Indigenous TK protection and enforcement, which parallels the IP framework set out in NAFTA.[25]

Under this mechanism, Indigenous Peoples would hold various rights over traditional practices and understandings, including biodiversity, culture, and medicinal practices, communally. The Indigenous authorities could also create binding rules for others accessing these knowledge rights and have a claim right to receive compensation for granting access to these rights. If consent or compensation is not received, the Indigenous members have the right and power to seek royalties, compensatory damages, and equitable relief. Indigenous Peoples also have certain powers of exempting and preventing copyright over TK, and have immunity against the expropriation of TK items listed in the agreement. Furthermore, all of these rights and powers are not time-bound and are of indefinite duration, subject to the People's discretion.[26]

The proposed mechanism addresses two types of TK protections within a domestic State setting that are considered necessary for robust protections of knowledge – positive protection and defensive protection. Positive protection of TK grants IP rights in the subject matter of TK while defensive protection does not grant IP rights over the subject matter of TK but instead aims to stop such rights from being acquired by third parties.[27]

Some consider such mechanisms to be quite ambitious schemes, while others argue they offer only a limited domestic 'band-aid' solution to the global challenge of valuing TK within the global IP system.[28] The challenge is to move beyond such domestic 'stop-gap' solutions, which some find to be designed to address only government policy challenges of effectively accommodating TK within the internationally enforced IP system.

[24] ibid; see also Christina Binder, 'UNDRIP and Interactions with International Investment Law' in Hohmann and Weller (n 13); Stoll (n 13).

[25] ibid. See also Stephen R Munzer, 'A Framework for Managing Disputes over Intellectual Property Rights in Traditional Knowledge' (2024) 29(1) Michigan Journal of Race & Law 31.

[26] ibid.

[27] WIPO, 'Background Brief No. 3, Developing a National Strategy on Intellectual Property, Traditional Knowledge and Traditional Cultural Expression' (WIPO 2016) <www.wipo.int/edocs/pubdocs/en/wipo_pub_tk_3.pdf> accessed 4 February 2025.

[28] ibid; see also Chidi Oguamanam, 'Wandering Footloose: Traditional Knowledge and the "Public Domain" Revisited' (2018) 21(5–6) Journal of World Intellectual Property 306.

5.3 NATIONAL EFFORTS FOR TRADITIONAL KNOWLEDGE

WIPO, in their guiding documentation, appears to recognize the difficulties of attempting to shift entire worldviews to accommodate TK in IP on a global stage, noting specifically that TK 'are matters primarily for national governments' and that 'National laws are currently the prime mechanism for achieving protection of TK.'[29] Under WIPO, countries spent many years negotiating a new international treaty on intellectual property, TK, and cultural heritage, as is discussed further below. WIPO experts have also sought to raise awareness about TK in relation to IP and to recommend domestic solutions that internally address TK issues within the boundaries of each willing country. The recommended pathways follow the protectionary measures usually applicable to IP, namely:

- **Legislative initiatives**, including strengthening existing legal tools and creating new ones;
- **Policy initiatives**, including political decisions to give greater attention and value to TK and traditional cultural expressions and their protection, as well as policy statements that set overall directions on key issues;
- **Infrastructure**, especially inventories, databases, and other information systems, can complement and support the implementation of legal systems;
- **Practical tools**, including the use of contracts, guidelines and protocols, as well as capacity-building and awareness-raising, if and when appropriate.[30]

National efforts to protect TK through any combination of the above four systems can be adopted as specialized measures or laws aimed to address the characteristics of specific subject matter, as well as inter-related challenges and conflicts within the domestic legal, policy, or legislative systems. As such, each country has the freedom to choose both whether and how to implement these four systems, which creates a voluntary framework that does not necessarily address the needs for TK protection which can fully dismantle barriers to Indigenous participation in business and trade.

Nonetheless, as examples from the United States and Canada can demonstrate, IP measures have been interpreted and applied to TK. It is possible to

[29] ibid; for further reference, see Mauro Barelli, 'Development Projects and Indigenous Peoples' Lands' in Short and Lennox (n 2); Binder (n 24).

[30] ibid.

examine the context and experiences in both these countries, as well as an example of the failure of these IP regimes for Indigenous People.

5.3.1 *The US Case for Traditional Knowledge*

While specific constitutional provisions may not directly provide protection for Indigenous or treaty rights in the US, the US Supreme Court in the 1830s recognized the US Tribal Nations as 'domestic dependent nations' with sovereignty and governance that pre-exists that of the United States.[31] As such, constitutionally three sovereign entities cohabitate in the same geographic space: the US federal government, the state governments, and the Tribal governments. Tribal sovereignty is protected against the states and is still valid in US law today. Tribes, through this sovereignty, can tax, create laws, and manage their citizens and territorial jurisdiction like any of the fifty US states. TK on Tribal lands is clearly enforced through Tribal courts, and in some states, there is also state judicial enforcement of some elements of TK.

At a federal level, the application of the protection of Indigenous TK is mostly found in federal legislation titled *The Indian Arts and Crafts Act* (IACA). Initially passed in 1935, the IACA focused on the purposes of 'educating the Indian craftsman in modern commercial methods, of expanding the market for Indian goods, and of protecting both the consumer and the Indian producer from cheaply imitated wares.'[32] The IACA provided for a review board, the Indian Arts and Crafts Board (IACB), with the powers to determine counterfeit Indian arts and crafts and render fines of up to US$2,000 for each offence and/or imprisonment for up to six months.[33]

In 1990 the legislation was revised and modestly updated but still mostly prohibits false advertising in the marketing of Indian arts or crafts.[34] The most significant upgrades came in the size of the fine which was increased for first-time violations of the IACA. Individuals can face civil or criminal penalties of up to US$250,000 in fines, a five-year prison term, or both for a first offence and up to US$ 1 million in fines and fifteen years maximum imprisonment for subsequent violations. If a business violates the IACA, it can face fines of up to

[31] See the three cases known as the Marshall Trilogy, 1823–1832: *Cherokee Nations v Georgia* 30 US 1 (1831); *Johnson v M'Intosh* 21 US (8 Wheat) 543 (1823); *Worcester v Georgia* 31 US (6 Pet) 515 (1832).

[32] Secretary of the Interior, 'Annual Report of the Department of the Interior, 1940' (U.S. Government Printing Office, 1940) 394.

[33] ibid 224.

[34] The Indian Arts and Crafts Act of 1990 (P.L. 101-644).

US$1 million for the first offence with a maximum of US$5,000,000 for subsequent violations.[35]

While the penalties appear serious and the revisions may have been welcome, the IACA of 1990 has been described as merely a 'truth-in-advertising law' which prohibits misrepresentation in the marketing of American Indian or Alaska Native arts and crafts products; it is also limited to the United States in its application.[36] As such, many Indigenous jurists conclude that IACA fails to cover the width and breadth of TK protection.[37] Nevertheless, IACA does provide a starting point and some domestic protection and enforcement for select aspects of TK.

5.3.2 *The Canadian Case for Traditional Knowledge*

Notwithstanding certain negotiations and limited experiments in delegated First Nation governance autonomy, jurists argue that in Canada the concept of Indigenous sovereignty is virtually non-existent.[38] In a formal sense, First Nations still operate under the federally imposed Indian Band system, where Chiefs and band councils report all resolutions for approval by the federal government in accordance with the *Indian Act* as per the fiduciary duty imposed on the Crown by section 91(24) of the *Constitution Act, 1867* which vests federal authority of 'Indians and lands reserved for Indians' within the federal jurisdiction.[39] Of further relevance to efforts to secure recognition of Indigenous sovereignty in Canada, section 88 of the *Indian Act* holds that provincial laws shall be enforceable on Indian reserve lands.[40] Notwithstanding the various treaties signed between Indigenous Peoples and

35 ibid ss 1159(b)(1) & (2).

36 'The Indian Arts and Crafts Act of 1990' (U.S. Department of the Interior, Indian Arts and Craft Board, Legislative Explanation, 2022) <www.doi.gov/iacb/act> accessed 4 February 2025.

37 William J Hapiuk Jr, 'Of Kitsch and Kachinas: A Critical Analysis of the Indian Arts and Crafts Act of 1990' (2001) 53(4) Stanford Law Review 1009. For a more recent comment since the 2023 sentencing of Jerry Van Dyke under the IACA, see Jemima Gravatt, 'The Indian Arts and Crafts Act of 1990: Fit for Purpose?' (Center for Art Law, 8 November 2023) <https://itsartlaw.org/2023/11/08/the-indian-arts-and-crafts-act-of-1990-fit-for-purpose/> accessed 13 February 2025.

38 For a discussion on how Britain argues its sovereignty over Indigenous Peoples, see Kent McNeil, 'Indigenous and Crown Sovereignty in Canada' (Talk given at the University of Saskatchewan College of Law, 24 October 2019) Osgoode Legal Studies Research Paper (9 December 2019, last revised 10 March 2020). See also, for further reading, John Borrows, *Braiding Legal Orders* (McGill-Queen's University Press 2023); and John Borrows, *Recovering Canada: The Resurgence of Indigenous Law* (University of Toronto Press 2002).

39 Constitution Act 1867 s 91(24).

40 Indian Act 1985, c. I-5 s 88.

the Crown, section 91(24) and section 88 can be characterized as effectively suppressing residual Indigenous sovereignty in Canada.[41]

In an effort to provide some level of protection to Indigenous rights, even if the sovereignty of the nature found in the United States cannot be obtained under the current regime, in the *Constitution Act, 1982*, which includes the *Charter of Rights and Freedom*, Canadian law-makers provided a constitutionally protected Aboriginal and treaty rights clause.[42] The clause has been met with mixed reactions. On the one hand, it codifies constitutionally enshrined Aboriginal rights, but on the other hand, it has been critiqued by some, including an Indigenous Justice Minister, as a 'black box' where neither the Crown nor Indigenous Peoples clearly know the extent of the rights that section 35 protects.[43]

Section 35 of the *Constitution Act, 1982* states, 'existing aboriginal and treaty rights are [. . .] recognized and affirmed'.[44] It aims to provide distinct recognition and affirmation of existing Aboriginal and treaty rights, which is important for harmonizing the common, civil, and Aboriginal legal tapestry found in Canadian law for Indigenous justice.

In essence, according to this section, for an Aboriginal right to exist in Canadian law, it must never have been expressly extinguished,[45] and it must have been exercised continuously since the point of entrance into the confederation.[46] While section 35 acknowledges and protects the 'existing Aboriginal and treaty rights', leading scholars and jurists suggest that the Government of Canada, with the provinces following suit, has devoted most of its case law efforts to establishing a reverse onus on Indigenous Peoples to provide absolute proof that any right they might claim was indeed 'existing' and continuously exercised, thus protected by section 35.[47]

41 Olthuis Kleer Townshend LLP, *Aboriginal Law Handbook* (5th edn, Thomson Reuters 2018); see also Kent McNeil, 'Aboriginal Title and Section 88 of the Indian Act' (2000) 34 University of British Columbia Law Review 159–194.

42 Constitution Act 1982 s 35.

43 Jody Wilson Raybould, '2016 AFN Annual General Assembly – Jody Wilson Raybould' (CPAC, 2016) <www.cpac.ca/cpac-special/episode/2016-afn-annual-general-assembly–jody-wilson-raybould?id=c1f73fdf-2b57-4906-b2db-b9461473b0ad> accessed 4 February 2025; Brian J Barth, 'What Jody Wilson-Raybould Really Thinks' (The Walrus 2019) <https://thewalrus.ca/what-jody-wilson-raybould-really-thinks/> accessed 4 February 2025.

44 Constitution Act (n 42) s 35.

45 Unilaterally extinguishing Aboriginal rights, including title by the Crown, requires 'clear and plain' legislative intent. *Calder v Attorney-General of British Columbia* [1973] SCR 313 (CAN), affirmed *R. v Sparrow* [1990] 1 SCR 1075 (CAN), affirmed *Delgamuukw v British Columbia* [1997] 3 SCR 1010 (CAN).

46 *Sparrow* (n 45); *Delgamuukw* (n 45).

47 ibid. See, generally, James [Sákéj] Youngblood Henderson, *Proving a Constitutional Right to the Land for Aboriginal Peoples of Canada* (Centre for First Nations Governance 2020). See

The reality of this reverse-onus Aboriginal and treaty rights policy was that a worthy Aboriginal rights case would invariably take decades to make its way through the Canadian justice system, costing millions which might instead have been dedicated to other needs such as on-reserve uncontaminated potable water, improved housing, and education.[48] Further, many of the requirements for Indigenous funds and attention were created, experts argue, by other forms of federal and provincial governmental neglect.[49] To make matters worse, the federal and provincial governments appear to mainly accept and follow decisions supporting Indigenous rights when rendered by the highest court, typically the Supreme Court of Canada, further inflating the costs and timelines required to affirm Aboriginal and treaty rights through the Canadian legal system. To date only a few cases have reached this level and received reluctant deference from the Crown: *Delgamuukw v British Columbia*[50] and *Williams Lake Indian Band v Canada*[51] are two important examples.

In Canada, domestic optimism for the free exercise and protection of TK persists. On 21 June 2021, the Parliament of Canada adopted the *United Nations Declaration on the Rights of Indigenous Peoples Act* [*UNDRIP Act*].[52]

also Kent McNeil, *The Onus of Proof of Aboriginal Title* (Centre for First Nations Governance 1999).

48 Some of the most polluting industrial works are located near reserve lands, which some have documented as 'environmental racism' of contaminated community lands. Contaminated water was then provided to the Indigenous People of Attawapiskat First Nation (Treaty 9) in Northern Ontario, Canada. Attawapiskat elders, from the beginning, advised against the source of water chosen for the reserve by INAC/AAND experts when the Indigenous community was moved to Attawapiskat, even as authorities seized the rest of their lands which extend beyond the present reserve and include various sources of pure water. The Attawapiskat water and infrastructure crisis offers on example of the consequences of ignoring Indigenous traditional ecological knowledge. See Rachel Arsenault, 'Water Insecurity in Ontario First Nations: An Exploratory Study on Past Interventions and the Need for Indigenous Water Governance' (2021) 13(5) Water 717; on this governmental and industrial practice in Canada, see Ingrid Waldron, *Environmental Racism in Canada* (Canadian Commission for UNESCO's IdeaLab 2020); on the biological and ecological impacts of this practice, see James Stinson and Elizabeth Lunstrom, *Biocultural Nation Making: Biopolitics, Cultural-Territorial Belonging, and National Protected Area* (Sage 2021); on the cultural impact of this practice in Canada, see Jodi Simkin, *Creating a New Reality: Repatriation, Reconciliation and Moving Forward* (Canadian Commission for UNESCO's IdeaLab 2020); K Aird and G Fox, *Indigenous Living Heritage in Canada* (Canadian Commission for UNESCO's IdeaLab with the First Peoples' Cultural Council 2020).

49 Arsenault (n 48).

50 *Delgamuukw* (n 45).

51 *Williams Lake Indian Band v Canada (Aboriginal Affairs and Northern Development)* [2018] S.C.C. 4 (SCC).

52 United Nations Declaration on the Rights of Indigenous Peoples Act, SC 2021, c 14; see also Kevin Gray, 'Change by Drips and Drabs or No Change at All: The Coming UNDRIP Battles in Canadian Courts' (2023) 11(2) American Indian Law Journal; Nigel Bankes, 'Implementing UNDRIP: An Analysis of British Columbia's Declaration on the Rights of Indigenous Peoples Act' (2021) 53(4) UBC Law Review.

Article 31 directly addresses and supports Indigenous protection for TK, stating as follows:

> Article 31 (1) Indigenous [P]eoples have the right to maintain, control, protect and develop their cultural heritage, Traditional Knowledge and traditional cultural expressions, as well as the manifestations of their sciences, technologies and cultures, including human and genetic resources, seeds, medicines, knowledge of the properties of fauna and flora, oral traditions, literatures, designs, sports and traditional games and visual and performing arts. They also have the right to maintain, control, protect, and develop their intellectual property over such cultural heritage, Traditional Knowledge, and traditional cultural expressions.
>
> (2) In conjunction with [I]ndigenous [P]eoples, States shall take effective measures to recognize and protect the exercise of these rights.[53]

By bringing this Act into force, some argue, it is possible to ensure that TK protections should be domestically enforced not only to culturally protect Indigenous People in Canada but also possibly provide a source of economic revenue for Indigenous People.[54] A grand majority of the economic wealth of Indigenous Peoples in Canada is tied to both the land and the TK associated with the use of the land and its resources. This new legislation, which is further discussed later in this volume, may hold the potential to help enable and protect such TK which furthers environmentally sustainable resources stewardship so as to advance sustainable economic development.

5.3.3 *The Cowichan Sweater Case for Traditional Knowledge*

With regard to the protections necessary for TK in Canada, it is possible to highlight one experience along with lessons learned. During the build-up to the 2010 Vancouver Winter Olympics, the Hudson's Bay Company was critiqued for marketing inauthentic Cowichan-style weaving, in the form of sweaters with appropriated traditional motifs, to commemorate the event.[55] The uproar and disputes that ensued provide a useful example of how Aboriginal rights in Canada are addressed against the backdrop of the current failings of TK within the global IP system.

[53] United Nations Declaration on the Rights of Indigenous People (adopted 13 September 2007) UN Doc A/RES/61/295 (UNDRIP) art 46 and art 31.

[54] ibid. This would further align with Truth and Reconciliation Commission of Canada, 'Calls to Action' (Winnipeg: Truth and Reconciliation Commission of Canada, 2015), Recommendation 50.

[55] See Regan Shrumm, 'Knitting for Our Lives: The Appropriation of Cowichan Sweaters by the Hudson's Bay during the 2010 Vancouver Olympics' (2019) 2(2) ARTiculate 120.

Pre-European contact, weaving was a fundamental part of Coast Salish identity, including that of the Cowichan First Nations whose traditional territories are found on the east coast of Vancouver Island in British Columbia. The Cowichan people made blankets of wool composed of mountain goat hair mixed with the hair of the now-extinct Coast Salish wool dogs. The creation of one blanket took months or even years of work to produce as it was finely made to be warm, rain repellent, and a work of cultural significance, often a masterpiece of art.[56] The quality of the Cowichan blankets has been described as comparable to Southwestern Navajo blankets and Northern Tlingit Chilkat blankets.[57]

During the early nineteenth century, cheap, mass-produced blankets gradually replaced traditional blankets. Coast Salish women took up knitting needles, spinning machines, and sheep's wool. Adapting designs from their woven blankets and baskets, they knit warm sweaters, socks, and toques for their families.[58] The Cowichan sweater, hats, and mittens remain unique because of the heavy, unprocessed hand-spun wool, and the unique geometric patterns, colour, and design that adorned the garments and re-defined how the original blankets could be expressed as contemporary traditional artworks.[59] Cowichan sweaters are now knit from natural, hand-spun, undyed sheep's wool, one that keeps its shape and due to high lanolin content of the wool, makes a water-repellent, stain-resistant sweater which, if cared for, can last for decades and be passed down from generation to generation.[60] Coast Salish artisans have created an authentic Indigenous garment industry and the modern Cowichan sweaters are marketed both nationally and internationally.

To protect the Cowichan TK, the Cowichan First Nation registered 'Cowichan', 'Genuine Cowichan', and 'Genuine Cowichan Approved' trademarks for goods that

> . . . have been hand-knit in one piece in accordance with the traditional tribal methods by members of the Coast Salish Nation using raw, unprocessed, undyed, hand-spun wool, also made and prepared in accordance with traditional tribal methods.[61]

[56] Marianne P Stopp, 'The Coast Salish Knitters and the Cowichan Sweater – An Event of National Historic Significance' (2012) 76 Material Culture Review 9.

[57] ibid.

[58] ibid.

[59] Sylvia Olsen, *Working with Wool: A Coast Salish Legacy and the Cowichan Sweater* (Sono Nis Press 2010) 8.

[60] ibid 8–9.

[61] Canadian Trademarks Database, 'Genuine Cowichan & Design –0792174' (Government of Canada, 1997) <https://ised-isde.canada.ca/cipo/trademark-search/0792174?lang=eng> accessed 27 March 2022.

However, in preparing for the 2010 Vancouver Winter Olympics, the Hudson's Bay Company began to market inauthentic Cowichan-style sweaters to commemorate the event. The company had initially entered negotiations with the Cowichan First Nation to produce authentic Cowichan sweaters, which would be hand-knit using the distinctive five Olympic rings symbol in each sweater and produced with natural, undyed wool. Ultimately, the deal fell through, with the Hudson's Bay Company claiming, some argue falsely, that the Cowichan Nation could not produce the quantities of product required in the allotted time.[62] Instead, the company outsourced the manufacturing of a fake Cowichan sweater to a third party in China with access to mechanized knitting equipment and cheaper materials.[63]

The sweaters produced by the Chinese manufacturer bore a striking resemblance to authentic Cowichan sweaters and were referred to as 'knock-offs' in the media. Members of the Cowichan First Nation were angered by the violation of their registered trademarks, the appropriation of their TK and cultural history, and the diversion of a potential source of income to a non-Aboriginal company whose products appeared intended to be confused with their own.[64] In the end, the court of public opinion forced an uneasy settlement. Facing significant opposition and public pressure, the company agreed to a last-minute licensing deal, allowing the Cowichan Nation to sell their own sweaters at the First Nations Pavilion and in the Bay's flagship store in Vancouver. There was, however, no profit-sharing arrangement for the manufacturing and sale by the Bay of the fake Cowichan sweaters that were made in China, calling into question the value of TK protections at the time.[65] Indeed, as descendants of the original designers, weavers, and artisans, the Cowichan people still claim the distinctive collective TK and IP rights for their knitted products and art. No one person or family claims the design nor technique or art; it has been held by the Cowichan People as collective since time immemorial. The practice will be carried forward through generations to come, even if at present the commodification of this art leads to little legal recourse until through future

[62] Stopp (n 56).

[63] Courtney Doagoo, 'Navajo Nation Sues Urban Outfitters Inc.' (IP Osgoode Intellectual Property & Technology Program, 2012) <www.iposgoode.ca/2012/06/navajo-nation-sues-urban-outfitters-inc/> accessed 4 February 2025.

[64] ibid. See also Shrumm (n 55).

[65] ibid.

determination of laws such as the *United Nations Declaration on the Rights of Indigenous Peoples Act*, Article 31.[66] In essence, the challenges faced by this First Nation underline that IP laws were unable to adequately protect TK – the TK for the Cowichan sweater was not fixed in time and the TK was not owned by one individual, but rather by the Coast Salish people at large. This example further emphasizes the need to redefine the knowledge, and the property of knowledge, that legal protections should encompass to enable Indigenous trade.

5.4 THE WIPO TREATY ON TRADITIONAL KNOWLEDGE

In May 2024, after decades of negotiations that first began at WIPO in 2001, the WIPO Member States adopted the WIPO Treaty on Intellectual Property, Genetic Resources and Associated Traditional Knowledge (GRATK Treaty) addressing the interface between intellectual property, genetic resources, and TK, as the first WIPO Treaty to include provisions specifically for Indigenous Peoples and local communities.[67] As noted above in this chapter, while genetic resources themselves cannot be directly protected as intellectual property, inventions developed using them can, most often through a patent. Some genetic resources are also associated with TK through their use and conservation by Indigenous Peoples as well as local communities, often over generations.

This knowledge is sometimes used in scientific research and, as such, may contribute to the development of a protected invention. The WIPO GRATK Treaty seeks to establish in international law a new disclosure requirement for patent applicants whose inventions are based on genetic resources and/or associated TK. According to WIPO, discussions were notable for their inclusion of Indigenous Peoples as well as local communities. WIPO and its Member States seek to demonstrate, through the agreement, that the global

66 UNDRIP Act (n 53) art 31. For more generally on TK in international trade, see Moody (n 7) 164.

67 WIPO Treaty on Intellectual Property, Genetic Resources and Associated Traditional Knowledge (adopted 24 May 2024). For more, see David J Jefferson, 'The World Intellectual Property Organization Treaty on Genetic Resources and Associated Traditional Knowledge: Implications for Plant Breeding and Scientific Research' (2024) Plants, People, Planet <https://nph.onlinelibrary.wiley.com/doi/epdf/10.1002/ppp3.10615> accessed 20 February 2025; Ayla do Vale Alves, 'WIPO's New Treaty on Intellectual property, Genetic Resources and Traditional Knowledge: A Turning Point for Indigenous Heritage?' (2024) 13(11) ESIL Reflections <https://esil-sedi.eu/wp-content/uploads/2024/09/Do-Vale-Alves-Vol.13-Issue-11.pdf> accessed 20 February 2025.

IP system can continue to incentivize innovation while evolving in a more inclusive way, responding to the needs of all countries and their communities. Broadly, as WIPO notes, the treaty governs situations in which a claimed invention in a patent application is based on genetic resources, and commits that each Contracting Party 'shall require applicants to disclose the country of origin or source of the genetic resources. Where the claimed invention in a patent application is based on Traditional Knowledge associated with genetic resources, each [C]ontracting [P]arty shall require applicants to disclose the Indigenous Peoples or local community, as applicable, who provided the Traditional Knowledge'.[68] The treaty addresses genetic resources that are contained in, for example, medicinal plants, agricultural crops, and animal breeds.

In the 2024 WIPO GRATK Treaty Preamble, Parties acknowledge 'the United Nations Declaration on the Rights of Indigenous Peoples (UNDRIP) and commitment to achieving the ends set forth therein', and affirm that 'best efforts should be made to include Indigenous Peoples and local communities, as applicable, in implementing this Treaty'.[69] Then, at Article 3.2, Parties agree that:

> Where the claimed invention in a patent application is based on Traditional Knowledge associated with genetic resources, each Contracting Party shall require applicants to disclose: (a) the Indigenous Peoples or local community, as applicable 3, who provided the Traditional Knowledge associated with genetic resources, or, (b) in cases where the information in Article 3.2(a) is not known to the applicant, or where Article 3.2(a) does not apply, the source of the Traditional Knowledge associated with genetic resources.[70]

Furthermore, in Article 6.1, States recognize that 'Contracting Parties may establish information systems (such as databases) of genetic resources and Traditional Knowledge associated with genetic resources, in consultation, where applicable, with Indigenous Peoples and local communities, and other stakeholders, taking into account their national circumstances.'[71] However, while at Article 9.1 'Contracting Parties undertake to adopt the measures necessary to ensure the application of this Treaty', the domestic challenges

[68] World Intellectual Property Organization, WIPO Treaty on Intellectual Property, Genetic Resources and Associated Traditional Knowledge Adopted' (24 May 2024) <www.wipo.int/pressroom/en/articles/2024/article_0007.html> accessed 20 February 2025.

[69] WIPO Treaty on Intellectual Property, Genetic Resources and Associated Traditional Knowledge (n 67).

[70] ibid preamble.

[71] ibid art 6.1.

discussed above are still relevant, as at 9.2 they also note that 'Nothing shall prevent Contracting Parties from determining the appropriate method of implementing the provisions of this Treaty within their own legal systems and practices.'[72]

Furthermore, at Article 10.1(c), the Parties agree that 'The Assembly shall encourage the effective participation of representatives from Indigenous Peoples and local communities as accredited observers. The Assembly will invite Contracting Parties to consider financial arrangements for participation of Indigenous Peoples and local communities.'[73] As such, the Indigenous Peoples will be observers to a treaty about their own TK and genetic resources, rather than being fully included through more innovative and participatory governance mechanisms piloted, for instance, by bodies such as the Arctic Council.[74]

As an instrument to address 'bio-piracy' the treaty is, perhaps, still helpful – by establishing an obligation to ensure that patent applications disclose Traditional Knowledge, and noting that Parties may establish information systems, also by including Indigenous Peoples representatives and prioritizing efforts to find funding for them, the regime does address some of the challenges mentioned above.[75] Many Indigenous Peoples representatives participated in the decades of negotiations, and some have been cautiously optimistic about the agreement: as the Indigenous Caucus noted upon adoption, the accord offers a 'first step towards guaranteeing just and transparent access to these resources'.[76] WIPO's mission is to lead the development of a balanced and effective global intellectual property ecosystem to promote

[72] ibid arts 9.1 and 9.2.

[73] ibid art 10.1(c).

[74] For more, see Douglas C Nord, *The Arctic Council: Governance within the Far North* (Routledge 2016); Oran R Young, 'The Arctic Council at Twenty: How to Remain Effective in a Rapidly Changing Environment' (2016) 6 UC Irvine Law Review 99.

[75] Margo A Bagley, 'The GRATK Treaty: Understanding a Triumph of Multilateralism' (*Geneva Policy Outlook*, 2025) <www.genevapolicyoutlook.ch/the-gratk-treaty-understanding-a-triumph-of-multilateralism/#:~:text=But%20this%20failure%20created%20an,in%20a%20Changing%20Political%20Context> accessed 20 February 2025; Kriti Sharma, 'Missed Opportunities WIPO Treaty Falls Short of Protecting Traditional Knowledge' (Center for International Law, National University of Singapore, 15 July 2024) <https://cil.nus.edu.sg/blogs/missed-opportunities-wipo-treaty-falls-short-of-protecting-traditional-knowledge/#:~:text=On%20May%2024%2C%202024%2C%20twenty%20five%20years,Resources%20and%20associated%20Traditional%20Knowledge%20(%60%60the%20treaty")> accessed 20 February 2025.

[76] Indigenous Caucus, 'Closing Statement: International Treaty on Genetic Resources & Traditional Knowledge' (Cosmovisiones Healing, 28 May 2024) <www.cosmovisioneshealing.org/post/indigenous-caucus-closing-statement-international-treaty-on-genetic-resources-traditional-knowledge> accessed 21 February 2025.

innovation and creativity for a better and more sustainable future. The WIPO GRATK Treaty seeks to establish elements of a regime which, if implemented effectively in full and respectful collaboration with Indigenous Peoples and local communities, might hold potential to address some of the most important barriers to recognition and protection of Indigenous Peoples' TK. This treaty is further discussed in later chapters of this volume with regard to cultural heritage protection.

In addition to the WIPO GRATK Treaty and also reflecting Article 31 of the UNDRIP, Indigenous Peoples in countries signatory to the Nagoya Protocol (the Protocol)[77] to the Convention for Biological Diversity (CBD)[78] may be able to access a further international treaty framework to protect their rights to TK over genetic resources. At Article 8(j) of the CBD, the Parties commit to respect, preserve, and maintain the knowledge, innovations, and practices of Indigenous Peoples and local communities. The Parties further commit to the promotion of wider application of TK with the approval and involvement of the knowledge holders equitable sharing of the benefits arising from the utilization and the article also urges the Parties to encourage equitable sharing of the benefits arising from the utilization of the TK.[79]

Further, at Article 7 of the Protocol, Parties agreed that '[i]n accordance with domestic law, each Party shall take measures, as appropriate, with the aim of ensuring that Traditional Knowledge associated with genetic resources that is held by Indigenous and local communities is accessed with the prior and informed consent or approval and involvement of these Indigenous and local communities, and that mutually agreed terms have been established'. The Parties to the Protocol clearly recognize the need for prior and informed consent or approval, as well as mutually agreed terms which may include

[77] Nagoya Protocol on Access to Genetic Resources and the Fair and Equitable Sharing of Benefits Arising from Their Utilization to the Convention on Biological Diversity (adopted 29 October 2010, entered into force 12 October 2014) UN Doc UNEP/CBD/COP/DEC/X/1.

[78] Convention on Biological Diversity (adopted 5 June 1992, entered into force 29 December 1993) 1760 UNTS 79 (CBD) preamble, arts 8(j), 17. See also CBD, 'Kunming-Montreal Global Biodiversity Framework' (19 December 2022) UN Doc CBD/COP/DEC/15/4.

[79] CBD art 8(j); for further discussion, see Azmi Sharom, 'A Critical Study of the Laws Relating to the Indigenous Peoples of Malaysia in the Context of Article 8(j) of the Biodiversity Convention' (2006) 13(1) International Journal on Minority and Group Rights 53; Elsa Tsioumani, 'Convention on Biological Diversity: A Review of the post-2020 Global Biodiversity Framework Working Group Negotiations' (2020) 50(1–2) Environmental Policy and Law; Maria Yolanda Teran, 'The Nagoya Protocol and Indigenous Peoples' (2016) 7(2) *International Indigenous Policy Journal*. See also Marie-Claire Cordonier Segger and Damilola Olawuyi, *Sustainable Development Law: Principles, Practices, and Prospects* (Oxford University Press 2025 forthcoming).

respect, recognition, and compensation.[80] At the 16th Conference of the Parties (COP16) to the Convention on Biological Diversity (CBD) a new Programme of Work on Article 8(j) and related provisions of the Convention were adopted with specific tasks to ensure meaningful contribution of Indigenous Peoples and local communities and their TK.[81] The Parties in the conference further established a new permanent subsidiary body on Article 8(j) and other provisions to elevate issues related to the implementation of the article and enhancing the engagement and participation of Indigenous Peoples and local communities in all convention processes.

5.5 THE 'NEW NORM': TK IN INTERNATIONAL TRADE AGREEMENTS

At present in Canada, First Nations, Métis, and Inuit Peoples can pursue recognition of their TK through international trade and protectionary measures domestically, including through Article 31 of the UNDRIP.[82] This can largely be done by taking an active interest and maintaining involvement in Canada's development of submissions in international trade negotiations and the WIPO.

Canada's first FTA to include an Indigenous trade chapter is the Canada-Ukraine Free Trade Agreement (CUFTA). While there are no express provisions on TK in CUFTA, Chapter 25, Article 25.1.3 includes emphasis that 'trade is fundamental to Indigenous histories, identities, cultural heritage, and economic prosperity', and Article 25.4 outlines cooperation activities to foster Indigenous Peoples' participation in international trade and investment. In addition, Article 25.7 includes a dispute settlement non-derogation clause, noting that '[a] Party shall not have recourse to dispute settlement under

80 Nagoya Protocol (n 77) art 7.

81 Convention on Biological Diversity, 'Biodiversity COP 16: Important Agreements Reached Towards Making Peace with Nature' (CBD, 2 November 2024) <www.cbd.int/article/agreement-reached-cop-16> accessed 20 February 2025; Steven Grattan, 'At UN Summit, Historic Agreement to give Indigenous Groups Voice on Nature Conservation Decisions' (AP News, November 2024) <https://apnews.com/article/biodiversity-cop16-colombia-decisions-indigenous-53a8b16befaf621d75a2fc9b9828c2a8> accessed on 20 February 2025.

82 For more details on older free trade agreements referencing TK, see Canada–Peru Free Trade Agreement (signed 29 May 2008) ch 17; Canada–Colombia Free Trade Agreement (signed 21 November 2008) ch 17 (TK provisions are common, since 2006, in Peru and Colombia's FTAs); Comprehensive and Progressive Agreement for Trans-Pacific Partnership (signed 8 March 2018) art 18.16; many of China's FTAs also reference TK, including the Regional Comprehensive Economic Partnership (signed 15 November 2020) art 11.53; Brazil–Chile Free Trade Agreement (signed 21 November 2018) arts 17.9.6, 23.1.6; Australia–Peru Free Trade Agreement (signed 12 February 2018) arts 17.16–17, 19.4.5; and CARIFORUM–EC Economic Partnership Agreement (signed 15 October 2008) arts 150, 164.

Chapter 28 (Dispute Settlement) for any matter arising under this Chapter'.[83] While CUFTA's Indigenous trade chapter provides a foundation for ongoing cooperation between the Parties' Indigenous Peoples, particularly through a Committee on Trade and Indigenous Peoples in Article 25.5,[84] its silence on TK may be interpreted to mean the Parties did not wish to incorporate the same rights as in the UNDRIP Article 31, or those outlined in the Protocol's articles on TK, as Canada is not a Party to the latter. This leaves uncertainty as to CUFTA's potential to promote Indigenous knowledge systems; particularly, intellectual property or benefit-sharing arrangements. Nevertheless, the reference in Article 25.1.3 to 'histories, identities, [and] cultural heritage' leaves the door open to future TK recognition; moreover, Article 25.4 highlights cooperation activities that might support TK indirectly, such as building Indigenous capacity and skills, promoting e-commerce for Indigenous products and services, and expanding supply-chain integration for Indigenous-owned businesses.[85]

Canada's other Indigenous trade chapter pursuits have shown mixed results. Canada continues to pursue an Indigenous trade chapter in its FTA negotiations with MERCOSUR, engaging countries such as Argentina, Brazil, Bolivia, Paraguay, and Uruguay.[86] In Canada, a strong case was also initially made for the recognition and protection of TK in the post-NAFTA negotiations, which led to the development of the Government of Canada's

[83] Canada-Ukraine Free Trade Agreement (signed 22 September 2023, Ottawa), ch 25 'Trade and Indigenous Peoples', which came into force on July 1, 2024, see *Canada-Ukraine Free Trade Agreement Implementation Act*, 2023, SC 2024, c 3 (royal assent March 19, 2024); see also Global Affairs Canada, 'International Trade Agreements and Indigenous Peoples: The Canadian Approach' (2025) <www.international.gc.ca/trade-commerce/indigenous_peoples-peuples_autochtones/approach-approche.aspx?lang=eng> accessed February 14, 2025.

[84] ibid art 25.5.

[85] ibid arts 25.1.3, 25.4.

[86] Global Affairs Canada, 'Summary of Initial GBA+ for Canada-Mercosur Free Trade Agreement Negotiations' (2019) <www.international.gc.ca/trade-commerce/gender_equality-egalite_genres/gba_plus_summary-acs_plus_resume.aspx?lang=eng> accessed February 14, 2025. At the time of writing, Venezuela is suspended from MERCOSUR, and Bolivia is undergoing accession, see MERCOSUR, 'MERCOSUR Countries' <www.mercosur.int/en/about-mercosur/mercosur-countries/> accessed 13 February 2025; for more details on recommendations for Canada's trade position with MERCOSUR, see Parliamentary Standing Committee on International Trade, 'Report of the Parliamentary Standing Committee on International Trade – Canada and The Mercosur Countries: A Potential Agreement to Advance Trade Relations' (Speaker of the House of Commons [Canada], 2018) 42nd Parliament, 1st Session, 22 <www.ourcommons.ca/DocumentViewer/en/42-1/CIIT/report-14/> accessed 4 February 2025.

Indigenous trade policies.[87] Protection, as it was argued for, would be conferred through the development of measures specifically adapted to the nature and characteristics of Indigenous knowledge within the framework of a binding supplemental Indigenous trade chapter or side letter in NAFTA's successor, CUSMA or USMCA as it is known in the United States. This proposed chapter included policies and philosophies which could support and protect TK. The proposed measures would respect and be in keeping with customary and traditional Indigenous law and thus would be designed, not to confer economic benefits on individual creators, but for common group exploitation by Indigenous Peoples collectively. However, in 2018, the Parties to CUSMA did not incorporate the Indigenous trade chapter into the final free trade agreement; they agreed instead to a general carve out, in Article 32.5, allowing each Party to adopt or maintain measures deemed 'necessary to fulfill its legal obligations to [I]ndigenous [P]eoples'.[88]

The efforts of the Indigenous participants nonetheless enabled the Canadian government to have in place the makings of the Canadian policy for Indigenous international trade. These policy developments built on post-NAFTA and CUSMA negotiations and assisted the Government of Canada in developing Canada's Inclusive Trade Agenda, which expressly included support and protection for TK. In 2025, Canada's Inclusive Trade Agenda, including Canada's Indigenous trade policy, as expressed in the proposed Indigenous trade chapter, is deployed by the Government of Canada in international trade talks with other countries. Many of these developments involve active, sensitive, and ongoing trade negotiations, thus the specific details of the TK passages remain confidential.

Inclusive trade remains a priority for the Canadian government, jurists argue, whose negotiators helped to establish the Inclusive Trade Action Group (ITAG). ITAG was originally founded at the Asia-Pacific Economic Cooperation (APEC) Leaders' Summit in November of 2018, with State members Canada, Chile, Mexico, and New Zealand. The objective of ITAG is to 'help make trade policies more inclusive and ensure that the

[87] International Inter-tribal Trade and Investment Organization, 'NAFTA IP & Indigenous Traditional Knowledge' (International Inter-tribal Trade and Investment Organization, 2017) <https://iitio.org/nafta2/> accessed 4 February 2025.

[88] While less significant than the initially sought Indigenous trade chapter, this clause nevertheless marked a first for Canada. For discussion of this clause, see J Anthony VanDuzer and Melanie Mallet, 'Indigenous Rights and Trade Obligations: How Does CUSMA's Indigenous General Exception Apply to Canada?' (2021) 58 Canadian Yearbook of International Law 1.

benefits of trade and investment are more broadly shared'.[89] ITAG policies focus on increased international trade opportunities for women, small- and medium-sized enterprises (SMEs), and Indigenous People.[90] Part of the discussion on Indigenous trade issues includes protecting and supporting TK.

Learning and collaboration for TK continue in various formal and informal international discussions for Indigenous trade issues in the Pacific Alliance Trade Negotiations, as well.[91] As of writing, there have been few direct results, but the raising of the Indigenous trade topic for discussion is a first step for advancing these issues. The ongoing background discussions of Indigenous trade issues educated and empowered various States along the Pacific Rim to support the push from their own domestic Indigenous groups' home-grown Indigenous products to have greater access to global markets. In most States that are supportive of Indigenous international trade, there is also concern regarding the mechanisms, both legal and operational, necessary to support and protect domestic TK held by Indigenous Peoples within their borders.

The Government of New Zealand's approach to both protecting TK and securing policy space for the domestic implementation of Indigenous rights is evident in two recent agreements concluded by its negotiators. In October of 2021, the New Zealand-United Kingdom Trade Agreement (UK-NZ FTA) was finalized, notable for its inclusion of a Māori Trade and Economic Cooperation chapter with TK elements.[92] Building on New Zealand's Treaty of Waitangi Exception (which justifies 'measures [New Zealand] deems necessary to accord more favourable treatment to Māori', and which appears in all of NZ's FTAs since 2001), the Parties allow New Zealand to 'respect, preserve, and promote' Māori TK and traditional cultural expressions. However, there is no corresponding obligation on the United Kingdom to do the same: Article 26.2(10)(c)–(d) disclaims recognition of genetic resources,

[89] Inclusive Trade Action Group, 'Inclusive Trade Action Group, Work Program 2020–2022' (Government of New Zealand, 2020) <www.mfat.govt.nz/assets/Trade-General/Trade-policy/ITAG-Inclusive-Trade-Action-Group/ITAG-work-programme-2020-2022.pdf> accessed 4 February 2025.

[90] ibid.

[91] Global Affairs Canada, 'Pacific Alliance Backgrounder' <www.international.gc.ca/trade-commerce/trade-agreements-accords-commerciaux/agr-acc/pacific-alliance-pacifique/background-contexte.aspx?lang=eng> accessed 13 February 2025.

[92] Free Trade Agreement between New Zealand and the United Kingdom of Great Britain and Northern Ireland (signed 28 February 2022, entered into force 31 May 2023) ch 26 (UK-NZ FTA); see also Christian Riffel, 'Constitutional Law-making by International Law: The Indigenization of Free Trade Agreements' (2024) 35(2) European Journal of International Law 445.

TK, or traditional cultural expression as forms of intellectual property under UK law. Nevertheless, the UK-NZ FTA's TK provisions allow New Zealand to, without violating this FTA's obligations, carve out policy space for TK recognition and protection within its own market and regulatory regime.[93] In a side letter, the Parties also acknowledge the guardianship of New Zealand's Indigenous Peoples over performance of the Haka Na Mate, the 'Haka dance', composed around 1820 by Ngāti Toa chief Te Rauparaha, to help protect against its misuse or misappropriation.[94] Finally, the Parties to the UK-NZ FTA contemplate Māori representation in future trade matters in both the IP Working Group (which 'may include' Māori representatives) and the Inclusive Trade Sub-Committee (which 'shall' include Māori representatives).[95]

In June of 2022, the European Union-New Zealand Free Trade Agreement (EU-NZ FTA) was also concluded,[96] likewise featuring a dedicated Māori Trade and Economic Cooperation chapter with references to TK. Like the UK-NZ FTA, no provision requires the EU to recognize Māori TK, genetic resources, or cultural expression as distinct forms of intellectual property under EU law. The Parties agreed however, in Article 18.62, to potential cooperation on 'genetic resources, Traditional Knowledge and traditional cultural expressions', and to cooperation on '[I]indigenous knowledge, participation and leadership in food systems' in Article 7.4.[97] Further, in the Māori Trade and Economic Cooperation chapter, the Parties define 'Mānuka' as the New Zealand tree *Leptospermum scoparium* – whose honey and oil is culturally important to Māori as a traditional medicine and resource – and recognize the value of increased Māori participation in digital trade, including

[93] UK-NZ FTA (n 92) art 26.2.6; for more details on New Zealand's Treaty of Waitangi from a trade lens, see Amokura Kawharu, 'The Treaty of Waitangi Exception in New Zealand's Free Trade Agreements' in Borrows and Schwartz (n 7) 274; for a critical assessment of whether the UK-NZ FTA complies with NZ's Treaty of Waitangi obligations, see Ngā Toki Whakarururanga, 'Te Tiriti o Waitangi Assessment of the Free Trade Agreement between New Zealand and the United Kingdom'; for more on the benefits to New Zealand's Indigenous, see Government of New Zealand, 'NZ-UK FTA – Benefits for Māori' (NZ Benefits Statement) <www.mfat.govt.nz/assets/Trade-agreements/UK-NZ-FTA/NZ-UK-FTA-Benefits-for-Maori.pdf> accessed 19 February 2025.

[94] ibid, Side Letter on the Haka Ka Mate (Exchange of Letters between the Rt Hon Anne-Marie Trevelyan MP, Secretary of State for International Trade of the United Kingdom, and the Hon Damien O'Connor, Minister for Trade and Export Growth of New Zealand, 28 February 2022)'.

[95] ibid arts 17.14, 17.17, 30.8.1.

[96] Free Trade Agreement between the European Union and New Zealand (signed 9 July 2023, entered into force 1 May 2024) (EU-NZ FTA).

[97] ibid arts 7.4, 18.62.

through Māori relational approaches informed by TK and the Treaty of Waitangi.[98] On digital trade, in addition to New Zealand's Treaty of Waitangi exception, the EU-NZ FTA features a carve-out maintaining New Zealand's regulatory autonomy over Māori interests pertaining to digital trade. These include Article 12.1.2(c), excluding 'measures adopted or maintained by New Zealand that it deems necessary to protect or promote Māori rights, interests, duties and responsibilities [...], including in fulfilment of New Zealand's [Treaty of Waitangi] obligations', and the designation in Article 12.3 of the 'protection of the rights, interests, duties and responsibilities of Māori' as a legitimate policy objective for New Zealand.[99] Finally, the EU-NZ FTA contemplates Māori representation in various consultative mechanisms, such as domestic advisory groups and a Civil Society Forum, both of which must include Māori participants.[100]

Additionally, Australia concluded their negotiations for a free trade agreement with the UK (UK-AUS FTA) prior to the conclusion of the UK-NZ trade agreement. While it contains no standalone Indigenous trade chapter, the UK-AUS FTA contains provisions that recognize and protect Indigenous rights in the Australian market, and that leave room for integration with multilateral instruments that may provide additional protections. These include commitments for both Parties to collaborate at the WIPO Intergovernmental Committee on Intellectual Property and Genetic Resources, TK and Folklore, and for Australia to endeavour to accede to *The Hague Agreement Concerning the International Registration of Industrial Designs, Geneva Act*.[101] Additionally, for all investment and cross-border trade in services, Australia 'reserves the right to adopt or maintain any measure that accords preferences to any Indigenous [P]erson or organisation or providing for the favourable treatment of any Indigenous [P]erson or organisation'; for recreational, cultural, and sporting services, Australia more

[98] ibid arts 20.1(i), 20.2(6).

[99] ibid arts 12.1.2(c), 12.3.

[100] ibid 24.6.1.

[101] ibid arts 15.12, 15.55; The Hague Agreement Concerning the International Registration of Industrial Designs, Geneva Act (adopted 2 July 1999, entered into force 23 December 2003) WIPO TRT/HAGUE/006 (1999 Geneva Act). While the 1999 Geneva Act does not detail Indigenous rights or TK, the Australia view was that accession could have further 'facilitated access to design protection for Indigenous fashion', see Government of Australia, 'United Kingdom – Australia Free Trade Agreement: Benefits for Indigenous Businesses' <www.dfat.gov.au/trade-and-investment/benefits-indigenous-business>, accessed 19 February 2025. The Government of New Zealand, for its part, has likewise agreed to endeavour to accede to the 1999 Geneva Act, though this effort is not included in its own statement of benefits for Māori, see NZ Benefits Statement (n 93).

specifically reserves the right to 'adopt or maintain any measure' with respect to Indigenous traditional cultural expression.[102]

In May of 2022 Canada and the United Kingdom initiated trade negotiations wherein Canada proposed the inclusion of an Indigenous Trade chapter. This was accepted in principle by the UK, jurists and leaders underline, with the proviso that the UK does not recognize collective human rights in international law; only individual human rights and that the UK cannot accept any changes to its intellectual property regime. In January 2024 the UK suspended negotiations with Canada and no trade deal was agreed.[103] While beef hormones and cheese were given as official reasons for the pause in negotiations, contributing factors may have been the lack of acceptance of Indigenous collective rights and the lack of inclusion of Indigenous TK into the UK IP.

It may be challenging to include TK provisions in an Indigenous Peoples' trade chapter for cultural property and TK, but this can also be considered worthwhile. The protection of TK and indigenous trade practices might offer opportunities for sustainable development among Indigenous industries, overcoming some of the barriers outlined in Chapter 4. The respective Tribal Nations would be able to develop, economically, what they know best: their relationship with resources and culture, within their geographic territory.

As several jurists have argued, there remain significant political and economic obstacles to implementation of these commitments, including the vested corporate and other interests in protecting the status quo of IP rights, despite disadvantages for Tribal Nations' TK.[104] There are, however, domestic remedies that can accommodate the exercise of the inherent Indigenous economic right to protect TK.[105] A review of trade agreements that protect TK has found that 'a total of 41 agreements mention TK, most often enjoining [S]tates to put into place domestic measures to ensure its protection'. Among these, Nicaragua and Taiwan call for protecting 'the collective intellectual property rights and the Traditional Knowledge of Indigenous [P]eoples and local and ethnic

[102] ibid Annex II, Schedules of Non-Conforming Measures for Services and Investment (Schedule of Australia), schs 1, 9.

[103] Paul Seddon and Kate Whannel, 'UK Halts Trade Negotiations with Canada over Hormones in Beef Ban' (BBC News, 26 January 2024) <www.bbc.com/news/uk-politics-68098177 accessed 13 February 2025>; Janyce McGregor and John Paul Tasker, 'U.K. Walks Away from Trade Talks with Canada' (CBC News, 25 January 2024) <www.cbc.ca/news/politics/uk-canada-trade-talks-1.7094526> accessed 13 February 2025.

[104] A helpful overview of the status quo's inequity is included in Deepa Varadarajan, 'A Trade Secret Approach to Protecting Traditional Knowledge' (2011) 36 Yale Journal of International Law 361.

[105] See the domestic enforcement proposition by Professor Munzer and Raustiala (n 18).

communities in which any of their creations [...] are used commercially'.[106] In addition, over seventeen agreements require free, prior, and informed consent from Indigenous communities when accessing this knowledge,[107] and more than twenty-nine agreements encourage the sharing of benefits derived from the use of this knowledge.[108]

Also relevant to advancing international cooperation on protecting and supporting TK are provisions in the 2021 Indigenous Peoples Economic and Trade Cooperation Agreement (IPETCA) engaging Canada, Australia, New Zealand, and Taiwan, with space for further members. Participants to IPETCA agreed to specific provisions highlighting the need for TK protection, seeking to enhance Indigenous international trade. For instance, the Participants recognize in Article 7(a) 'the contribution Traditional Knowledge makes to innovation, sustainable development, and ecologically sound management of the environment'. While these commitments stop short of imposing hard obligations, they help inform a shared understanding of TK among Participants. Under Article 7(c) the participating economies 'will exchange views and explore options for implementing and supporting the right of Indigenous peoples to maintain, control, protect, and develop their cultural heritage, Traditional Knowledge, and traditional cultural expressions'.[109] The IPETCA and its implications as a modern tool for Indigenous economic empowerment and for the advancement of sustainable development is discussed later in this volume.

5.6 CONCLUSION

It is clear that IP laws were designed for protection of economic gain whereas TK, which was not considered as being a part of the IP model until at earliest the 1990s, was traditionally more a form of cultural heritage protection for each Indigenous Nation and only relatively recently considered by Indigenous Peoples for economic purposes.[110] Indigenous Nations around the world can

106 Jean-Frédéric Morin and Mathilde Gauquelin, 'Trade Agreements as Vectors for the Nagoya Protocol's Implementation' (Centre for International Governance Innovation (CIGI) Papers No 115, 2016) 2–3 <www.cigionline.org/sites/default/files/documents/Paper%20no.115.pdf> accessed 4 February 2025.

107 ibid 2–3, eg, Colombia Costa Rica, 2013.

108 ibid 2–3, eg, Caribbean Community European Community, 2008.

109 Arrangement on Indigenous Peoples Economic and Trade Cooperation (IPETCA) (2022) <www.mfat.govt.nz/assets/Trade-agreements/Indigenous-Peoples-Economic-and-Trade-Cooperation-Arrangement/IPETCA-Final-Text.pdf> accessed 24 January 2025.

110 Lyndel V Prott and Patrick J O'Keefe, '"Cultural Heritage" or "Cultural Property"' (1992) 1(2) International Journal of Cultural Property 310.

engage in the active protection of TK, specifically through prudent and cautious practices in governance, economic development, industries, and businesses.

Given the impracticality of changing the WIPO international order for IP protection, existing domestic laws can instead be supplemented by novel and new domestic legislation to protect and support TK within each willing State. Additionally, interested States can protect and support Indigenous Nations' TK through international trade provisions that address the specific needs of Indigenous Nations and the cultural heritage that falls outside the standard IP systems. As the square peg of TK does not fit into the round hole of IP, new concepts of ownership and control over TK can be created to address and protect existing and emerging expressions of Indigenous cultural identity. Protection within domestic State IP systems may be important, so that economic benefits can flow to Indigenous Peoples to continue breaking down barriers for economic empowerment and sustainable futures for both Indigenous Peoples and global populations.

6

Renewable Resources, Sustainable Development, and Indigenous Treaty Law

6.1 INTRODUCTION

Natural resources are critical to creating and sustaining life and livelihoods. Organic resources are sustained by ecosystems, the health of which is essential for biodiversity, a stable climate system, economies, and societies. Their health depends also on sustainable harvesting, stewardship, and governance, which are important for the responsible development and use of clean energy resources. The ability to harness clean energy and properly manage and balance the use and regeneration of renewable resources[1] is central to maintaining well-being: for humans, the flora and fauna with whom land and seas are shared, and the future generations of all life on Earth.[2]

[1] In the context of this book, renewable resources mean 'natural resources that, after exploitation, can return to their previous stock levels by natural processes of growth or replenishment'. Likewise, this also means that these are resources that, through exploitation, can potentially reach a level beyond which regeneration can become impossible. For more, see Claire Charters, 'Indigenous Peoples' Rights to Lands, Territories, and Resources in the UNDRIP: Articles 10, 25, 26, and 27' in Jessie Hohmann and Marc Weller (eds), *The UN Declaration on the Rights of Indigenous Peoples: A Commentary* (Oxford University Press 2018) 395; Stefania Errico, 'Control over Natural Resources and Protection of the Environment of Indigenous Territories: Articles 29, 30, and 32' in Hohmann and Weller (see above) 425.

[2] Inter-American Court of Human Rights, *Advisory Opinion AO-32/25 (Climate Emergency and Human Rights, Requested by Chile and Colombia, 29 May 2025)*, para 302, where the Court observes that the collective dimension of the right to a healthy climate "protects the collective interest of present and future generations of humans and other species . . . in maintaining a climate system fit to ensure their well-being . . ." See Deborah McGregor, 'Living Well with the Earth: Indigenous Rights and the Environment' in Damien Short and Corinne Lennox (eds), *Handbook of Indigenous Peoples' Rights* (Routledge 2016) 167. See also more generally Robin Wall Kimmerer, *Braiding Sweetgrass: Indigenous Wisdom, Scientific Knowledge, and the Teachings of*

Of course, renewable resources are just one aspect of this balance, and economists, also policy makers, seek ways to value myriad ecosystem services. As defined in the Millennium Ecosystem Assessment of 2006, ecosystem services encompass a holistic evaluation of the supporting mechanisms and regulating processes that interact not only for the benefit of human-nature dualities, but also for nature-nature modalities.[3] This includes supporting services necessary to produce all other ecosystem services such as nutrient cycling and soil formation, provisioning services for products obtained from ecosystems such as food and fresh water, regulating services providing benefits through the regulation of ecosystem processes such as climate regulation and pollination, and cultural services providing nonmaterial benefits such as cultural heritage, education, and recreation.[4]

These ecosystem services, however, are presently largely evaluated through anthropocentric views in contemporary scientific and legal literature. Humans are placed at the centre of service considerations, which focus primarily on the wants and needs of humankind.[5] These anthropocentric frameworks thus, intentionally or unintentionally, create a dominion over nature to extract and manage resources as *people* see fit. Distinctly, in Indigenous worldviews, nature is not under the dominion of human control but is rather vested with powers and gifts which humans can access by building relationships with nature.[6] People are stewards of nature and its services, and must abide by the laws of necessity and continuity, and the laws of respect, to only harvest and transform the land within the boundaries of necessity while respecting nature's agency and sacrifice.[7] Indigenous Traditional Knowledge (TK), laws, and practice thus create a biocentric view where all species are created equal and must share and respect the earth.[8] Commitments have been made,

Plants (Tantor 2016) and Robin Wall Kimmerer, *The Serviceberry: Abundance and Reciprocity in the Natural World* (Scribner 2024).

3 See Millennium Ecosystem Assessment, *Ecosystems and Human Well-being* (Millennium Ecosystem Assessment 2005); Environment Law Institute, Unlocking Nature's Potential: A Guide to Navigating Federal Permits and Environmental Reviews to Facilitate Use of Nature-Based Solutions (Environmental Law Institute, 2024).

4 Millennium Ecosystem Assessment (n 3) 57.

5 George Tyler Miller and Scott Spoolman, *Living in the Environment* (19th edn, Brooks/Cole Cengage Learning 2018) ch 25: Environmental Worldviews, Ethics and Sustainability.

6 For more, see McGregor (n 2); Paul Havemann, 'Mother Earth, Indigenous Peoples and Neo-Liberal Climate Change Governance' in Short and Lennox (n 2) 181.

7 Wapshkaa Mia'iingan (Aaron Mills), 'Aki, Anishinaabek, kaye tahsh Crown' (2010) 9(1) Indigenous Law Journal 120–123.

8 'Indigenous Peoples and the Nature They Protect' (UN Environment Programme, 2020) <www.unep.org/news-and-stories/story/indigenous-peoples-and-nature-they-protect> accessed 6 February 2025.

including in national laws and as settlements to court cases, as well as in 'traditional' and 'modern treaties' between Indigenous First Nations and the government of Canada.[9] As discussed earlier in this volume, during an era of reconciliatory practices, negotiations and agreements were negotiated. Although shaped by colonial and assimilatory practices, including residential schools, which many scholars note have caused a systemic loss of Indigenous cultures in communities across Canada and the United States,[10] the need to rectify historical wrongs on the part of Canadian federal, provincial, and territorial governments coupled with determined efforts among Indigenous Peoples to find ways to heal from the resulting deeply rooted intergenerational trauma. This led many communities across the country, which did not already have treaties negotiated with Canadian governments, to codify the relationships and obligations necessary for sustainable and healthy functioning of their communities and environments.[11] These treaties represented certain important steps for community agency in the era of reconciliation.[12]

Many of these treaties include provisions, negotiated by the Parties, which characterize or define the appropriate governance and co-management of natural resources.

9 As per earlier chapters, obligations may be fostered or frustrated in the implementation process of modern treaties. Although treaty articles may state that certain rights or obligations are recognized, the ultimate test for whether these treaties have created a positive outcome for the Nations or Peoples that have negotiated the agreements relates to the efficacy of their implementation. Gaps remain between the rights that have been respected and should be enforced for Indigenous Peoples in Canada and the Canadian reality in respecting said rights. For example, the Land Claims Agreements Coalition, which incorporates members from most of the modern treaties in Canada, have stated that although they negotiated and signed modern treaties in good faith, the federal government has refused to fully implement modern treaties and many necessary improvements outlined in these treaties over four decades have still not occurred. See 'Implementation Issues' (Land Claims Agreements Coalition, n.d.) <https://landclaimscoalition.ca/implementation-issues/> accessed 6 February 2025. Nonetheless, implementing the UNDRIP in domestic law presents a tangible avenue for accountability and continued respect for Indigenous rights in Canada. See also John Borrows, Larry Chartrand, Oonagh E. Fitzgerald and Risa Schwartz (eds), *Braiding Legal Orders: Implementing the United Nations Declaration on the Rights of Indigenous Peoples* (McGill-Queens University Press 2023).

10 Zebedee Nungak, *Wrestling with Colonialism on Steroids: Quebec Inuit Fight for Their Homeland* (Véhicule Press 2017) 13. See also Borrows and others (n 9); Edward Allen, 'Our Treaty, Our Inherent Right to Self-Government: An Overview of the Nisga'a Final Agreement' (2004) 11(3) International Journal on Minority and Group Rights 233–249; Nicole Spadotto, 'Jurisdiction Devolution: An Interim Transitional Arrangement on the Road to Indigenous Self-Government' (2024) 47(2) Dalhousie Law Journal 682.

11 Nungak (n 10). See also Sheryl Lightfoot and Sarah Maddison (eds), *Handbook of Indigenous Public Policy* (Edward Elgar 2024).

12 ibid.

In this chapter, natural resources governance specific to forestry and fisheries through timber harvesting, fish stocks, and aquaculture, in addition to the development of renewable energy technologies, is explored. To understand the urgent need for Indigenous consent and involvement in resource management and production and how treaties and legal obligations can facilitate this, this chapter first features an examination into international guidance and developments that may safeguard the sustainable, regenerative, use of renewable resources. Based on this understanding, three categories of resources, that is, forests, fisheries, and energy, are examined in this chapter to explore both how these international and domestic legal instruments apply to each domain of resource use, and also how these legal instruments are reiterated or expanded upon through Indigenous stewardship and benefit-sharing by way of treaties with their State. This analysis seeks to provide insights into the importance of consent and stewardship in renewable resource management, and the necessity for including Indigenous governance to enable sustainable development and economic empowerment for all who depend on these critical resources.

6.2 INTERNATIONAL GUIDANCE FOR RENEWABLES

In recent years, many international regulatory bodies and courts have recognized the need to consider serious questions about the state of natural resources globally.[13] Decisions, like those of the International Court of Justice in *Certain Activities carried out by Nicaragua in the Border Area* that awarded compensation taking into consideration damage to a wetland concerning transboundary natural resources,[14] highlight that stewardship of natural resources invokes both global and regional concern, and demonstrates how, despite international law, such resources can be increasingly degraded although many depend on their services.[15] Rising to the challenge of discerning global trends in the international regulation of the sustainable use of these

[13] Marie-Claire Cordonier Segger and Judge CG Weeramantry (eds), *Sustainable Development Principles in the Decisions of International Courts and Tribunals 1992–2012* (Routledge 2017).

[14] *Certain Activities carried out by Nicaragua in the Border Area (Costa Rica v Nicaragua)* [2015] ICJ 78. See also Jorge Cabrera Medaglia and Miguel Saldivia Olave, 'Sustainable Development Law Principles in the Costa Rica v Nicaragua Territorial Disputes' in Cordonier Segger and Weeramantry (n 13); Anon, 'Recognition of "Environmental Services" in the ICJ's First Award of Compensation for International Environmental Damage' (2018) 48(1) Environmental Policy and Law 36–41.

[15] Marie-Claire Cordonier Segger, 'Exploring the Role of International Law in Sustainable Natural Resources Management for Development' (Lauterpacht Centre for International Law, 2021) <www.lcil.cam.ac.uk/blog/exploring-role-international-law-sustainable-natural-resources-management-development-prof> accessed 6 February 2025. See also Marie-Claire Cordonier Segger, Ilaria Espa and Nicolaas Schrijver (eds), *Sustainable Development in International Law on Natural Resources* (Wolters Kluwer 2025 forthcoming).

resources, in 2021 after nearly a decade of dialogue and analysis, the International Law Association (ILA) unanimously adopted the Kyoto Guidelines on the Role of International Law in Sustainable Management of Natural Resources for Development (ILA Sustainable Natural Resources Guidelines), which present the rules and standards which currently define, guide, and direct how States manage natural resources of a global, regional, or transboundary nature, as well as national natural resources of global importance.[16] International law has also rapidly evolved to recognize that achieving greenhouse gas emissions targets, mitigating anthropocentric climate change, and adhering to commitments to limit temperature increases to 1.5°C above pre-industrial levels would require redoubled efforts towards sustainable management of natural resources, including promoting the regenerative use of renewable resources and securing a stable global climate system as a resource.[17] The importance of careful stewardship of natural resources was clearly underlined in the ambitious target 12.2 of the Sustainable Development Goals by 2030 to achieve the sustainable management and efficient use of natural resources, and reaffirmed by the adoption of the Kunming-Montreal Global Biodiversity Framework (GBF), a landmark agreement to guide global action on nature through to 2030, at the fifteenth Conference of the Parties to the Convention on Biological Diversity in 2022.[18] As one of its four overarching global goals, the GBF seeks to advance the sustainable use and management of biodiversity to ensure that nature's contributions to people are valued, maintained, and enhanced.[19]

16 International Law Association, 'The Role of International Law in Sustainable Natural Resources Management for Development' in *International Law Association Final Report of the 79th Biennial Conference* (International Law Association 2020) <www.ila-hq.org/en_GB/committees/role-of-international-law-in-sustainable-natural-resource-management-for-development>; Marie-Claire Cordonier Segger and Nico J. Schrijver, 'ILA Guidelines for Sustainable Natural Resources Management for Development' (2021) 68 Netherlands International Law Review 315.

17 Inter-American Court of Human Rights, *Advisory Opinion AO-32/25 (Climate Emergency and Human Rights, Requested by Chile and Colombia, 29 May 2025)* and International Court of Justice, *Obligations of States in respect of Climate Change (Advisory Opinion, 23 July 2025, General List No 187)*. United Nations Framework Convention on Climate Change (adopted 9 May 1992, entered into force 21 March 1994) 1771 UNTS 107 (UNFCCC) art 2; Paris Agreement (adopted 12 December 2015, entered into force 4 November 2016) UN Doc FCCC/CP/2015/L.9/Rev.1, 55 ILM 743 (Paris Agreement) arts 2.1 and 4.1.

18 Convention on Biological Diversity (adopted 5 June 1992, entered into force 29 December 1993) 1760 UNTS 142 (CBD); Kunming-Montreal Global Biodiversity Framework, CBD COP Decision 15/L.25 (2022).

19 UN Environment Programme (Convention on Biological Diversity), 'Kunming-Montreal Global Biodiversity Framework' (19 December 2022) UN Doc CBD/COP/DEC/15/4 (GBF) Goal B.

By supporting more sustainable resource management at national and regional levels, international law seeks to complement national instruments in promoting greater respect for interconnected ecosystems and cultures. This highlights the transboundary nature of natural resources, and how ecosystems and their services do not halt at arbitrary geopolitical lines drawn between human societies. By supporting and shaping regulations and institutions, international law has the potential to enable more cooperative and sustainable management of resources in today's globalized economy.[20] Additionally, as natural and renewable resources gain prominence at international forums, regional human rights courts, particularly the Inter-American Court of Human Rights, have also increasingly been called to consider the rights of Indigenous Peoples to sustainable use of natural resources.[21] For Indigenous Peoples, this has led to an extensive interpretation of the rights and duties associated with the use of natural and renewable resources, including rights associated with the use and management of resources on traditional lands.[22] The CBD and its GBF, for example, place Indigenous participation and affirmation of Indigenous rights to resources front and centre, both during the negotiations of the GBF and in the framework itself, stating the intention to 'ensure that the rights of [I]ndigenous [P]eoples and local communities are respected and given effect to in the implementation of the [GBF]', and this has been recognized in important cases including in the African and Inter-American human rights courts.[23]

20 Cordonier Segger (n 15).

21 See, for instance, *Santa Clara de Uchunya v Plantaciones de Pucallpa and the Regional Government of Ucayali* [2016] IACHR Case No 12,759; *Waorani of Pastaza v Ecuadorian State* (2019) IACtHR Series C No 398; Inter-American Court of Human Rights, Advisory Opinion OC-23/17 (15 November 2017) Series A No 23; *Case of the Kaliña and Lokono Peoples v Suriname*. Merits, reparations and costs, Judgment of November 25, 2015, Series C No 309, paras 177–181, especially at 181 where the Court reiterates that 'in principle, the protection of natural areas and the right of the indigenous and tribal peoples to the protection of the natural resources in their territories are compatible, and it emphasizes that, owing to their interrelationship with nature and their ways of life, the indigenous and tribal peoples can make an important contribution to such conservation. Thus, the criteria [ ] of a) effective participation,[ ] b) access and use of their traditional territories, and c) the possibility of receiving benefits from conservation [ ] – all of the foregoing provided that they are compatible with protection and sustainable use (*supra* para 177) – are essential elements to achieve this compatibility which should be evaluated by the State. Consequently, the State must have adequate mechanisms to implement these criteria as a means of guaranteeing the right to a dignified life and to cultural identity to the indigenous and tribal peoples in relation to the protection of the natural resources that are in their traditional territories'.

22 See, *infra*, MC Cordonier Segger with HE CJ Weeramantry (eds), *Sustainable Development in International Courts and Tribunals* (Routledge 2017). See also Marie-Claire Cordonier Segger and Damilola Olawuyi, *Sustainable Development Law: Principles, Practice and Prospects* (Oxford University Press 2025).

23 GBF (n 19) art 6, ibid.

Though these innovative and cooperative international regimes are expanding the recognition and the need to sustainably manage natural and renewable resources, compliance still falls short.[24] Advancing knowledge and respect for these decisions, guidelines, and accords is just the beginning in elaborating accountable and enforceable legal measures that place sustainable use of natural resources and ecosystems at the forefront. By extension, respect for Indigenous knowledge, participation, and consent remains vital to not only achieving the goals set out by these international laws, but also to respecting Indigenous rights and paving the path for more ambitious and impactful goals in future legal developments.

6.3 PRINCIPLES AND RULES FOR FORESTRY

Forests cover 31 per cent of land area globally, which is just over 4 billion hectares. They house most of Earth's biodiversity, and are crucial to reversing and halting climate change from their unparalleled capacity to store carbon, potentially providing up to 30 per cent of the solution to managing greenhouse gas emissions.[25] Forest ecosystems of many types provide important ecosystem services for all living species including valuable renewable resources, biological diversity, and natural disaster prevention and mitigation.[26] Forests additionally are of immense cultural and livelihood significance to many Indigenous Peoples.[27]

However, deforestation and forest degradation continue at an alarming rate, with deforestation exceeding the rate of forest expansion, which occurs through regeneration, afforestation, and reforestation. Cumulatively, estimates suggest that there has been a net loss of 178 million hectares of forest since 1990.[28] Though not the only factor in forest degradation,[29] unsustainable

[24] Cordonier Segger (n 15).

[25] 'Challenges and Opportunities in Turning the Tide on Deforestation – Joint Statement of the Collaborative Partnership on Forests' (n.d.) 3 <www.fao.org/3/cb5879en/cb5879en.pdf> accessed 6 February 2025; Jean-Christophe Vié, Craig Hilton-Taylor, and Simon N Stuart (eds), *Wildlife in a Changing World – An Analysis of the 2008 IUCN Red List of Threatened Species* (IUCN Red List of Threatened Species 2008) 64.

[26] Yvonne Walz and others, 'Disaster-Related Losses of Ecosystems and Their Services. Why and How Do Losses Matter for Disaster Risk Reduction?' (2021) 63 International Journal of Disaster Risk Reduction 7.

[27] Klaus Seeland, *Nature Is Culture: Indigenous Knowledge and Social-Cultural Aspects of Trees and Forests in Non-European Cultures* (Studies in Indigenous Knowledge 1997).

[28] HM Treasury, 'The Economics of Biodiversity: The Dasgupta Review – Abridged Version' (2021) London: HM Treasury 11–68.

[29] Agriculture is the main culprit for the majority of the world's deforestation. Yet, combined with forestry, these industries contribute strongly to the degradation of the world's forest ecosystems

forestry practices and overexploitation have contributed largely to the state of forest health. It has been underlined that forest degradation varies drastically based on the jurisdictions that set standards and regulations for the sustainable harvesting of lumber and other forest products, and the level of recognition of the need for renewable resource regeneration. Some sources suggest that Indigenous Peoples steward at least 36 per cent of the world's remaining intact forests, of which Indigenous-managed forests are the most biodiverse.[30] Furthermore, the free, prior, and informed consent (FPIC) principle is not always respected when it comes to timber and forestry extraction on Indigenous territories, which undermines conservation goals and reconciliation efforts with local Indigenous Peoples.[31]

In Canada for example, over 70 per cent of First Nations are located in or near forested lands; it is widely recognized that involving Indigenous Peoples in forestry-related decisions and practices is integral to both the livelihoods of Indigenous People and forest health, especially when considering decisions to be made on their traditional territories.[32] Federal forestry laws cover the management of forests on lands under federal jurisdiction. The main federal laws in this domain are the *Forestry Act*, Timber Regulations, *Indian Act*, *First Nations Land Management Act*, and *National Parks Act*.[33] However, provincial, territorial, and private lands fall under provincial and territorial laws that govern the regions Indigenous Peoples reside in, which may create gaps and shortfalls when it comes to involving Indigenous Peoples in decision-making

and damage the integrity, and thus the quality, of the ecosystem services that these biomes can provide. Noriko Hosonuma and others, 'An Assessment of Deforestation and Forest Degradation Drivers in Developing Countries' (2012) 7(4) Environmental Research Letters.

30 'World Leaders, Corporations at COP26, Take Major Step to Restore and Protect Forests' (United Nations, 2021) <https://news.un.org/en/story/2021/11/1104642> accessed 6 February 2025; Nicholas J Reo and others, 'Invasive Species, Indigenous Stewards, and Vulnerability Discourse' (2017) 41(3) American Indian Quarterly 201–223.

31 '1 Year into Injunction Enforcement at Fairy Creek Blockades, 100s of Protesters Await Trial' (CBC News, 2022) <www.cbc.ca/news/canada/british-columbia/rcmp-started-enforcing-the-injunction-against-the-fairy-creek-blockades-a-year-ago-49-sentenced-so-far-1.6456353> accessed 6 February 2025.

32 This sentiment is reflected through s 35(1) of the 1982 *Charter of Rights and Freedoms*, which enshrines Indigenous rights in the Canadian Constitution. See *Constitution Act* 1982, Canadian Charter of Rights and Freedoms; 'Indigenous Peoples and Forests' (Canadian Council of Forest Ministers, 2022) <www.ccfm.org/canadians-and-communities/indigenous-peoples-and-forests/> accessed 6 February 2025. See also Borrows and others (n 9).

33 'Canada's Forest Laws' (Natural Resources Canada, 2023) <www.nrcan.gc.ca/our-natural-resources/forests/sustainable-forest-management/canadas-forest-laws/17497> accessed 6 February 2025.

over the governance of traditional forests on lands outside federal jurisdiction.[34]

One mediating factor that may resolve certain current challenges is that Indigenous lands covered through treaties must respect the agreements inherent to those treaties. Many of these agreements include forestry provisions, specifically the management and use of resources, conservation measures, boundary setting, conditions of access including limitations, and the inherent right to hunting and gathering.[35] In these treaties, the Parties often also include stipulations for land ownership and resources, which provide a foundation for mutual, beneficial, and sustainable development of forestry resources between Indigenous landowners and Canadian governments.[36] For example, modern treaties between Indigenous Peoples and the Governments of Newfoundland and Labrador, Quebec, and Yukon (and the Government of Canada as the underlying federal Party) include revenue sharing and providing Indigenous ownership access to land and capital transfers.[37] The Parties to the Carcross/Tagish First Nation Final Agreement between Canada, Yukon, and Carcross/Tagish First Nation, for instance, negotiated an entire chapter dedicated to forestry provisions including addendums such as the right to sustainably harvest 'Forest Resources on Crown Land for purposes incidental to the exercise of their traditional pursuits of hunting, fishing, trapping and gathering ... and to the practice of their traditional customs, culture and religion or for the traditional production of handicrafts and implements.'[38]

Such treaties can also be deployed to negotiate terms for specified protected areas to enact an appropriate management plan for forests on land claims territories between governments and Indigenous rights holders. For example, in the Kwanlin Dun First Nation Final Agreement between the Government of Canada, the Kwanlin Dun First Nation, and the Government of the Yukon, the Parties consider conservation impacts in relation to different land use

[34] ibid. See also Borrows and others (n 9).

[35] Agreements in this context largely refers to modern treaties, or Comprehensive Land Claims Agreements, that are negotiated after the 1970s, and provide indigenous people with leverage and power in determining the priorities for natural resources, amongst many other priorities. 'Treaties and Agreements' (Government of Canada, 2020) <https://perma.cc/M2DP-6GZG> accessed 6 February 2025. See also Borrows and others (n 9).

[36] 'Indigenous Peoples and Forestry in Canada' (Government of Canada, 2016) <https://perma.cc/3UG9-K66C> accessed 6 February 2025.

[37] ibid.

[38] The Carcross/Tagish First Nation Final Agreement (Khà Shâde Héni of the Carcross/Tagish First Nation–Government of Canada–Government of the Yukon) (adopted 22 October 2005) arts 17.3.1.1 and 17.3.1.3.

types. These provisions enable co-management in special management areas that can include but are not limited to wildlife areas, national and territorial parks, migratory bird or wildlife sanctuaries, designated heritage sites, and watershed protection areas.[39]

In the absence of modern treaties, at times provincial, territorial, and/or federal governments along with interested timber companies have introduced consultation practices and revenue-sharing agreements so that Indigenous Peoples can, in some way, still economically benefit from the activities that occur in their traditional territories, most popularly in British Columbia where timber harvesting has abundant economic opportunity.[40] However, the level of involvement of Indigenous Peoples in decision-making, including through respect and recognition of TK, in the management of the forest resources before, during, and after forestry activities; the due diligence and politics involved in achieving FPIC (where FPIC is the end goal for negotiating Parties); and how governments and industries alike abide by their legally binding treaty and contractual obligations remain largely open questions.[41]

6.4 PRINCIPLES AND RULES FOR FISH HABITATS

Fish habitats provide numerous economic benefits and ecological services. Much like forests, oceans and lakes can provide significant sinks for carbon storage and also support important and potentially sustainable industries through aquaculture and fisheries.[42] The waters, including surrounding deltas and riparian areas, also hold substantial cultural significance to Indigenous

[39] Kwanlin Dun First Nation Final Agreement (Kwanlin Dun First Nation–Government of Canada–Government of the Yukon) (adopted 19 February 2005).

[40] Government of Canada (n 36). Tara Dawn Atleo, 'Local Indigenous Planning Instruments for Intergenerational Equity in Ahousaht Traditional Territories of Canada' in Marie-Claire Cordonier Segger, Marcel Szabo and Alexandra Harrington (eds), *Intergenerational Justice in Sustainable Development Treaty Implementation: Advancing Future Generations Rights through National Institutions* (Cambridge University Press 2021) 528–544.

[41] Marie-Claire Cordonier Segger, Wayne Garnons-Williams, and Eva Wu, 'Indigenous Treaties with Canada: Obstacles or Opportunities to Realizing the Sustainable Development Goals in Light of the United Nations Declaration on the Rights of Indigenous Peoples across Canada' (2023) 3(1) Inter Gentes <https://intergentes.com/wp-content/uploads/2023/09/indigenous-treaties-with-canada_ew-updates.pdf> accessed 6 February 2025. See also Borrows and others (n 9).

[42] For reference, see Mauro Barelli, 'Development Projects and Indigenous Peoples' Lands' in Short and Lennox (n 2) 69; Jérémie Gilbert and Corinne Lennox, 'Towards New Development Paradigms: The United Nations Declarations on the Rights of Indigenous Peoples as a Tool to Support Self-Determined Development' in Damien Short, Corinne Lenox, Julian Burger and Jessie Hohmann (eds), *The United Nations Declaration on the Rights*

communities and serve as habitats for many species, including at risk and cultural keystone species, as well as being critical for the protection and restoration of ecological systems more generally. Conservation of salt and freshwater aquatic systems has also been demonstrated to provide significant benefits for both marine environments and those whose lives and livelihoods depend on them.[43]

Due to the transboundary nature of marine ecosystems and resources, large bodies of international law generally form the foundation governing oceans and freshwater bodies. These laws and conventions focus heavily on fisheries and fish stock management, as these renewable resources are heavily impacted by nearly all the extractive industries that exist in marine environments.[44] Frameworks for internationally managing fisheries and oceans emerge from the United Nations and include the rules under the United Nations Convention on the Law of the Sea (UNCLOS), including the United Nations Agreement on Straddling and Highly Migratory Fish Stocks (UN Fish Stocks Agreement or UNSFA).[45] Important further provisions related to establishing jurisdictions, parameters of governance, management of fish stocks, and conservation measures are carried out worldwide by Regional Fisheries Management Organizations (RFMOs).[46] The Food and Agriculture Organization (FAO) has also developed numerous agreements to conduct appropriate fisheries management, including the Code of

of Indigenous Peoples: A Contemporary Evaluation (Routledge 2021). See also Borrows and others (n 9).

43 For further reference see, Samira Idllalène and Hicham Masski, 'Biodiversity and Marine Protected Areas: An Analysis of the Fishing-Oriented MPA Legal Framework in Morocco' in Damilola Olawuyi and Riyad Fakhri (eds), *Biodiversity and Nature Conservation Law and Policy in the Middle East and North Africa Region* (Routledge, forthcoming); Karen Scott, 'SDG 14: Conserve and Sustainably Use the Oceans, Seas and Marine Resources for Sustainable Development' in Jonas Ebbesson and Ellen Hey (eds), *The Cambridge Handbook of the Sustainable Development Goals and International Law* (Cambridge University Press 2020).

44 See Moritaka Hayashi, 'The 1995 UN Fish Stocks Agreement and the Law of the Sea' in Davor Vidas and Willy Ostreng (eds), *Order for the Oceans at the Turn of the Century* (Brill/Nijhoff 1999) 37.

45 Agreement for the Implementation of the Provisions of the United Nations Convention on the Law of the Sea of 10 December 1982, Relating to the Conservation and Management of Straddling Fish Stocks and Highly Migratory Fish Stocks (adopted on 4 December 1995, entered into force 11 December 2001) 2167 UNTS 3 (UN Fish Stocks Agreement). See also 'International Treaties and Agreements' (Fisheries and Oceans Canada, 2020) <https://perma.cc/7WXB-Z7ZX> accessed 6 February 2025.

46 UN Fish Stocks Agreement art 12, 13 and 14. For reference, see David D. Caron, 'Revisiting the Freedom of Fishing and Legal Obligations on States Not Participating in Regional Fisheries Management Organizations' (2008) 23(1) The International Journal of Marine and Coastal Law 1.

Conduct for Responsible Fisheries, the International Plan of Action for the Management of Fishing Capacity, and the International Plan of Action to Prevent, Deter and Eliminate Illegal, Unreported and Unregulated Fishing.[47] FAO furthermore plays a role in developing international fisheries legislation, while also providing legal advisory services to RFMOs and governments to assist in creating national legislation.[48]

Through multiple international instruments, States have agreed on the need for more sustainable fisheries management and conservation. Adopted by the UN in 2015, under Sustainable Development Goal 14 Life Below Water, countries have prioritized the need to 'conserve and sustainably use the oceans, seas and marine resources for sustainable development'.[49] For example, in the GBF under the CBD, States specifically call for more sustainable management, conservation, and restoration of marine ecosystems in Targets 2 and 3, while highlighting fisheries as an industry that if mismanaged or unsustainably exploited can significantly impact progress towards sustainability and biodiversity.[50] Additionally, the Rio Declaration on Environment and Development, and the Declaration of the UN Conference on the Human Environment (the Stockholm Declaration) similarly highlight fisheries and marine management as critical to the environment and ecosystems.[51] Widely considered 'soft law' internationally, the principles identified in these Declarations are important in public policy and practice, informing standards and priorities when an RFMO or national governing body is determining laws, policies, or treaties for their own fishery management.

For example, in 1992 the Atlantic seaboard experienced a major decline of Northern cod populations due to decades of overfishing caused by deficient regulatory regimes. In Canada, this resulted in a moratorium set by the Government of Canada to allow the near-extinct fish stocks of the Northern

[47] UN, FAO Code of Conduct for Responsible Fisheries (FAO 1995) <www.fao.org/4/v9878e/v9878e00.htm>; UN, International Plan of Action for the management of Fishing Capacity (FAO 1999) <www.fao.org/4/i0318e/i0318e03.pdf > ; UN, International Plan of Action to Prevent, Deter and Eliminate Illegal, Unreported and Unregulated Fishing (FAO 2001) <https://openknowledge.fao.org/server/api/core/bitstreams/a80c3bfb-1d5b-4ee6-9c85-54b7e83986a2/content >; for further reference, see Caron (n 46).

[48] Carolin Anthes and Olivier de Schutter, 'The Food and Agriculture Organization of the United Nations' in Benjamin Mason Meier and Lawrence O Gostin (eds), *Human Rights in Global Health: Rights-Based Governance for a Globalizing World* (Oxford University Press 2018).

[49] UN General Assembly Res 70/1, 'Transforming Our World: The 2030 Agenda for Sustainable Development' (21 October 2015) UN Doc A/RES/70/1 SDG 14.

[50] GBF (n 19).

[51] Anthes and Schutter (n 48). See also Cordonier Segger and Olawuyi (n 22).

Cod to replenish. Although domestic fishers were provided a Total Allowable Catch (TAC) quota, scholars and jurists note, international fishing fleets with activities beyond Canada's 200 nautical mile Exclusive Economic Zone (EEZ), exploiting the same fish stocks, continued to force the species into decline.[52] This forced Canada to establish even lower TACs for domestic harvesters and ended most foreign fishing within its coastline limits. As illegal fishing and overexploitation continued, the Northwest Atlantic Fisheries Organization (NAFO) imposed more restrictions on fishery quotas and allowable technology. Still, in Atlantic regions beyond Canadian and US coastlines, concerns were raised that foreign fishing operators continued to harvest five times the NAFO quota. The Atlantic cod populations as expected thus dwindled to near extinction and international legislation had to be implemented to prevent an unrecoverable tragedy of the commons.[53] The resulting United Nations Fish Stocks Agreement thus committed States to use a precautionary approach when managing their domestic and shared fish stocks.[54] Based on the United Nations Fish Stocks Agreement, the Department of Fisheries and Oceans (DFO) developed the Canadian Sustainable Fisheries Framework (SFF) in 2009, which outlines the tools and policies required to ensure the well-being and reproductive levels of Canada's fish stocks through the protection of biodiversity and fishery habitats.[55] However, a 2016 federal government audit by the Canadian Commissioner of the Environment and Sustainable Development (CESD) found that though DFO had identified the tools needed for fisheries management, they were unsuccessful in their implementation.[56]

Much like in the forestry industry, modern treaties in the Canadian context allow for TK-driven management practices and sustainable use in places where international cooperation and domestic frameworks fall short. Many modern treaties, especially those negotiated for Indigenous Peoples whose culture and livelihoods depend on marine ecosystems, also include sections or chapters related to fishing rights and entitlements.[57] These include but are not limited to the management and use of fishery resources based on Total

[52] Fred Mason, 'The Newfoundland Cod Stock Collapse: A Review and Analysis of Social Factors' (2002) 1(17) UCLA Electronic Green Journal.

[53] ibid; Garrett Hardin, 'The Tragedy of the Commons' (1968) 162 Science.

[54] 'Report 2 – Sustaining Canada's Major Fish Stocks – Fisheries and Oceans Canada' in *2016 Fall Reports of the Commissioner of the Environment and Sustainable Development* (Office of the Auditor General of Canada 2016) 2.3.

[55] ibid.

[56] DW Archibald, R McIver, and R Rangeley, 'The Implementation Gap in Canadian Fishery Policy: Fisheries Rebuilding and Sustainability at Risk' (2021) 129 Marine Policy.

[57] For more, see Jeremy Patzer, 'Indigenous Rights and the Legal Politics of Canadian Coloniality: What Is Happening to Free, Prior and Informed Consent in Canada?' in Short

Allowable Catch (TAC) and basic need levels, conditions of access with overlapping national and provincial or territorial parks, conservation measures, and species considerations. Limits are often set to protect and conserve fish resources including establishing boundaries, harvest levels, fishing licences, and creating Joint Fishery Committees, boards, and/or councils.[58]

As an example, section 16.9 of the 2005 Carcross/Tagish First Nation Final Agreement on Fish and Wildlife Harvests outlines harvesting management established through TK for both treaty beneficiaries and other harvesters, and notes that the Fish and Wildlife Management Board has the power to establish, modify, or remove Total Allowable Harvests in situations required for 'conservation, public health or public safety; . . . to meet sustainable yield requirements as determined by scientific research and surveys and the special knowledge of Yukon Indian People; or . . . to achieve the goals and objectives identified by species and population management plans'.[59] Similar to the Fish and Wildlife Management Board for the Carcross/Tagish People, the Tsawwassen First Nation in their modern treaty stipulate similar management powers, though adding as well that for fisheries matters managed by the Government of Canada, there will be a Joint Fisheries Committee with both Tsawwassen and government representatives that 'will seek to operate by consensus' on management decisions.[60] As jurists underline, these terms provide the Indigenous Parties with codified powers in managing not only the renewable resources present on their lands, but also those that are transboundary beyond their land claims territory, which the federal government thus manages. However, this recognizes that the federal government as the deciding authority for fishery management decisions in these cases. In some cases, such as that in the Labrador Inuit Land Claims Agreement, the Government of Newfoundland and Labrador and the Government of Canada, Indigenous rights holders appear to have a more significant role in the decision-making arena. For instance, in the accord,

and others (n 42); see also John Borrows (ed), *Braiding Legal Orders* (McGill-Queen University Press 2023). See also Borrows and others (n 9).

58 For reference, see Yong Wang and Xin Pan, 'Reasonable Restrictions on the Freedom of Fishing in High Seas Marine Protected Areas from an International Law Perspective: An Analysis' (2023) 10 Frontiers in Marine Science <www.frontiersin.org/journals/marine-science/articles/10.3389/fmars.2023.1030646/full?utm_source=chatgpt.com> assessed 20 February 2025; Borja Nogue-Alguero, Giorgos Kallis and Miquel Ortega, 'Limits to Fishing: The Case for Collective Self-Limitation Illustrated with an Example of Small-Scale Fisheries in Catalonia'(2023) 10 Frontiers in Marine Science <www.frontiersin.org/journals/marine-science/articles/10.3389/fmars.2023.1134725/full?utm_source=chatgpt.com> assessed 20 February 2025.

59 Carcross/Tagish First Nation Final Agreement (n 38) ch 16: Fish and Wildlife.

60 Tsawwassen First Nation Final Agreement (Tsawwassen First Nation–Government of Canada–Government of British Columbia) (adopted 6 December 2007) ch 9: Fisheries.

Parties commit that with respect to inter-jurisdictional fisheries management of 'any species or stock of Fish or Aquatic Plants, Fish Habitat or the management of fisheries in or affecting the Labrador Inuit Settlement Area shall ... extend beyond those generally available to non-governmental organizations'.[61] In practice, some suggest, this has primarily enabled the Inuit to have a respected role in the decisions surrounding the sustainable management of fishers in their territory, though to what extent these decisions are taken into account, especially if there are economic pressures for Canadian governments to set their own agenda, can be questioned. FPIC thus remains a crucial underlying principle especially for natural resource economies like Canada.

6.5 PRINCIPLES AND RULES FOR RENEWABLE ENERGY

Transitioning to renewable energy-dominated economies is crucial to meeting climate and sustainable development targets.[62] These sources of energy, such as solar, wind, hydroelectric, biomass, geothermal and tidal energy, are hailed as a saving force in international agreements and governing bodies when it comes to achieving global temperature rise reduction targets. Multilateral treaties on sustainable development such as the Paris Agreement under the United Nations Framework Convention on Climate Change (UNFCCC)[63] have led the dialogue in promoting the use of renewable energy. In order to offer a way to highlight and include the voices and views of Indigenous Peoples, platforms like the International Indigenous Peoples' Forum on Climate Change (IIPFCC), established in 2008, recognize that Indigenous Peoples have close relationships with supportive ecosystems and are holders of unique TK that can shape the sustainable development of renewable resources, including for energy, as well as to ensure that renewable energy infrastructure is more resilient to the impacts of climate change.[64]

[61] Labrador Inuit Land Claims Agreement (Inuit of Labrador–Government of Canada–Government of Newfoundland and Labrador) (adopted 21 January 2005) ch 13: Fisheries.

[62] International Renewable Energy Agency (IRENA), *World Energy Transitions Outlook: 1.5°C Pathway* (2022).

[63] Paris Agreement to the United Nations Framework Convention on Climate Change (adopted 12 December 2015, entered into force 4 November 2016) 3156 UNTS 54113 (Paris Agreement); United Nations Framework Convention on Climate Change (adopted 09 May 1992, entered into force 21 March 1994) 1771 UNTS 107 (UNFCCC).

[64] International Indigenous Peoples' Forum on Climate Change, Center for International Environmental Law, 'Indigenous Peoples and Traditional Knowledge in the context of the UN Framework Convention on Climate Change' (n.d.) 6 <www.ciel.org/wp-content/uploads/2018/12/Indigenous-Peoples-and-Traditional-Knowledge-in-the-Context-of-the-UNFCCC.pdf> accessed 6 February 2025. For more, see Gilbert and Lennox (n 42); Paul Patton, 'Philosophical Justifications for Indigenous Rights' in Short and others (n 42); Corinne Lewis,

In Canada, First Nations, Inuit, and Métis are partners or beneficiaries of almost 20 per cent of Canada's renewable energy market, participation in which has exponentially grown in the last two decades.[65] This has been largely attributed to Indigenous Peoples asserting a presence and participation in project developments that have implications on ancestral lands in recognition of legal treaty rights and federal and provincial governments requiring projects to adhere to the norms of FPIC.[66] Benefits to this expansion are threefold: joint jurisdiction between Indigenous groups and governments for clean energy projects provides shared revenues for renewable energy projects on traditional territories, partnership and collaboration creates employment and economic development opportunities for the Indigenous Peoples involved, and respect for Indigenous participation and consent in resource development projects impacting the communities complies with FPIC and modern treaties stipulations, as applicable. Clean and renewable energy near communities also provides decarbonization pathways for traditionally diesel and carbon-heavy power generation that communities have been forced to rely on.[67]

In part, this shift in including, and even pushing for, Indigenous participation on the part of the governments in Canada and by the energy industry can be attributed to the *Canadian Energy Regulator Act* (CERA), which sets the conditions under which current and future regulations can have legal standing.[68] Multiple sections of the CERA relate to Indigenous regulation and participation in the energy sector, specifically calling for the duty to 'consider any adverse effects that the decision, order or recommendation may have on the rights of the Indigenous Peoples of Canada recognized and affirmed by section 35 of the *Constitution Act, 1982*'.[69] To achieve this, the project regulator must also 'establish an advisory committee to enhance [Indigenous] involvement … in respect of pipelines, power lines and offshore renewable energy projects as well as abandoned pipelines' which must include at least one of each First Nations, Inuit, and Métis representative recommended by the respective Indigenous organization.[70] This is all to be conducted under

'Indigenous Peoples and the Corporate Responsibility to Respect Human Rights' in Short and Lennox (n 2) 201; Tobias Stoll, 'Intellectual Property and Technologies-Article 31' in Hohmann and Weller (n 1). See also Borrows and others (n 9).

65 Canadian Institute for Climate Choices, 'Wave of Change – Indigenous Clean Energy Leadership for Canadas Clean, Electric Future' (2022) 1 <https://climateinstitute.ca/wp-content/uploads/2022/02/ICE-report-ENGLISH-FINAL.pdf> accessed 6 February 2025.

66 ibid 6.

67 ibid 10.

68 CERA 2019.

69 ibid s 56.

70 ibid s 57.

the commitment to taking both scientific and Indigenous knowledge into account during decision-making;[71] more specifically, authorizing a proposed project requires both Indigenous knowledge and scientific information and data to be considered in the project decision.[72]

Further augmenting the CERA are specific stipulations if the Indigenous community has a treaty in place. For example, in 2022 the Government of British Columbia funded Doig River First Nation, under Treaty 8, at least $150,000 in equity towards developing clean-energy projects.[73] Additionally, for Indigenous communities with a modern treaty, certain provisions stipulated within these agreements can require additional requirements for participation, economic allocations, and governance. The Little Salmon/Carmacks First Nation Final Agreement, for instance, includes a section entitled 'Economic Development Measures', which provides that the First Nation takes 'advantage of economic development opportunities generated by that Settlement Agreement',[74] through a plan that covers the training and experience that is required by the First Nation, pathways to maximizing the financial and technical resources related to the opportunity and identifies the 'funding requirements and measures necessary to stimulate community level economic activity'.[75] Benefits of this form, at face value, provide the Little Salmon/Carmacks First Nation with the financial revenue to compensate for the renewable energy and other resources harvested from their land, but also serve as funding that can support the community, cultural revitalization, and reconciliation to some degree. These considerations mirror the aforementioned wave of Indigenous involvement in the renewable energy industry, and the Little Salmon/Carmacks First Nation has prioritized their interest in making 'strategic investments' in both renewable resource services and energy resources.[76] This dynamic may also be reflected in other modern treaties in the Yukon, as this type of clause is applied through the framework set out by the Umbrella Final Agreement (UFA).[77]

[71] ibid preamble.

[72] ibid ss 183, 198, 262.

[73] 'Indigenous Clean-Energy Projects Funded in Northern B.C.' (Ministry of Indigenous Relations and Reconciliation, 2022) <https://news.gov.bc.ca/releases/2022IRR0002-000019> accessed 6 February 2025.

[74] Little Salmon/Carmacks First Nation Final Agreement (Little Salmon/Carmacks First Nation–Government of Canada–Government of the Yukon) (adopted 21 July 1997) art 22.3.0.

[75] ibid. See also Borrows and others (n 9).

[76] ibid art 22.3.3.4.

[77] The Umbrella Final Agreement (1990) is the overall 'umbrella' agreement of the Yukon Land Claims package that stipulates the general agreement made between the Yukon First Nations,

However, as scholars and leaders note, treaties in other government jurisdictions adopted prior to the UNDRIP often do not include complete consent for project development on treaty lands. The previously mentioned Tsawwassen First Nation Final Agreement includes merely that 'Canada will Consult with Tsawwassen First Nation in respect of any proposed new legislation or regulation, or amendment' but does not mandate clearly how much weight this consultation will hold in the final decision-making process.[78] There also remains concern about how much these modern treaties are respected as legally binding obligations and whether or not the communities have the resources and capacity to adequately respond to requests for consultation and provide adequate input into what is sometimes a bombardment of proposals sent their way.[79] This in essence reverts the onus to federal legislation like CERA to keep governments and industries accountable for applying the norms of FPIC and delivering equitable benefits for profits and proceeds gleaned from the proposed activity.

As one further illustrative example of modern treaties and their recognition of Indigenous sovereignty over renewable resources including forests and lands, with discussions of oceans and fisheries to proceed, in 2025 the President of the Haida Nation, Gaagwiis *Jason Alsop*, together with the Prime Minister of Canada the Rt Hon Justin Trudeau and the Minister of Crown-Indigenous Relations, Hon Gary Anandasangaree, announced the signing of the *Chiix̱uujin/Chaaw K̲aawgaa 'Big Tide (Low Water)' Haida Title Lands Agreement*. As explained in the announcement, the Agreement includes Canada's recognition of Haida Aboriginal title to lands on Haida Gwaii and marks a significant milestone in the journey to reconciliation.[80]

the Government of Yukon, and the Government of Canada. Though this document is not legally binding, it acts as a political agreement that creates a framework through which each of the fourteen Yukon First Nations can conclude a land claims agreement with the territorial and federal governments. All the provisions set out in the UFA are automatically a part of each of the First Nations' modern treaties, with specific provisions added to their agreement based on the individual negotiations. See The Umbrella Final Agreement (Council for Yukon Indians–Government of Canada–Government of the Yukon) (adopted 29 May 1993). See also Borrows and others (n 9).

78 Tsawwassen First Nation Final Agreement (n 60) s 29.

79 Cordonier Segger, Garnons-Williams, and Wu (n 41). See also Borrows and others (n 9).

80 *Chiix̱uujin / Chaaw K̲aawgaa 'Big Tide (Low Water)' Haida Title Lands Agreement* (2025). At a Special House of Assembly on 24 November 2024, Haida citizens voted 97 per cent in favour of the *Chiix̱uujin / Chaaw K̲aawgaa 'Big Tide (Low Water)' Haida Title Lands Agreement*. As a result, the Agreement was signed by the Haida Nation and Canada on 4 December 2024. See Council of the Haida Nation, 'The Haida Nation and Canada Announce a First-of-Its-Kind Agreement Recognizing Aboriginal Title on Haida Gwaii (17 February 2025) HlGaagilda (Skidegate), Haida Gwaii and Prime Minister's Office, Ottawa,

According to the Parties, Canada's recognition of Haida Aboriginal title on Haida Gwaii includes the foreshore and extends to the low-water mark, but does not affect private property interests or local and municipal governments on Haida Gwaii. The Agreement confirms the continued delivery of federal public services, and notes that the Haida-Canada Archipelago Management Board continues to cooperatively manage Gwaii Haanas through a transition period, during which both governments will work to reconcile jurisdictions and laws. As recognized in the Agreement, the Haida Nation collectively holds inherent Haida title and rights as described in the *Constitution of the Haida Nation*.[81] Over a transition period, the Haida Nation and Canada have committed to continue to work respectfully and cooperatively on matters relating to Haida Gwaii, in an orderly and incremental way, providing ongoing stability for all island residents and other interest holders on Haida Gwaii. This Agreement builds on previous reconciliation accomplishments, including the *Nang K̲'uula/Nang K̲'úulaas Recognition Agreement* signed by the Haida Nation, Canada, and British Columbia in 2023, as well as the *Gaayhllxid/Gíihlagalgang 'Rising Tide' Haida Title Lands Agreement* signed by the Haida Nation and British Columbia in April 2024.[82] According to the Parties, the *Chiix̲uujin/Chaaw K̲aawgaa 'Big Tide (Low Water)' Haida Title Lands Agreement* can be seen as demonstrating Canada's commitment to implement and advance the *United Nations Declaration on the Rights of Indigenous Peoples*.[83] As the announcement recognizes, Canada's recognition of Haida Aboriginal title results from Gud ad T'alang HlG̲ang.gulx̲a Tll Yahda/Tll yá'adee G̲ii gud ahl t'álang hlG̲ángulaang (*People Working Together to Make it Right*) and, in this way, upholds the duty and honour of the Crown based on a principled and respectful nation-to-nation relationship.[84] On announcing the agreement,

Canada <www.haidanation.ca/for-immediate-release-the-haida-nation-and-canada-announce-a-first-of-its-kind-agreement-recognizing-aboriginal-title-on-haida-gwaii/>.

81 ibid. See Council of the Haida Nation, Constitution of the Haida Nation (30 May 2021) <www.haidanation.ca/haida-constitution>.

82 ibid. For further reading, see Louise Takeda, *Islands' Spirit Rising: Reclaiming the Forests of Haida Gwaii* (University of British Columbia Press 2015) 4–5; Louise Takeda and Inge Røpke, 'Power and Contestation in Collaborative Ecosystem-Based Management: The Case of Haida Gwaii' (2010) 70 Ecological Economics 178, 180; Michaela M McGuire, 'We Can Do Our Own Thing Here on Haida Gwaii' (2023) 14(3) The International Indigenous Policy Journal 1–25; Nang K̲aa Klaagangs, Ernie Gladstone, and Brady Ruyin Yu, 'One Beat in the Infinite Heart of Haida Gwaii' (2023) 39(1) Parks Stewardship Forum 60–72.

83 Ibid. For further discussion of UNDRIP in the Canadian context, see Jessie Hohmann and Marc Weller (eds), *The UN Declaration on the Rights of Indigenous Peoples: A Commentary* (Oxford University Press 2018); Short and others (n 42).

84 ibid.

Gaagwiis *Jason Alsop* declared that '[t]he recognition of Haida title to Haida Gwaii by Canada acknowledges historic injustices and illustrates the transformative possibilities of working together for what is right. It takes leadership to recognize a wrong, begin the process of healing from a troubled history, and trust in the ability to forge a new relationship based on respect. This recognition of title by Canada – which was initiated in 1913 by our past leaders – means that we can begin a new era of peaceful co-existence knowing that we can look after Haida Gwaii and ensure the well-being of all who call these shining islands home'.[85]

In line with Article 26(1) of UNDRIP, which affirms Indigenous peoples' rights to lands and resources historically used,[86] the Agreement underscores the importance of Nation-to-Nation negotiations. In Paragraph 1.1(b), the Parties to the *Chiix̱uujin/Chaaw K̲aawgaa Big Tide (Low Water) Agreement* 'set out an orderly process for reconciliation of jurisdictions and laws on Haida Gwaii'.[87] This clause appears to align with SDG 15 to '[p]rotect, restore and promote sustainable use of terrestrial ecosystems, sustainably manage forests, combat desertification, and halt and reverse land degradation and halt biodiversity loss' by affirming Indigenous stewardship over lands and natural resources. In the *Chiix̱uujin/Chaaw K̲aawgaa Big Tide (Low Water)* Agreement at para 6.1(d), the Parties further prioritize discussions of 'fisheries and related matters' to reconcile governance of Haida Gwaii's marine and forest resources, reflecting SDG 14 to '[c]onserve and sustainably use the oceans, seas and marine resources for sustainable development'. This also echoes Article 26(2) of UNDRIP, where its drafters agreed 'Indigenous [P]eoples have the right to own, use, develop and control … their lands, territories and resources'.[88] Accordingly, the *Chiix̱uujin/Chaaw K̲aawgaa Big Tide (Low Water) Agreement* appears to signal the Haida Nation's continued stewardship of ecological integrity and resources in their territory, through title sovereignty.

6.6 CONCLUSION

In considering the rapidly changing and evolving fields of forestry, fishing, and energy, these potentially renewable resources industries clearly play an important role in supporting local economies, advancing achievement towards climate, biodiversity, and environmental targets, while supporting sustainable

[85] ibid.
[86] UNDRIP, for discussion supra (n 83).
[87] *Chiix̱uujin / Chaaw K̲aawgaa Big Tide (Low Water) Haida Title Lands Agreement* (n 80).
[88] UNDRIP, for discussion (n 83).

development as a whole.[89] Additionally, the consensus remains clear throughout these agreements: the input of TK and the participation of Indigenous Peoples in renewable resource ventures not only respect norms of FPIC, but also respect the fact that Indigenous Peoples themselves have a wealth of knowledge and contributions that are invaluable in managing the use of the renewable resources in question.[90] In essence, it is of utmost importance that the original inhabitants and stewards of the traditional territories are provided with the continued use of the resources on those territories. Treaties may play a crucial role in augmenting international and domestic law to provide Indigenous communities with the authority and the autonomy to drive negotiations, planning, and decision-making necessary to support sustainable and just industries.

[89] See Havemann (n 6).

[90] See Barelli (n 42); Havemann (n 6), Borrows and others (n 9).

7

Indigenous Rights, Cultural Heritage, and Indigenous Treaty Law

7.1 INTRODUCTION

'Culture' is crucial for human needs, contributes to social stability, and is essential to human well-being, and cultural heritage specifically can be seen as encompassing both tangible natural and cultural heritage, along with intangible heritage.[1] In academic literature, these forms of heritage offer an intersecting and complementary dichotomy to understanding of culture, whereby tangible heritage encapsulates the material aspects of built and natural environments,[2] and is coupled with intangible cultural heritage constituting the incorporeal elements that create 'living heritage'.[3] According to the UN Expert Mechanism on the Rights of Indigenous Peoples, the tangible and intangible manifestations of Indigenous ways of life, achievements, and creativity are expressions of self-determination, specifically in relation to spiritual and physical relationships with the lands, territories, and resources.[4]

1 Sylvia Maus, 'Hand in Hand against Climate Change: Cultural Human Rights and the Protection of Cultural Heritage' (2014) 27(4) Cambridge Review of International Affairs 699.

2 Tangible heritage also includes 'cultural landscapes'. See 'Convention concerning the Protection of the World Cultural and Natural Heritage' (UNESCO, 2003); 'Operational Guidelines for the Implementation of the World Heritage Convention' (UNESCO, 2021) WHC.21/01 II(A).

3 Federico Lenzerini, 'Intangible Cultural Heritage: The Living Culture of Peoples' (2011) 22(1) European Journal of International Law 101.

4 'Promotion and Protection of the Rights of Indigenous Peoples with Respect to the Cultural Heritage' (UNHR, 2015) A/HRC/30/53 [7]. See also, for further discussion, Felipe Gómez Isa, 'The UNDRIP: An Increasingly Robust Legal Parameter' in Damien Short, Corinne Lennox, Julian Burger and Jessie Hohmann (eds), *The United Nations Declaration on the Rights of Indigenous Peoples: A Contemporary Evaluation* (Routledge 2021); Alexandra Xanthaki, 'Culture – Articles 11(1), 12, 13(1) and 34' in Jessie Hohmann and Marc Weller (eds), *The UN*

Thus, the two are deeply inter-dependent.[5] The Convention for the Safeguarding of the Intangible Cultural Heritage in 2003 (ICH Convention), a United Nations Educational, Scientific and Cultural Organization (UNESCO)-adopted Resolution that serves as a protective instrument to safeguard intangible heritage,[6] defines intangible heritage as cultural 'practices, representations, expressions, knowledge and skills – as well as the instruments, objects, artifacts and cultural spaces associated therewith – that communities, groups and, in some cases, individuals recognize as part of their cultural heritage'.[7] This, according to the ICH Convention, is manifested as, '(a) oral traditions and expressions, including language as a vehicle of the intangible cultural heritage; (b) performing arts; (c) social practices, rituals and festive events; (d) knowledge and practices concerning nature and the universe; and/or (e) traditional craftsmanship'.[8] With respect to traditional practices, both tangible and intangible cultural heritage is deeply rooted in many Indigenous practices, including ceremony, craftsmanship, stewardship of territories, and subsistence hunting and gathering practices.[9]

International legal mechanisms like the ICH Convention are one of many advances that have been made to protect Indigenous cultural heritage, traditions, and practices, and to affirm Indigenous Peoples' ability to have a greater voice to advocate for respect and realization of human rights. These advances are particularly impactful through major international instruments and agreements that garnered broad international acceptance, such as the *United Nations Declaration on the Rights of Indigenous Peoples* (UNDRIP) and the Indigenous and Tribal Peoples Convention, 1989 No. 169 (ILO 169).[10] This progress may facilitate the legal framework through which Indigenous Peoples

Declaration on the Rights of Indigenous Peoples: A Commentary (Oxford University Press 2018); Jessie Hohmann, 'The UNDRIP and the Rights of Indigenous Peoples to Existence, Cultural Integrity and Identity, and Non-Assimilation – Articles 7(2), 8 and 43' in Hohmann and Weller, ibid; Lee Swepston, 'Indigenous and Tribal Peoples' Culture and Work under the ILO' in Damien Short and Corinne Lennox (eds), *Handbook of Indigenous Peoples' Rights* (Routledge 2016).

5 UNESCO, 'Convention for the Safeguarding of the Intangible Cultural Heritage' (UNESCO, 2003) preamble (ICH Convention).

6 Safeguarding, per the ICH Convention, means 'measures aimed at ensuring the viability of the intangible cultural heritage, including the identification, documentation, research, preservation, protection, promotion, enhancement, transmission, particularly through formal and non-formal education, as well as the revitalization of the various aspects of such heritage'. ibid art 11.

7 ibid art 2(1).

8 ibid art 2(2).

9 Isa (n 4), Xanthaki (n 4); Hohmann (n 4); Swepston (n 4).

10 The details about these two agreements and how they came to be ratified by most Nations globally can be found in Chapter 2; see also Isa (n 4), Xanthaki (n 4); Hohmann (n 4); Swepston (n 4).

and communities can govern the use and practice of culture and tradition as they deem fit. This is of utmost importance in an era of burgeoning demand for Indigenous experiences in art and tourism, even as climate change and biodiversity loss impact the cultural dichotomy in which cultural heritage can thrive, and economic development pressures drive the use, and often the appropriation of Indigenous cultural heritage, practices, and craftsmanship. Declarations like the UNDRIP and treaties such as ILO 169 provide guidelines hold potential to govern how cultural industries should operate in Indigenous communities. As such, they could protect Indigenous Peoples' rights and interests while retaining the ability to participate in economic opportunities, in particular cultural industries like tourism and arts.

This chapter explores the ways that international legal mechanisms, treaties, and domestic law seek to facilitate the protection of cultural heritage for sustainable development. It begins by considering commitments enshrined in the UNDRIP and ILO 169 that, when implemented by the States which drafted and consented to these instruments , can support the protection of cultural heritage. The impact of this protection is also analysed through a climate change and biodiversity loss lens to highlight the importance of safeguards in an era where these forms of global change disproportionately impact Indigenous Peoples' tangible and intangible cultural heritage, with a case study to explain the concern. The chapter then examines how cultural heritage protection commitments enshrined in international instruments like the UNDRIP and ILO 169 can be augmented through domestic treaties and legal doctrines, through illustrative examples of US legal and historical developments and Canadian negotiations and implementations of modern treaties. Finally, Indigenous trade treaty commitments in relation to the protection of tangible and intangible cultural heritage, including in relation to cultural industries and tourism, are briefly highlighted, underlining the need for more research and dialogue to support Indigenous rights to self-identification and cultural heritage, as a foundation for cultural survival and revival, and to advance key SDGs for Indigenous Peoples.

7.2 UNDRIP AND ILO 169 GUIDANCE ON CULTURAL HERITAGE

In the UNDRIP and the ILO 169 Convention, the drafters recognized corroborating principles that affirm and explain Indigenous Peoples' rights, affirming that these rights are 'inherent' or pre-existing.[11] These rights reflect,

[11] UN Res 61/295, 'United Nations Declaration on the Rights of Indigenous Peoples' (2007) UN Doc A/RES/61/295 art 37(1) and preamble [7] (UNDRIP); Isa (n 4), Xanthaki (n 4); Hohmann (n 4); Swepston (n 4).

for instance, global consensus that Indigenous Peoples hold inherent and inalienable human rights. By supporting and corroborating the inherent rights of Indigenous People to protect their cultural heritage, to apply these rights to social and economic development if they so choose, and to use these rights to protect their land and territories as a function of the interconnected nature of their tangible and intangible cultural heritage, the drafters of both instruments built a foundation for promoting Indigenous Peoples' rights globally and continue to influence the relationship between Indigenous Peoples and their ability to practise, revitalize, and maintain their cultures. Specifically, as recognized in the Declaration at Article 11(1):

> Indigenous [P]eoples have the right to practise and revitalize *their cultural traditions and customs.* This includes the right to maintain, protect and develop the past, present and future manifestations of their cultures, such as archaeological and historical sites, artefacts, designs, ceremonies, technologies and visual and performing arts and literature.[12]

These rights include, as recognized in Article 13, the ability to 'revitalize, use, develop and transmit to future generations their histories, languages, oral traditions, philosophies, writing systems and literature, and to designate and retain their own names for communities, places and persons'.[13] As further elaborated in Article 31, Indigenous Peoples have the right to 'maintain, control, protect and develop their cultural heritage, Traditional Knowledge and traditional cultural expressions'.[14] Articles 8, 15(1), and 16(2) further corroborate these rights to cultural heritage protection. This self-determination enables Indigenous Peoples to have autonomy, and to foster practices that allow their cultural heritage and Traditional Knowledge (TK) to flourish.[15]

In this respect, Articles 3, 5, 20(1), and 23 of the UNDRIP and ILO Articles 2(b), 5(a), and 7(1) further reaffirm that Indigenous Peoples have the right to manage institutions which contribute to Indigenous societies through economic, social, and cultural development. This forms a positive application of choice for Indigenous self-determination in how to pursue the practice and revitalization of cultural heritage. With respect to outside interests that potentially encroach on Indigenous Peoples' tangible heritage, and thus by extension the ability to maintain intangible manifestations of culture, Articles 25, 29 (1), and 32(1) and (2) in the UNDRIP and Articles 7(2), 14(1), 15(1), and

[12] UNDRIP (n 11) art 11(1) (emphasis added).
[13] ibid art 13.
[14] ibid art 31.
[15] UNDRIP (n 11).

23(1) and (2) of ILO 169 establish Indigenous People's rights to give or withhold consent and control the use of resources in traditional territories. This also entails that free, prior, and informed consent[16] is required when cultural heritage is impacted.[17] This is especially evident through Article 11 (2), which states that 'States shall provide redress through effective mechanisms, which may include restitution, developed in conjunction with [I]ndigenous [P]eoples, with respect to their cultural, intellectual, religious and spiritual property taken without their free, prior and informed consent or in violation of their laws, traditions and customs'.[18]

Establishing these rights through international legal frameworks, including through the principles enshrined in UNDRIP and agreed in ILO 169, is seen by many to be key in acknowledging the interdependence of tangible and intangible cultural heritage for Indigenous People and enabling ratifying countries to implement these articles through domestic legal regimes.[19] Furthermore, for many jurisdictions that have not fully accepted or implemented the UNDRIP to its full extent,[20] the UNDRIP still remains a substantial international interpretive instrument. Nonetheless, as an international Declaration that upholds Indigenous cultural practices and a full range of associated mechanisms, it has enormous weight and potential, especially in the age of the triple planetary crisis, as discussed in the following subsection.

7.2.1 *Cultural Heritage in the Age of Triple Planetary Crisis*

According to the United Nations, the world faces triple planetary crises: climate change, nature (biodiversity) loss, and pollution and waste.[21] As scholars and jurists argue, effects of these crises are disproportionately felt by the world's most vulnerable people, including Indigenous Peoples.[22] Climate change, for example, is linked to land erosion, crop destruction, community

[16] Further discussion of free, prior, and informed consent (FPIC) can be found in Chapter 2. See also Mauro Barelli, 'Free, Prior and Informed Consent in the United Nations Declaration on the Rights of Indigenous Peoples – Articles 10, 19, 29(2) and 32(2)' in Hohmann and Weller (n 4).

[17] UNDRIP (n 11) arts 10, 11(2), 28(1), 29(2).

[18] ibid art 11(2).

[19] See Isa (n 4), Xanthaki (n 4); Hohmann (n 4); Swepston (n 4).

[20] See, eg, Deborah McGregor, 'Living Well with the Earth' in Short and Lennox (n 4).

[21] UNEP, 'Making Peace with Nature: A Scientific Blueprint to Tackle the Climate, Biodiversity and Pollution Emergencies' (UNEP, 2021) <www.unep.org/resources/making-peace-nature> accessed 6 February 2025.

[22] Noelle Higgins, 'Changing Climate; Changing Life – Climate Change and Indigenous Intangible Cultural Heritage' (2022) 11(3) Laws 47.

dispersal and relocation, and changes in animal migration and behaviours which impact subsistence hunting and harvesting amongst many other effects. For cultural heritage, this could mean that knowledge and practices passed down for generations may be lost due to the loss of land, biodiversity, and the accumulation of waste stemming from development.[23] As the 2007 International Union for Conservation of Nature (IUCN) Assessment Report explains, communities living on marginal lands, e.g., low-lying or coastal lands, and whose livelihoods depended on natural resources are among the most vulnerable to climate change.[24] Indeed, as the International Council on Monuments and Sites (ICOMOS) has highlighted, Indigenous Peoples are the most vulnerable to the adverse effects of climate change because, among other reasons, their existence is often inextricably tied to the land.[25]

As an illustrative example, also discussed elsewhere in this volume, Haida Gwaii, the group of over 200 islands totalling approximately one million hectares, is located approximately 100 kilometres west of the northern coast of mainland British Columbia. The Haida have been stewards of Haida Gwaii for millennia, and enduring tangible cultural heritage of the Haida including SG̲ang Gwaay Llnagaay (Red Cod Island, commonly known by its English name Ninstints), a village site of the Haida people and part of the Gwaii Haanas National Park Reserve and Haida Heritage Site, is renowned worldwide as a UNESCO World Heritage Site,[26] a National Historic Site,[27] and a National Marine Conservation site,[28] celebrated for ancient, majestic lodges and giant cedar carved totem poles. The Council of the Haida Nation (CHN) was formed as a national government in 1974, and the *Constitution of the*

[23] Mauro Barelli, 'Development Projects and Indigenous Peoples' Lands' in Short and Lennox (n 4); Jérémie Gilbert and Corinne Lennox, 'Towards New Development Paradigms: The United Nations Declaration on the Rights of Indigenous Peoples as a Tool to Support Self-Determined Development' in Short and others (n 4); Lindsay Borrows, *Otter's Journey Through Indigenous Language and Law* (UBC Press 2018).

[24] Mirjam Macci and others, 'Indigenous and Traditional Peoples and Climate Change' (International Union for Conservation of Nature, 2008) 4.

[25] Climate Change and Cultural Heritage Working Group, 'The Future of Our Pasts: Engaging Cultural Heritage in Climate Action' (International Council on Monuments and Sites, July 2019) 19 (hereafter 'Future of Our Pasts').

[26] UNESCO, 'UNESCO World Heritage Site' <www.UNESCO.org> accessed February 25, 2025; UNESCO, 'SGang Gwaay' <www.UNESCO.org> accessed February 25, 2025.

[27] Parks Canada, 'Nan Sdins National Historic Site of Canada' (Parks Canada Directory of Federal Heritage Designations, 2025).

[28] Parks Canada, 'Gwaii Haanas National Park Reserve, National Marine Conservation Area Reserve, and Haida Heritage Site' (Parks Canada, October 10, 2024); 'Ninstints' (BC Geographical Names).

Haida Nation was formally adopted in 2003, mandating CHN to conduct the external affairs and steward the lands and waters of Haida Gwaii on behalf of the Haida Nation, ensuring that the Haida relationship with Haida Gwaii continues in perpetuity. In 2021, Canada, the Haida Nation, and British Columbia signed the *GayG̱ahlda/Kwah.hlahl.dáyaa 'Changing Tide' Framework for Reconciliation*, setting out an incremental approach to negotiating reconciliation agreements. The *Nang K̲'uula/Nang K̲'úulaas Recognition Agreement* is the first tripartite agreement reached under this renewed process of negotiations. Through the *Nang K̲'uula/Nang K̲'úulaas Recognition Agreement*, Canada and British Columbia recognized the Haida Nation as the holder of inherent rights of governance and self-determination, and the Council of the Haida Nation as the governing body of the Haida Nation. On 7 November 2024, Bill S-16, *An Act respecting the recognition of the Haida Nation and the Council of the Haida Nation* received royal assent. As noted earlier in this volume, in 2025 the President of the Haida Nation, Gaagwiis *Jason Alsop*, together with the Prime Minister of Canada Rt Hon Justin Trudeau and the Minister of Crown-Indigenous Relations, Hon Gary Anandasangaree, announced the signing of the *Chiix̲uujin/Chaaw K̲aawgaa 'Big Tide (Low Water)' Haida Title Lands Agreement*. As explained in the announcement, the Agreement includes Canada's recognition of Haida Aboriginal title to lands on Haida Gwaii and marks a significant milestone in the journey to reconciliation.[29] The Haida-Canada Archipelago Management Board continues to cooperatively manage Gwaii Haanas through a transition period, during which both governments will work to reconcile jurisdictions and laws. As recognized in the Agreement, the Haida Nation collectively holds inherent Haida title and rights as described in the *Constitution of the Haida Nation*.[30] As noted above, this Agreement builds on previous reconciliation accomplishments, including the *Nang K̲'uula/ Nang K̲'úulaas Recognition Agreement* signed by the Haida Nation, Canada, and British Columbia in 2023, as well as the *Gaayhllxid/Gíihlagalgang*

[29] *Chiix̲uujin / Chaaw K̲aawgaa 'Big Tide (Low Water)' Haida Title Lands Agreement* (2025). At a Special House of Assembly on 24 November 2024, Haida citizens voted 97 per cent in favour of the *Chiix̲uujin / Chaaw K̲aawgaa 'Big Tide (Low Water)' Haida Title Lands Agreement*. As a result, the Agreement was signed by the Haida Nation and Canada on 4 December 2024. See Council of the Haida Nation, 'The Haida Nation and Canada Announce a First-of-Its-kind Agreement Recognizing Aboriginal Title on Haida Gwaii (17 February 2025) HlGaagilda (Skidegate), Haida Gwaii and Prime Minister's Office, Ottawa, Canada <www.haidanation.ca/for-immediate-release-the-haida-nation-and-canada-announce-a-first-of-its-kind-agreement-recognizing-aboriginal-title-on-haida-gwaii/>.

[30] ibid. See Council of the Haida Nation, Constitution of the Haida Nation (30 May 2021) <www.haidanation.ca/haida-constitution>.

'Rising Tide' Haida Title Lands Agreement signed by the Haida Nation and British Columbia in April 2024.[31] According to the Parties, the *Chiix̱uujin/Chaaw K̲aawgaa 'Big Tide (Low Water)' Haida Title Lands Agreement* can be seen as demonstrating Canada's commitment to implement and advance the *United Nations Declaration on the Rights of Indigenous Peoples*.[32] Indeed, the Parties to the *Chiix̱uujin/Chaaw K̲aawgaa Big Tide (Low Water)* Agreement also seek to advance SDG 11.4 to: '[s]trengthen efforts to protect and safeguard the world's cultural and natural heritage'. At sections 4.4–4.7, Parties do so by safeguarding cultural heritage, placing emphasis on maintaining Gwaii Haanas 'primarily for its natural function, cultural continuity of the Haida Nation, and appreciation of its intrinsic values'. By recognizing and protecting significant Haida sites, the Parties also appear to affirm the provisions of UNDRIP such as Article 31(1), which states 'Indigenous [P]eoples have the right to maintain, control, protect and develop their cultural heritage, Traditional Knowledge and traditional cultural expressions'.[33]

As another example, Alaskan communities, like Shishmaref situated on the Bering Strait, not only face relocation due to rapidly eroding shorelines but also suffer from barriers to subsistence hunting and fishing that nourish the communities due to melting sea ice, shorter winters, and severe weather events.[34]

As such, Indigenous advocates have also been among the first to reference the interconnected nature of how *both* landscapes and cultural identity are impacted by climate change, and continue to be so as the triple planetary crises inevitably worsen.[35] This linkage between land, identity, and climate

[31] ibid. For further reading, see Louise Takeda, *Islands' Spirit Rising: Reclaiming the Forests of Haida Gwaii* (2015) 4–5; Louise Takeda and Inge Røpke, 'Power and Contestation in Collaborative Ecosystem-Based Management: The Case of Haida Gwaii' (2010) 70 Ecological Economics 178, 180; Michaela M McGuire, 'We Can Do Our Own Thing Here on Haida Gwaii' (2023) 14(3) The International Indigenous Policy Journal 1–25; Nang K̲aa Klaagangs, Ernie Gladstone, and Brady Ruyin Yu, 'One Beat in the Infinite Heart of Haida Gwaii' (2023) 39(1) Parks Stewardship Forum 60–72.

[32] ibid. For further discussion of UNDRIP in the Canadian context, see Hohmann and Weller (n 4); Short and others (n 4).

[33] ibid.

[34] Christopher Mele and Daniel Victor, 'Reeling from Effects of Climate Change, Alaskan Village Votes to Relocate', *The New York Times* (New York, 20 August 2016) <www.nytimes.com/2016/08/20/us/shishmaref-alaska-elocate-vote-climate-change.html> accessed 6 February 2025; Josie Holtzman and Isaac Kestenbaum, 'Subsistence, A Way of Life: How Climate Change Is Affecting Alaskan Traditions' (The Arctic Institute, January 2018) <thearcticinstitute.org/subsistence-way-life-climate-change-affecting-alaskan-traditions/> accessed 6 February 2025. For further reading on the unique challenges facing Indigenous peoples in Nordic countries, see Peter Johansson, 'Indigenous Self-determination in the Nordic Countries: The Sami, and the Inuit of Greenland' in Short and Lennox (n 4).

[35] Future of Our Pasts (n 25).

change is further reiterated by experts, who underline that '[c]limate displacement has been closely associated with land, sense of place, and identity'.[36] As further experts explain: 'Indigenous ontological worldviews and cultural heritage are outcomes of the complex interaction between people and their environments. The unique expressions of connection to land, whether through material culture, livelihoods, knowledge, identity, songs, ritual and religion derive foremostly from socioecological relationships.'[37] Forced dispersion and relocation have additional psychological impacts on community well-being, which is passed on to future generations.[38] Much of the diverse intangible cultural heritage of Indigenous Peoples, which includes traditional cultural expressions, skills (e.g., in hunting and fishing), and land management practices may be lost in the face of climate change.[39] Additionally, as noted earlier, elements of TK are recognized as vital to mitigating the effects of climate change and biodiversity loss, with the Kunming-Montreal Global Biodiversity Framework acknowledging 'the important roles and contributions of [I]ndigenous [P]eoples and local communities as custodians of biodiversity and as partners in its conservation, restoration and sustainable use'.[40] Safeguarding this heritage is thus even more critical, with UNESCO stating that '[s]afeguarding living heritage is very crucial for [I]ndigenous [P]eoples because their heritage is the basis of their identity, the basis of their cultures

36 Gül Aktürk and Martha Lerski, 'Intangible Cultural Heritage: A Benefit to Climate-Displaced and Host Communities' (2021)11 Journal of Environmental Studies and Sciences 305, 307.

37 Jasmine Pearson, Guy Jackson, and Karen E McNamara, 'Climate-Driven Losses to Indigenous and Local Knowledge and Cultural Heritage' (2021) 1 The Anthropocene Review 1.

38 E Ferris and J McAdam, 'Planned Relocations in the Context of Climate Change: Unpacking the Legal and Conceptual Issues' (2015) 4 Cambridge Journal of International and Comparative Law 137.

39 Maus (n 1).

40 United Nations Environment Programme (Convention on Biological Diversity), 'Kunming-Montreal Global Biodiversity Framework' (19 December 2022) UN Doc CBD/COP/DEC/15/4 (GBF) art 7(a). The Framework additionally recognizes that the knowledge held through Indigenous cultural practices must be respected in light of the world's growing biodiversity challenges and that this respect comes as reciprocal protection and affirmation of Indigenous rights. Specifically, art 7(a) states that 'The Framework's implementation must ensure that the rights, knowledge, including Traditional Knowledge associated with biodiversity, innovations, worldviews, values and practices of [I]ndigenous [P]eoples and local communities are respected, and documented and preserved with their free, prior and informed consent, including through their full and effective participation in decision-making, in accordance with relevant national legislation, international instruments, including the United Nations Declaration on the Rights of Indigenous Peoples, and human rights law. In this regard, nothing in this framework may be construed as diminishing or extinguishing the rights that [I]ndigenous [P]eoples currently have or may acquire in the future'. For more on TK, see Chapter 5.

and, of course, it is the continual transmission of this heritage that is going to strengthen [I]ndigenous [P]eoples' identities and cultures'.[41]

7.3 CULTURAL HERITAGE IN INDIGENOUS TREATIES

Recognizing the importance of protecting Indigenous cultural heritage, and affirming the right to protection through international instruments, is only the first phase of concretely implementing the pathways necessary for safeguarding Indigenous cultural heritage. It is also necessary to understand the role that actors play in this implementation, specifically what States are, and must be, doing in advancing heritage. To understand this, it is possible to consider examples of cultural protection in the United States and Canada and how the advent of UNDRIP and relevant national legal mechanisms can foster or frustrate the ability to protect culture and heritage. First, the US example outlines the country's policies and legal history regarding respecting the UNDRIP and treaty interpretation as related to cultural heritage. Then, the Canadian example distinguishes how the Canadian modern treaties have the potential to both affirm and be affirmed by the UNDRIP when highlighting the inherent rights related to the protection of cultural heritage.

7.3.1 *US Legal and Historical Perspectives on Cultural Heritage*

Modern US history includes a fraught relationship with Indigenous Peoples, characterized by policies and practices of assimilation and discrimination at both state and federal levels.[42] Furthermore, in the United States many policies can be highlighted for 'exceptionalist and self-serving interpretations of international positive (treaty and convention) and customary law'.[43] In a 2013 US Report submitted to the Committee on the Elimination of Racial Discrimination (CERD) the United States argues that it 'does not consider that the Declaration – a non-legally binding, aspirational instrument that was not negotiated for the purpose of interpreting or applying the CERD – should be

[41] United Nations Educational, Scientific, and Cultural Organization, 'Living Heritage and Indigenous Peoples' (UNESCO, 2019) <https://ich.unesco.org/en/indigenous-peoples> accessed 6 February 2025.

[42] More context regarding the US application of treaty law and jurisdiction with regard to Indigenous Peoples can be found in Chapter 10. For more on Indigenous rights to existence and non-assimilation, see Hohmann (n 4).

[43] National Indian Youth Council, 'Commentary on the Periodic Report of the United States of America on the Elimination of Racial Discrimination Pursuant to the International Convention' (National Indian Youth Council, 2013) 1 <https://cendoc.docip.org/collect/cendocdo/index/assoc/HASH0139/b8ee14dc.dir/other_sources_INT_CERD_NGOUSA_17638_E.pdf> accessed 6 February 2025.

used to reinterpret Parties' obligations under the treaty'.[44] This is argued despite an affirmation that underlined the government's 'support for the Declaration's recognition in the preamble that [I]ndigenous individuals are entitled without discrimination to all human rights recognized in international law, and that [I]ndigenous [P]eoples possess certain additional, collective rights'.[45] The 2021 periodic report affirms this political position, furthermore arguing that 'the United States understands "free, prior, informed consent" to call for a process of meaningful consultation with [T]ribal leaders, but not necessarily the agreement of those leaders, before the actions addressed in those consultations are taken'.[46] Many express concern that such views not only relegate the UNDRIP, and thereby the inherent Indigenous rights captured in its articles, to an aspirational declaration that can be set aside when Indigenous views contradict outsider positions, but also diminish the impact of free, prior, and informed *consent* to one of mere *consultation* that ultimately does not require Indigenous agreement (consent) to a decision or project before the governments of the United States or their industry can unilaterally continue their pursuits that may infringe on Indigenous decisions and/or rights.[47]

These responses are especially important for understanding the US position on the UNDRIP and affirming indigenous rights and cultural heritage. The 2013 report was submitted in response to CERD's recommendations for proper consideration of the impacts that extractive and other potentially damaging activities may have on areas of spiritual and cultural significance. Instead of presenting concrete solutions to protecting cultural heritage, the authors instead point to statutes as their solutions,[48] even though these statutes

[44] CERD, 'Periodic Report of the United States of America to the United Nations Committee on the Elimination of Racial Discrimination' (2013) [176] <https://2009-2017.state.gov/j/drl/rls/cerd_report/210605.htm> accessed 6 February 2025.

[45] ibid.

[46] CERD, 'Combined Tenth to Twelfth Periodic Reports Submitted by the United States of America under art 9 of the Convention, due in 2017' (2021) UN Doc CERD/C/USA/10-12 [128] <https://tbinternet.ohchr.org/_layouts/15/treatybodyexternal/Download.aspx?symbolno=CERD/C/USA/10-12&Lang=en> accessed February 2025.

[47] The issues that arise when distinguishing between *consent* and *consultation* are explored in Chapter 2. Please refer to this chapter for context regarding the importance of valuing consent in contrast to consultation.

[48] The statutes in question include U.S. American Indian Religious Freedom Act 1978, the Native American Graves Protection and Repatriation Act 1990, the Religious Freedom Restoration Act 1993, the National Historic Preservation Act 1966 and other legal provisions. See also CERD, 'Reports Submitted by States Parties under art 9 of the Convention – Seventh to Ninth Periodic Reports of States Parties due in 2011 – United States of America' (2013) UN Doc CERD/C/USA/7-9 [168–169]. <https://tbinternet.ohchr.org/_layouts/15/treatybodyexternal/Download.aspx?symbolno=CERD/C/USA/7-9&Lang=en> accessed February 2025.

are limited in their power and apply restrictive approaches which were developed before the general recognition of the scope of Indigenous rights as outlined by the UNDRIP.[49] Restrictive interpretations of the UNDRIP such as those outlined by the US government in CERD submissions can allow judicial decisions that disregard or fail to respect Indigenous cultural rights.[50] This can be contrasted, in 2025, with the positions of the Canadian government after passing domestic legislation to implement the UNDRIP into law.[51] The US policy stipulated that such declarations as UNDRIP are not binding, and are merely used as 'a guide to interpret[ing] the State Party's obligations under the Convention relating to [I]ndigenous [P]eoples'.[52] In part, this may be a reflection of measures the United States government has adopted to limit direct legal enforcement of international treaties. Such limitations, for instance under the Treaty Clause of the US Constitution, may work to insulate policies with discriminatory effects from the obligations of Conventions and other instruments adopted to build protection of and respect for Indigenous rights.[53] Specifically, such policies may not necessarily be deemed illegal or in violation of the definition of 'racial discrimination' applied in US courts, since their effects can fall in the category of 'disparate impact discrimination'.[54] This may enable policies and judicial interpretations by US courts that fall short of the UNDRIP's full expression of rights and *obligations to be considered valid and reasonable in the circumstances.*[55] The requirement to adopt national legislation, like the Canadian government sought to do through the *UNDRIP Act* in Canada, is typically necessary to implement these treaties domestically.[56]

Responses from the United States government that show support for Indigenous rights and cultural heritage are likely to continue to allow *de facto* discrimination to pervade the US legal and political system so long as Congress or state legislatures fail to implement UNDRIP rights into domestic

49 CERD, ibid.

50 *Lyng v Northwest Indian Cemetery Protective Association* [1988] 485 US 439; *Navajo Nation v United States Forest Service* [2008] 535 F.3d 1058 (9th Cir); *Rayellen Resources, Inc. v New Mexico Cultural Properties Review Committee* [2014] No. 33497 (N.M. Sup. Ct.).

51 United Nations Declaration on the Rights of Indigenous Peoples Act 2021 (UNDRIP Act), as outlined in Chapter 2.

52 NIYC (n 43) 13.

53 See also, on the right to cultural integrity, Hohmann (n 4).

54 NIYC (n 43) 16.

55 See also Martin Scheinin and Mattias Åhrén, 'Relationship to Human Rights, and Related International Instruments' in Hohmann and Weller (n 4).

56 NIYC (n 43) 13.

law.[57] Refusing to accept the UNDRIP even as 'guidelines' might, some suggest, enable the United States government to categorize groups as 'Indian' or 'Indigenous' and argue that they fall under the protection and benefits of their domestic rights.[58] This issue in a sense is mitigated through the UNDRIP, which does not define the term 'Indigenous [P]eoples' but instead creates the framework for protecting both individual and collective rights.[59] This empowers substantive rights holders and keepers of cultural heritage to navigate and express identity on their own terms.[60] Specifically, regarding cultural heritage in this respect, Article 9 recognizes that 'Indigenous [P]eoples and individuals have the right to belong to an [I]ndigenous community or nation, in accordance with the traditions and customs of the community or nation concerned. No discrimination of any kind may arise from the exercise of that right'.[61] This recognizes that authority for defining a given community or Nation lies with Indigenous Peoples themselves, essentially a self-identification right. In such contexts, implementing the UNDRIP, specifically Article 9, could come into direct conflict with the US practice of unilateral Tribal 'recognition'.

Additionally, in relation to American Indian treaty law, there is added ambiguity as to whether religious and cultural claims were surrendered when the Indigenous individuals were required to cede land claims, and whether residual forms of property may affirm the existence of religious and cultural rights that are so often quashed.[62] It may be possible to leverage this form of affirming Indigenous cultural rights in the absence of US acceptance of the relevance of UNDRIP. For example, in the case of *Minnesota v Mille Lacs Band of Chippewa Indians*, the Court upheld the usufructuary treaty rights of Minnesota Indians in relation to land use outside of their ceded treaty area.[63]

[57] See also Scheinin and Åhrén (n 55).

[58] For example, there have been ongoing efforts to recognize Native Hawaiians as Indigenous since they are not part of Indian 'Tribes'. This exclusion is in part to limit funding opportunities of that group, an effort that began with the Indian Reorganization Act 1934 with subsequent statues limiting the benefits of individuals living in Indian Country who are not part of 'recognized' Indian Tribes. James W Zion, 'Time for a New Paradigm for American Indian Policy and Law?' in Jeffrey Ian Ross (ed), *American Indians at Risk* (2nd edn, Bloomsbury 2014) 665; NIYC (n 43) 4.

[59] UNDRIP (n 11).

[60] For further reading, see Shin Imai and Kathryn Gunn, 'Indigenous Belonging: A Commentary on Membership and Identity in the United Nations Declaration on the Rights of Indigenous Peoples – Articles 9, 33, 35 and 36' in Hohmann and Weller (n 4).

[61] UNDRIP (n 11) art 9.

[62] For further reading, see also Xanthaki (n 4).

[63] *Minnesota v Mille Lacs Band of Chippewa Indians* [1999] 526 US 172; See also Michael R Newhouse, 'Recognizing and Preserving Native American Treaty Usufructs in the Supreme Court: the Mille Lacs Case' (2000) 21 Public Land & Resources Law Review 169.

Modern-day ramifications of how such treaty rights are preserved do raise other questions about the efficacy of this treaty's implementation. Nonetheless, these legal tools can potentially affirm Article 12 of the UNDRIP, recognizing and supporting the right to cultural property that can help rights-holders 'maintain, protect, and have access in privacy to their religious and cultural areas'.[64]

At present, while concerns persist that the American perception of 'property' prevails over the rights bestowed through Tribal and international treaties[65] and statutory power for unilateral recognition of US Tribes discriminates against Indigenous rights and their sovereignty over cultural heritage, there remains also optimism for efforts to continue affirming the inherent Indigenous rights that must be respected in UNDRIP and through domestic law going forward.[66]

7.3.2 *Canadian Modern Treaties and Constitutional Interpretations for Cultural Heritage*

Presently in Canada, treaty obligations outline many of the prevailing methods for affirming cultural heritage.[67] Though many of these treaties were negotiated prior to the codification and Canadian ratification of the UNDRIP, many of the clauses pertaining to the rights of Indigenous Peoples in the context of the modern treaties can nonetheless be seen as UNDRIP-enabling and also crucial to efforts to advance the SDGs, due to the alignment between the desired outcomes from the treaty, principles reflected in the UNDRIP, and targets under various SDGs.

Regarding cultural heritage, in modern treaties the Canadian government and Indigenous signatories have agreed to important commitments to preserve Indigenous self-determination and protection for cultural practices and TK expression.[68]

Examples of modern treaties taking these steps toward cultural heritage protection can be found throughout the myriad agreements negotiated before 2025. Though each agreement takes on its own approach depending on the interests and situations of the negotiating Parties, the underlying representation of cultural protection, determination, and dissemination for well-being

64 UNDRIP (n 11) art 12. See also Xanthaki (n 4).
65 NIYC (n 43) 12.
66 UNDRIP (n 11) art 37(1), preamble [7]. For further reading, see also Barelli (n 16).
67 Modern and historic treaties can be challenging constructs to analyse, as discussed in Chapter 3.
68 See ibid for a brief introduction of modern treaties and the legal and historical developments that necessitated these legal instruments.

and sustainable development is a common thread between each of the treaties. The stipulated obligations range from tourism, park and environmental management, and the expression and revitalization of artistic culture.

For example, in the James Bay and Northern Quebec Agreement (JBNQA), which was signed in 1975 by the Grand Council of the Crees (of Quebec), the Parties reference 'artistic culture' throughout the agreement. Not only is JBNQA considered the first 'modern' treaty, but in the accord, the Parties also recognize specific territorial and cultural rights for the Cree and Inuit signatories to preserve their independence, to include them in the region's economic development, and to protect traditional harvesting activities.[69] Specifically, the agreement, amongst a variety of other innovations, created obligations for art, culture, and traditional ways of life to be respected and uplifted through the treaty's implementation. For example, section 11(6) of the Kativik Act stipulates that municipal corporations must '[a]ssist in the undertaking and furtherance, in the municipality and elsewhere, of works of charity, education, scientific, *artistic or literary culture*, youth training, and generally of any social welfare enterprise of the population'.[70]

Similarly, in the Tsawwassen First Nation Final Agreement (TFNA) signed by the Tsawwassen First Nation, the Government of Canada, and the Government of British Columbia in 2007, the Parties adopted numerous provisions related to cultural heritage, including language, tangible cultural heritage, and cultural industries. These include chapter 14 of the Agreement, which gives the Tsawwassen Government the right to make laws respecting 'the preservation, promotion and development of the culture of Tsawwassen First Nation and the Hun'qum'i'num language';[71] it also addresses archaeological sites, artifacts, and heritage resources on Tsawwassen Lands.[72]

Further, in the Kluane First Nation Final Agreement (KFNA), signed in 2003 between the Kluane First Nation and the Governments of Canada and the Yukon,[73] the Parties created a new standard for Indigenous rights and title related to land management and co-governance. The KFNA stipulated the

69 James Bay and Northern Québec Agreement and Complementary Agreements (Cree Nation of Eeyou Istchee–Inuit of Nunavik–Government of Canada–Government of Quebec–Hydro-Quebec) (adopted 11 November 1975) (JBNQA).

70 'Act respecting certain municipalities and the Regional Government of Northern Québec' 1987 (Kativik Act) s 11(6) (emphasis added).

71 Tsawwassen First Nation Final Agreement (Tsawwassen First Nation–Government of Canada–Government of British Columbia) (adopted 6 December 2007) ch 14: Culture and Heritage art 2(a) (TFNA).

72 ibid arts 2(b)–(d).

73 Kluane First Nation Final Agreement (Kluane First Nation–Government of Canada–Government of the Yukon) (adopted 18 October 2003) (KFNA).

designation of Special Management Areas to preserve and protect natural resources and associated areas of *environmental and cultural* significance.[74] A direct outcome of this arrangement is the Kluane National Park and Reserve.[75] Though established in 1943 for gaming, this park (mentioned earlier in this volume) is managed under the joint responsibility of Kluane First Nation, the Champagne and Aishihik First Nations, which are Party to the Champagne and Aishihik First Nations Final Agreement of 1992,[76] and Parks Canada, the government agency responsible for managing national parks and historic sites across the country. Enabling, or perhaps more accurately *re-enabling* this connection to the land with the First Nations, who have a vast knowledge of the ways of life in this territory, allows collaborative priority-setting for the resources and environments located in the national park.[77] Not only does it foster the principles behind the UNDRIP and other international conventions on amplifying Indigenous stewardship for cultures and environments, the arrangements also advance efforts to achieve SDG 15: Life on Land.[78] This may support and affirm both the tangible and intangible forms of cultural heritage as discussed in Section 7.1. However, the KFNA is one example of an agreement that remains vulnerable to outside interests pursuing activities in the absence of free, prior, and informed consent, should the UNDRIP not be fully implemented in Canada.[79] The KFNA appears to only bind the Government of Yukon or any other entity deemed an 'authority' by virtue of legislation to consult with the Kluane: there is concern that absent an explicit provision for a First Nation to put a stop to development under the terms of the KFNA, the agreement only requires that consultation occurs and complies with the outlined procedures.[80] Many might argue that it is even more important that UNDRIP principles be fully and rapidly respected in contexts like these, ensuring that consent from the Indigenous Party is recognized as necessary prior to undertaking activities, in order to respect Indigenous rights.

[74] ibid ch 10: Special Management Areas.

[75] For further reading on the evolution of Canada's relationship with its Indigenous, see Jeremy Patzer, 'Indigenous Rights and the Legal Politics of Canadian Coloniality: What Is Happening to Free, Prior and Informed Consent in Canada?' in Short and others (n 4).

[76] Champagne and Aishihik First Nations Final Agreement (Champagne and Aishihik First Nations–Government of Canada–Government of the Yukon) (adopted 19 June 1992).

[77] Patzer (n 75).

[78] UN General Assembly Res 70/1, 'Transforming Our World: The 2030 Agenda for Sustainable Development' (21 October 2015) UN Doc A/RES/70/1SDG 15.

[79] For more on the slow progress of UNDRIP realization in Canada, see T Mitchell and C Enns, 'The UN Declaration on the Rights of Indigenous Peoples: Monitoring and Realising Indigenous Rights in Canada' (2014).

[80] KFNA (n 73) ch 7: Expropriation.

In the context of modern treaties, the underlying collective and inherent sovereignty and rights held by Indigenous Peoples, as reaffirmed in the UNDRIP,[81] are not dependent on explicit grants from the British nor Canadian legislatures.[82] Although these treaties codify specific rights, like the territorial and cultural rights that the JBNQA outlines,[83] as the Supreme Court of Canada has found, these rights also pre-existed the colonial domain.[84] Indigenous Nations maintain, that Indigenous rights were not transferred or surrendered by treaty, whether modern or historical, nor through clear legislative acts,[85] despite important efforts of government representatives. Indigenous Nations maintain, despite important efforts of government representatives. For example, in Treaty 4, one of the numbered treaties that spanned the now provinces of western Manitoba and southeastern Alberta, many historians argue that government negotiators sought to ensure that the Cree and Saulteaux Tribes had ceded, released, surrendered, and yielded up all their rights, titles, and privileges to certain lands.[86]

However, Indigenous Parties to the treaty do not agree with government interpretation, stating that from their point of view, there was never an intention to surrender sovereignty or jurisdiction.[87] Similar challenges have been advanced with regard to the interpretation and negotiation of repugnant clauses in other historic treaties. In Treaty 6, First Nations Parties have argued that their representatives were placed under duress to sign an agreement ceding their rights, including through threats of starvation largely stemming from disappearance of the buffalo due to settlement and increasing non-Indigenous, often illegal, encroachments.[88] Similarly,

[81] UNDRIP (n 11) art 37(1), preamble [7].

[82] *Delgamuukw v British Columbia* [1997] 3 SCR 1010 (SCC) [133], where the SCC recognized that s 35(1) of the Constitution Act 1982 did not create Aboriginal rights; instead, it accorded constitutional status to those inherent rights that were already 'existing' in 1982. See also *Mitchell v MNR* [2001] 1 SCR 911 (SCC) [9–11].

[83] JBNQA (n 69).

[84] *Delgamuukw* (n 82).

[85] Siku Allooloo and others, 'Treaty Relations as a Method of Resolving IP and Cultural Heritage Issues' (University of Victoria and Intellectual Property Issues in Cultural Heritage, 2014) 11 <www.sfu.ca/ipinch/sites/default/files/resources/reports/treatyrelations_finalreport_2014.pdf> accessed 6 February 2025. For further reading, see also L Cameron, D Courchene, S Ijaz and I Mauro, 'The Turtle Lodge: Sustainable Self-Determination in Practice' (2019) 15(1) AlterNative: An International Journal of Indigenous Peoples 13.

[86] Treaty No 4 (Cree and Saulteaux Tribes of Indians at the Qu'appelle and Fort Ellice–Her Majesty the Queen) (adopted 15 September 1874). See also Cameron and others (n 85).

[87] Allooloo and others (n 85). For further reading, see also Dominic O'Sullivan, *Sharing the Sovereign: Indigenous Peoples, Recognition, Treaties and the State* (Palgrave Macmillan 2021).

[88] 'Letters from Charlie N. Bell to Morris, from the Laird Papers' (National Archives of Canada, 1874). For further reading, see Matthew LM Fletcher, 'The Insidious Colonialism of the

in Treaty 11, First Nations and other experts argue, government representatives made false promises and forced symbolic elections of chiefs to fulfil the minimum technical requirements of treaty negotiation, likely motivated by interest in exploiting oil-rich Mackenzie District, and expanding Canadian territory.[89] This type of interpretational dispute could have been mitigated. In New Zealand, for instance, the Treaty of Waitangi was drafted as a dual treaty – it was drafted and signed in both English and Māori, with both versions fixed forever as texts of equal import for the interpretation of this treaty.[90]

Considering histories of misinterpretation, flawed negotiations, and duress during negotiations, it can be persuasively argued that Indigenous Peoples in Canada have collective arrangements and cultural heritage, including language, routines, and ceremonies of each Nation that exist regardless of historic and numbered treaties.[91] These inherent rights thus also exist in the context of modern treaties, which reinforce arguments that Indigenous Peoples have an inherent right to reserve and regulate their holistic heritages, knowledge systems, and languages in Canada.[92] Canadian federal, provincial, and territorial governments are, from this perspective, obligated to implement the rights and obligations, all of which have been further affirmed through constitutional interpretation.[93] If an infringement of these rights is necessary or desired, then Indigenous Peoples are further entitled to free, prior informed consent and to compensation.[94]

The UNDRIP is additionally helpful in the interpretation, and guiding the implementation, of treaty obligations to explain the extent of Indigenous Peoples' constitutional rights particularly given the recognition, in the seventh

Conqueror: The Federal Government in Modern Tribal Affairs' (2005) 19 Washington University Journal of Law and Policy.

89 René Fumoleau and Arctic Institute of North America, *As Long as This Land Shall Last: A History of Treaty 8 and Treaty 11, 1870–1939* (University of Calgary Press 2004) 265–269.

90 Alan K Melby, Arle Lommel, and Lucía Morales Vàzquez, 'Bitext' in Chan Sin-Wai (ed), *Routledge Encyclopedia of Translation Technology* (Routledge 2015) 409. For more information about the Treaty of Waitangi and about the use of treaty for advancing Māori while fostering sustainable development, see Chapter 11.

91 For further reading, see John Borrows, *Braiding Legal Orders* (McGill-Queen's University Press 2023).

92 Erica-Irene Daes, 'Protection of the Heritage of Indigenous People: Final Report of the Special Rapporteur of the Commission on Human Rights' (United Nations, 1995) UN Doc E/CN.4/Sub.2/26 12.

93 *R. v Marshall* [1999] 3 SCR 456 (SCC) [45–48]; *R. v Bernard* [2005] 2 SCR 220 (SCC) [38–39]; others like *Delgamuukw* (n 82) and *Mitchell* (n 82).

94 *R. v Sparrow* [1990] 1 SCR 1075 (SCC) [1109–1120].

preambular paragraph, of 'inherent' and pre-existing rights,[95] which many recognize reflects global consensus that Indigenous Peoples are the bearers of inherent and inalienable human rights.[96] Specifically, Articles 11, 12, 13, and 31 are vital for affirming the protection of cultural heritage in the context of modern treaties in Canada. They clearly outline that Indigenous Peoples have the right to 'practice and revitalize ... cultural traditions and customs';[97] to 'manifest, practice, develop and teach their spiritual and religious traditions, customs and ceremonies';[98] to 'revitalize, use, develop and transmit to future generations their histories, languages, oral traditions, philosophies, writing systems and literatures';[99] and to 'maintain, control, protect and develop their cultural heritage, Tradititonal Knowledge and traditional cultural expressions'.[100]

Furthermore, per International Human Rights lawyer, advocate, and educator James Sákéj Youngblood Henderson, cultural heritage protection can be augmented for Indigenous rights-holders and artists by establishing 'protective legislation that gives intellectual property-style[101] protection to Indigenous heritage, knowledge systems, and cultural expressions'.[102] Such protections may constitute a minimum first step, including (as argued in previous chapters) the need for the Canadian intellectual property regime to explicitly 'protect and promote Indigenous [P]eoples' knowledge and cultural and artistic expressions'.[103] As Henderson explains, this can be accomplished with a non-derogation clause, which acts as a 'shield' to protect and affirm

95 UNDRIP (n 11) preamble [7].

96 Samuel Moyn, *The Last Utopia: Human Rights in History* (Harvard University Press 2012). For the link between human rights and intellectual property rights, see Laurence R Helfer, 'Toward a Human Rights Framework for Intellectual Property' (2007) 40 UC Davis Law Review 975.

97 UNDRIP (n 11) art 11.

98 ibid art 12.

99 ibid art 13.

100 ibid art 14.

101 For more on the need to protect Indigenous TK, see Chapter 5. Additionally, it is also important to recognize that the use of the western intellectual property rights regime requires TK to conform to intellectual property's western standards and protocols, while disclosing knowledge that is privileged and sacred to the communities that have been the stewards of this knowledge for millennia. TK additionally is held communally, rather than by one individual person or legal entity. This is an additional component that would need to be remedied between the two legal orders. Aman K Gebru, 'International Intellectual Property Law and the Protection of Traditional Knowledge: From Cultural Conservation to Knowledge Codification' (2015) 15 Asper Review of International Business and Trade Law 298, 312–16.

102 James Sákéj Youngblood Henderson, 'The Indigenous Domain and Intellectual Property Rights' (2021) 4(2) Lakehead Law Journal 113.

103 ibid.

Indigenous rights in the framework of Canadian constitutional law, and might for instance underline that:

> For greater certainty, nothing in this Act shall be construed to abrogate, derogate, or infringe from any existing aboriginal or treaty rights of the Aboriginal [P]eoples of Canada under section 35 of the Constitution Act, 1982, but it shall be construed to protect and promote these constitutional rights.[104]

This form of a clause to protect cultural heritage could be further augmented based on the outcomes of various international pushes for protecting Indigenous TK, as explained earlier in this volume. Proponents of intellectual property-style protections for TK had recommended inclusion of such a clause in a formal treaty at the World Intellectual Property Organization (WIPO) on intellectual property and genetic resources, TK, and traditional cultural expressions.[105] As noted above, such protections were eventually adopted in the context of the 'Diplomatic Conference to Conclude an International Legal Instrument relating to Intellectual Property, Genetic Resources and Traditional Knowledge Associated with Genetic Resources', held at WIPO headquarters from 13 to 24 May 2024.[106] Such international treaty-style affirmations of Indigenous plant heritage as part of Indigenous Peoples' intellectual property could support the vital step of implementing these rights within Canada's legislative framework. As experts argue, Canada needs such a strategy and federal legislation to protect Indigenous Peoples' heritage and knowledge systems.[107] Canadian public domains, from this perspective, should not continue to be used as a universal way of justifying the appropriation or denial of Indigenous Peoples' knowledge and cultural rights,[108] especially in the face of the treaty obligations that explicitly stipulate the need

[104] ibid.

[105] Wend Wendland, 'Is an International Agreement on IP, Genetic Resources and Associated Traditional Knowledge Finally in Sight?' (WIPO Magazine, 2023) <www.wipo.int/wipo_magazine_digital/en/2023/article_0003.html> accessed 6 February 2025; and mandatory disclosure requirements in WIPO, 'Decisions of the Thirty-Fourth Session of the Committee' (WIPO, 2017) art 3 <www.wipo.int/edocs/mdocs/tk/en/wipo_grtkf_ic_34/wipo_grtkf_ic_34_decisions.pdf> accessed 6 February 2025.

[106] WIPO Treaty on Intellectual Property, Genetic Resources and Associated Traditional Knowledge, adopted on 24 May <www.wipo.int/edocs/mdocs/tk/en/gratk_dc/gratk_dc_7.pdf> accessed 21 February 2025; for more details on this treaty, see María Vásquez Callo-Müller, Diego F Ortega Sanabria, and Alejandro Matsuno Remigio, 'The WIPO Treaty on Intellectual Property, Genetic Resources and Associated Traditional Knowledge: Situating a Landmark Development in International Intellectual Property Governance' (2024) 73(12) GRUR International 1128.

[107] For further reading, see also Tobias Stoll, 'Intellectual Property and Technologies – Article 31' in Hohmann and Weller (n 4).

[108] Youngblood Henderson (n 102) 113–114.

to advance and amplify the practice and revitalization of Indigenous cultural practices and knowledge.[109]

While inherent rights that are accorded to Indigenous Peoples in Canada, coupled with the provisions within modern treaties, serve as strong foundations for enabling the implementation of the UNDRIP, there remain key gaps in legislation and issues with modern treaty implementation that still frustrate components of protecting cultural heritage through these legal tools.

7.4 TOURISM, CULTURAL HERITAGE, AND TRADE TREATIES

In the Indigenous trade chapters described earlier in this volume, cultural heritage and the potential for cultural industries are recognized as integral to Indigenous economic aspirations. For example, the Parties to the Canada-Ukraine Free Trade Agreement state that 'trade is fundamental to Indigenous histories, identities, cultural heritage, and economic prosperity' (Article 25.1 (3)), while the United Kingdom-New Zealand FTA highlights the 'significance of the Haka Ka Mate to Ngāti Toa Rangatira, and as an integral part of its history, culture, and identity' (Article 26.6(1)). Similarly, in Article X.1(g) of the EU-New Zealand FTA, honey and oil derived from the Mānuka tree are described as culturally important to Māori traditional medicine.[110]

For its part the Arrangement on Indigenous Peoples Economic and Trade Cooperation (IPETCA) likewise encourages cross-border measures that preserve cultural heritage and expression, though IPETCA is an arrangement and

[109] Additionally, art 4 of the TFNA states: 'For the purposes of subclause 2.a, the culture of Tsawwassen First Nation includes its history, feasts, ceremonies, symbols, songs, dances, stories and traditional naming practices. For greater certainty, and in accordance with clause 22 of the General Provisions chapter, Tsawwassen Government does not have the power to make laws in respect of Intellectual Property or the official languages of Canada.' This is a clear example that the modern treaty seeks to provide greater protection for their cultural practices, especially in the face of increasing tourism and greater prevalence of appropriation of traditional cultures, however, they lack the power to protect such cultural heritage due to the limitations of their powers within the Canadian intellectual property regime, which is exclusively within the federal jurisdiction. TFNA (n 71).

[110] Canada-Ukraine Free Trade Agreement (signed 22 September 2023, Ottawa), ch 25 'Trade and Indigenous Peoples', entered into force on 1 July 2024, see *Canada-Ukraine Free Trade Agreement Implementation Act*, 2023, SC 2024, c 3 (royal assent March 19, 2024); Free Trade Agreement between New Zealand and the United Kingdom of Great Britain and Northern Ireland (signed 28 February 2022, entered into force 31 May 2023) ch 26; see also ibid, Side Letter on the Haka Ka Mate (Exchange of Letters between the Rt Hon Anne-Marie Trevelyan MP, Secretary of State for International Trade of the United Kingdom, and the Hon Damien O'Connor, Minister for Trade and Export Growth of New Zealand, 28 February 2022); Free Trade Agreement between the European Union and New Zealand (signed 9 July 2023, entered into force 1 May 2024) ch X.

not an agreement. First, participating economies underscore that under UNDRIP, the responsibility falls on States 'in conjunction with Indigenous peoples [. . .] to recognise and protect the exercise of Indigenous peoples' right to maintain, control, protect, and develop their cultural heritage, Traditional Knowledge, and traditional cultural expressions' (IPETCA s1(a)(xiii)). Second, they commit to 'explore options for implementing and supporting the right of Indigenous peoples to maintain, control, protect, and develop their cultural heritage, Traditional Knowledge, and traditional cultural expressions' (IPETCA 7(c)) and to 'share information, experiences, and approaches' designed to protect against misuse and misappropriation' (IPETCA 7(d)).[111] Accordingly, the text of this Indigenous trade chapter, together with IPETCA, signal a willingness to undertake to respect and facilitate Indigenous control over their heritage, including how heritage is marketed or otherwise shared internationally, and how to protect forms of Indigenous heritage from misappropriation.

7.5 CONCLUSION

As countries strive to implement the UNDRIP and advance the SDGs, the importance of protecting tangible and intangible forms of Indigenous Peoples' cultural heritage remains vital, not just for survival, but also as a crucial corollary of recognizing and advancing the inherent rights of Indigenous Peoples globally. The interconnected nature of cultural and environmental heritage, especially in the age of climate change and sustainable development, serves as a reminder that Indigenous rights and treaty obligations are necessary to achieve equitable and just transitions for not only the Indigenous stewards of lands and waters, but also for all others who are responsible for fulfilling treaty obligations that help enable the protection of cultural heritage of communities around the world. The onus is on all countries, as well as domestic legislative bodies, to advance the rights to cultural heritage that have been recognized in the UNDRIP and through other pieces of international, domestic, and regional agreements.

[111] Arrangement on Indigenous Peoples Economic and Trade Cooperation (IPETCA) (2022) <www.mfat.govt.nz/assets/Trade-agreements/Indigenous-Peoples-Economic-and-Trade-Cooperation-Arrangement/IPETCA-Final-Text.pdf> accessed 24 January 2025.

8

Extractive Industries, Sustainable Development, and Indigenous Treaty Law

8.1 INTRODUCTION

Globally, there has been a growing focus on the environmental and human rights impacts of growth and development of extractive industries, including coal, oil, and gas, but also metals and minerals of many types. Concurrently, the need for climate change mitigation places green technologies at the centre of many national decarbonization strategies and regulations, even as across several regions of the world, consumer preferences, popular concern, and other pressures on private industries drive transitions.[1] Many countries are turning to renewable energy, indeed as of 2019 95 per cent of Costa Rica's energy comes from renewable sources.[2] Legacy internal combustion engine vehicle manufacturers have, for instance, announced a shift to electric

[1] Jonathan Watts, 'Growing Number of Global Insurance Firms Divesting from Fossil Fuels' (*The Guardian*, 15 November 2017) <www.theguardian.com/environment/2017/nov/15/growing-number-of-global-insurance-firms-divesting-from-fossil-fuels> accessed 7 February 2025; Clare Church and Alec Crawford, 'Minerals and the Metals for the Energy Transition: Exploring the Conflict Implications for Mineral-Rich, Fragile States' in Manfred Hafner and Simone Tagliapietra (eds), *The Geopolitics of the Global Energy Transition*, vol 73 (Lecture Notes in Energy, Springer 2020). The authors are grateful to Dr Cecilia Campero for her insights and contributions to this chapter, building on her leading research in, for instance, Cecilia Campero, Nathan Andrews and Tracy Smith-Carrier, 'Mining, the Sustainable Development Goals and Impact Assessments: A Review of Governance and Local Impacts' (2024) 42(5) Impact Assessment and Project Appraisal 423.

[2] Sebastian Rodriguez, 'Despite Drought, Costa Rica's Electricity Stays Clean – But Not Cheap' (*Reuters*, 19 June 2019) <www.reuters.com/article/us-costa-rica-electricity-drought-analys/despite-drought-costa-ricas-electricity-stays-clean-but-not-cheap-idUSKCN1TK1VZ> accessed 7 February 2025.

vehicles.[3] According to Bloomberg, at the current rate, 50 per cent of the world's electricity will be made up of renewables like wind and solar by 2050.[4] However, in addition to continuing use of coal, oil, gas, and other extracted non-renewable resources like uranium in many countries, the growing demand for green technologies drives a corresponding demand for materials and minerals used in these technologies. The World Bank predicts that minerals needed for solar panels will increase by 300 per cent by 2050 to meet global 2°C warming targets, and minerals like cobalt, lithium, and rare earth metals face similar increases in demand.[5] Such booms in demand can, and already do, imply a corresponding cost. Many minerals necessary for decarbonization are found in areas stewarded by Indigenous Peoples and can thus impact communities.[6] Additionally, an increase in the use of renewables and clean energy sources does not mean that older energy production technology immediately grinds to a halt. The need to move away from oil, gas, and other non-renewable resources extraction remains a real concern for equitably managing the green transition.

3 This includes Volvo, stating that since 2019 all their vehicles contain an electric motor. Volvo, 'Electrification' (28 October 2023) <https://web.archive.org/web/20231028162309/https://group.volvocars.com/company/innovation/electrification> accessed 6 February 2024. Ford, too, has embraced mass adoption of EV technology, Ford Motor Company, 'Mass Production of New All-Electric Explorer Starts at Ford's EV Assembly Plant in Cologne' (4 June 2024) <https://media.ford.com/content/fordmedia/fna/us/en/news/2024/06/04/mass-production-of-new-all-electric-explorer-starts-at-fords-ev-.html> accessed 6 February 2025.

4 BloombergNEF, 'Electric Vehicle Outlook 2019' (Long-Term Electric Vehicle Outlook, Bloomberg Finance LP, 2019); BloombergNEF, 'New Energy Outlook 2019' (Bloomberg Finance LP, 2019).

5 John Richard Drexhage and others, 'The Growing Role of Minerals and Metals for a Low Carbon Future' (2017) World Bank Group Working Paper 117581 <http://documents.worldbank.org/curated/en/207371500386458722/The-Growing-Role-of-Minerals-and-Metals-for-a-Low-Carbon-Future> accessed 7 February 2025.

6 For further reading, see Stefania Errico, 'Control over Natural Resources and Protection of the Environment of Indigenous Territories – Articles 29, 30 and 32' in Jessie Hohmann and Marc Weller (eds), *The UN Declaration on the Rights of Indigenous Peoples: A Commentary* (Oxford University Press 2018); Claire Charters, 'Indigenous Peoples' Rights to Lands, Territories and Resources in the UN Declaration on the Rights of Indigenous Peoples – Articles 25, 26, 27 and 10' in Hohmann and Weller, ibid; Janeth Warden-Fernandez, 'Indigenous Communities Rights and Mineral Development' (2005) 23(4) Journal of Energy & Natural Resources Law 395; Jérémie Gilbert and Corinne Lennox, 'Towards New Development Paradigms: The United Nations Declaration on the Rights of Indigenous Peoples as a Tool to Support Self-Determined Development' in Damien Short, Corinne Lennox, Julian Burger and Jessie Hohmann (eds), *The United Nations Declaration on the Rights of Indigenous Peoples: A Contemporary Evaluation* (Routledge 2021); Mauro Barelli, 'Development Projects and Indigenous Peoples' Lands' in Damien Short and Corinne Lennox (eds), *Handbook of Indigenous Peoples' Rights* (Routledge 2016); Lindsay Borrows, *Otter's Journey through Indigenous Language and Law* (UBC Press 2018).

Given the long history of tense, indeed often confrontational and antagonistic relationships between Indigenous Peoples and resource extraction industries, identifying meaningful and robust solutions which uphold Indigenous rights is even more crucial.[7]

This chapter explores the complex relationship between extractive industries, sustainable development, and Indigenous treaty law, with an emphasis throughout on how this relationship impacts the current green transition. First, the chapter examines the international law guidance available for extractive industries; this includes analysing frameworks and principles that promote responsible and sustainable practices in resource extraction while considering the social, economic, and environmental dimensions. Second, the analysis shifts to carbon-intensive forms of resource extraction, notably coal, oil, and natural gas, which have had significant impacts on Indigenous communities. The focus is on the importance of meaningful consultation, consent, or the right to withhold it, and fair benefit-sharing in alignment with Indigenous treaty rights; especially frameworks and concepts from the United Nations Declaration on the Rights of Indigenous Peoples (UNDRIP) such as free, prior, and informed consent (FPIC). Third, this chapter examines two core drivers behind the need for FPIC in the twentieth and twenty-first centuries – oil and gas extraction – highlighting a Canadian example of the need for consent and more in these extractive industries that have been so pervasive on many Indigenous lands. Lastly, this chapter explores the mining sector's implications for sustainable development, considering social, economic, and environmental aspects and emphasizing the role of Indigenous treaty law in ensuring responsible practices, equitable resource distribution, and the protection of Indigenous rights and lands. Overall, this chapter emphasizes the need for a balanced approach that respects Indigenous rights, integrates Indigenous perspectives and recognizes non-consent, while also promoting sustainable practices to collaboratively achieve Sustainable Development Goals.

8.2 IMPACTS OF EXTRACTIVE INDUSTRIES AND INDIGENOUS RIGHTS

Extractive industries such as those exploiting coal, oil, gas, and minerals including uranium and other radioactive ores have often proven to be devastating to ecosystems, cultures, and livelihoods on Indigenous

[7] ibid; See also, for instance, Clinton N Westman and Tara L Joly, 'Oil Sands Extraction in Alberta, Canada: A Review of Impacts and Processes Concerning Indigenous Peoples' (2019) 47 Human Ecology 233.

territories.[8] Experts describe the impacts as amplifying the effects of colonization through forced urbanization, territorial displacement and worse.[9] Due to these impacts, many Indigenous Peoples have been continuously fighting for rights to land and resources, voicing clear opposition to activities that degrade natural resources, the environment, and sovereignty.[10] Through legal and political developments such as recognition of Aboriginal title, comprehensive land claims, or modern treaties in countries like Canada, Indigenous Peoples' ability to assert authority and stewardship over resource management and extraction on their ancestral territories may be strengthened.[11] Where ancestral territories are not recognized or are contested by the State, including in key areas of the Americas and Australia, Indigenous Peoples and many allies have sought other political and decision-making strategies to resolve resource use and extraction conflicts that impact ecosystems, well-being, and ways of life.[12]

Indigenous Peoples have made progress through these conflicts to enable institutional spaces for protecting and advancing territorial

[8] ibid; See also, for instance, Leah S Horowitz and others, 'Indigenous Peoples' Relationships to Large-Scale Mining in Post/Colonial Contexts: Toward Multidisciplinary Comparative Perspectives' (2018) 5 The Extractive Industries and Society 404 <www.sciencedirect.com/science/article/abs/pii/S2214790X1830039X> accessed 7 February 2025.

[9] ibid; See also, for instance, Debra M Stokes, Bruce G Marshall, and Marcello M Veiga, 'Indigenous Participation in Resource Developments: Is It a Choice?' (2019) 6 The Extractive Industries and Society 50 <www.sciencedirect.com/science/article/abs/pii/S2214790X18301576> accessed 7 February 2025; Arn Keeling and John Sandlos, 'Introduction: Critical Perspectives on Extractive Industries in Northern Canada' (2016) 3 The Extractive Industries and Society 265 <www.sciencedirect.com/science/article/abs/pii/S2214790X15001392> accessed 7 February 2025.

[10] ibid; See also, for instance, Michael J Dockry, 'Indigenous Rights and Empowerment in Natural Resource Management and Decision Making as a Driver of Change in US Forestry' (2020) Gen Tech Rep NRS-P-197: Drivers of change in US forests and forestry over the next 20 years 76 <www.fs.usda.gov/nrs/pubs/gtr/gtr-nrs-p-197papers/08-dockry-gtr_nrs-p-197.pdf> accessed 7 February 2025.

[11] John Borrows, *Recovering Canada: The Resurgence of Indigenous Law* (University of Toronto Press 2017); Rauna Kuokkanen, 'At the Intersection of Arctic Indigenous Governance and Extractive Industries: A Survey of Three Cases' (2019) 6 The Extractive Industries and Society 15 <www.sciencedirect.com/science/article/abs/pii/S2214790X18301345> accessed 7 February 2025.

[12] Kirsten Maclean, Catherine J Robinson, and David C Natcher, 'Consensus Building or Constructive Conflict? Aboriginal Discursive Strategies to Enhance Participation in Natural Resource Management in Australia and Canada' (2015) 28 Society and Natural Resources 197 <www.tandfonline.com/doi/abs/10.1080/08941920.2014.928396> accessed 7 February 2025. For further reading, see also Dominic O'Sullivan, *Sharing the Sovereign: Indigenous Peoples, Recognition, Treaties and the State* (Palgrave Macmillan 2021); Valerie J Phillips, 'Parallel Worlds: A Sideways Approach to Promoting Indigenous-Nonindigenous Trade and Sustainable Development' (2006) 14 Michigan State Journal of International Law 521; Errico (n 6).

rights.[13] For the past several decades, it is possible to trace certain (hard won) advances in Indigenous voices in tackling the impacts of resources extraction in the United States. For example, as experts noted in 2020, Indigenous Peoples may increasingly have 'the potential to influence major environmental issues like climate change, fossil fuel extraction and transport, timber harvesting, and water management.'[14] It can be argued that this is due in part to increasing assertion of sovereign Indigenous rights in the US constitutional framework, which encompasses original jurisdiction over lands, cultures, and communities.[15] It may also reflect increasing global recognition of Indigenous sovereignty and culture by national governments, courts, and broader societies.[16] Significant elements of this recognition may be reflected in existing treaty obligations between governments and Indigenous Peoples.[17]

However, such advances are not reflected uniformly for all Indigenous Peoples, nor are all States equally engaged. Many Indigenous groups continue to resist energy and mineral extraction projects that proceed without consent, including through the courts, as well as protests and barricades.[18] As Prof James Anaya, the former United Nations Special Rapporteur on the Rights of Indigenous Peoples, recognized in his 2015 report, Indigenous Peoples have a right to oppose extractive industry activities in their territories.[19] Yet, in many areas around the globe, Indigenous stewardship and authority over territories –

[13] David C Natcher and Nicolas D Brunet, 'Extractive Resource Industries and Indigenous Community-Based Monitoring: Cooperation or Cooptation?' (2020) 7 The Extractive Industries and Society 1279 <www.sciencedirect.com/science/article/pii/S2214790X20302732> accessed 7 February 2025.

[14] Dockry (n 10) 77.

[15] Joanne Barker, 'For Whom Sovereignty Matters' in Joanne Barker (ed), *Sovereignty Matters* (University of Nebraska Press 2006); Kevin Bruyneel, *The Third Space of Sovereignty: The Postcolonial Politics of US–Indigenous Relations* (University of Minnesota Press 2007) 320.

[16] Dockry (n 10) 77.

[17] Affirmations of Indigenous rights have created various legal innovations globally. For example, the Māori of New Zealand successfully fought to have the Waitangi River declared as having the same rights as people based on the Treaty of Waitangi. For more information, see Chapter 11 in this volume. See also David E Wilkins and K Tsianina Lomawaima, *Uneven Ground: American Indian Sovereignty and Federal Law* (University of Oklahoma Press 2002) 336.

[18] For further reading, see Mauro Barelli, 'Free, Prior and Informed Consent in the United Nations Declaration on the Rights of Indigenous Peoples: Articles 10,19, 29(2) and 32(2)' in Jessie Hohmann and Marc Weller (eds), *The UN Declaration on the Rights of Indigenous Peoples* (Oxford University Press 2018); Matthew LM Fletcher, 'The Insidious Colonialism of the Conqueror: The Federal Government in Modern Tribal Affairs' (2005) 19 Washington University Journal of Law and Policy; Errico (n 6).

[19] S James Anaya, 'Report of the Special Rapporteur on the Rights of Indigenous Peoples on Extractive Industries and Indigenous Peoples' (2015) 32 Arizona Journal of International and Comparative Law 116 <https://scholar.law.colorado.edu/cgi/viewcontent.cgi?article=1033&

including to ensure sustainable use of natural resources as prioritized under SDG 12 on Sustainable Consumption and Production in target 12.2 to achieve the sustainable management and efficient use of natural resources by 2030 – remains disrupted due to mining, coal, petroleum, gas, and other extractive industries.[20] Resulting resurgences and disputes ultimately concern more than environmental impacts, raising questions about Indigenous sovereignty, stewardship and co-management rights, respect for cultural heritage, and opportunities for reconciliation or revitalization, as well as the longer-term interests of future generations.[21] This is especially crucial, considering that Anaya's report states that '[w]hile [I]ndigenous [P]eoples potentially have much to gain from resource development within their territories, they also face the highest risks to their health, economy and cultural identity from any associated environmental degradation'.[22] Indeed, as has been documented by the UN Special Rapporteur on Environmental Defenders under the Aarhus Convention and other experts, in some cases the defenders of Indigenous rights and territories have been forced to pay a terrible price for their resistance, leading to worldwide calls to 'defend the defenders' across justice, human rights, and sustainable development circles.[23]

context=faculty-articles> accessed 7 February 2025; International Covenant on Civil and Political Rights (adopted 16 December 1966, entered into force 23 March 1976) 999 UNTS 171 (ICCPR) arts 19, 22, 25.

20 Liam Downey, Eric Bonds, and Katherine, 'Natural Resource Extraction, Armed Violence, and Environmental Degradation' (2010) 23 Organization & Environment 417 <http://doi.org/10.1177/1086026610385903> accessed 7 February 2025; United Nations Economic and Social Council, 'Decrying Violence against Indigenous Rights Defenders, Speakers Urge Protection of Native Lands from Development Aggression, as Permanent Forum Continues' (HR/5388, United Nations 2018) <www.un.org/press/en/2018/hr5388.doc.htm> accessed 7 February 2025.

21 Dockry (n 10) 78.

22 United Nations Human Rights Council, 'Report of the Special Rapporteur on the Rights of Indigenous Peoples, James Anaya' (4 July 2014) UN Doc A/HRC/27/52/Add.2.

23 Marie-Claire Cordonier Segger, Thalsa-Thiziri Mekaouche, Zunaida Moosa-Wadiwala, Tejas Rao and Hugh Travis, 'Defending the Defenders: State Responsibilities to Respect Climate Justice, Rule of Law and Rights of Counsel in Climate Litigation Worldwide' in Ezio Costa Cordella and Pilar Moraga Sariego (eds), *State Responsibilities in the Climate Crisis: Legal Standards and Global Litigation* (Tirant Lo Blanch 2024); Micheal Forst, 'State Repression of Environmental Protest and Civil Disobedience: A Major Threat to Human Rights and Democracy' (UN Special Rapporteur on Environmental Defenders under the Aarhus Convention 2024) <https://unece.org/sites/default/files/2024-02/UNSR_EnvDefenders_Aarhus_Position_Paper_Civil_Disobedience_EN.pdf>. See also Sumudu Atapattu, 'Linking International Human Rights Law and Climate Change' in Marie-Claire Cordonier Segger and Christina Voigt (eds), *Routledge Handbook of Climate Law and Governance, Courage, Contributions and Compliance* (Routledge, 2024); Zunaida Moosa

8.3 INTERNATIONAL LAW GUIDANCE FOR EXTRACTIVES

The basis of Indigenous Peoples' rights in the context of natural resource extraction is largely centred around the legal nature and implementation of free prior and informed consent (FPIC).[24] FPIC is a human rights norm that is integral to Indigenous Peoples' rights and self-determination.[25] Specifically, as the UNDRIP stipulates in Article 19, States are required to 'consult and cooperate in good faith with the [I]ndigenous [P]eoples concerned through their own representative institutions in order to obtain their free, prior and informed consent before adopting and implementing legislative or administrative measures that may affect them.'[26] Additionally, as Article 32 of the UNDRIP recognizes, 'Indigenous [P]eoples have the right to determine and develop priorities and strategies for the development or use of their lands or territories and other resources'.[27] Further, according to UNDRIP, FPIC mandates good faith consultation and cooperation with Indigenous Peoples 'prior to the approval of any project affecting their lands or territories and other resources, particularly in connection with the development, utilization or exploitation of mineral, water or other resources.'[28]

Both substantive and procedural elements of FPIC, as defined by the UN Working Group on Indigenous Populations, may be crucial in the application of FPIC for resource extraction:

> ... the right of free, prior and informed consent is grounded in and is a function of [I]ndigenous [P]eoples' inherent and prior rights to *freely determine their political status, freely pursue their economic, social and cultural development and freely dispose of their natural wealth and resources* – a complex of inextricably related and inter-dependent rights encapsulated in the right to self-determination, to their lands, territories and resources, where applicable, from their treaty-based relationships, and their legitimate

Wadiwala, 'The Impact of Climate Change on Human Rights and the Legal Obligations of States to Protect Them – A Comparative Jurisdictional Analysis' (2023) 17 Carbon & Climate Law Review 123–135.

24 For further discussions on FPIC in this volume, please see Chapter 2, see also Barelli (n 18). See also Charters (n 6); Errico (n 6). See also United Nations Expert Mechanism on the Rights of Indigenous Peoples, Thirty-Ninth Session 10–28 September 2018, 'Free, Prior and Informed Consent: A Human Rights-Based Approach' (10 August 2018) A/HRC/39/62 (UNEMRIP).

25 UNEMRIP (n 24) paras 3–5.

26 United Nations Declaration on the Rights of Indigenous People (adopted 13 September 2007) (2007) 46 ILM 1013) (UNDRIP) art 19.

27 ibid art 32(1).

28 ibid art 32(2).

> authority to require that third parties enter into an equal and respectful relationships with them based on the principle of informed consent [sic]. Procedurally, free, prior and informed consent requires processes that allow and support meaningful and authoritative choices by [I]ndigenous [P]eoples about their development paths.[29]

As such, the right of FPIC is part of the State's duty to consult when Indigenous Peoples may be affected by any proposed resource extraction activities. Special Rapporteur Anaya, for instance, is of the opinion that the FPIC principle creates this obligation as a matter of customary international law.[30] It offers some protection to Indigenous Peoples' resource claims and lays the foundations for new resource management and stewardship governance models based on notions of shared sovereignty and partnership.[31]

However, despite the intention to protect and advance Indigenous rights, a nuanced analysis of the impacts of FPIC reveals that it does not have the same degree of intended impact implied by its textual ambitions.[32] Specifically, some argue that FPIC falters due to patchy and unsatisfactory implementation coupled with aspirational, but ambiguous, content.[33] While there has been wide endorsement of the UNDRIP, commentators also signal concern that FPIC alone cannot resolve 'a number of challenges related to resource extraction such as sovereignty over resources, access to justice, and local implementation'.[34] Although there may be a duty to consult, from this perspective, the scope and content of this duty remain unclear. Once an FPIC implementation regime has been put in place, several additional

[29] UNHRC, 'Expanded working paper offering guidelines to govern the practice of implementation of the principle of free, prior, and informed consent of indigenous peoples in relation to development affecting their lands and natural resources / submitted by Antoanella-Iulia Motoc and the Tebtebba Foundation' (14 July 2005) UN Doc E/CN.4/Sub.2/AC.4/2005/WP.1, para 56 (emphasis added).

[30] James Anaya, 'Indigenous Peoples' Participatory Rights in Relation to Decisions About Natural Resource Extraction: The More Fundamental Issue of What Rights Indigenous Peoples Have in Lands and Resources' (2005) 22 Arizona Journal of International and Comparative Law 7, 7.

[31] René Dussault and Georges Erasmus, *Report of the Royal Commission on Aboriginal Peoples*, vol 5 (Renewal: A Twenty-Year Commitment, Canada Communication Group 1996) 58–61.

[32] See generally Daria Shapovalova, 'Indigenous Rights and Resource Extraction: One Step Forward Two Steps Back' *Environmental Policy and Law* (Aberdeen, 7 December 2020) <https://environmentalpolicyandlaw.com/news-blog/indigenous-rights-and-resource-extraction-one-step-forward-two-steps-back> accessed 12 June 2022.

[33] Barelli (n 18); Martin Papillon and Thierry Rodon, 'Proponent-Indigenous Agreements and the Implementation of the Right to Free, Prior, and Informed Consent in Canada' (2017) 62 Environmental Impact Assessment Review 216.

[34] Shapovalova (n 32); see Chapter 7 for a discussion of a US government position on whether UNDRIP and FPIC is binding in US domestic law.

questions remain, including who is ultimately entitled to FPIC rights,[35] how consent is achieved and what said consent entails,[36] and how those affected can handle logistical issues such as constraints in time and funding.[37] Additional risks faced by the FPIC process include accountability for decision-making, vulnerabilities for manipulation, increased conflicts within and/or between Indigenous communities, and the potential to generate unrealistic expectations for benefits during the consent-seeking process.[38]

There also remains the question of whether Indigenous communities have the right to refuse consent and prevent State activity on their traditional lands. If so, what are the circumstances that would enable this refusal?[39] Without the ability to withhold consent, FPIC cannot guarantee Indigenous Peoples' right to self-determination, right to development, and right to protect their land, territories, and resources. From this perspective, FPIC thus constitutes a compromise on behalf of Indigenous Peoples; it falls short of fully challenging States' predominant claims of exclusive ownership over resources in Indigenous territories through doctrines such as *jura regalia*.[40] Additionally, some proponents of this perspective may argue, the International Labour Organization Convention No 169 (ILO 169) is the legally binding instrument that recognizes Indigenous Peoples' FPIC rights and is only applicable to the twenty-four countries that have ratified this treaty, leaving aside considerations of customary law or human rights.[41]

[35] Forest Stewardship Council, 'FSC Guidelines for the Implementation of the Right to Free, Prior, and Informed Consent (FPIC)' (Version 1, FSC International Center GmbH 2012) 7–8 <www.grassrootsjournals.org/assets/fls/FSC-GUI-30-003-V1-0-EN-FPIC.pdf> accessed 7 February 2025. See also Barelli (n 18); see also Elvira Pulitano, *Indigenous Rights in the Age of the UN Declaration* (Cambridge University Press 2012).

[36] Boreal Leadership Council, 'Free, Prior, and Informed Consent in Canada: A Summary of Key Issues, Lessons, and Case Studies Towards Practical Guidance for Developers and Aboriginal Communities' (2012) 9–10 <https://fpic.info/media/library/resources/free-prior-and-informed-consent-canada-summary-key/FPICReport-English-web.pdf> accessed 7 February 2025. See Barelli (n 18); for further reading, see also John Borrows, *Law's Indigenous Ethics* (University of Toronto Press 2019).

[37] Forest Stewardship Council (n 35) 45.

[38] ibid 15; Barelli (n 18); Fletcher (n 18).

[39] Anaya (n 30) 7.

[40] Cathal M Doyle, *Indigenous Peoples, Title to Territory, Rights and Resources* (Routledge 2017) 4.

[41] ILO, 'Ratifications of C169 – Indigenous and Tribal Peoples Convention, 1989 (No 169)' (NORMLEX) <https://normlex.ilo.org/dyn/nrmlx_en/f?p=NORMLEXPUB:11300:0::NO:11300:P11300_INSTRUMENT_ID:312314:NO> accessed 7 February 2025. See also Chapter 2, ILO 169 and UNDRIP for more information about the legally binding nature of ILO 169. For further reading, see Lee Swepston, 'Indigenous and Tribal Peoples' Culture and Work under the ILO' in Short and Lennox (n 6); Barelli (n 18).

Some authors suggest that FPIC can be, in the absence of positive State enforcement of the full extent of this right, upheld by corporate entities through their commitment to obtaining community consent for resource extraction.[42] However, others argue that though pursuing voluntary FPIC may align with commercial interests in certain scenarios, there remain other situations where FPIC can come at the expense of business values and profitability.[43] It is in these circumstances that robust and enforceable legal safeguards in international and domestic legal systems could be considered necessary to protect community rights; otherwise, these rights risk being 'granted or withdrawn at the behest of the company.'[44] While voluntary FPIC processes are indisputably desirable, maximizing the impact of FPIC as a right for resource governance and self-determination would require that State governments enforce the full application of FPIC criteria.

Based on this understanding of the powers and limitations of FPIC as a right, UNDRIP and FPIC, in their original construction, appear crucial to upholding Indigenous Peoples' rights against resource extraction industries. Yet, their success is ultimately reliant on their full and binding implementation within legal systems worldwide.

8.4 FPIC IN THE FACE OF OIL AND GAS EXTRACTION

As corporations in the oil and gas industry search for new resources globally, they find themselves frequently operating in Indigenous lands. For the most part, legal certainty is useful, and these industries seek to operate based on obtaining permissions through permits and licences, with resource rights secured from a national, sub-national, or non-Indigenous government in the form of leases and concessions.[45] In many of these situations, the oil and gas industry will conduct these activities in Indigenous Peoples' territories where there are known claims to land and resources, but the claims are either unresolved or contested by non-Indigenous counterparts.[46] Where activities

42 Lisa J Laplante and Suzanne A Spears, 'Out of the Conflict Zone: The Case for Community Consent Processes in the Extractive Sector' (2008) 11 Yale Human Rights and Development Law Journal 69.

43 Connie K Chan, 'Lisa J. Laplante & Suzanne A. Spears, *Out of the Conflict Zone: The Case for Community Consent Processes in the Extractive Sector*' (2008) 11 Yale Human Rights and Development Law Journal 117, 118.

44 ibid.

45 Ketil Fred Hansen and Nigel Bankes, 'Human Rights and Indigenous Peoples in the Arctic: What Are the Implications for the Oil and Gas Industry?' in Aslaug Mikkelsen and Oluf Langhelle (eds), *Arctic Oil and Gas: Sustainability at Risk?* (Routledge 2008) 293–294.

46 ibid 294.

occur on lands with recognized claims, such as in Alaska and many areas of northern Canada, the non-Indigenous governments will look to the settlement agreements which are found largely as modern treaties in Canada,[47] and legislation to identify the land and resource rights associated with the Indigenous claims. Such treaties and settlements define ownership based on the specific terms of the agreements, with some recognizing full ownership of oil and gas rights including sub-surface rights within all or parts of their traditional territories.[48] Should such types of claims exist, interested companies would negotiate with the Indigenous landowners for concessions or leases. Nonetheless, these companies may still need to coordinate between multiple owners and/or usufruct holders, who may or may not be Indigenous. However, if Indigenous Peoples only own surface rights, the industry generally needs to resolve access issues and negotiate Impact and Benefit Agreements (IBAs) or look to co-management structures and regulatory authorities on how power is shared between the Indigenous Peoples and the regional or national governments.[49]

Thus, operating on Indigenous lands creates complexities for resource extraction industries that directly impact the implementation of FPIC as a right. In this section, the ongoing importance of FPIC is examined following the oil and gas extraction booms of the twentieth and twenty-first centuries, even amid the green transition. Specifically, experiences in Canada are offered as an example to illustrate how oil and gas extraction affects the nature and necessity of FPIC.

Canada's potential crude oil reserve is the largest in the world; its natural gas exportation is second only to Russia's.[50] Canada has a long history of treaty-making with Indigenous Peoples, including modern treaties that seek to provide predictability for land and resources rights in roughly 40 per cent of Canada's land mass, including in areas that are rich in oil and gas reserves.[51] However, the Crown can contradict its treaty-making efforts by asserting its sovereignty to authorize extractive projects on Indigenous territories while

47 See Chapter 3 for further discussion of modern treaties.

48 Hansen and Bankes (n 45) 294. See also generally *supra* (n 6).

49 ibid.

50 Jerome Dean Davis, 'North American Oil and Natural Gas: Current Trends, Future Problems?' (2005) 60 International Journal 429.

51 Crown-Indigenous Relations and Northern Affairs Canada, 'Modern Treaties' (Government of Canada 2024) <https://perma.cc/8SEA-UD2D> accessed 7 February 2025; Rebecca Macias Gimenez, 'Book Review: To Share, Not Surrender: Indigenous and Settler Visions of Treaty Making in the Colonies of Vancouver Island and British Columbia, Peter Cook, Neil Vallance, John Sutton Lutz, Graham Brazier & Hamar Foster, eds. (Vancouver: UBC Press, 2021)' (2022) 59 ALR 1051, 1053.

denying Aboriginal title claims.[52] To better understand this contradiction, it is possible to consider the legal framework that guides jurisdiction over natural resources in Canada.

Canada as a federal State divides powers between the federal government, provincial governments, and territories as stipulated by the *Constitution Act, 1867*.[53] Section 109 of the *Constitution* gives provinces ownership and jurisdiction over the natural resources within their borders, including 'all lands, mines, minerals, and royalties',[54] and enables provinces to enact laws regarding the management, control, and exploitation of these natural resources.[55] The federal government retains authority over natural resources in portions of the three territories, the continental margin, national parks, and Indigenous reservations, along with regulatory power over international and interprovincial oil, gas, and electric utilities that are of public interest.[56] However, this delineation is complicated in cases of resource development on Indigenous lands.[57] Through section 91(24) of the *Constitution Act, 1867*, the federal government has responsibility for 'Indians and lands reserved for the Indians', for which land is held by the Crown for the use and benefit of the First Nations band.[58] This remains the case today, though modern treaty agreements have shifted the jurisdictional power for the land and resources encompassed by the agreement to the local Indigenous government.[59]

With respect to activities on Indigenous lands, section 35(1) of the *Constitution Act, 1982* affirms Aboriginal and treaty rights which are inherent, collective rights that are based on original Indigenous occupancy of the

52 Gimenez (n 51).

53 *Constitution Act, 1867* (UK), 30 & 31 Vict, c 3, reprinted in RSC 1985, App II, No 5; for further reading, see also John Borrows, 'Indigenous Legal Traditions in Canada' (2005) 19 Washington University Journal of Law and Policy 167; Jeremy Patzer, 'Indigenous Rights and the Legal Politics of Canadian Coloniality: What Is Happening to Free, Prior and Informed Consent in Canada?' in Short and others (n 6); see also Jane Dickson, 'The Indian Specific Claims Commission as a Mechanism of Transitional Justice in Canada' in Short and Lennox (n 6).

54 ibid s 109.

55 Laura Wright and Jerry P White, 'Developing Oil and Gas Resources On or Near Indigenous Lands in Canada: An Overview of Laws, Treaties, Regulations and Agreements' (2012) 3(2) The International Indigenous Policy Journal 1.

56 ibid.

57 See generally *supra* (n 6); *supra* (n 53).

58 *Constitution Act, 1867* s 91(24). For further reading, see Borrows (n 53); Patzer (n 53).

59 Marie-Claire Cordonier Segger, Wayne Garnons-Williams, and Eva Wu, 'Indigenous Treaties with Canada: Obstacles or Opportunities to Realizing the Sustainable Development Goals in Light of the United Nations Declaration on the Rights of Indigenous Peoples across Canada' (2023) 3(1) Inter Gentes <https://intergentes.com/wp-content/uploads/2023/09/indigenous-treaties-with-canada_ew-updates.pdf> accessed 6 February 2025.

land.[60] Furthermore, Aboriginal title, as confirmed by the Supreme Court of Canada decision *Calder et al v Attorney General of British Columbia*, is a legal right derived from traditional occupation and use of tribal lands.[61] It is a sui generis interest in land that differs from traditional common and civil law notions of property.[62] This interest in land was further clarified through *Delgamuukw v British Columbia*, which concluded that Aboriginal title is a collective interest that cannot be alienated, except to the Crown.[63] This reinforces the important notion that government considerations and accommodations of Indigenous interests 'must always be in accordance with the honour and good faith of the Crown.'[64]

Aboriginal title disputes may arise where there is no pre-existing treaty between the Indigenous Peoples and the British Crown, or where title may have been extinguished. In the post-*Calder* era after 1973, this has largely been remedied through the negotiation of modern treaties. Modern treaties give Indigenous communities jurisdiction over their traditional territories and guarantee that these communities can participate in decision-making related to these lands. These negotiated agreements are thus able to codify undefined rights for the Indigenous community, with these rights including title to land and additional treaty-specific rights.[65]

Scholars and jurists underline that the Crown has a legal duty to consult Indigenous groups when there is potential Crown conduct that could give rise to adverse impacts on a potential or established Aboriginal or treaty right.[66] Treaties, including modern treaties, do not negate this duty to consult. The duty applies to both federal and provincial governments, as decided in the rulings of *Haida Nation v British Columbia (Minister of Forests)* and *Taku River Tlingit First Nation v British Columbia (Project Assessment Director)*.[67] Further, the legal duty to consult requires the Crown to act honourably in its dealings with Indigenous Parties and establishes that the ultimate legal duty of

60 *Constitution Act*, 1982, being Schedule B to the *Canada Act 1982* (UK), 1982, c 11, s 35(1); for further reading, see Borrows (n 53); Patzer (n 53); generally *supra* (n 6) and (n 53).

61 *Calder et al v Attorney-General of British Columbia* [1973] SCR 313 at 328–329 [*Calder*].

62 ibid.

63 *Delgamuukw v British Columbia* [1997] 3 SCR 1010 at para 31.

64 ibid para 203.

65 Wright and White (n 55) 3.

66 Chris Sanderson, Keith Bergner, and Michelle Jones, 'The Crown's Duty to Consult Aboriginal Peoples: Towards an Understanding of the Source, Purpose, and Limits of the Duty' (2011–12) 49 Alberta Law Review 821.

67 *Haida Nation v British Columbia (Minister of Forests)*, 2004 SCC 73 (CAN) at paras 67, 77; *Taku River Tlingit First Nation v British Columbia (Project Assessment Director)*, 2004 SCC 74 (CAN).

consultation still rests with the Crown, even if consultations are delegated to third parties and industry project proponents.[68]

In addition to Aboriginal rights and title, legislation can impact the consideration of oil and gas development projects given the potential impacts for Indigenous Peoples.[69] The *Indian Oil and Gas Act, 1985* gave the then Department of Indian Affairs and Northern Development the power to regulate and manage the exploitation of oil and gas on 'land reserved for the Indians.'[70] Additionally, the *Indian Oil and Gas Regulations*, adopted in 1995 and amended in 2019, set procedures for those looking to develop oil and gas on land reserved for Aboriginal People.[71] These regulations provide for exploratory licences, permits, leases, royalties, drilling monitoring and regulation, surface rights, and other activities related to resource exploitation.[72] The *Framework Agreement on First Nation Land Management Act, 2022* which has over 200 signatories, encompasses over 100 Nations seeking to establish their own management codes to govern their lands, communities, and resources.[73] The *Canadian Environmental Assessment Act* adopted in 1992 further required an environmental assessment to determine the potential impact that the project may have on the environment and the inhabitants in the region before a federal authority authorized or carried out a project, though this legislation was repealed in 2019 and replaced with an *Impact Assessment Act*.[74] Finally, certain provinces, including British Columbia, have adopted policies and procedures for

[68] Guy Régimbald and Dwight Newman, *The Law of the Canadian Constitution* (2nd edn, LexisNexis Canada 2017) 145–146.

[69] For further reading, see Borrows (n 53); Patzer (n 53).

[70] *Indian Oil and Gas Act*, RSC 1985, c I-7, s 2; Indian Oil and Gas Canada, 'About IOGC' (Government of Canada, 2024) <https://perma.cc/KT4T-7KCM> accessed 7 February 2025.

[71] *Indian Oil and Gas Regulations*, SOR/2019-196.

[72] *Indian Oil and Gas Act* (n 70); Indian Oil and Gas Canada (n 70).

[73] *Framework Agreement on First Nation Land Management Act*, SC 2022, c 19, s 121; Land Advisory Board Resource Centre, 'Framework Agreement' <https://labrc.com/framework-agreement/> accessed 7 February 2025.

[74] *Canadian Environmental Assessment Act*, SC 2012, c 19, s 52; *Impact Assessment Act*, SC 2019, c 28, s 1. According to some civil society jurist, the 2019 rules are not necessarily stronger or more effective. See West Coast Environmental Law, 'Making the Grade: A Report Card on Canada's New Impact Assessment Act' (28 August 2019) <www.wcel.org/publication/making-grade-report-card-canadas-new-impact-assessment-act> accessed 7 February 2025. Under the new act, federal entities such as the National Energy Board can issue licenses and permits without an impact assessment, whereas under the old act, no federal bodies can bypass the impact assessment process. The new act can also limit public input into the assessment process.

consulting with Indigenous groups for land management and resource development on Crown land.[75]

Despite the legal obligations for consultation in Canada, the right to FPIC is still vitally important in securing the Indigenous right to self-determination.[76] Though the Canadian legal framework mandates environmental assessments and consultation before extraction, many scholars and Indigenous leaders argue that implementing the FPIC regime under a consent paradigm, rather than simply an intention to consult, remains necessary to uphold the right of self-determination for Indigenous Peoples and the integrity of the democratic process.[77] Some argue that local consent should be standard for all major natural resource development projects for four main reasons: '(1) the need to give due weight to local interests; (2) the need to apportion risk according to stake; (3) the need to give voice to local knowledge; and (4) the need to enhance legitimacy and acceptance of the resulting decision'.[78] Additionally, as leading scholars argue, 'governments can help corporations achieve the benefits of community acceptance [for resource extraction projects] and avoid the risks of community dissent by implementing FPIC regimes.'[79] This sentiment was backed by the Special Representative of the UN Secretary-General for Business and Human Rights who warned:

> Governments should not assume that they are helping business by failing to provide adequate guidance for, or regulation of, the human rights impacts of corporate activities. On the contrary, the less governments do, the more they increase reputational and other risks to business.[80]

If FPIC serves as an engagement and consultation model for development projects, from this perspective, the Crown's duty to consult may be more likely

[75] See Government of British Columbia, 'Ministry of Indigenous Relations and Reconciliation' (8 March 2024) <www2.gov.bc.ca/gov/content/governments/organizational-structure/ministries-organizations/ministries/indigenous-relations-reconciliation> accessed 7 February 2025.

[76] For further reading, see Borrows (n 53); Patzer (n 53).

[77] Grace Nosek, 'Re-imagining Indigenous Peoples' Role in Natural Resource Development Decision-Making: Implementing Free, Prior and Informed Consent in Canada through Indigenous Legal Traditions' (2017) 50 UBC Law Review 95, 131–135.

[78] Nicholas A Fromherz, 'From Consultation to Consent: Community Approval as a Prerequisite to Environmentally Significant Projects' (2013) 116 West Virginia Law Review 100, 145.

[79] Nosek (n 77) 138.

[80] UNHRC, 'Protect, Respect and Remedy: A Framework for Business and Human Rights: Report of the Special Representative of the Secretary-General on the Issue of Human Rights and Transnational Corporations and Other Business Enterprises, John Ruggie' (2008) UN Doc A/HRC/8/5, para 22.

to be respected, and there may also be less dissent and other downstream risks to the community and environment.[81]

As one illustrative example, according to scholars and Indigenous sources, in Northern Alberta Indigenous communities raised concerns over the oil sands (also known as 'tar sands') impacts on their health and environment, and these challenges intensified after revelations of toxic tailings water seepage from Imperial Oil Ltd's Kearl mining site.[82] As Chief Allan Adam of the Athabasca Chipewyan First Nation noted, for years, communities experienced elevated rates of cancer, autoimmune disease, skin irritations, and severe arthritis; the Indigenous Nation and others first called for a health study in 1992, and a federally funded study of Fort Chipewyan began to investigate such concerns in 2024.[83]

As another challenging experience, Talisman Energy's shale gas project, located on the West Moberly First Nations' traditional territories in north-eastern British Columbia, voluntarily incorporated FPIC principles after reviewing the risks and benefits associated with its adoption. They concluded that FPIC, despite its present 'soft law' status, will shift normative frameworks within corporate operations and gain legal force to bolster claims made by Indigenous communities. A review conducted for Talisman Energy concluded:

> [I]n the long-term, the benefits for oil and gas companies of obtaining community agreement based on FPIC principles, and thereby both supporting their social licence to operate and reducing legal and reputation risks, may outweigh the substantial challenges of securing consent.[84]

[81] For further reading, see Sullivan (n 12); Borrows (n 53); Patzer (n 53).

[82] Nathalie J Chalifour, 'Bringing Justice to Environmental Assessment: An Examination of the Kearl Oil Sands Joint Review Panel and the Health Concerns of the Community of Fort Chipewyan' (2010) 21 Journal of Environmental Law and Practice 33 at 35–36; Monique M Passelac-Ross and Karin Buss, 'Water Stewardship in the Lower Athabasca River: Is the Alberta Government Paying Attention to Aboriginal Rights to Water?' (2011) 2011 CanLIIDocs 622 (Canadian Institute of Resources Law Occasional Paper #35). See also for further reading, Christopher Nowlin, 'Indigenous Capitalism and Resource Development in an Age of Climate Change: A Timely Dance with the Devil?' (2020) 17(1) McGill Journal of Sustainable Development Law 73.

[83] Nia Williams, 'Canada to Fund Health Study on How Oil Sands Impact Indigenous Communities' (*Reuters*, 9 August 2024). In addition to rare human diseases, Fort Chippewyan residents also attribute wildlife mutations to oil sands industrial pollution flowing downstream through the Athabasca River.

[84] Amy K Lehr and Gare A Smith, 'Implementing a Corporate Free, Prior, and Informed Consent Policy: Benefits and Challenges' (Foley Hoag LLP, 2010) 8 <https://justice-project.org/wp-content/uploads/2017/07/foley-hoag-for-talisman.pdf> accessed 7 February 2025.

Certain scholars have also argued that obtaining consent, specifically FPIC, can safeguard community interests in a robust and localized manner to provide value, beyond purely monetary gains, for the long term, suggesting that:

> Non-renewable resources like oil and gas are not only exhaustible, but the income they produce is also subject to the volatility of world markets. Extractive industries are generally controlled by multi-national corporations that are more responsive to global forces than to local concerns.[85]

In the context of extractive industries like oil and gas, it seems clear in the Canadian realm that at the very least, FPIC implementation is imperative to protect and amplify community interests that are not only backed by treaty, but also grounded in, and may augment, existing domestic legal regimes. Indeed, given concerns about world market volatility as well as many countries' Nationally Determined Contributions and other decarbonization commitments under the Paris Agreement, even as Indigenous decision-makers gain increased access to information about the many social and environmental impacts of extractive technologies both locally and globally, companies and others may need to be increasingly prepared for exploration and development consent to be withheld, particularly for coal, oil, and gas extraction.[86]

8.4 MINING AND MINERALS IN THE AGE OF SUSTAINABLE DEVELOPMENT

The mining and minerals sector can present similar FPIC opportunities as those raised in other extractive industries, but during an era of sustainability transitions, as the demand for critical minerals such as lithium, cobalt, and rare earth metals has increased, careful regulation and respect for Indigenous rights may become even more important.[87] For much of contemporary history, experts argue, minerals such as gold were major drivers of colonial conquest

[85] Oran R Young and Níels Einarsson, 'A Human Development Agenda for the Arctic: Major Findings and Emerging Issues' in Níels Einarsson and others (eds), *Arctic Human Development Report* (Stefansson Arctic Institute 2004) 239.

[86] For further reading, see Marie-Claire Cordonier Segger and Christina Voigt (eds), *Routledge Handbook of Climate Law and Governance: Courage, Contributions and Compliance* (Routledge 2025); Sumudu Atapattu, *Human Rights Approaches to Climate Change Challenges and Opportunities* (Routledge 2018).

[87] Drexhage and others (n 5).

in relation to the invasion of Indigenous Peoples' lands.[88] Indeed, historians note, the lure of gold in particular was a documented factor in the decimation of the Taíno People of Hispaniola, Hernán Cortés' destruction of the Aztec Empire, and in the desecration of Tlingit territory during the Klondike gold rush.[89] Experts and leaders note that indigenous land rights continue to face terrible pressures, worldwide: though Indigenous Peoples claim customary rights to over half of our world's lands, some studies suggest that jurisdiction is only acknowledged with the legal rights to use or own – over just 18 per cent of said land.[90] Tensions that result from determining jurisdiction over mineral extraction on Indigenous territories present unique challenges for collaboration, cooperation, and consent. As one illustrative example, in Central Queensland, Australia, the Carmichael coal mine and rail project by Adani Mining Pty Ltd (Adani) has faced considerable legal and moral opposition from the Wangan and Jagalingou Family Council (W&J). As traditional owners, the W&J led an unsuccessful court challenge against the National Native Title Tribunal for authorizing the issuance of a mining lease despite their express rejection of an Indigenous Land Use Agreement relating to the mine. According to scholars and W&J, the mining lease is perceived as a form of dispossession authorized by Queensland State on the basis of false consent, with the coal extraction threatening local ecology and water resources.[91]

As noted earlier in this chapter, under ILO 169 Parties recognized that Indigenous Peoples have a right to participate in the use, management, and conservation of natural resources associated with their lands.[92] In most cases,

[88] Hamid Maskawati and Harlina Sitti, 'Implementation of Indigenous People Values in Environmentally Sustainable Development' (2018) 78 Journal of Law, Policy and Globalization 106; Errico (n 6); Warden-Fernandez (n 6).

[89] Irving Rouse, *The Tainos: Rise and Decline of the People Who Greeted Columbus* (Yale University Press 1992); Hugh Thomas, *Rivers of Gold: The Rise of the Spanish Empire, From Columbus to Magellan* (Random House 2003);Charles F Wilkinson, *Blood Struggle: The Rise of Modern Indian Nations* (Norton 2005).

[90] Ford Foundation, 'Natural Resources and Climate Change' <www.fordfoundation.org/work/challenging-inequality/natural-resources-and-climate-change/> accessed 7 February 2025.

[91] Stephen M Young, 'The Material Costs of Claiming International Human Rights: Australia, Adani and the Wangan and Jagalingou' (2020) 20(2) Melbourne Journal of International Law; Wangan & Jagalingou Family Council, '"Healing Country" Won't Happen While Adani Proceeds to Destroy Our Lands and Waters' (8 July 2021) <https://wanganjagalingou.com.au/healing-country-wont-happen-while-adani-proceeds-to-destroy-our-lands-and-waters/> accessed 28 February 2025; Wangan & Jagalingou Family Council, 'Fed Court Decision: Adani Leases Issued Despite Traditional Owners' Express Rejection' (25 August 2017) <https://wanganjagalingou.com.au/fed-court-decision-adani-leases-issued-despite-traditional-owners-express-rejection/> accessed 28 February 2025.

[92] It is key to note that though ILO 169 constitutes binding international law, only nineteen countries have ratified this treaty. It nonetheless serves as crucial guidance for how countries,

integral to this right is an environmental impact assessment, providing the necessary information for consultations and benefit-sharing negotiations between the industry, government, and Indigenous Peoples, and facilitating cooperation on environmental management and impact issues on Indigenous territories.[93] These assessments, along with FPIC and benefit-sharing agreements, are often identified as holding greater potential to safeguard Indigenous self-determination for social, cultural, and economic development against proposed extractive industry activities.[94] Such obligations are particularly important when proposed projects are deemed to threaten the physical or cultural survival of the Indigenous and local communities.[95] This could be because the proposed activities may impact natural resources *traditionally* used by these Indigenous Peoples or because extracting resources that are *not traditionally* used could impact other resources or areas of socio-cultural, spiritual, or ecological importance.[96]

Additionally, ILO 169 rights include the ability to participate in the benefits that arise from such activities whenever possible, including in situations where the State retains ownership or other rights associated with these resources.[97] This form of benefit-sharing results from the obligation to assess the social, spiritual, cultural, and environmental impacts of the proposed resource extraction project. It encompasses the good-faith consultation requirements imposed on the States involved in the respective projects.[98] Negotiating an impact benefit agreement (IBA) is an increasingly piloted method to ensure equitable

even those that have not ratified this treaty, should operate in relation to the clauses stipulated in its articles. For more information about ILO 169, refer to Chapter 2, ILO 169 and UNDRIP.

93 Pia Marchegiani, Elisa Morgera, and Louisa Parks, 'Indigenous Peoples' Rights to Natural Resources in Argentina: The Challenges of Impact Assessment, Consent and Fair and Equitable Benefit-Sharing in Cases of Lithium Mining' (2020) 24 The International Journal of Human Rights 224.

94 *Saramaka People v Suriname*, Preliminary Objections, Merits, Reparations, and Costs, Inter-American Court of Human Rights Series C No 172 (28 November 2007) paras 93–95; *Kaliña and Lokono Peoples v Suriname*, Merits, Reparations and Costs, Inter-American Court of Human Rights Series C No 309 (25 November 2015) para 124; Mattias Åhrén, *Indigenous Peoples' Status in the International Legal System* (Oxford University Press 2016) 93.

95 *Case of the Saramaka People v Suriname*, paras 122–123; Patrick Thornberry, *Indigenous Peoples and Human Rights* (Manchester University Press 2002) 282.

96 *Saramaka People v Suriname* (n 94) paras 155–158; Stefania Errico, 'The Controversial Issue of Natural Resources: Balancing States' Sovereignty with Indigenous Peoples' Rights' in Stephen Allen and Alexandra Xanthaki (eds), *Reflections on the UN Declaration on the Rights of Indigenous Peoples* (Hart 2011) 329–366.

97 Convention Concerning Indigenous and Tribal Peoples in Independent Countries (adopted 27 June 1989, entered into force 5 September 1991) (1989) 28 ILM 1382 (ILO 169) art 15.

98 ibid arts 5–6, 7(3), 7(4).

sharing of project costs and benefits.[99] Also known as community benefits agreements, benefit-sharing agreements, and impact and benefit agreements, IBAs are contracts between project proponents, governments, and communities that determine how Parties will mitigate the impacts of a proposed project and provide benefits respectively. These agreements can require the project proponents to provide monetary payments to the community and may include provisions for employment, training, infrastructure, and opportunities for local businesses.[100] These agreements can be used to share project benefits and obtain FPIC, though achieving the IBA's objectives and measuring its success remains highly dependent on the context and structure of the agreement.[101]

These forms of discussions and agreements in the context of environmental justice may be particularly important for minerals like lithium. Though it can be difficult to extract, lithium is at the forefront of discussions for transitioning away from fossil fuel-based economies due to its role in renewable energy technologies, such as being the core component in lithium-ion battery anodes for many electric cars.[102] In this context, lithium and other mineral extraction debates focus on whether the positive impact of low-carbon societies can be obtained while simultaneously ensuring accountability for Indigenous Peoples' rights and ecosystems.[103]

This dynamic is most evident in South America's 'Lithium Triangle', a cluster of salt planes located high in the Andes spanning parts of Argentina, Bolivia, and Chile which is estimated to hold more than half of the world's lithium reserves, largely underneath Indigenous lands.[104] Since 2016, Argentina has become the fastest-growing provider of lithium.[105]

99 Maggie Cascadden, Thomas Gunton, and Murray Rutherford, 'Best Practices for Impact Benefit Agreements' (2021) 70 Resources Policy 1, 1.

100 Energy and Mines Ministers' Conference, *Good Practices in Community Engagement and Readiness: Compendium of Case Studies from Canada's Minerals and Metals Sector* (Natural Resources Canada 2014).

101 Jennifer Loutit, Jacqueline Mandelbaum, and Sam Szoke-Burke, 'Emerging Practices in Community Development Agreements' (2016) 7 Journal of Sustainable Development Law and Policy 64.

102 Drexhage and others (n 5).

103 For further reading, see Errico (n 6); Warden-Fernandez (n 6).

104 The Economist, 'A Battle for Supremacy in the Lithium Triangle' *The Economist* (London, 17 June 2017) <www.economist.com/the-americas/2017/06/15/a-battle-for-supremacy-in-the-lithium-triangle> accessed 7 February 2025; Alexander Villegas and Ernest Scheyder, 'Chile Plans to Nationalize Its Vast Lithium Industry' (*Thomas Reuters*, 21 April 2023) <www.reuters.com/markets/commodities/chiles-boric-announces-plan-nationalize-lithium-industry-2023-04-21/> accessed 7 February 2025; Errico (n 6); Warden-Fernandez (n 6).

105 Pía Marchegiani, Jasmin Höglund Hellgren, and Leandro Gómez, 'Lithium Extraction in Argentina: A Case Study on the Social and Environmental Impacts' (Fundación Ambiente y

The government spurred the growth of Argentina's mining sector by removing export taxes on mined minerals and by creating public companies.[106] Though lithium mining operations can produce jobs and benefits for the region's inhabitants, many Indigenous communities have expressed concerns about the risks and ultimate benefits that they receive, especially given the large influence of foreign companies in joint ventures.[107] For example, beneath the ancestral lands of the Atacama is the world's largest reserve of lithium, estimated to contain 9.3 million tons.[108] One company involved, Minera Exar, a joint venture between Ganfeng Lithium Co. Ltd., a Chinese company, and Lithium Argentina (whose stake was formerly held by Lithium Americas Corp., a Canadian company), has made agreements with six Indigenous communities to extract US$250 million in resources each year, promising annual benefit payments of US$9,000 to US$60,000 per community in return. However, local community leaders have raised concerns that these payments are not being received in full, with some Indigenous leaders arguing that 'lithium companies are taking millions of dollars from our lands … they ought to give something back. But they're not.'[109] Additional concerns are raised by communities and allies in these regions as lithium extraction, which pumps soluble lithium from underground reserves up to surface level for mineral precipitation, creates the potential for pollution, and risks increasing water shortages in an area that is already one of the world's driest deserts.[110]

Recursos Naturales, 2018) <https://goodelectronics.org/wp-content/uploads/sites/3/2019/05/DOC_LITHIUM_ENGLISH.pdf> accessed 7 February 2025. See also Errico (n 6); Warden-Fernandez (n 6).

[106] Marchegiani, Morgera, and Parks (n 93) 228.

[107] For further reading, see Errico (n 6); Warden-Fernandez (n 6).

[108] Patricia I Vásquez, 'All Eyes on Chile amid Global Scramble for Lithium' (*Wilson Center*, 7 April 2023) <www.wilsoncenter.org/blog-post/all-eyes-chile-amid-global-scramble-lithium> accessed 7 February 2025.

[109] Minera Exar was originally a Canadian-Chilean joint venture between Sociedad Química y Minera de Chile S.A. (SQM) and Lithium Americas Corp. Samar Ahmad, 'The Lithium Triangle: Where Chile, Argentina, and Bolivia Meet' (2020) 41 Harvard International Review 51, 52. In 2019, the purchase of SQM's stake by a Chinese investor, Ganfeng Lithium Co. Ltd. through its Netherlands subsidiary, Ganfeng Lithium Netherlands Co., B.V., was announced: Ganfeng Lithium Co. Ltd., 'Acquisition of Equity Interest in Minera Exar' (Hong Kong Stock Exchange, 1 April 2019) 4 <www1.hkexnews.hk/listedco/listconews/sehk/2019/0401/ltn201904013100.pdf> accessed 7 February, 2025. Today, the project is between Ganfeng Lithium Co. Ltd. (46.7 per cent), Lithium Argentina (44.8 per cent) and Jujuy Energia y Mineria Sociedad del Estado (8.5 per cent): Lithium Argentina, 'Our Projects: Cauchari-Olaroz' <https://lithium-argentina.com/our-projects/cauchari-olaroz/default.aspx> accessed 7 February 2025.

[110] Gonzalo Gajardo and Stella Redón, 'Andean Hypersaline Lakes in the Atacama Desert, Northern Chile: Between Lithium Exploitation and Unique Biodiversity Conservation' (2019) 1(9) Conservation Science and Practice 1.

Furthermore, in Argentina, the lack of formal processes for negotiation between Indigenous communities and mining companies often complicates the beginning stages of the natural resources value chain,[111] which includes obtaining consent from the affected communities. These mining operations have been underway since 1997 and are ramping up to meet global demand.[112] Even when negotiations proceed smoothly and consent is obtained, community leaders still do not feel that the result adequately compensates the communities for the extraction of these valuable resources.[113] For example, a study by Professors Pia Marchegiani, Elisa Morgera, and Louisa Parks looked at two lithium mining projects that began in 2015: the Minera Exar project discussed above and another, named Sales de Jujuy. These projects are located on the traditional territories of ten Indigenous Atacama communities.[114] These communities, located 4,300 metres above sea level, were reliant on a fragile, closed water basin. The possibility of having this exhaustible and limited supply contaminated by mining activities would drastically impact the communities' ability to live in the area and pursue their traditional activities. However, studies note, the communities are also in need of employment and basic services, which makes investments in the area attractive to them, despite the possible social and environmental damage.[115] One study of three communities impacted by the two projects revealed concerns over whether the mining companies properly obtained FPIC, even with the communities holding communal land title.[116] Concerns expressed included that mining companies used lengthy reports and highly technical language during meetings to convey assessment findings and answer questions from community members, that relevant information was not made available to communities early enough before assemblies for proper consideration, and all the information provided was from company sources, with limited third-party sources that could provide alternative opinions.[117] In addition, according to community leaders, State agencies were not always present to facilitate the dialogue between companies and communities to

[111] The natural resource value chain, in the context of this chapter, is the entire life cycle of resource extraction, which begins with the decision to extract natural resources, from the decision to extract natural resources, the contracts governing the terms of extraction, the production itself, and the revenue generated by extraction and spent by governments.

[112] Marchegiani, Morgera, and Parks (n 93) 228.

[113] Ahmad (n 109) 52.

[114] Marchegiani, Morgera, and Parks (n 93); Marchegiani, Hellgren, and Gómez (n 105).

[115] Miguel Ángel Marazuela and others, 'Hydrodynamics of Salt Flat Basins: The Salar de Atacama Example' (2019) 651 Science of the Total Environment 668.

[116] For further reading, see also Errico (n 6); Warden-Fernandez (n 6).

[117] ibid.

ensure fairness and impartiality throughout the proceedings, and once the community provided initial consent for the project, they felt the company personnel greatly decreased their presence and availability for community members to continue engaging in the consultation process.[118] These factors among others appear to fall short of the community-level research necessitated by obligations under ILO 169, which includes: the reliability, accessibility, and framing of information; the need for continuous, good-faith dialogue on FPIC and benefit-sharing; and engaging the State as an actor in the consultation process. According to the community and other civil society leaders, challenges with domestic laws on environmental impact assessments, FPIC, and benefit-sharing were also difficult in this regard.[119]

Tactics employed by mining companies to obtain consent may reveal unbalances in community-industry relationships even when efforts may be made to respect environmental impact assessments, FPIC, and benefit-sharing obligations. Companies do have significant sway over defining the communities that fall within the scope of consultation, how those consultations proceed, and the result of the consultation. As experts have noted, '[e]ven when communities proactively set the terms for engagement through community protocols, companies may prefer other routes . . .'[120] Challenging experiences underscore the importance of ensuring robust and detailed domestic rules that adhere to FPIC rights and standards set by ILO 169 and UNDRIP principles, if only to ensure that 'substandard practices by private companies can be effectively monitored, identified as unlawful, and feasibly challenged within the domestic legal system.'[121] Experiences such as those documented in Argentina suggest that detailed provisions are crucial to capture the priorities, worldviews, and consent of Indigenous Peoples for all projects, including 'green transition' mining project development. Creating opportunities to exercise control and to share in the benefits of these projects may be necessary if FPIC is to be obtained for community well-being, especially in the era of green transitions where minerals and resources remain vital for securing low-carbon societies.

8.5 CONCLUSION

As many have noted, the ability to live in a healthy and sustainable society should not be a right reserved for select individuals within today's globalized

[118] ibid.
[119] Marchegiani, Morgera, and Parks (n 93) 228–231.
[120] ibid 235.
[121] ibid.

economies. The patterns of exploitation linked to extraction of traditional coal, oil, gas, mineral, and metals resources has revealed many flaws in public policy and law, leading to conflicts. Extraction of new resources necessary for green infrastructure and clean energy transitions requires new and accountable approaches which respect the rights of the local communities and Indigenous Peoples whose lands may be impacted. As demonstrated throughout this chapter, prioritizing mechanisms for FPIC is vital in the international and domestic legal regimes that safeguard Indigenous Peoples' rights to self-determination. Many of the treaties, laws, and doctrines that make this possible reveal shortcomings in the implementation of legal requirements on all levels. Nonetheless, such legal instruments are required and can be improved, if founded upon the right to healthy environments, the right to self-determination, and the right to participate in more sustainable development. It is thus critical for companies and States to jointly participate and fully engage with these requirements for a just and sustainable clean energy transition.

PART IV

Indigenous Treaty Implementation for Sustainable Development in Key Countries

9

Treaty Rights throughout History in Canada

9.1 INTRODUCTION

As the United Nations Special Rapporteur on the Rights of Indigenous Peoples has noted: 'Canada consistently ranks near the top among countries concerning human development standards, and yet amidst this wealth and prosperity, Aboriginal People live in conditions akin to those in countries that rank much lower and in which poverty abounds.'[1] Scholars highlight historical and current governance, social, economic, and environmental failures including legacies of colonization, legal and systemic discrimination, destruction of territories and livelihoods, and other pressures leading to intergenerational trauma, disadvantage and lower well-being for Indigenous Peoples in Canada compared to the broader Canadian population.[2] The Report of Canada's Truth and Reconciliation Commission (TRC) provides roadmaps for advancing reconciliation through listening and urgent and ambitious

[1] James Anaya, 'Statement upon Conclusion of the Visit to Canada by the United Nations Special Rapporteur on the Rights of Indigenous Peoples' (OHCHR, 15 October 2013) <www.ohchr.org/en/statements/2013/10/statement-upon-conclusion-visit-canada-united-nations-special-rapporteur-rights> accessed 7 February 2025.

[2] See, eg, Lisa Monchalin, *The Colonial Problem: An Indigenous Perspective on Crime and Injustice in Canada* (University of Toronto Press 2016); Michelle Good, *Truth Telling: Seven Conversations about Indigenous Life in Canada* (HarperCollins 2023); Deborah McGregor, 'Mino-Mnaamodzawin: Achieving Indigenous Environmental Justice in Canada' (2018) 9(1) Environment and Society; Jeremy Patzer, 'Indigenous Rights and the Legal Politics of Canadian Coloniality: What Is Happening to Free, Prior and Informed Consent in Canada?' in Damien Short, Corinne Lennox, Julian Burger, and Jessie Hohmann (eds), *The United Nations Declaration on the Rights of Indigenous Peoples: A Contemporary Evaluation* (Routledge 2021).

implementation of the TRC Calls to Action, as required to realize the rights of Indigenous Peoples across Canada.[3] This would also help advance Sustainable Development Goal (SDG) target 10.2, to empower and promote the social, economic, and political inclusion of all.

Additionally, Indigenous Peoples are stewards of knowledge and landscapes crucial for climate resilience and biodiversity protection.[4] Many Indigenous communities also harbour immense economic potential that can transform business and trade both for the Nations and communities themselves, as well as for the country and global economies working with these Indigenous economies.[5] Sustainable development, particularly United Nations (UN) SDG 15 on promoting and restoring sustainable use of terrestrial ecosystems,[6] SDG target 17.10 on equitable trade, and SDG 17.16 on multi-stakeholder partnerships, requires Indigenous participation and reconciliation for past and present harms.[7] As such, achieving the SDGs

[3] TRC, *Final Report of the Truth and Reconciliation Commission of Canada: Volume One: Summary: Honouring the Truth, Reconciling for the Future* (Truth and Reconciliation Commission of Canada 2015). More generally, see John Borrows, Larry Chartrand, Oonagh E Fitzgerald, and Risa Schwartz, *Braiding Legal Orders: Implementing the United Nations Declaration on the Rights of Indigenous Peoples* (McGill-Queen's University Press 2023); John Borrows, *Canada's Indigenous Constitution* (University of Toronto Press 2010).

[4] UN Environment Programme (Convention on Biological Diversity), 'Kunming-Montreal Global Biodiversity Framework' (19 December 2022) UN Doc CBD/COP/DEC/15/4; Deborah McGregor, 'Living Well with the Earth' in Damien Short and Corinne Lennox (eds), *Handbook of Indigenous Peoples' Rights* (Routledge 2016); Adriana Giunta, 'Looking Back to Move Forward: The Status of Environmental Rights under the UN Declaration on the Rights of Indigenous Peoples' in Short and others (n 2).

[5] See Chapter 4, see also Jérémie Gilbert and Corinne Lennox, 'Towards New Development Paradigms: The United Nations Declaration on the Rights of Indigenous Peoples as a Tool to Support Self-Determined Development' in Short and others (n 2); John Borrows and Risa Schwartz, *Indigenous Peoples and International Trade – Building Equitable Inclusive International Trade and Investment Agreements* (Cambridge University Press 2020); Mauro Barelli, 'Development Projects and Indigenous Peoples' Lands' in Short and Lennox (n 4).

[6] United Nations General Assembly, 'Transforming Our World: The 2030 Agenda for Sustainable Development' (21 October 2015) UN Doc A/RES/70/1.

[7] See Elena Pribytkova, 'Global Obligations for Sustainable Development: Harmonizing the 2030 Agenda for Sustainable Development and International Human Rights Law' (2020) 41 University of Pennsylvania Journal of International Law 1031; Matthew F Jaksa, 'Putting the Sustainable Back in Sustainable Development: Recognising and Enforcing Indigenous Property Rights as a Pathway to Global Environmental Sustainability' (2006) 21 Journal of Environmental Law and Litigation 157.

and the UN Declaration on the Rights of Indigenous Peoples (UNDRIP)[8] is firmly a joint endeavour.[9]

This chapter examines historical and legal factors that have led to the current treatment of Indigenous Peoples; through a case study of Indigenous rights in the context of Canada's treaties and policies with Indigenous Peoples. Subsequently, the focus in this chapter shifts to engaging with current advancements for the rights of Indigenous People and the enforcement of those rights with the implementation of the law; namely, through the domestic implementation of the UNDRIP and instruments such as the *UNDRIP Act* in Canada. Overall, this examination provides a baseline to understanding next steps on Canada's path to achieving reconciliation and, subsequently, sustainable development, in partnership with Indigenous Peoples. Finally, this chapter turns to examine the modern effects in Indigenous trade in relation to Canada.

9.2 INDIGENOUS PEOPLES WITHIN THE DOMINION OF CANADA FRAMEWORK

To create a foundation for understanding how reconciliation and sustainable development can occur in Canada, it is first necessary to consider Indigenous legal traditions, and the historic policies governing Indigenous rights in Canada that brought the country to its current relationship with Indigenous Peoples.[10] Prior to Canada becoming an independent country, historians and elders note, Indigenous Peoples, including the First Nations, Métis, and Inuit living in the region that became Canada, agreed varying historical treaties and trade arrangements with colonial settlers and the Crown.[11] Indigenous

[8] United Nations General Assembly, '*United Nations Declaration on the Rights of Indigenous Peoples*' (2 October 2007) UN Doc A/RES/61/295.

[9] Hamid Maskawati and Harlina Sitti, 'Implementation of Indigenous People Values in Environmentally Sustainable Development' (2018) 78 Journal of Law, Policy and Globalization 106; Mandy Li-Ming Yap and Krushil Watene, 'The Sustainable Development Goals (SDGs) and Indigenous Peoples: Another Missed Opportunity?' (2019) 20 Journal of Human Development and Capabilities 451.

[10] For further reading see, eg, John Borrows, 'Indigenous Legal Traditions in Canada' (2005) 19 Washington University Journal of Law and Policy 167; John Borrows, *Recovering Canada: The Resurgence of Indigenous Law* (University of Toronto Press 2002); Sébastien Grammond, *The Reception of Indigenous Legal Systems in Canada* (Routledge 2009); Richard Stacey, 'The Dilemma of Indigenous Self-Government in Canada: Indigenous Rights and Canadian Federalism' (2018) 46(4) Federal Law Review 669–688.

[11] ibid; TRC (n 3); see also Borrows and others (n 3), John Borrows, 'Ground-Rules: Indigenous Treaties in Canada and New Zealand' (2006) 22 New Zealand Universities Law Review 188; Dominic O'Sullivan, *Sharing the Sovereign: Indigenous Peoples, Recognition, Treaties and the*

Peoples, it is noted, were integral to British and French success in establishing themselves in the new world, even in light of effects created through colonial measures like *terra nullius* and the Doctrine of Discovery.[12] Colonial transformation intensified in the 1860s, which turned Indigenous Peoples from partners in establishing successful colonies to Peoples that needed to be removed from the Canadian vision.

In the 1866 drafting of the *British-North America Bill*, proponents sought to raise the colonies up, in colonial classification terms, to the status of Dominion within the British Empire and once passed in the House of Parliament as the *British-North America Act*, this became the Canadian Constitution.[13] The drafters classified 'Indians and lands reserved for Indians' as being the jurisdictional responsibility of the federal government.[14] Thereafter since 1867, when the colonies of what is now Canada were consolidated as a Dominion subject to British Crown, the government characterized Indigenous Peoples, whose territories it had seized, as wards under the Crown and in 1876 subjected Indigenous People to the Indian Act.[15]

State (Palgrave Macmillan 2021); Angelique Eaglewoman, 'Indigenous Historic Trade in the Western Hemisphere' in Borrows and Schwartz (n 5) 43.

[12] First found in the decision written by Chief Justice Marshall in the 1823 US Supreme Court case of *Johnson v McIntosh*. In this case, Chief Justice Marshall proposes the legal notion of the Doctrine of Discovery, *Johnson v McIntosh* [1823] 21 US 543. The doctrine is then applied in the leading 1887 Supreme Court of Canada case of *St. Catherines Milling and Lumber Co. v R* [1887] 13 SCR 577. In short, according to experts, the 'Doctrine of Discovery' was a factual fraud upon a legal fiction upon an international misapplication, see Lindsay G Robertson, *Conquest by Law: How the Discovery of America Dispossessed Indigenous Peoples of Their Lands* (Oxford University Press 2007); Jennifer Reid, 'The Doctrine of Discovery and Canadian Law' (2010) 30(2) The Canadian Journal of Native Studies 335–359.

[13] See the private and official papers of the fourth Earl of Carnarvon, who was Secretary of State for the Colonies from 1866 to 1867, at the National Archives, 'The Discovery Service' (*The National Archives*, 12 August 2009) <https://discovery.nationalarchives.gov.uk/details/c/F257356> accessed 7 February 2025; TRC (n 3); see generally Borrows and others (n 3); Borrows, 'Indigenous Legal Traditions in Canada' (n 10); Borrows, *Recovering Canada* (n 10); Grammond (n 10); Stacey (n 10).

[14] Constitution Act 1867 s 91 (24) (CAN); TRC (n 3); see generally Borrows and others (n 3); Borrows, 'Indigenous Legal Traditions in Canada' (n 10); Borrows, *Recovering Canada* (n 10); Grammond (n 10); Stacey (n 10).

[15] TRC (n 3); see generally Borrows and others (n 3); Borrows, 'Indigenous Legal Traditions in Canada' (n 10); Borrows, *Recovering Canada* (n 10); Grammond (n 10); Stacey (n 10). This contrasts to events in the United States, where in the 1830s the US Supreme Court determined that American Tribes were 'domestic dependent Nations' who hold a form of sovereignty in relation to the US states, with said sovereignty being outside the confines of the US Constitution, see *Cherokee Nation v Georgia* [1831] 30 US 1; *Worcester v Georgia* [1832] 31 US 515 which was recently affirmed in *McGirt v Oklahoma* [2020] 591 US. For further reading see Roxanne Dunbar-Ortiz, *An Indigenous Peoples' History of the United States* (Beacon Press 2014); Alice Nash, 'Indigenous Peoples' in *The Routledge Handbook to the*

Until the 1950s the Canadian federal government, through the *Indian Act* did not allow Indigenous individuals or Nations to take legal action in court for recognition of their sovereignty over provincial governments.[16] However, Indigenous Nations and Tribes persisted, and in landmark 1985 and 1990 cases, courts found that for outstanding issues regarding Canada's treaty obligations, the rules of Indigenous interpretation of treaties must be applied.[17] When there is ambiguity, the decision must fall in favour of an Indigenous interpretation.[18] Further, for ambiguous treaty clause interpretation, the decision must provide a large and liberal interpretation in favour of Indigenous People.[19] Despite these rulings, for much of the subsequent history of Canada, the exercise of the Crown's fiduciary duty to protect Indigenous economic interests remained underimplemented, with hardly any engagement for trade or international affairs that reach beyond colonial borders.[20] In later efforts to respect the inherent Indigenous rights, the Government of Canada took measures, including through the commissions explained below, to understand the breadth of their impact and ways to begin repairing some of the damage.

More than a century later, an update to the BNA created the *Constitution Act, 1982*, where Part I section 25 of the *Charter of Rights and Freedoms* and Part II section 35 of the *Rights of Aboriginal Peoples of Canada* sought to provide greater constitutional protection for Indigenous Peoples.[21] Under Section 25, titled 'Aboriginal, treaty or other rights and freedoms', the law guarantees that no rights protected under the Charter will be used to abrogate or derogate from section 35 rights belonging to Aboriginal

History and Society of the Americas (Routledge 2019); S James Anaya, 'Indigenous Peoples in the United States: Justice Still Needed' in W Michael Reisman and Roza Pati (eds), *Human Flourishing: The End of Law* (Brill 2023).

16 An Act to Amend the Indian Act 1927 s 141 (repealed 1951).

17 The Supreme Court of Canada determined that 'treaties and statutes relating to Indians should be liberally construed and uncertainties resolved in favour of the Indians'. *R. v Sioui* [1990] 1 SCR 1025, 1035, 1042–1043, applying *Simon v The Queen* [1985] 2 SCR 387, 410; TRC (n 3); see generally Borrows and others (n 3); Borrows, 'Indigenous Legal Traditions in Canada' (n 10); Borrows, *Recovering Canada* (n 10); Grammond (n 10); Stacey (n 10).

18 *Simon* (n 17).

19 *Sioui* (n 17).

20 See, generally, Borrows, 'Indigenous Legal Traditions in Canada' (n 10); Borrows, *Recovering Canada* (n 10); Grammond (n 10); Stacey (n 10).

21 Constitution Act 1982, Part I Canadian Charter of Rights and Freedoms, s 25; Part II Rights of Aboriginal Peoples of Canada, s.35; TRC (n 3); see, generally, Borrows and others (n 3); Borrows, 'Indigenous Legal Traditions in Canada' (n 10); Borrows, *Recovering Canada* (n 10); Grammond (n 10); Stacey (n 10).

Peoples, including the protection of Indigenous rights provided under the Royal Proclamation.[22]

Section 35, in particular, can be regarded as a means to enshrine and affirm existing Aboriginal rights 'in federal law, allowing First Nations to reconstitute their governance structures outside the Indian Act'.[23] Nonetheless, though treaty rights may be reasonably clear what a treaty right is, the scope and breadth of existing 'Aboriginal rights' remain elusive. While section 35 acknowledged and protected the 'existing Aboriginal and Treaty Rights', the Government of Canada, with the provinces following suit, devoted most of its case law efforts to establishing a reverse onus on Indigenous Peoples to provide absolute proof, through the Canadian judicial system, that any right Indigenous People might claim was indeed 'existing' and was thus inescapably protected by section 35 of the 1982 Constitutional amendment.[24] As documented, such reverse-onus Aboriginal and treaty rights approaches led many Aboriginal rights cases decided through the Canadian justice system to cost decades and millions in expenses, funds urgently required for pressing needs for Canada's Indigenous Peoples, such as on-reserve uncontaminated potable water,[25] improved housing, and education.[26] Though seen as an imperfect solution, these constitutional protections still provided an entryway into an additional inquiry into Indigenous and treaty rights and Indigenous policy development in subsequent years.

In 1991, the Canadian government formed a Royal Commission on Aboriginal People,[27] whereby seven commissioners were appointed to explore

[22] King George III, 'Proclamation' (1763), reprinted in RSC 1985, App II, No. 1; TRC (n 3); see, generally, Borrows and others (n 3); Borrows, 'Indigenous Legal Traditions in Canada' (n 10); Borrows, *Recovering Canada* (n 10); Grammond (n 10); Stacey (n 10).

[23] Jorge Barrera, 'Wilson-Raybould Battled Bennett, Other Ministers over Indigenous Rights Framework' CBC News (Toronto, 22 February 2019) <www.cbc.ca/news/indigenous/raybould-wernick-framework-1.5029144> accessed 7 February 2025; see also TRC (n 3); see, generally, Borrows and others (n 3); Borrows, 'Indigenous Legal Traditions in Canada' (n 10); Borrows, *Recovering Canada* (n 10); Grammond (n 10); Stacey (n 10).

[24] Department of Justice Canada, *'Principles Respecting the Government of Canada's Relationship with Indigenous Peoples'* (2017) <https://perma.cc/YJV2-B459> accessed 7 February 2025 (DOJ UNDRIP Principles).

[25] Rachel Arsenault, 'Water Insecurity in Ontario First Nations: An Exploratory Study on Past Interventions and the Need for Indigenous Water Governance' (2021) 13(5) Water 717; Jodi Simkin, 'Creating a New Reality: Repatriation, Reconciliation and Moving Forward' (Canadian Commission for UNESCO's IdeaLab, 2020).

[26] Assembly of First Nations, *Royal Commission on Aboriginal People at 10 Years: A Report Card* (AFN Publication 2006) 15, 16, 17 <www.cbc.ca/news2/background/aboriginals/pdf/afn_rcap.pdf> accessed 7 February 2025 (RCAP Report Card).

[27] A Canadian Royal Commission is a special investigative committee tasked by the Governor in Council with the mandate to conduct extensive study into a particular issue that must be

the issues relating to First Nations People. The 4,000-page Report of the Royal Commission on Aboriginal People (RCAP) was released in 1996 after five years of consultations in ninety-six communities, and sets forth a twenty-year action plan and 440 recommendations. Though only a first step in investigating the harms affecting Indigenous Peoples in Canada, the report was seen as a milestone in official acknowledgement and redress. Professor Lynda Grey, for example, in her textbook *First Nations 101*, comments that many Indigenous leaders believed that if implemented, the recommendations of the RCAP would greatly improve the living conditions of Indigenous People.[28]

As the RCAP noted, the impact of international treaties on Indigenous Peoples raises important questions for trade, including the negotiation of trade rules. Certain RCAP recommendations, specifically those listed under 'First Nation Economic Development and Trade',[29] highlight the importance of Indigenous trade amongst the framework of issues that impact Indigenous Peoples covered by the Commission. The report underlines the need to '[expand] trade, both among Aboriginal communities and with non-Aboriginal customers', noting that '[t]hese intercommunity links can also be extended to the international level, and indeed some examples are emerging in different parts of the country'.[30]

Fast and effective implementation of these recommendations offered an opportunity for the government to play a constructive role in revitalizing Indigenous economies, bringing back levels of cooperation seen before the BNA. However, the formal response to the RCAP report by the federal government, which itself took over a year to be issued, was seen as broadly disappointing by Indigenous Peoples, international observers, and human rights organizations following the progress of RCAP. At face value, the Government's response, titled *Gathering Strength: Canada's Aboriginal Action Plan*, appeared to address the challenges highlighted by the RCAP report in four broad objectives: 'Renewing the Partnership, Strengthening

addressed and that is beyond the immediate scope of the Parliamentary standing committees. The Royal Commission is clothed in significant investigative authority and typically has the mandate to report back to Parliament with a series of findings and recommendations for the government of the day to choose, or not to choose to act upon. See Public Inquiries Act (1985) c. I-11 ss 4–8.

[28] Lynda Grey, 'First Nations 101' (Adaawx Publishing 2011) 88.

[29] Royal Commission on Aboriginal Peoples, 'Economic Development' in *Report of the Royal Commission on Aboriginal Peoples* (vol 2, Ottawa 1996) 868 (RCAP Report).

[30] ibid.

First Nations Governance, Developing a New Fiscal Relationship, and Supporting Strong Communities, People and Economies'.

However, the government's response to RCAP in their policy document *Gathering Strength* was seen by many as merely a watered-down version of the recommendations found in the RCAP report; its objectives were critiqued as window dressing.[31] The policies received poor to failing marks in almost every category, in the *Royal Commission on Aboriginal People at 10 Years: A Report Card* review released by the Assembly of First Nations in 2006.[32] Very little was concretely accomplished or advanced by the federal government concerning the RCAP Indigenous trade recommendations, though the recommendations did provide invaluable context and influence.

9.3 POTENTIAL FOR AFFIRMING RIGHTS THROUGH TREATIES, INVESTMENT, AND TRADE

Since the Dominion of Canada was created, important trade and investment agreements were signed by the Government of Canada on behalf of the State without sufficient consultation or consideration of potential impacts on the Indigenous interests at stake.[33] Most notably, agreements affecting Indigenous intellectual property and Traditional Knowledge (TK), stewardship of renewable resources, cultural heritage and tourism, and free prior and informed consent over extractives projects, including other aspects of trade and investment, were made without adequate Indigenous consultation or inclusion.[34] According to jurists, on international trade law, the Government of Canada began late in consulting with Indigenous Peoples on cases where Indigenous inherent rights, treaty rights, or interests in more sustainable development

[31] Grey (n 28) 88–89.

[32] RCAP Report Card (n 26) 2; Grey (n 28) 89.

[33] Borrows and others (n 3); TRC (n 3); see, generally, Borrows, 'Indigenous Legal Traditions in Canada' (n 10); Borrows, *Recovering Canada* (n 10); Grammond (n 10); Stacey (n 10).

[34] Significant agreements struck without consultation and potentially impacted Indigenous People in free trade agreements and intellectual property law regimes. Canada-United States Free Trade Agreement (Canada-United States) (adopted 2 January 1988, entered into force 1 January 1989); North American Free Trade Agreement (Mexico-Canada-United States) (adopted 17 December 1992, entered into force 1 January 1994); Canada-United States-Mexico Agreement (Mexico-Canada-United States) (adopted 30 November 2018, entered into force 1 July 2020) (CUSMA). Leah Sarson, 'You Cannot Trade What Is Not Yours: Indigenous Governance and the NAFTA Negotiations' (2019) 49(2) American Review of Canadian Studies 332–347; Brenda Gunn, 'International Investment Agreements and Indigenous Peoples' Rights' in Borrows and Schwartz (n 5) 194.

opportunities might be eroded by the substantive commitments in a trade or investment accord.[35]

Part of this inclusion can be traced back to the RCAP report, despite Canada's overall shortcomings in the Action Plan response. Though the report dismissed the idea of creating a specific Aboriginal Trade Commission, which the Commission had suggested as an option, the RCAP recommended direct regional collaboration with the provinces and federal government instead. These recommendations provided evidence for the need for inclusion of Indigenous Peoples in trade and international treaties. Included in the recommendations at 2.5.19, 2.5.20, and 2.5.21, are calls for:

> The capacity for trade promotion to be built into the sectoral and other economic development organizations of Aboriginal nations, as appropriate. (2.5.19)
>
> The international trade promotion agencies of the federal and provincial governments, in cooperation with Aboriginal producers and economic development institutions, to actively seek out markets for Aboriginal goods and services abroad. (2.5.20)
>
> Provincial and territorial governments to join the federal government in establishing effective set-aside programs to benefit Aboriginal businesses and municipal governments with large proportions of Aboriginal residents also undertaking these programs. (2.5.21)[36]

Of importance, despite possibilities for alignment with SDGs, particularly SDG 17.10 on equitable trade and SDG 17.16–17 on multi-stakeholder partnerships, many have noted that to address these recommendations have not yet been fully realized, in many respects.

In addition to the RCAP recommendations, modern domestic treaty obligations between the government and Indigenous Peoples also set consultation obligations. The wave of post-1970s treaties, also known as Comprehensive Land Claims Agreements (CLCAs), includes many clauses negotiated by First Nations and Inuit requiring the Canadian federal government to respect specific consultation obligations for any international trade

[35] Marie-Claire Cordonier Segger, *Crafting Trade and Investment Accords for Sustainable Development: Athena's Treaties* (Oxford University Press 2021); see also more generally S James Anaya, *Indigenous Peoples in International Law* (2nd edn, Oxford University Press 2004); John Borrows, 'Indigenous Diversities in International Investment and Trade' in Borrows and Schwartz (n 5) 1; O'Sullivan (n 11); William David, 'Recognizing the Rights of Indigenous Peoples in International Trade and Environment' in Borrows and Schwartz (n 5) 133.

[36] RCAP Report (n 29) 870.

agreements affecting Indigenous Peoples. Two examples of modern treaties that exercise this form of Indigenous economic rights are the Nunavut Agreement and the Nisga'a Final Agreement.

The Nunavut Agreement, which became Canadian law in 1993, provides for an express federal legal obligation of consultation about any reasonably foreseeable impact in international treaty negotiations relating to Inuit wildlife harvesting rights. Article 5.9.2 states, 'The Government of Canada shall include Inuit representation in discussions leading to the formulation of government positions in relation to an international agreement relating to Inuit wildlife harvesting rights in the Nunavut Settlement Area'.[37] The level of consultation required through this agreement is also noteworthy. Specifically, consultations of this nature are often performed with input from stakeholders, which can include industry, trading partners, and members of the public. In this case, the Nunavut Agreement through Article 5.9.2 calls for an additional level of participation afforded to Inuit stakeholders, stating that 'discussions [involving Inuit] shall extend beyond those discussions generally available to non-governmental organizations'.[38]

The 1999 Nisga'a Final Agreement also demonstrates a similar clause to this effect, though the accord does not call for heightened consultation. Through section 115, the Nisga'a treaty requires the proactive duty that 'Canada will consult with the Nisga'a Nation with respect to the formulation of Canada's positions about international discussions or negotiations that may significantly affect fisheries resources referred to in this Agreement'.[39] As discussed in Chapter 6 of this book on renewable resources, stewardship of the oceans and fisheries relates to crucial Indigenous rights under the UNDRIP, particularly Articles 20 and 26, as well as important targets for life below water (SDG 14), and zero hunger (SDG 2), among other key SDGs. This consultation requirement and the Indigenous right to participate in decision-making in Canada can also be triggered by the negotiation of international agreements, as acknowledged by the federal government in its duty--to-consult guidelines.[40] In many modern treaties, similar to the Nunavut and

[37] The Nunavut Agreement (The Inuit of the Nunavut Settlement Area as represented by the Tungavik Federation of Nunavut–Her Majesty The Queen in Right of Canada) (adopted 6 November 1992, entered into force 31 December 1993) s 5.9.2.

[38] ibid.

[39] Nisga'a Final Agreement (Nisga'a Nation–Her Majesty the Queen in Right of Canada–Her Majesty the Queen in Right of British Columbia) (adopted 27 April 1999, entered into force 11 May 2000) s 68, 90.

[40] 'Officials should assess whether provisions in land claim agreements or self-government agreements require that consultation take place in relation to legally binding international instruments. Second, officials must determine whether legislation requires Canada to consult

Nisga'a Agreements, the Parties have agreed provisions requiring consultation before Canada consents to be bound by a new international treaty giving rise to new international legal obligations that might adversely affect the rights of the Indigenous Parties.[41]

Additionally, the Supreme Court of Canada (SCC) and appellate courts, through the lengthy legal process necessary to affirm Aboriginal rights, have clarified the extent of Indigenous Peoples' right to participate in decision-making and the government responsibilities associated with the 'duty to consult'. The SCC, in *Rio Tinto Alcan Inc. v Carrier Sekani Tribal Council* (*Rio Tinto*), for example,[42] has provided guidance as to whether the duty to consult extends beyond individual projects that impact Aboriginal territory. According to the SCC, 'government action is not confined to decisions or conduct which have an immediate impact on lands and resources. Potential for adverse impact suffices. Thus, the duty to consult extends to "strategic, higher level decisions" that may have an impact on Aboriginal claims and rights'.[43]

In *Hupacasath First Nation v Minister of Foreign Affairs Canada*, the Federal Court of Appeal (FCA), however, ruled that the duty to consult did not extend to ratification of a bilateral investment treaty with China; while 'strategic, higher level decisions' may be reviewable as outlined in *Rio Tinto*, a 'causal relationship between the Crown conduct and potential adverse impacts on pending Aboriginal claims or rights' must also be demonstrated for a duty to consult to arise.[44] In so ruling, the FCA appears to preclude a legal obligation to include Indigenous Peoples in broad, international framework treaties that protect foreign investors in Canada. This runs contrary to the obligations for the participation of Indigenous Peoples in decisions that

on international instruments. Officials should seek legal advice, which will support the broader departmental or agency assessments and decision-making processes'. Minister of the Department of Aboriginal Affairs and Northern Development Canada, *Aboriginal Consultation and Accommodation – Updated Guidelines for Federal Officials to Fulfill the Duty to Consult – March 2011* (Public Works and Government Services Canada, Ottawa 2011) 23 <https://perma.cc/AAC5-E6EX> accessed 7 February 2025.

41 For an additional example, see art 24 of the Tla'amin Final Agreement (Tla'amin Nation–Her Majesty the Queen in Right of Canada–Her Majesty the Queen in Right of British Columbia) (adopted 11 April 2014, entered into force 5 April 2016). For further reading, see Borrows (n 11); Anaya (n 35).

42 *Rio Tinto Alcan Inc v Carrier Sekani Tribal Council* [2010] 2 SCR 650.

43 ibid 44.

44 *Hupacasath First Nation v Canada (Foreign Affairs and International Trade Canada)* [2015] FCA 4 (CAN) 7, 58, 84, 379. ibid 105, where the FCA ruled '[a]ny adverse impact on rights stemming from the [Bilateral Investment] Agreement, if any, can be addressed later when they rise beyond the speculative and trigger the duty to consult'. See also Gunn (n 34) 1.

impact their rights as set out in the UNDRIP, although Canada's endorsement of its requirements in 2010 and the promise to implement the Declaration was made in 2016, only a short while after the FCA's decision. Nevertheless, an Indigenous group's right to inter-Tribal trade with another Tribal Nation is still very much open to judicial recognition, especially since the FCA ultimately determined treaty-making, an exercise of Crown prerogative, to be a judicially reviewable government power. Conversely, it remains to be seen whether the finding in *R. v Mitchell*,[45] in which the SCC found that a claimed Aboriginal right (to unmolested cross-border trade) never came into existence, due to its ruling that the exercise of this right flies in the face of Canadian sovereignty,[46] remains unchanged. Such gaps in the law have left the door open to the possibility of future clarifications regarding the extent and terms of consultation requirements.[47]

The breadth of the Indigenous participation that occurs and the degree to which these agreements are implemented continues to vary with each government and the unique circumstances of each negotiation process.[48] Nevertheless, this still marks a new era of Indigenous participation in international trade and treaty negotiation. Following the recommendations set forth by the RCAP and the requirements of Indigenous participation through domestic treaties, the beginnings of a new era of relationships may be possible between the Indigenous Peoples and the State. It forms only a first step towards reconciliation of the acts by the latter, having adhered to their Nation State-to-Tribal Nation treaties more in the breach than in the observance, and many argue would not erase the prior violations of rights, including colonial policies of dispossession, cultural assimilation, and other historical injustices which occurred and continue to this day. From this view, further steps remain necessary to satisfying Indigenous rights to redress under Article 28 of UNDRIP and advancing SDGs 16.7 on inclusive decision-making, 17.10 on equitable trade, 17.16–17 on multi-stakeholder partnerships, and 10.2 on promoting social, economic, and political inclusion.

45 *R. v Mitchell* [2001] 1 SCR 911.

46 ibid 62, 172–173.

47 *Hupacasath* (n 44).

48 IPETCA involved direct Indigenous negotiation of the trade agreement which is a sharp contrast to art 3 of the Jay Treaty of 1763 which directly impacted Indigenous People, but did not consult or involve them in the development or negotiation of the clauses. IPETCA (Ministry of Foreign Affairs and Trade, 2022) <www.mfat.govt.nz/assets/Trade-General/Trade-policy/Indigenous-Peoples-Economic-and-Trade-Cooperation-Arrangement-IPETCA-FINAL-VERSION.pdf> accessed 7 February 2025.

9.4 CANADIAN DOMESTIC ENFORCEMENT OF THE UNITED NATIONS DECLARATION ON THE RIGHTS OF INDIGENOUS PEOPLES

In addition to the work of commissions like the RCAP, as well as the obligations set by modern treaties, international law has helped to enforce, or at the very least catalyse conversations on, Indigenous rights in the Canadian context. Although the UNDRIP may appear to be aspirational – exerting a political, persuasive, and moral force rather than binding legal obligations the Indigenous rights once recognized can and indeed should be found enforceable against governments through the justice system, then giving that declaration the force of domestic law.[49] In countries like Canada, the decision to ensure that UNDRIP is reflected in domestic law through the UNDRIP Act of Canada[50] may provide further opportunities to catalyse Indigenous rights and participation in decision-making related to sustainable development on the ground. This aligns with SDG 16.7 on inclusive decision-making, in addition to UNDRIP Article 38 on taking legislative measures to achieve its aims.

However, it is not completely straightforward to ensure that UNDRIP becomes domestic and enforceable law particularly given the changes in sustainable development related decision-making that 'Doctrine of Discovery'-based,[51] colonial States like the United States, New Zealand, and Australia would face if the full force of Articles 19 and 46, relating to free, prior, and informed consent and self-determination came into effect.[52] After more than eight years in UN committees, the UNDRIP draft was finally acceptable for a vote on the UN General Assembly floor.[53] Still, when the original draft provided by the Working Group on Indigenous Populations (WGIP) was circulated,[54] these countries raised significant concerns over the potential for loss of government control and political autonomy. Many

[49] Nigel Bankes, 'Implementing UNDRIP: An Analysis of British Columbia's Declaration on the Rights of Indigenous Peoples Act' (2020) 53(4) UBC Law Review 971 citing *Nevsun Resources Ltd v Araya* [2020] SCC 5, 77.

[50] *United Nations Declaration on the Rights of Indigenous Peoples Act*, SC 2021, c 14 (UNDRIP Act).

[51] David Getches and others, 'Chapter 14, Section B Emerging Voices: Indigenous Rights and International Law' in *Cases and Materials on Federal Indian Law* (7th edn, West Academic Publishing 2017) 1100.

[52] Note that UNDRIP Act (n 50) art 46 (1) still provides a State overriding mechanism.

[53] James Sákéj Youngblood Henderson, *Indigenous Diplomacy and the Rights of Peoples: Achieving U.N. Recognition* (Purich Publishing 2008) 119.

[54] Erica-Irene Daes, UN Subcommission on Prevention of Discrimination and Protection of Minorities and the Working Group on Indigenous Populations 'Draft Declaration on the Rights of Indigenous Peoples' (8 June 1993) UN Doc E/CN.4/Sub.2/1993/26.

Indigenous representatives refused to change the draft, stating that the wording of the text merely extended rights to the Indigenous Peoples that were already guaranteed to colonial others.[55]

The final version endorsed by the UN General Assembly was significantly changed from the original wording, reflecting compromise between representatives, the most dramatic edit found in Article 46 of the UNDRIP: 'Nothing in this Declaration may be interpreted as implying for any State, people, group or person any right to engage in any activity or to perform any act contrary to the Charter of the United Nations'.[56] From many Indigenous perspectives, only once section 46 had been weakened enough to reassure these State representatives that their countries' current governing regimes could not be adversely affected was a full vote permitted in the UN General Assembly. To Article 46(1) was added 'or any action which would dismember or impair, totally or in part, the territorial integrity or political unity of sovereign and independent States'.[57]

The full vote of the UN General Assembly finally took place on 13 September 2007, after nearly forty years of advocacy and intense and consistent efforts by numerous Indigenous Peoples and international bodies. In the end, 144 States voted in favour and four did not (Canada, the United States, New Zealand, and Australia), countries which some Indigenous and other experts observed would be most impacted economically, particularly their resource extraction sectors, if decision-making power for resource development projects were weakened by Indigenous self-determination.[58] Among arguments advanced were, for instance, statements by the opposing countries that as they have strong records of upholding human rights, in particular Indigenous rights within the State governance system they did not need the international standards in this form. By contrast, as suggested by another perspective, merely claiming to observe so-called soft rights (such as language and cultural rights) can act as a systemic obstacle to realizing 'hard rights',

[55] Youngblood Henderson (n 53) 70.

[56] UN Res 61/295, 'United Nations Declaration on the Rights of Indigenous Peoples' (2007) UN Doc A/RES/61/295 art 46 (UNDRIP); Sheryl Lightfoot, 'Indigenous Mobilization and Activism in the UN System' in Short and Lennox (n 4); Marc Weller, 'Self-determination of Indigenous Peoples – Articles 3, 4, 5, 18, 23 and 46(1)' in Jessie Hohmann and Marc Weller (eds), *The UN Declaration on the Rights of Indigenous Peoples: A Commentary* (Oxford University Press 2018).

[57] Felipe Gómez Isa, 'The UNDRIP: An Increasingly Robust Legal Parameter' in Short and others (n 2); Dorothée Cambou, 'The UNDRIP and the Legal Significance of the Right of Indigenous Peoples to Self-Determination: A Human Rights Approach with a Multidimensional Perspective' in Short and others (n 2).

[58] Getches and others (n 51) 1100, 1105.

including land rights.[59] While some Canadian intervenors argued that the Canadian Charter of Rights and Freedoms was already upholding rights, and that the UNDRIP would be inconsistent with the Constitution by putting Indigenous rights above those of other Canadians, however, many disagreed with this characterization of the legal position.[60]

Eventually, positions were reversed, and the four opponents did declare support for the UNDRIP. Canada endorsed the Declaration in 2010, with full acceptance in 2016.[61] Critics called attention to the processes involved, objecting to the non-binding, 'lukewarm' reception of the Declaration and expressing concern as to the actual effects of the recognition of Indigenous rights, and related commitments.[62] For the full effect of the UNDRIP to apply in Canada, in particular through Article 38 on measures to achieve the Declaration's ends, provincial and federal legislation was needed to align the legal framework itself with the UNDRIP.

At the provincial level, after the Government of Canada endorsed the Declaration in 2016, British Columbia released its *Declaration on the Rights of Indigenous Peoples Act* and this was followed by the Government of Canada's *UNDRIP Act*. These acts, as stated by the Government of Canada, serve as a 'range of important measures that contribute to renewed, respectful Crown-Indigenous relationships, in partnership with Indigenous [P]eoples'.[63] These measures additionally make specific reference to Indigenous participation in trade and treaties, thereby adding an additional level of legal obligation for inclusion in these fields.

In November 2019, the Government of British Columbia passed its *Declaration on the Rights of Indigenous Peoples Act* to implement the UN Declaration.[64] Article 41 of this *Act* sets out key provisions for free, prior, and informed consent, while Article 29(1) recognizes the right to environmental protection. Specific to inter-Tribal trade, Articles 20(1) and 36(1) stipulate that

59 Sheryl R Lightfoot, 'Emerging International Indigenous Rights, Norms and Overcompliance in New Zealand and Canada' (2010) 62(1) Political Science 84 96.

60 Sasha Boutilier, 'Free, Prior, and Informed Consent and Reconciliation in Canada: Proposals to Implement Articles 19 and 32 of the UN Declaration on the Rights of Indigenous Peoples' (2017) 7-1 Western Journal of Legal Studies 5.

61 Getches and others (n 51) 1100, 1105.

62 Sheryl R Lightfoot, 'A Sea Change on the U.N. Declaration – Or Is It?' (*Indian Country Today*, 3 May 2010) <https://ictnews.org/archive/a-sea-change-on-the-un-declaration-or-is-it> accessed 7 February 2025.

63 Government of Canada, 'The UN Declaration Explained' (*Implementing the United Nations Declaration on the Rights of Indigenous Peoples Act*, 23 July 2023) <https://perma.cc/8ZYV-9U9M> accessed 7 February 2025 (UNDRIP Explanation).

64 Declaration on the Rights of Indigenous Peoples Act BC Bill (2019-41) 41 4th Session, 41st Parliament (UNDRIP Bill 41).

'Indigenous [P]eoples have the *right to maintain and develop their economic institutions*, and *to engage freely in all their traditional and other economic activities*',[65] and that 'Indigenous [P]eoples, in particular those divided by international borders, have *the right to maintain and develop* contacts, relations and cooperation, including activities for spiritual, cultural political, *economic* and social *purposes, with their own members as well as other [P]eoples across borders*'.[66]

At the federal level, the *UNDRIP Act*, according to the Government of Canada, was intended to 'provide a roadmap for the Government and Indigenous Peoples to work together to implement the Declaration fully'.[67] This Act, which became law in 2021 and responds to the TRC's Calls to Action 43, requires that the Government of Canada work in consultation and cooperation with Indigenous Peoples to take measures to ensure Canadian law is consistent with the UNDRIP, prepare and implement an action plan to achieve the objectives of the Declaration, and develop and submit to Parliament annual reports on the progress of implementation.[68] The adoption of this act, aligning with UNDRIP's Article 38 on legislative measures to realizing the Declaration, may provide a step towards supporting Indigenous sustainable development,[69] as well as cultural preservation and protection of Indigenous TK, by supporting – or at least not hindering – the exercise of the inherent right of inter-Tribal trade. For the development of a Indigenous international trade economy, many argue governments may need to pull together, consult, and include Indigenous Peoples more fully in discussions of the international issues impacting them. The *UNDRIP Act* serves as one way to consistently have policy and industry reflect this need across the country while respecting Aboriginal and Treaty rights.

9.5 CANADA-INDIGENOUS TREATIES IN THE CONTEXT OF TRADE AND SUSTAINABLE DEVELOPMENT

Building on the momentum created through domestic inquiries and international agreements, Indigenous participation in treaties in the Canadian

[65] ibid art 20 (1) (emphasis added).

[66] ibid art 36 (1) (emphasis added).

[67] UNDRIP Explanation (n 63).

[68] Government of Canada, 'About the Act' (Implementing the United Nations Declaration on the Rights of Indigenous Peoples Act, 23 July 2023) <https://perma.cc/VB6Y-N4UH> accessed 7 February 2025.

[69] As in the Federal Indigenous Relationship Principles Statement issued July 2017, art 8, which states: 'Reconciliation and self-government require a renewed fiscal relationship, developed in collaboration with Indigenous Nations, that promotes a mutually supportive climate for economic partnership and resource development'. DOJ UNDRIP Principles (n 24).

context has advanced significantly in recent years as part of Canada's 'Inclusive Trade Agenda'.[70] Organizations and Indigenous bodies, including the Assembly of First Nations, the International Inter-tribal Trade and Investment Organization (IITIO), and all other national Indigenous political bodies and organizations worked with the Government of Canada through the Global Affairs Canada Indigenous Working Group (IWG) to develop this policy, mandated to collaborate on the development of international instruments for furthering Indigenous trade.[71] The outcomes included Canada's Indigenous Trade Chapter, the country's playbook in global trade talks with various other States in which Indigenous Peoples are interested in developing trade opportunities with Canada's First Nations, Métis, and Inuit Peoples.[72] This agenda operates within the global context for Indigenous trade, in particular with the work of New Zealand and Australia, as well as the Pacific Trade Alliance, Mercosur, the Inclusive Trade Action Group,[73] and a number of side letters of understanding. It represents a novel and innovative means to advancing equitable trade as outlined in SDG 17.10 and the UNDRIP's Article 36 on maintaining cross-border contacts with other Indigenous Peoples.

In addition to the Inclusive Trade Agenda, in 2017, the IWG set into motion the engagement process and means of developing an Indigenous trade policy. Trade chapters for Indigenous Peoples are essential to their inclusion in international economic opportunities as they promote and enhance cooperation in

[70] Government of Canada, 'Canada's Inclusive Approach to Trade' (9 February 2023) <https://perma.cc/Y269-ZARJ> accessed 7 February 2025; see also Borrows (n 35) 1; Risa Schwartz, 'Developing a Trade and Indigenous Peoples Chapter for International Trade Agreements' in Borrows and Schwartz (n 5) 248.

[71] ibid.

[72] *Hupacasath* (n 44) aptly demonstrated the interest of Indigenous Peoples in the development or renewal of international trade and investment agreements. Hupacasath First Nation, supported by other First Nations in British Columbia and Ontario, including Serpent River First Nation and the Tsawwassen First Nation, along with the Union of BC Indian Chiefs and the Chiefs of Ontario, intervened in the matter of a China/Canada foreign investment agreement. Canada's inclusive approach to trade, 'First Nation Loses Bid to Block Canada-China FIPA Treaty' *CBC News* (Coast Salish Territory, Vancouver, BC, 27 August 2013) <www.cbc.ca/news/politics/first-nations-loses-bid-to-block-canada-china-fipa-treaty-1.1344065> accessed 7 February 2025. Interest in Indigenous Peoples' participation in international trade and investment agreements has since then only grown, both in Canada and internationally, through creation of organizations examining how to increase cross-border trade and investment among Indigenous communities.

[73] The Inclusive Trade Action Group (ITAG) is an organization of currently three countries, Canada, Chile, and New Zealand that are dedicated to advancing inclusive trade initiatives. Government of Canada, 'Overview: The Inclusive Trade Action Group' (International trade and investment, 13 October 2021) <https://perma.cc/KBK3-5LWB> accessed 7 February 2025 (Inclusive Trade Agenda).

trade and investment among like-minded States.[74] Such cooperation can improve global capacity and conditions for Indigenous Peoples to engage successfully in cross-border inter-Tribal trade. An Indigenous trade policy, supplemented with cross-border trade engagement activity, is thus essential to develop an Indigenous trade chapter in international trade negotiations.

The Indigenous trade chapter's lead negotiators from IITIO according to jurists, sought to meaningfully participate in trade through this new USMCA. The chapter detailed Canada's larger approach to renegotiating a modernized accord and the implications for traditional elements of a trade agreement, such as intellectual property, government procurement and services, and non-conforming measures, while drawing on Canada's inclusive approach to Indigenous trade. The negotiations themselves offered a unique opportunity to better align international trade and investment with international Indigenous and Human Rights Law. Discussions between the United States, Canada, and Mexico evolved, with some representatives seeking a chapter that would recognize the important role of Indigenous Peoples in trade, both historically and in the context of facilitating sustainable growth and prosperity for Indigenous communities, facilitate cooperative activities between the Parties, enhance the ability of Indigenous Peoples to participate in and benefit from the opportunities created by this Agreement, and establish a committee to oversee the implementation of the Chapter and consider matters of relevance to Indigenous Peoples across the Agreement.[75] Such provisions, if included, would align with the UNDRIP Article 20, which notes that 'Indigenous peoples have the right to [...] their own means of subsistence and development, and to engage freely in all their traditional and other economic activities,' and could advance SDG 8.3, which prioritizes 'promot [ing] development-oriented policies that support productive activities, decent job creation, entrepreneurship, creativity and innovation', together with SDG 17.10, on equitable multilateral trading.

Additionally, the advocates of an Indigenous trade chapter proposed that all exceptions found in the original NAFTA to preserve preferences for Indigenous trade should be retained, and called for contain stronger exceptions that are more proactive in effectively protecting Aboriginal rights, treaty rights, and Aboriginal title interests in land, referencing Section 35 precedent on the duty to consult and accommodate Indigenous concerns and

74 Borrows (n 35); Schwartz (n 70).

75 Jorge Barrera, 'Canada Proposes "Groundbreaking" NAFTA Chapter on Indigenous Rights' *CBC News* (Toronto, 1 December 2017). <www.cbc.ca/news/indigenous/nafta-indigenous-chapter-1.4429145> accessed 7 February 2025.

international Indigenous and human rights instruments, such as the UNDRIP, in particular Article 19 on consultation and FPIC.[76]

Though the draft Indigenous trade chapter did not in the end include all points sought by the Indigenous representatives,[77] nor was it incorporated wholesale into the final text of this iteration of the Agreement, it nonetheless offered as a strong starting point.[78] Notably, the chapter included a clause that prevented any other clause in the agreement from eroding the legal rights of Canada's Indigenous Peoples through the USMCA Article 32.5, Exemptions and General Provisions. The proposed 'Indigenous Peoples Rights' clause states that '... nothing in this Agreement [...] preclude[s] a Party from adopting or maintaining a measure it deems necessary to fulfill its legal obligations to [I]ndigenous [P]eoples'.[79] This general exception in the USMCA provides extra clarity and assurance that should there be a conflict between USMCA and Indigenous Rights, the dispute should be resolved to minimally impact Indigenous People's rights.

Likewise, Chapter 24 of the USMCA on environment recognizes the specific importance of the environment for Indigenous Peoples, and the role Indigenous People play in long-term environmental conservation helping advance SDG 15.5 ('take urgent and significant action to reduce the degradation of natural habitats [...]').[80] It preserves the pre-existing NAFTA 'carve-out' (exception) for Aboriginal harvesting of natural resources,[81] and encourages enterprises to voluntarily follow standards, guidelines, and principles of corporate social responsibility.[82] Likewise, Indigenous protections are also found in Chapter 6 'Textiles and Apparel Goods', through Article 6.2 'Handmade, Traditional Folklore, or Indigenous Handicraft Goods',[83] and Article 22.1 under Chapter 22, 'State-Owned Enterprises and Designated Monopolies', allowing State-owned enterprises to give preferential treatment

76 UNDRIP (n 56).

77 Jay Treaty Principles of 'unmolested inter-tribal trade' and inclusion of Indigenous Traditional Knowledge protection in Intellectual Property regimes in North America had been expressly kept off the table by the Government of Canada, as it was felt that these concepts would potentially slow down progress in getting the US and Mexican negotiators to agree to the chapter.

78 Although the negotiating teams were receptive to the 'Aboriginal Peoples Chapter', it was ultimately rejected by senior US officials because it was not consistent with the direction or vision of the Trump administration. Canada's Inclusive Trade Agenda remains, however, as part of various trade negotiations underway at the time of this writing. Inclusive Trade Agenda (n 73).

79 CUSMA (n 34).

80 ibid arts 24.2; 24.15; 24.17; 24.19; 24.23.

81 ibid.

82 ibid art 24.13.

83 ibid art 6.2.

in buying goods and services from Indigenous-owned businesses, amongst many other provisions.[84]

The chapter was also the first to be developed collaboratively with broad-based Indigenous consultative membership, including national groups such as the Assembly of First Nations, Inuit Tapiriit Kanatami, and the Métis Federation as participating members.[85] These negotiations also included rights-holder organizations representing treaty-holding Nations and non-treaty-holding Nations, as well as interested stakeholders such as the IITIO, the Canadian Council of Aboriginal Business, the Canadian Economic Development Officers Association (CANDO), the National Aboriginal Capital Corporations Association, and the Indigenous Peoples' Commission. Concepts developed during the process can be found in several chapters of the USMCA. Further, jurists note, the Indigenous Trade Chapter was shared with other countries working on integrating Indigenous rights into their trade agreements, such as New Zealand.

9.6 CONCLUSION

The rights of Indigenous Peoples in Canada, including economic, social, land, and cultural rights have long been challenged. Recognition is slowly improving. The codification of Aboriginal rights through section 35 of the *Charter of Rights and Freedoms*, the ratification of the UNDRIP (particularly Article 32 on project approval and resource use), and the adoption of the *UNDRIP Act* in Canada have all contributed to progressive intentions for the rights and liberties of Indigenous Peoples that build on decades of consultations, advocacy, and treaty negotiation. Additionally, Indigenous trade practices and perspectives will only further help bring innovation to international trade concepts and expand legal frameworks for Indigenous rights and consultations, thus allowing a fresh view of how to effectively blend environmental stewardship with economic development that is both sustainable and equitable. Especially in an age where economic expansion and international collaboration remain at the forefront of political agendas globally, a fresh economic approach that allows the peoples of the world to enjoy the Earth's bounty without destroying its source is crucially necessary. Indigenous economic perspectives and their contribution to the legal framework of Canada present a timely, new foundation in international treaty-making.

[84] ibid ch 22: State Owned Enterprises and Designated Monopolies.
[85] ibid; see also Borrows (n 35).

10

Treaty Rights to Economic Sovereignty in the United States

10.1 INTRODUCTION

Indigenous sovereignty in the United States manifests differently than in Canada due to differing historical and legal developments in the two countries. Much like in Canada, Tribal Nations do not have a Nation-to-Nation relationship with the State, despite Indigenous Peoples being the land's original inhabitants. This marginalization and oppression led to limitations, but also innovations, in the ways that Indigenous Peoples could participate in the economy and trade.

This chapter begins by examining the legal doctrines and State actions that have enabled the modern level of sovereignty seen by US Tribal Nations regarding self-governance, treaty negotiations, and trade. As explained bu jurists, two aspects of Indigenous and settler-colonial legal history predisposed colonizing States to place Indigenous Peoples below the standard of a Nation-to-Nation relationship: (1) a legal fiction known as the 'Doctrine of Discovery' and (2) the disempowerment of Tribal sovereignty through the breaking up of Tribal Nations' communally held property guaranteed by treaty. The current situation related to Indigenous sovereignty also merits examination, specifically how sovereignty continues to be affirmed through Indigenous participation in US treaties and trade, as reflected in jurisprudence and legislation.

10.2 THE UNITED STATES AND THE TREATMENT OF INDIGENOUS PEOPLES, INDIGENOUS SOVEREIGNTY, AND ECONOMIC RIGHTS

Many aspects of legal history greatly contributed to Indigenous Peoples' fraught relationships with the United States, but one of the most significant stems from the 'Doctrine of Discovery' (Doctrine) of the fifteenth century, granting for European colonizers a religious and legal basis to claim lands in overseas territories. This doctrine took its shape in the form of a 1493 Papal Bull, issued by Pope Alexander VI, granting to Spain lands 'discovered' by Columbus upon his return from the Americas, and further granting other explorers the right to claim any 'discovered' land for their respective nation if not already occupied by Christians. As detailed by scholars, the Doctrine thus sought to invalidate the sovereignty of any Indigenous Nations that were present, and subjugating and confiscating their lands. In particular, the former British colonies in Canada, Australia, New Zealand, and the United States of America repeatedly relied on this doctrine to rationalize the racial, cultural, and rights erasure of Indigenous Peoples in these jurisdictions.[1]

In the United States, the Doctrine of Discovery is referenced in the foundational history of Indian law through the Marshall Trilogy.[2] In *Johnson v M'Intosh*, US Supreme Court Chief Justice Marshall invokes the Doctrine of Discovery as a principal justification for Indigenous removal and seizure of Native lands. This sought to give the United States and others, that is, the 'discoverer', the right and title to all lands in the New World, while Indigenous Peoples would only be recognized as holding a 'right of occupancy' over such land.[3] The Doctrine provided a legal justification for attempts to subordinate Indigenous People to allow the new inhabitants to continue their westward expansion uninhibited by Indigenous claims to title.[4] As documented by Indigenous and other historians, effects for Indigenous Peoples in the US included forced removals (such as during the Trail of Tears), the seizure of lands and natural resources, the intentional destruction of traditional languages, education and cultures, and the disruption of

1 Pope Alexander VI, 'Demarcation Bull Granting Spain Possession of Lands Discovered by Columbus' (Rome, 4 May 1493); Holy See Press Office, 'Joint Statement of the Dicasteries for Culture and Education and for Promoting Integral Human Development on the "Doctrine of Discovery"' (30 March 2023); for a discussion of the 'Doctrine of Discovery', see Lindsay Robertson, *Conquest by Law: How the Discovery of America Dispossessed Indigenous Peoples of Their Lands* (Oxford University Press 2007).

2 The Marshall Trilogy included three cases: *Johnson v M'Intosh*, *Cherokee Nation v Georgia*, and *Worcester v Georgia*. Each of these cases provides some understanding of how the United States began at its inception to interpret and continues to this day to interpret the existence of Tribal sovereignty. *Johnson v McIntosh* [1823] 21 US 543; *Cherokee Nation v Georgia* [1831] 30 US 1; *Worcester v Georgia* [1832] 31 US 515.

3 *Johnson* (n 2).

4 Robertson (n 1); see also S James Anaya, 'Indigenous Peoples in the United States: Justice Still Needed' in W Michael Reisman and Roza Pati (eds), *Human Flourishing: The End of Law* (Brill/Nijhoff 2023) 677–707.

Indigenous families and communities – as justified by the Doctrine of Discovery.[5] The Doctrine ultimately represents a deliberate decision, and failure, to recognize or respect local Indigenous populations as Nations, among the community of nations of the world.

A second main aspect that further eroded Indigenous sovereignty involved disempowerment and dispossession of territories – the breaking up of Tribal Nations' communally held property guaranteed by treaty. In particular, the seizure of lands and natural resources highlighted above also led, in the US, to the imposition of allotment systems – the carving of communal lands into privately owned allotments, along with the dissolution of land holdings despite reservation and Indigenous community ownership having been guaranteed by treaty.[6] These historical injustices form only part of the story behind the commitments contained in UNDRIP aimed at reconciliation, particularly Article 7 on the right to security of the person, Article 10 against forced removal, and Article 8 on redress for attempts at land dispossession, assimilation and cultural erasure, together with Articles 11 and 28 on restitution and redress. Measures to realize such commitments may also align with SDG 10.2, promoting social, economic, and political inclusion of all, and SDG 16.3 on equal access to justice for all; as discussed below, Indigenous Peoples were denied equal treatment before courts during centuries of institutionalized dispossession.

Prior to the arrival of colonial groups, and partly even during the early period of their settlement, Indigenous Peoples of what was to become America possessed a form of inherent sovereignty which involved, among other aspects, the free exercise of international and inter-Tribal trade.[7] Most European States, experts suggest, established good trading relations with North American Indigenous Peoples when they arrived on the continent: many saw the trade discussions, negotiations, and agreements taking place between equals.[8]

However, with increased colonial population growth in North America, coupled with technological and governance changes to land acquisition and

[5] ibid; see also Kenneth M Casebeer, 'Subaltern Voices in the Trail of Tears: Cognition and Resistance of the Cherokee Nation to Removal in Building American Empire' (2014) 4 University of Miami Race & Social Justice Law Review 1.

[6] ibid; Claire Charters, 'Indigenous Peoples' Rights to Lands, Territories and Resources in the UN Declaration on the Rights of Indigenous Peoples – Articles 25, 26, 27 and 10' in Jessie Hohmann and Marc Weller (eds), *The UN Declaration on the Rights of Indigenous Peoples: A Commentary* (Oxford University Press 2018).

[7] For a discussion of pre-European contact inter-Tribal trade see Felix S Cohen, 'A Brief History of Inter-Tribal Trade in Canada and the United States' in *Handbook of Federal Indian Law* (United States Government Printing Office 1945).

[8] ibid; Anaya (n 4).

resource consumption practices, many underscore that the balance of equals shifted to a relationship of exploitation, dominance, and attempts to establish cultural superiority over the Indigenous values and culture.[9] Then, the early to mid-1800s led to the 'Removal Era'. Though suppressed, jurists argue, indigenous sovereignty remained as an 'inherent power of a limited sovereignty which has never been extinguished.'[10]

It was also during this period that the US legal framework surrounding Indigenous rights and sovereignty began to become codified in jurisprudence. The Marshall Trilogy US Supreme Court decisions forms the basic framework for federal Indian law in the United States. The three related decisions, *Johnson v M'Intosh*, *Cherokee Nation v Georgia*, and *Worcester v Georgia*, written by Chief Justice John Marshall of the US Supreme Court, each provide some understanding of how the United States began, and continues, to interpret the existence of Tribal sovereignty.

In the infamous first case of *Johnson v M'Intosh*, the court characterized Tribal Nations as substandard, declining to see Indigenous Peoples as sovereign North American Nations.[11] Concerns underline that the law of the time refused to consider contemporary legal instruments that were widespread and according to many, also widely respected, insisting instead that Indigenous Nations cannot be States as from this view 'Indians' are sub-human. In the name of political expediency, the court chose to ignore the existing international body of laws addressing the laws of Nations and treaty obligations. Rather than basing his decision on precedent, the court fabricated a new category of 'domestic dependent [N]ations', that, being Tribal Nations, have a certain level of sovereignty that places them outside the Constitution of the United States, but that is also nonetheless under the power of the United States of America.[12]

The decisions also found that Tribes were Nation-States which could not be on equal footing with countries of the world at that time, creating a new form of title, known as Indian or Aboriginal Title, tantamount to an Indigenous

9 The evolution of the Indigenous-settler relationship is clearly documented in the gradual transition in imbalance when one compares the Revolutionary Era (1750–1785) decisions to the Trade and Intercourse Era (1785–1817) to the Removal era (1817–1848) and so on. The loss of respect by the settler governments for Indian culture, land, Indigenous languages, and traditional laws is well documented.

10 Robert Anderson, Sarah Krakoff, and Bethany Berger, *American Indian Cases and Commentary* (4th edn, West Academic Publishing 2020) 132;David Getches and others, *Cases and Materials on Federal Indian Law* (7th edn, West Academic Publishing 2017) 417.

11 *Johnson* (n 2).

12 ibid; Anaya (n 4).

right of occupancy.[13] The court's line of reasoning was a rationale based on a merger of the Doctrines of Discovery and Conquest, both of which diminished an American Tribe's ability to conduct commerce with whomever they chose. Based on this outcome, title to Indian lands could be taken only by the federal government: states, corporations, and individuals could not take title to Indian lands. This aspect of the ruling hints, according to some scholars, as a method of protecting Indians from unscrupulous land speculators as well as a recognition of previous colonial abuse regarding the illegitimate taking of Indian lands.[14]

The second case in the Marshall Trilogy on Indigenous sovereignty is *Cherokee Nation v Georgia*.[15] In this case, the US Supreme Court elaborated on the definition of a 'domestic dependent [N]ation' by referring to the Commerce Clause of the US Constitution.[16] The Cherokee Nation sought to declare that two laws passed by the Georgia State Legislature were unconstitutional based on treaties between the Cherokee Nation and the US government. These laws declared that Tribal territory could be inspected, divided up, and distributed to white citizens, and that the government could penalize and punish anyone who did not comply.[17] The Cherokee Nation argued that the Supreme Court had jurisdiction over this case, since their treaties provide for sovereignty and federal protection, thus placing their lands outside the scope of the state laws, and the Court concluded that the Cherokee Nation was neither a domestic state nor a foreign Nation, but a unique sovereign.[18] Citing Article III of the US Constitution, the Court provided that they had jurisdiction over cases that are 'between a State or the citizens thereof, and foreign [S]tates, citizens, or subjects.'[19] The relationship between the United States and the Tribes was thus held to be unique, and like that of a guardian to a

[13] For further reading on Indigenous self-government and autonomy, see Dorothée Cambou, 'The UNDRIP and the Legal Significance of the Right of Indigenous Peoples to Self-Determination: A Human Rights Approach with a Multidimensional Perspective' in Damien Short, Corinne Lennox, Julian Burger and Jessie Hohmann (eds), *The United Nations Declaration on the Rights of Indigenous Peoples: A Contemporary Evaluation* (Routledge 2021); Jérémie Gilbert and Corinne Lennox, 'Towards New Development Paradigms: The United Nations Declaration on the Rights of Indigenous Peoples as a Tool to Support Self-Determined Development' in Short and others, ibid; Alexandra Tomaselli, 'Exploring Indigenous Self-Government and Forms of Autonomy' in Damien Short and Corinne Lennox (eds), *Handbook of Indigenous Peoples' Rights* (Routledge 2016).

[14] ibid.

[15] *Cherokee Nation* (n 2).

[16] For further reading, see Cambou (n 13); Gilbert and Lennox (n 13); Tomaselli (n 13).

[17] *Cherokee Nation* (n 2); Cambou (n 13); Gilbert and Lennox (n 13); Tomaselli (n 13).

[18] *Cherokee Nation* (n 2).

[19] ibid 30.

ward. As experts note, this decision marks the beginning of federal fiduciary duty to American Indians.[20]

The last case in the Marshall Trilogy, *Worcester v Georgia*,[21] was decided the following year, where the Supreme Court further consolidated federal power vis-à-vis the states and confirmed the sovereign status of the Cherokee Nation. The Court held that the laws of the State of Georgia could have no effect in Indian country, for two reasons. First, the inherent, pre-constitutional sovereignty of the Cherokee Nation precluded it.[22] According to the decision, 'the Indian Nations had always been considered as distinct, independent political communities, retaining their original natural rights as the undisputed possessors of the soil'.[23] Though Native American Tribes were now under the protection of the United States, this 'protection does not imply the destruction of the protected'.[24] Second, the Supremacy Clause found in Article 6 Clause 2 of the US Constitution made Indian treaties part of the 'supreme law of the land', pre-empting state law.[25] The Cherokee Nation is thus a distinct community with its own territory, where Georgian law cannot be applied and where the citizens of Georgia could not enter without Cherokee approval.[26] President Andrew Jackson refused to enforce the ruling, however, allowing states to enact further legislation harming Native Americans, most notably forcing the Cherokee off their land in 1838 in what would later be known as the Trail of Tears, where some 15,000 Cherokee were driven from their land, causing over 4,000 deaths.[27] Despite this atrocity, *Worcester v Georgia* nonetheless helped form the basis for subsequent US law related to Native Americans and enabled them to retain some areas of political autonomy.[28]

In summation, four salient principles derived from the Marshall Trilogy which shape attempts to implement the UNDRIP and advance the SDGs among Indigenous Peoples in the United States today include:

- Only the federal government can take title to Indian lands;
- Aboriginal title is tantamount to an Indigenous right of occupancy;

20 For further reading, see Cambou (n 13); Gilbert and Lennox (n 13); Tomaselli (n 13).
21 *Worcester* (n 2).
22 Cohen (n 6); Anderson, Krakoff, and Berger (n 10); Getches and others (n 10).
23 *Worcester* (n 2) 519.
24 ibid 518.
25 US Constitution, art 6, cl 2 states: 'This Constitution, and the laws of the United States which shall be made in pursuance thereof; and all treaties made, or which shall be made, under the authority of the United States, shall be the supreme law of the land.'
26 For further reading, see Cambou (n 13); Gilbert and Lennox (n 13); Tomaselli (n 13).
27 Casebeer (n 5).
28 For further reading, see Cambou (n 13); Gilbert and Lennox (n 13); Tomaselli (n 13).

- A Tribal Nation is neither a domestic state nor a foreign Nation, but a unique sovereign, a 'domestic dependent [N]ation'; and
- Laws of the States have no effect in Indian Country.[29]

For the most part, these core principles have withstood the test of time. Subsequent decisions and incremental State legal challenges have to some degree attempted to encroach on Tribal sovereignty, but the Marshall Trilogy remains as the framework outlining Indigenous rights and sovereignty.[30]

10.2.1 *Recognition and Affirmation of Tribal Nation Sovereignty*

While Tribes may exist outside the federal sphere as outlined by the Marshall Trilogy, it is far more advantageous legally for a Tribe to have official federal recognition as a 'domestic dependent [N]ation'. Without such recognition, a claim of Tribal sovereignty can be unacknowledged by the federal government, and its members will be denied access to federal benefits, programmes, and policies that support the Tribe's existence.[31] To enable this recognition and define how Tribal sovereignty is to be exercised in the United States in relation to implementing UNDRIP and advancing the SDGs, two core concepts of 'Tribe' and of 'Indian Country' can be considered. In federal Indian law, these concepts determine which Tribal Nations are officially recognized and where their precise jurisdictional borders are placed by the federal government. Congress alone has the authority to regulate both concepts through statute.[32] In respect of this chapter's assessment on whether such measures help or hinder the SDGs, it is worthwhile to note that ensuring legal recognition of Tribal autonomy helps advance SDG 16.7, building inclusive decision-making processes, and can align with SDG 10.2, promoting social, economic, and political inclusion of all. Ensuring such recognition also furthers the commitment, in Article 5 of the UNDRIP, to strengthen and maintain distinct Indigenous institutions, in addition to Article 4 committing to the rights to autonomy, self-determination, and self-government

Firstly, 25 United States Code (U.S.C.) § 450b(e) provides that an 'Indian [T]ribe' means 'any Indian [T]ribe, band, [N]ation, or other organized group or community … which is recognized as eligible for the special programs and services provided by the United States to Indians because of their status as

[29] ibid.
[30] ibid.
[31] For further reading, see Cambou (n 13); Gilbert and Lennox (n 13); Tomaselli (n 13).
[32] 18 United States Code § 1151; *Solem v Bartlett* [1984] 465 US 463; *McGirt v Oklahoma* [2020] 591 US.

Indians [. . .]'.[33] This creates a special legal relationship between the federal government and the Indian Tribes that it recognizes, which allows federally recognized [T]ribes to exercise Tribal sovereignty over their Tribal membership and over the lands within 'Indian Country'.[34] The power to enact this recognition is exercised by Congress as affirmed by *United States v Sandoval*.[35]

Additionally, the legal definition of 'Indian Country' as stated in 18 U.S.C. § 1151 means

> (a) all land within the limits of any Indian reservation under the jurisdiction of the United States Government, notwithstanding the issuance of any patent, and, including rights-of-way running through the reservation, (b) all dependent Indian communities within the borders of the United States whether within the original or subsequently acquired territory thereof, and whether within or without the limits of a state, and (c) all Indian allotments, the Indian titles to which have not been extinguished, including rights-of-way running through the same.[36]

The concept of 'Indian country' thus delineates the geographical extent to which the Indian Tribe's recognized rights may apply.[37] As with defining an 'Indian Tribe', only Congress has the power to diminish or extinguish 'Indian country'. This was first confirmed in *Solem v Bartlett*, which stated the central governing principle that only Congress could divest a reservation of its lands and diminish its boundaries.[38] This was later reinforced in the recent case of *McGirt v Oklahoma*[39] when the State of Oklahoma attempted to assert that the State had the power to diminish Tribal lands.[40]

Once the concepts of 'Indian Tribe' and 'Indian Country' have been established for the Tribe seeking federal recognition, the relationship between the United States and Indian Tribal Nations is clarified as one of Nation-to-'domestic dependent' Nation. This enables the US federal government to exercise three powers over Indian Tribes, reciprocated with corresponding federal obligations towards these Tribes when exercising these powers.

33 25 United States Code § 450 b(e). For further discussion, see Anderson, Krakoff, and Berger (n 10) 251–255.
34 Anderson, Krakoff, and Berger (n 10).
35 *United States v Sandoval* [1913] 231 US 28.
36 18 United States Code (n 32).
37 For further reading, see Cambou (n 13); Gilbert and Lennox (n 13); Tomaselli (n 13).
38 *Solem* (n 32) 470.
39 *McGirt* (n 32).
40 For further discussion on Indian Country jurisdiction see Anderson, Krakoff, and Berger (n 10) 273–294; Getches and others (n 10) 510–531.

The obligations toward Tribal Nations can be seen as three legal doctrines: the Reserved Rights Doctrine, the Congressional Plenary Power Doctrine, and the Trust Doctrine.

First, as jurists explain the Reserved Rights Doctrine recognizes certain inherent rights retained by Indian Tribes despite the loss of their original lands or other aspects of Tribal sovereignty. The doctrine establishes that Tribes retain all the powers of any sovereign unless those powers have been expressly removed via treaty, congressional edict, or implicit divestment.[41] Under this doctrine, when a Tribe ceded or sold land to the United States through a treaty or other agreement, certain rights and privileges were expressly reserved for the Tribe.[42] The doctrine is rooted in the concept that the Tribes' rights to engage in traditional activities on their ancestral lands are not automatically extinguished by the transfer of ownership to the federal government. It has been recognized and affirmed by various court decisions, including the landmark case of *United States v Winans* (1905).[43] In that case, the US Supreme Court held that Tribal members possessed a reserved right to fish in their usual and accustomed fishing grounds, even after those lands were ceded to the United States. It has been influential in shaping the legal framework for the protection of Tribal rights, particularly in the context of natural resource management and environmental regulations.[44] It acknowledges the importance of preserving Tribal cultural practices, sustenance activities, and Tribal self-governance.[45]

Second, as noted by scholars, the Congressional Plenary Power Doctrine gives Congress broad authority and control over Indian Tribes. Under this doctrine, Congress can regulate Tribal affairs and make decisions that impact Tribal sovereignty without being restricted by constitutional limitations that apply to other areas of federal power.[46] The doctrine derives from the US Constitution's Indian Commerce Clause, which grants Congress the authority to regulate commerce with Indian Tribes.[47] *United States v Kagama*[48] and *Lone Wolf v Hitchcock*[49] have interpreted this doctrine to give Congress

[41] For further reading, see Cambou (n 13); Gilbert and Lennox (n 13); Tomaselli (n 13).

[42] Anderson, Krakoff, and Berger (n 10); Getches and others (n 10).

[43] *United States v Winans* [1905] 198 US 371.

[44] For further reading, see Cambou (n 13); Gilbert and Lennox (n 13); Tomaselli (n 13).

[45] Judith Royster, Michael Blumm, and Elizabeth Ann Kronk, *Native American Natural Resources Law* (3rd edn, Carolina Academic Press 2002) 367–369, 372–373.

[46] For further reading, see Cambou (n 13); Gilbert and Lennox (n 13); Tomaselli (n 13).

[47] US Constitution, art 1, s 8, Commerce clause which states that the United States Congress shall have power '[t]o regulate Commerce with foreign Nations, and among the several States, and with the Indian Tribes'.

[48] *United States v Kagama* [1886] 118 US 375.

[49] *Lone Wolf v Hitchcock* [1903] 187 US 553.

extensive power over Tribal Nations, including the ability to legislate on matters such as Tribal membership, land use, jurisdiction, and the relationship between Tribes and non-Tribal entities. Specifically, this is through Congress' power over Indian Tribes in three ways: subject matter, the exclusivity of states, and the quality of being beyond the courts' review. The authority of Congress to have absolute power over Indian Tribes is a concept that is based on the merger of the doctrines of discovery and conquest in the Marshall Trilogy.

According to the Congressional Plenary Power Doctrine, experts maintain, Congress can abrogate or diminish Tribal sovereignty, alter reservation boundaries, and regulate Tribal governance. This doctrine has been used historically to pass laws that have significantly affected Tribal communities, such as the Indian Removal Act of 1830 and the General Allotment Act of 1887.[50] However, it is worth noting that the application and scope of the Congressional Plenary Power Doctrine have been subject to ongoing legal debate and evolving interpretations. US District Judge Louis Oberdorfer in his 1990 case[51] was highly critical of the plenary power doctrine and asserted that it should be re-evaluated to ensure a more balanced and respectful approach to Tribal self-governance and sovereignty rather than bestowing Congress with absolute power over Indian Tribes.[52] This opinion has been supported by leading Indigenous law professors, as an opportunity to revisit the balancing of sovereign interests.[53]

Finally, it is argued, the Trust Doctrine establishes a fiduciary relationship between the federal government and Indian Tribes.[54] Under this doctrine, the federal government has a legal and moral responsibility to protect the interests and welfare of Indian Tribes and their members. Specifically, these obligations can include:

- Protecting [T]ribal lands and resources: The government must manage and protect [T]ribal lands, natural resources, and other assets for the benefit of [T]ribes and their members. This includes safeguarding against unauthorized use, depletion, or exploitation.

[50] For further reading, see Cambou (n 13); Gilbert and Lennox (n 13); Tomaselli (n 13).

[51] *Red Lake Band of Chippewa Indians v Swimmer* [1990] 740 F Supp 9, 11, 12.

[52] For further reading, see Cambou (n 13); Gilbert and Lennox (n 13); Tomaselli (n 13).

[53] Lindsay Robertson, 'Freedom 101: How the Constitution Address Native Americans' (Lecture Series, University of Oklahoma College of Law, 29 October 2012); for further reading, see Cambou (n 13); Gilbert and Lennox (n 13); Tomaselli (n 13).

[54] Mary Christina Wood, 'Indian Land and the Promise of Native Sovereignty: The Trust Doctrine Revisited' (1994) 4 Utah Law Review 1471.

- Upholding treaty obligations: The government is responsible for honouring the terms of treaties and agreements made with [T]ribes, including the protection of treaty rights, such as hunting, fishing, and gathering rights.
- Promoting [T]ribal self-governance: The government must support and facilitate [T]ribal self-governance, allowing [T]ribes to exercise their inherent sovereign powers and make decisions regarding their internal affairs.
- Providing essential services and programs: The government has a duty to provide essential services and programs to [T]ribes, such as healthcare, education, housing, and infrastructure development, to promote the well-being of [T]ribal communities.[55]

The Trust Doctrine originates from the historical relationship between the United States and Native American Tribes, characterized by treaties, agreements, and laws.[56] It is based on the notion that the federal government, as the trustee, has a duty to act in the best interests of Tribes and ensure the protection of Tribal lands, resources, and rights. Stemming from *Cherokee Nation v Georgia*,[57] In the Marshall cases, the US Supreme Court emphasized that the US federal government's relationship with Indian Tribes was held to be akin to that of a 'guardian and his ward'. In underlining the guardian-ward model, the Court notes the existence of a fiduciary relationship governed by trust law. The government thus has an obligation to act as a trustee for Tribes and uphold its fiduciary responsibilities. The case of *United States v Kagama*,[58] while finding plenary power of Congress over Indian Tribes, also underlined the obligation of Congress to protect Indian Tribes:

> These Indian [T]ribes are the wards of the [N]ation. They are communities dependent on the United States ... From their very weakness and helplessness, so largely due to the course of dealing of the Federal Government with them and the treaties in which has been promised, there arise the duty of protection, and with it the power.[59]

Congress and the federal government are, as a corollary obligated to exercise plenary power in the best interest of the Indian Tribes. Applying this trust

[55] Janice Aitken, 'The Trust Doctrine in Federal Indian Law: A Look at Its Development and at How Its Analysis under Social Contract Theory Might Expand Its Scope' (1997) 18 Northern Illinois University Law Review 115, 115 to 119.

[56] For further reading, see Cambou (n 13); Gilbert and Lennox (n 13); Tomaselli (n 13).

[57] *Cherokee Nation* (n 2); Aitken (n 55) 117–122.

[58] *Kagama* (n 48).

[59] ibid 383–384.

doctrine in federal Indian law thus also has possibilities for creative applications in the law of equity beyond the scope of this brief case study.[60]

The three legal doctrines underline a significant power imbalance that has existed and continues to exist because of findings such as the 'domestic dependant [N]ation' and 'plenary power doctrine' by Congress over Indian Tribes.[61] To address this, the courts have developed canons of construction – tools that aid in striking an equitable balance in the federal/Indian relationship.[62] As Anderson, citing Cohen's *Handbook of Federal Indian Law* from 2012, explains, these Indian law canons of construction as follows:

> The basic Indian law canons of construction require that treaties, agreements, statutes, and executive orders be liberally construed in favor of the Indians; all ambiguities are to be resolved in favor of the Indians; in addition, treaties and agreements are to be construed as the Indians would have understood them; and [T]ribal property rights and sovereignty are preserved unless Congress's intent to the contrary is clear and unambiguous. [63]

Such canons of construction are not exclusive to US Tribal law.[64] In Canada Rules of Indigenous Interpretation of Treaties, discussed earlier in this volume, stipulate that, first, judgment must favour an Indigenous interpretation if there is ambiguity, and that there should be a large and liberal interpretation which likewise must be provided in favour of the affected Indigenous People.[65]

[60] For a detailed discussion on the Trust Doctrine see Royster Blumm, and Kronk (n 45) 76–78; Anderson, Krakoff, and Berger (n 10) 164–166; Getches and others (n 10) 361–363.

[61] For further reading, see Cambou (n 13); Gilbert and Lennox (n 13); Tomaselli (n 13).

[62] Getches and others (n 10) 154–156.

[63] Anderson, Krakoff, and Berger (n 10) 168 (citations omitted).

[64] For example, these canons have been applied in Canadian Indigenous law. There, the Crown has an obligation to follow these rules of construction in denying or extinguishing a treaty right when in relation to trade. There must be a clear, express, and unambiguous extinguishment of the right to cross-border inter-Tribal trade for it to apply. If an unambiguous clause is in question, then an interpretation using the Rules of Indigenous Interpretation of Treaties should apply. For more on inter-Tribal trade and Jay Treaty principles, see Chapter 9; see also John Borrows and Risa Schwartz (eds), *Indigenous Peoples and International Trade: Building Equitable and Inclusive International Trade and Investment Agreements* (Cambridge University Press 2020).

[65] ibid; *R. v Sioui* [1990] 1 SCR 1025, 1035, 1042–1043; *Simon v The Queen* [1985] 2 SCR 387, 410; the Supreme Court of Canada determined that 'treaties and statutes relating to Indians should be liberally construed and uncertainties resolved in favour of the Indians', as discussed in earlier chapters.

10.3 TRIBAL NATION SOVEREIGNTY: PAST AND PRESENT

Tribal sovereignty and the right to self-government is a practical affair centred around the day-to-day operations of Tribal Nations. Although the courts constantly push and pull at the fringes of Tribal sovereignty, the ever-shifting jurisdictional boundary between the Tribes and the other two sovereign entities, that is federal and state, is not the reality of Tribal sovereignty and governance. Tribal Nations' rightful sovereign focus is on core matters uncontestably within the purview of Tribal governance, which generally concerns domestic and internal operations. These uncontested core matters include good governance,[66] the power to tax, the regulation of the defined property within the jurisdiction, the administration of justice, and rule-making for inheritance and probate.[67] Like other measures identified above, these governance powers also align with SDG 16.7, promoting inclusive and participatory governance.

The United States has expressly acknowledged, since 1832, the Tribal right of sovereignty. The right has been contested constantly, through struggles in the courts, in Congress, and in the state legislatures – alongside constant efforts to educate decision-makers and to protect against the legislative and judicial erosion of Tribal sovereignty.[68] As one example of the violations of Indigenous sovereignty and identity, for which redress and restitution are committed to in UNDRIP Articles 8, 11, and 28, together with SDG 16.3 on justice for all, the allotment policy in the nineteenth and twentieth centuries mentioned above sought to remove Indigenous sovereignty by weakening Indigenous rights guaranteed through treaties.[69] The allotment in US Tribal law refers to a historical federal policy implemented primarily through the General Allotment Act of 1887, also known as the Dawes Act.[70] The allotment policy aimed to break up and destroy Tribal lands held in common and distribute them to individual Tribal members.[71] The goal of the allotment policy was to assimilate Native Americans into mainstream American society, promote private land ownership, and encourage agricultural

[66] Which includes choosing its own form of government, determining its own membership, and regulating its own domestic relations.

[67] Anderson, Krakoff, and Berger (n 10) 147, 151, and 152; William C Canby, 'Tribal Sovereignty Today – Its Meanings and Limits' in *American Indian Law in a Nutshell* (6th edn, West Academic Publishing 2015) 78, 79.

[68] For further reading, see Cambou (n 13); Gilbert and Lennox (n 13); Tomaselli (n 13).

[69] ibid.

[70] 25 United States Code (n 33) ch 32, which includes the General Allotment Act (the Dawes Act) and subsequent amendments.

[71] For further reading, see Cambou (n 13); Gilbert and Lennox (n 13); Tomaselli (n 13).

practices among Native communities.[72] The allotment was viewed as one of the chief remedies to the 'Indian Problem' by taking the existing Tribe and transforming it from a sovereign Nation, endowed in perpetuity with vast Tribal land holdings guaranteed to the Indigenous Nation by treaty, into a manageable set of individuals.[73] These individuals were Christianized but were not citizens of the United States, instead characterized as merely farmers whose lands have been seized by the United States.[74] As such, they were bereft of the rights of an Indigenous sovereign Nation; specifically, they no longer held the collective group land rights that are similar to those of the citizens of a State. It is thus unsurprising that 'no panacea for the Indian problem was more persistently proposed than the allotment of land to the Indians in severalty.'[75] From the late 1880s onward, the reservation system was characterized as an impediment to attempts to secure the assimilation of 'the Indian' into American society.[76] The allotment policy, experts note, was viewed as a means to 'Americanize the Indian' while getting rid of the inconvenient Indigenous groups that held Tribal sovereignty rights. This enabled a 'powerful drive then underway for general allotment of land in severalty and for extending United States law over the Indians was intended ultimately to destroy the reservation system.'[77]

Under the policy, Tribal lands were divided into smaller parcels and allocated to individual Tribal members, typically with the intention of transitioning them from a communal landholding system to a system of individual land ownership.[78] It primarily featured three dimensions. First, the allotment of land divided Tribal lands into individual allotments, typically ranging from 40 to 160 acres per individual, depending on various factors such as Tribal membership and availability of land. Each Tribal member was assigned an allotment, and the remaining 'surplus' lands were opened for non-Native settlement.[79] Secondly, there was assimilation and citizenship. This policy encouraged Native Americans to adopt a farming lifestyle and conform to American cultural norms. Allottees were granted US citizenship, and often,

72 Delos Sacket Otis, 'Chapter II Aims and Motives' in *The Dawes Act and the Allotment of Indian Lands* (University of Oklahoma Press 1973).

73 Indian General Allotment Act, 1887, NADP Document A1887 (otherwise known as 'Dawes Act') 24, 388–391.

74 For further reading, see Cambou (n 13); Gilbert and Lennox (n 13); Tomaselli (n 13).

75 Paul Francis Prucha, *The Great Father, The United States Government and the American Indians* (University of Nebraska Press 1988) 224.

76 For further reading, see Cambou (n 13); Gilbert and Lennox (n 13); Tomaselli (n 13).

77 Prucha (n 75) 223.

78 Otis (n 72).

79 For further reading, see Cambou (n 13); Gilbert and Lennox (n 13); Tomaselli (n 13).

the distribution of land was tied to requirements such as abandoning Tribal practices and adopting Western agricultural methods.[80] Lastly, land ownership restrictions were put in place. Allotted lands were subject to various restrictions and regulations, including a period of trust status during which the lands were held in trust by the federal government for a specified period, typically twenty-five years, and could not be sold or transferred.[81] This period was intended to provide time for Native individuals to learn agricultural practices and become self-sufficient.[82] This allowed the allotted Indian lands to change from an occupancy interest to a clear fee simple title.[83] Thus, historians and jurists note, the 'Indians' were forcibly expelled from both their communally held treaty lands and their ancient group identity, and they were made to pay, with that same act, for their own destitution.[84]

To facilitate the land allotment process and Tribal citizenship enrolment in 1893, Congress passed the 'Dawes Commission Act' or the 'Curtis Act', which established a special commission to negotiate with the 'Five Civilized Tribes' (Five Trading Tribes) in Oklahoma, namely the Cherokee, Chickasaw, Choctaw, Creek (Muscogee), and Seminole Nations.[85] A three-member Dawes Commission met and unsuccessfully negotiated with the Five Trading Tribes until 1895 when Congress ordered that the Five Trading Tribes' lands be surveyed.[86] To do so, they passed the 1898 *Curtis Act* setting up a harsh and rigorous land allotment process.[87] This forced the Five Trading Tribes to negotiate in haste before the strict rules of the 1898 *Curtis Act* took effect.[88]

There was a great deal of resistance to being forced into an allotment, experts observe, given that the Five Tribes had been promised treaty protection.[89]

80 ibid.
81 ibid.
82 David A Chang, 'Enclosures of Land and Sovereignty: The Allotment of American Indian Lands' (2011) 109 Radical History Review 108.
83 Prucha (n 75) 226.
84 Paul Francis Prucha, *Documents of United States Indian Policy General Allotment Act, February 8, 1887, Section 1* (University of Nebraska Press 1975) 17 and 171–172.
85 The term 'Five Civilized Tribes' derives from the colonial period in the history of the United States. It refers to five Indigenous Tribal Nations – the Cherokee, Chickasaw, Choctaw, Creek, and Seminole. These are the first five Tribes that European Americans called 'civilized'. These Tribes had always had active, wealthy, and powerful trading systems, and they chose to involve the European colonials in their commerce as opposed to engaging in hostile acts of war. This author is of the opinion that the term 'Five Trading Tribes' is more apt.
86 For further reading, see Cambou (n 13); Gilbert and Lennox (n 13); Tomaselli (n 13).
87 W David Baird and Danney Goble, *The Story of Oklahoma* (2nd edn, University of Oklahoma Press 2013) 261.
88 ibid 261–262.
89 For further reading, see Cambou (n 13); Gilbert and Lennox (n 13); Tomaselli (n 13).

As Baird and Boble note, 'Oklahoma's Five Tribes were losing the sovereignty that had been promised to them for as long as the grass grew and the waters ran.'[90] Specifically, open resistance to allotment came from the Four Mothers Society. Active in almost every Tribe except the Seminole, it claimed to have as many as 24,000 members, every one of them a person resolved not to let go of the old promises. Then, in 1901, 'an elderly full-blood Creek named Chitto Harjo (Crazy Snake) organized a shadow government with its own council and passed its own laws – laws that forbade Creeks to accept allotment, rent land to non-Creeks or employ White Labour.'[91] The local Indian Agent, upon learning of the separate anti-allotment council, called in the US Army, which rounded up 94 Creeks, most of them elderly, calling their protest 'the Crazy Snake Rebellion' and sending them off to prison.[92]

Ultimately, historians note, the Tribal lands were divided into allotments, with surplus lands opened for non-Native settlement.[93] The process disrupted traditional Tribal land tenure systems and communal landholding practices, causing a loss of Tribal territory and cultural disruption.[94] Additionally, Tribal membership rolls were created, which had implications for Tribal citizenship and benefits. This forcibly took away Tribal sovereignty from the Five Trading Tribes and eroded the right to self-government.[95]

As referenced in part above, ensuring restitution or recognition of these rights would align with SDG 10.2, fostering social, economic, and political inclusion, 10.3 and 16b on non-discriminatory laws and policies, and SDG 16.7 on responsive, inclusive, participatory, and representative decision-making at all levels, in addition to the commitments in the UNDRIP Articles 8, 11, and 28.

10.3.1 McGirt v Oklahoma: *Righting Past Legal Wrongs and Establishment of Tribal Reservation Boundaries and Tribal Jurisdiction*

On 9 July 2020, the US Supreme Court issued its decision in *McGirt v Oklahoma*,[96] seen as one of the most important Indigenous rights decision in the twenty-first century, which clarified the extent of proof required to constitute treaty land (reservation) disestablishment by the State. The case

[90] Baird and Goble (n 87) 262.
[91] ibid 263.
[92] ibid.
[93] ibid.
[94] For further reading, see Cambou (n 13); Gilbert and Lennox (n 13); Tomaselli (n 13).
[95] Baird and Goble (n 87).
[96] *McGirt* (n 32).

challenged the prosecution of Jimcy McGirt, a citizen of the Seminole Nation, by the State of Oklahoma for a crime committed on land that, according to the accused, at the time of the alleged crime was on Muscogee (Creek) Nation reservation land.[97] As such, it was argued, Oklahoma had no jurisdiction under federal law, and the crime should have instead been prosecuted at the federal level. The Court examined whether the land was, as McGirt purported, Muscogee (Creek) Nation reservation land or had the land been disestablished by Congress more than a century ago even though the land had once been reservation land?[98]

The Muscogee (Creek) Nation was forcibly removed from their traditional lands in the south-eastern United States to what is now Oklahoma in the 1830s, and the reservation lands, McGirt argued, included all or part of eleven Oklahoma counties and most of the city of Tulsa.[99] As a result of the Allotment Act,[100] the treaty guaranteed that communally held Tribal reservation land had been carved up against the will of the Muscogee (Creek) Nation. The federal government created allotments of individual farms and ranches, distributing them to individual Muscogee (Creek) citizens, with the remainder being either sold to non-Indigenous settlers, ranchers, and farmers or held by the federal government as trust lands.

The court majority sided with McGirt and decided that the text of the Allotment Act did not clearly disestablish the Muscogee (Creek) reservation and Oklahoma had no jurisdiction to prosecute on those lands. The failure to disestablish the reservation meant that the Muscogee (Creek) was and always had been their reservation.[101] The McGirt Decision re-acknowledged the Muscogee (Creek) Nation reservation in accordance with the treaty boundaries and within those boundaries, in accordance with the original sovereign jurisdiction in relation to the State of Oklahoma.[102] This decision, while jurisdictional in nature, serves as an important boundary re-acknowledgement, one which aligns with SDG 16.3 on the rule of law and equal access to justice, SDG 16.6 on effective and accountable institutions, and the UNDRIP, particularly Articles 4 on self-governance, 5 on the right to strengthen distinct Indigenous institutions, 26 on the right to traditional lands, 27 on land adjudication, and 37 on respect for treaties concluded with States.

97 For further reading, see Cambou (n 13); Gilbert and Lennox (n 13); Tomaselli (n 13).
98 ibid.
99 For further reading, see Cambou (n 13); Gilbert and Lennox (n 13); Tomaselli (n 13).
100 25 United States Code (n 33) § 5, 24 Stat. 389–390; Creek Allotment Agreement, ch 676, 31 Stat. 861.
101 For further reading, see Cambou (n 13); Gilbert and Lennox (n 13); Tomaselli (n 13).
102 25 United States Code (n 33) § 5, 24 Stat. 389–390; Creek Allotment Agreement (n 100).

This decision, incidentally, effectively revised the Court's opinion in another disestablishment case, *Nebraska v Parker*, in which a small non-Indigenous town in Nebraska was held to be within a reservation.[103] The rationale of the judgment was that a post-treaty event had somehow rendered the lawful treaty irrelevant. The *McGirt* decision ended the prior flawed and irrational justification for disestablishment by placing the burden of proof squarely on the State to perfect its intention to dissolve a reservation.[104] The decision reinforces that externalities are irrelevant in disestablishment cases and that clear language from statutes alone (the express and clear intention of Congress) should answer questions of intent.[105] Post-*McGirt*, Indigenous Tribes can make claims based on historic promises without fear that subsequent, often unjust events will defeat them.

10.4 US TRIBAL SOVEREIGNTY THROUGH INTERNATIONAL INDIGENOUS TRADE

Grounded in an understanding of Tribal rights concerning both economic rights and sovereignty, the current situation for Indigenous Peoples in the United States can largely be interpreted by analysing their participation in treaties and trade, examined through the lenses of jurisprudence and legislation, and informed by the UNDRIP; particularly, Articles 3 on pursuing economic development, 5 and 20 on distinct economic institutions, and 36 on the right to develop and maintain contacts and cross-border cooperation with other Indigenous Peoples. Treaties and trade are also salient to this chapter's analysis of SDGs, particularly SDG targets 10.2 to empower and promote the social, economic, and political inclusion of all, 17.10 on equitable trade, and 17.16 on multi-stakeholder partnerships.

In the United States, Indigenous Peoples still hold to some extent the unextinguished right to domestic and international inter-Tribal trade. At a minimum, Indigenous People need to be consulted, but above all, they need to be involved in trade negotiations. In the absence of guidance from the US Supreme Court on whether trade negotiations trigger consultation requirements with Indigenous Peoples, the US federal government needs to fill this policy gap and develop a framework for meaningful participation and for increased involvement of Indigenous peoples in trade negotiations.[106] As an

[103] *Nebraska v Parker* [2016] 577 US.
[104] For further reading, see Cambou (n 13); Gilbert and Lennox (n 13); Tomaselli (n 13).
[105] *McGirt* (n 32) 8.
[106] For further reading, see Cambou (n 13); Gilbert and Lennox (n 13); Tomaselli (n 13).

example, trade chapters may be considered essential to Indigenous inclusion in international economic opportunities. They have potential to promote and enhance cooperation in trade and investment among like-minded States, which improves global capacity and conditions for Indigenous Peoples to engage successfully in cross-border inter-Tribal trade. Coupling a good domestic trade policy with trade engagement activity is thus essential to developed trade chapter in an international trade agreement.[107]

Trade agreements, between Canada and the United States, for example, could include provisions allowing free movement of Indigenous Peoples and goods traded by Indigenous Peoples across the Canada-US border. This would be consistent with the Jay Treaty, formerly known as the Treaty of Amity, Commerce, and Navigation,[108] which was entered into force by the United States and Great Britain on 19 November 1794. Article III of the Jay Treaty states that the Parties would allow First Nations Peoples to live on either side of the newly established border and to freely cross the border for, among other things, inter-Tribal trade:

> It is agreed that at all Times be free to His Majesty's Subjects, and to the Citizens of the United States, and also to the Indians dwelling on either side of said Boundary Line freely to pass and re-pass by Land, or Inland Navigation, into the respective Territories and Countries of the Two Parties on the Continent of America (the Country within the Limits of the Hudson's Bay Company only excepted) and to navigate all the Lakes, Rivers and waters thereof, and *freely to carry on trade and commerce with each other* [...] No Duty of Entry shall ever be levied by either Party on Peltries brought by Land, or Inland Navigation into the said Territories respectively, nor shall the Indians passing or re-passing with their own proper Goods and Effects of whatever nature, pay for the same any Import or Duty whatever. But Goods in Bales, or other large Packages unusual among the Indians shall not be considered as Goods belonging bona fide to Indians.[109]

Two recent pieces of jurisprudence indicate that inter-Tribal trade is within the rights held by Tribal Nations in the United States. The first case, *Grand River Enterprises Six Nations Ltd. v United States* [*Grand*

[107] The Canadian government worked with Indigenous partners to develop and refine Canada's Indigenous trade policy, which is reflected in the Indigenous trade mechanisms, including IPETCA, to which Canada is a Participant.

[108] Treaty of Amity, Commerce, and Navigation (His Britannic Majesty–United States of America) (adopted 19 November 1794, entered into force 29 February 1796) (Jay Treaty). Additional context relating to the Jay Treaty, including Canada's failure to honour the Jay Treaty, can be found in Chapter 4.

[109] ibid art III (emphasis added).

River],[110] demonstrates that regular inter-Tribal trade for Indigenous products, spanning Canada and the United States, for example, is accepted and legitimate, so long as it stays within the inter-Tribal realm. *Grand River* is a case brought under NAFTA's chapter 11 investor-State dispute settlement mechanism involving the inter-Tribal trade of Canadian Indigenous cigarettes transported and sold outside the scope of US Tribal sales. The claimants produced tobacco products on Haudenosaunee territory claimed by Canada. The tobacco products were distributed on sovereign Indigenous lands located throughout the United States, through a facility owned by one of the claimants located on Seneca territory claimed by the United States.[111] Because the Canadian Indigenous tobacco was regularly sold on US Tribal lands, it received no state or provincial sales tax or duties, which constitutes a favourable treatment, and was exempt from the tobacco taxes generally imposed for all other tobacco products sold outside of Indian lands. This greatly reduced the cost of the Indigenous tobacco product in comparison to non-Indigenous tobacco products sold 'off-reserve' and thus made the Canadian Indigenous tobacco products considerably cheaper. However, the Indigenous tobacco products were also distributed or sold 'off-reserve' by an exclusive, third-party distributor at prices below that of duty-paid tobacco products, threatening the State's excise tax revenues from non-Indigenous tobacco companies.[112] Though the Tribunal Members declined to resolve competing interpretations of the Jay Treaty presented to them, which they held did not confer 'absolute immunity' from state regulation, they did acknowledge the detailed argument and historical narrative in favour of such immunity, together with the 'importance of the Jay Treaty for protecting cross-border movement and trade among [I]ndigenous [P]eoples in North America'. They also agreed that there are rights and interests for Indigenous Nations to maintain and develop cross-border trade relations in accordance with longstanding traditions in promoting economic development opportunities for Indigenous communities.[113] An important finding was thus the recognition of a nexus between rights in Indigenous treaty law, including rights to inter-Tribal trade found in the Jay

[110] *Grand River Enterprises Six Nations Ltd and Others v United States of America*, Award, ICSID (International Center for Settlement of Investment Disputes) (2011) Case No ARB/10/5, IIC 481.

[111] Keeping Indigenous tobacco trade within the inter-Tribal realm, that is among Tribal Nations, offers the considerable economic advantage of greatly reduced taxes and duties, with favourable conditions for competition. To sell the Indigenous product outside the realm of Indigenous sales to non-Indigenous People would give a significant price advantage to the Indigenous company, disadvantaging the non-Indigenous company.

[112] *Grand River* (n 110) 23–26, 119.

[113] ibid 143, 186.

Treaty, and an Indigenous investor's reasonable expectations of treatment associated with First Nations Status.

The second case, *Washington State Department of Licensing v Cougar Den, Inc.* from the US Supreme Court in 2019,[114] confirmed inter-Tribal trade rights for the Yakama Nation, located in the general region just south of British Columbia in Washington State.[115] The US Supreme Court found that the *Yakama Treaty of 1855* confirmed the express treaty right of the Yakama People to conduct inter-Tribal trade and the right to travel outside their Nation for the purposes of bringing their goods to and from market.[116] Justice Gorsuch, for the major decision brief, stated that 'this Court has considered this treaty four times previously; each time it has considered language very similar to the language now before the Court; and each time it has stressed that the language of the treaty should be understood as bearing the meaning that the Yakamas understood it to have in 1855'.[117] As to the 'understood' meaning, the US Supreme Court construes that, '[t]he 1855 treaty guarantees Tribal members the right to move their goods, including fuel, to and from market freely. When dealing with a Tribal treaty, a court must "give effect to the terms as the Indians themselves would have understood them"'.[118] Thus, the majority concluded that the treaty right to inter-Tribal trade remains cogent.[119] Should there be any doubt, the courts have the tools to aid in the clarification of this protected treaty right.

The US Senate also passed the *Native American Business Development, Trade Promotion, and Tourism Act 2000* to support international Indigenous trade.[120] The official legislative 'Findings' and 'Purpose' refer to promoting Indigenous and inter-Tribal international trade. Articles like 4301(a)(4) and

[114] *Washington State Department of Licensing v Cougar Den, Inc.* (2019) 586 US.

[115] For further reading, see Cambou (n 13); Gilbert and Lennox (n 13); Tomaselli (n 13).

[116] *Washington State Department* (n 114).

[117] ibid 3, 10. To discern the meaning of the language, the US Supreme Court expressly applied its rules of treaty interpretation. In the case of *United States ex. rel Hualpai Indians v Santa Fe Pacific Railway Co.* [1941] 314 US 339 the Court determined that doubtful expressions in acts relating to Indians, instead of being resolved in favour of United States, are to be resolved in favour of the Indians. In the US Supreme Court case of *United States v Shoshone Tribe of Indians* [1938] 304 US 111, the following sage analysis was applied: 'Treaties (recognized title) made by the United States with Indian [T]ribes are not to be interpreted narrowly but are to be construed in the sense in which naturally the Indians would understand them [...]. Doubts, if any, as to the ownership of land, minerals, or timber, would be resolved in favor of the [T]ribe, since transactions between a guardian and his wards are to be construed favorably to the ward.'

[118] *Washington State Department* (n 114) 3 and 10 citing *Minnesota v Mille Lacs Band of Chippewa Indians* [1999] 526 US 172, 196.

[119] For further reading, see Cambou (n 13); Gilbert and Lennox (n 13); Tomaselli (n 13).

[120] 25 United States Code (n 33) ch 44, Native American Business Development, Trade Promotion, and Tourism Act 2000.

(b)(5) shed light on the necessity to furnish trade opportunities for American Indians, noting that 'Indian Tribes retain the right to enter into contracts and agreements to trade freely, and seek enforcement of treaty and trade rights',[121] and that the Act encourages 'inter[T]ribal, regional, and international trade and business development in order to assist in increasing productivity and the standard of living of members of Indian Tribes and improving the economic self-sufficiency of the governing bodies of Indian Tribes'.[122] Additionally, Article 4304 specifically addresses 'Native American trade and export promotion', where subsection (c) legislates the creation of certain programs to 'develop the economies of Indian [T]ribes [...] and stimulate the demand for Indian goods and services[...]'.[123] These statutory priorities are to ensure 'the greatest degree of economic benefits to Indians; and [...] foster long-term stable international markets for Indian goods and services'.[124] While the legislation seems worthwhile and reasonably straightforward, finding actual application of these statutory sections, in the form of active support for American Indian International trade opportunities, remains something of a challenge.[125]

Effective judicial recognition of the Jay Treaty, together with legislation in support of Indigenous trade, represent important measures in support of Tribal self-governance, and inter-Tribal trade. As discussed above, these developments align with the UNDRIP's commitments in Articles 3 on pursuing economic development, 5 and 20 on distinct economic institutions, and 36 on the right to develop and maintain contacts and cross-border cooperation with other Indigenous Peoples. They also further support SDG targets 10.2, 17.10, and 17.16.

10.5 CONCLUSION

This chapter has explored the intricate interplay between Tribal sovereignty and economic rights to trade within the context of the United States. The examination of Tribal sovereignty has shed light on arguments for more sustainable and equitable affirmations of Indigenous rights in the United States. However, it is crucial to acknowledge that the journey toward reconciliation, sustainable development, and economic self-sufficiency for Tribal Nations is an ongoing process. Challenges persist, including navigating

[121] ibid § 4301 (a)(4).
[122] ibid § 4301 (b)(5).
[123] ibid § 4304 (b) 'Coordination of Federal programs and services'.
[124] ibid § 4304 (e) 'Priorities'.
[125] For further reading, see Cambou (n 13); Gilbert and Lennox (n 13); Tomaselli (n 13).

complex legal frameworks, addressing social and economic disparities, and balancing cultural preservation with economic growth. Policymakers, legal practitioners, and Tribal leaders must continue to collaborate, striving to develop inclusive and equitable frameworks that empower Tribal Nations to pursue sustainable economic development while safeguarding their cultural and natural resources.

In Chapter 11, attention turns to New Zealand's experiences to continue illuminating the diverse approaches different countries and Indigenous Peoples take to reconcile the imperatives of sustainable development with the demands of international trade and uncover valuable practices that may promote sustainable development within the context of Indigenous treaties.

11

Legal Standing for Nature in New Zealand

11.1 INTRODUCTION

Indigenous philosophies tend to place people within, not above, the environment and see it not as a commodity to be plundered but as an ongoing relationship. Such a relationship with the environment is one of harvesting and reciprocity – giving back to protect its long-term viability for future generations. Additionally, human guardians or *kaitiaki* have specific roles to play in representing the interests of nature and adequately protecting the environment. Indigenous Peoples' Traditional Knowledge (TK) is a repository of knowledge, values, philosophy, and understanding necessary for providing this *kaitiaki* guardianship role. As the World Economic Forum's Global Risk Report 2020 states 'humanity relies on [I]ndigenous communities to be stewards of ecosystems, protecting and preserving environmental resources. Indigenous [P]eoples comprise less than 5% of the world's population but protect 80% of its biodiversity'.[1] Because Indigenous Peoples have never ceased teaching and practising their Traditional Knowledge of living in balance with nature, they are often best placed as *kaitiaki* to speak on behalf of nature and to represent its best interests.

New Zealand (Aotearoa, or Aotearoa New Zealand) sets an example of how a country can protect nature by adopting an alternative to the inherently human-centric, anthropocentric approach to ownership in most Western legal

[1] World Economic Forum, 'The Global Risks Report 2020' (15th edn, 2020) 49. The authors are grateful to Dr Robert Joseph for his insights and contributions to this chapter.

systems.[2] Specifically, the co-governance structure of the Te Urewera National Park with the local Māori tribe and the guardianship structure surrounding the Whanganui River are sources of inspiration for countries seeking alternatives for conservation, as they embrace the Indigenous Māori philosophy of quasi-kinship with nature. By providing legal personhood to a national park and river, this New Zealand statutory experiment has the potential to give nature the power and authority to protect itself, with the aid of Indigenous *kaitiaki* guardians, in courts while advancing conservation.

This chapter provides an overview of how Aotearoa (New Zealand's) treaty and legislative innovations have evolved over time through the relationships between the New Zealand Government and the Māori Tribes to enable cutting-edge sustainable development practices. First, this chapter begins with an examination into specific aspects of Māori culture, practices, and TK, especially in terms of the Māori philosophy of kinship with Nature and the *tikanga Māori* form of Māori governance. *Tikanga Māori* (customary law) applies Indigenous systems of values and laws in Māori trade governance and stewardship of nature. This analysis next examines how treaty interpretation advanced specific Māori rights, specifically through the lens of the *Treaty of Waitangi*. Building on those interpretive insights, the discussion then turns to the case study of the Tuhoe Māori of Te Urewera lands negotiation, culminating in the *Te Urewera Act 2014*, followed by an examination of the Whanganui River case study, which gave rise to the *Te Awa Tupua (Whanganui River Claims) Settlement Act 2017*. New Zealand's best practices in environment and trade thus emerge as a functional whole – a synthesis of Indigenous Traditional Knowledge in philosophy and New Zealand common law. In this respect, this chapter also features a discussion of how Māori Indigenous TK is paving the way for sustainable development through the additional example of the *Agreement between New Zealand and the Separate Customs Territory of Taiwan, Penghu, Kinmen, and Matsu on Economic Cooperation* (ANZTEC) and New Zealand's new methodology for measuring gross domestic product (GDP). The analysis in this chapter points to how these approaches on Aotearoa align with the commitments made in the UNDRIP, particularly Articles 25–26, rights to land and maintaining spiritual connections thereto, 29 on conservation and protection of the environment, and 36 on the development of contacts with other Indigenous Peoples across borders; likewise, the chapter details how these approaches also advance the SDGs, particularly SDGs 6.6 on protecting and restoring water-related

[2] Anne De Vries-Stotijn, Ilon Van Ham, and Kees Bastmeijer, 'Protection through Property: From Private to River-Held Rights' (2019) 44 Water International 736.

ecosystems, 11.4 on safeguarding the world's cultural and natural heritages, 15 on the preservation of terrestrial ecosystems, 16.7 on inclusive decision-making, and 17.16 on enhancing global partnerships for sustainable development.

11.2 THE MĀORI PHILOSOPHY OF A RELATIONSHIP WITH NATURE

In the individualist capitalistic model, there is the overarching premise that success and relationships are founded on the goals of ever-increasing accumulation of wealth and power for the sole benefit of oneself or one's corporation. Contrast this with the philosophy and worldview behind Indigenous Peoples' role as advocates or *kaitiaki* for the Earth, where Indigenous Peoples see themselves as having an obligation to protect the ecosystem for the benefit of future generations. Such a situation creates the comprehensive rationale behind the Māori traditional rules for guardian relationships, called *tikanga Māori*,[3] which are central to understanding the legal personality that constitutes the natural order of Aotearoa.

Fundamental to any discussion of tikanga Māori, however, is the necessity to appreciate its functioning within te ao Māori – Māori worldviews. As the New Zealand Law Commission recently opined:

> Understanding tikanga requires a journey through the Māori world, one that outlines the knowledge systems, values and beliefs, and that locates tikanga in its natural environment. To try to build an understanding of tikanga outside

[3] Te Aka Māori Dictionary, 'tikanga' (2023) <https://maoridictionary.co.nz/search?keywords=tikanga> accessed 7 March 2025. For other tikanga Māori references, see House of Lords, 'Report from the Select Committee of the House of Lords Appointed to Inquire into the Present State of the Islands of New Zealand and the Expediency of Regulating the Settlement of British Subjects Therein' in British Parliamentary Papers 1838 (No 680, 7 August 1838); Edward Durie, 'Custom Law' (Unpublished Draft Paper, Address to the New Zealand Society for Legal and Social Philosophy, January 1994); Hirini Mead, *Tikanga Māori: Living by Māori Values* (Huia 2003); Joseph Williams, 'Lex Aotearoa: A Heroic Attempt at Mapping the Māori Dimension in Modern New Zealand Law' in Robert Joseph and Richard Benton (eds), *Waking the Taniwha: Māori Governance in the 21st Century* (Thomson Reuters 2021) ch 9; Richard Boast and others, *Māori Land Law* (Butterworths 1999); Robert Joseph, 'Re-creating Space for the First Law of Aotearoa-New Zealand' (2009) 17 Waikato Law Review 74; Richard Benton, Alex Frame, and Paul Meredith, *Te Mātāpunenga: A Compendium of References to the Concepts and Institutions of Māori Customary Law* (Te Mātāhauariki Research Institute, University of Waikato, Victoria University Press 2013); C Fox, 'Ko Te Mana Te Utu. Narratives of Sovereignty, Law and Tribal Citizenship in the Potikirua ki Te Toka-a-Taiau District' (PhD thesis, Te Whare Wānanga o Awanuiārangi 2023); Te Aka Matua o te Ture, Law Commission, *He Poutama* (Law Commission Purongo Rangahau Study Paper 24, Wellington, September 2023) (New Zealand Law Commission).

of that framework runs the risk of it becoming decontextualised and abstract, and where its authentic meaning becomes distorted.[4]

Worldviews generally orientate the human being and their community to their world so that it is rendered understandable and their experience of it is explainable. The Reverend Māori Marsden, a late twentieth century Ngāpuhi tribal *tohunga* (expert), scholar and philosopher, articulated an economical definition of a culture's worldview when he opined:

> Cultures pattern perceptions of reality into conceptualisations of what they perceive reality to be, of what is to be regarded as actual, probable, possible or impossible. These conceptualisations form what is termed the 'world view' of a culture. The world view is the central systematisation of conceptions of reality to which members of its culture assent and from which stems their value system. The worldview lies at the very heart of the culture, touching, interacting with and strongly influencing every aspect of the culture.[5]

The late Māori Law Professor, Nin Tomas, explored further the understanding of *tikanga Māori* and a Māori worldview as forming a 'view of ultimate reality', which includes three foundational ideas:

> (1) that humans are part of an ongoing process that originates from a world of nonphysical existence or 'wairua' that is beyond consciousness, time, or space; (2) that natural connections exist between 'te ao wairua' (the realm of nonphysical or spiritual being) and 'te ao marama' (the material world of physical being); and (3) that 'whakapapa' (genealogy) informs and links all things into a natural order.[6]

By understanding the worldview and such foundational ideas of a culture, we can come to an understanding of its values and behaviour. Worldviews then are invisible sets of ideas about the world that lie deep within a culture.

Consequently, such tikanga Māori worldviews and foundational form three fundamental tenets of the Māori rules governing relationships with the environment:

1. That *Papatuanuku*, or Earth mother, possesses a powerful personality completely independent of human existence.

[4] New Zealand Law Commission (n 3) 25.

[5] Charles Royal, *The Woven Universe: Selected Writings of Rev. Maori Marsden* (Estate of Rev. Maori Marsden, 2003) at 56.

[6] Nin Thomas, 'Maori Concepts of Rangatiratanga, Kaitiakitanga, the Environment, and Property Rights' in David Grinlinton and Prue Taylor (eds), *Property Rights and Sustainability: The Evolution of Property Rights to Meet Ecological Challenges* (Koninklijke Brill 2011) 219, 222–223.

2. Humans are subjects of the environment, rather than its masters and as such, we are part of an interrelated living whole.
3. Finally, *whakapapa*, which is the maintenance of genealogical links to the land, anchors *kaitiaki*, who are caretakers, stewards, and guardians, to fulfill obligations to future generations.[7]

Tikanga Māori as a legal system then is a conception based on relationships through: (1) *Whakapapa* (genealogy) or the physical descent of everything; and (2) *Wairuatanga* or the spiritual connection of everything. *Tikanga Māori* thus considers people, particularly Māori, in general as *kaitiaki* (guardians, stewards), who are interrelated amongst themselves with nature and the natural elements. All Māori are therefore in a relationship with the environment, which is both spiritual and ancestral, and is of utmost importance to survival. This forms the idea of Kaitiakitanga,[8] a guardianship or stewardship, which is one of the fundamental principles underlying Māori worldviews and society, tikanga Māori laws, beliefs, and practices. The stewardship role does not entail individual reward or profit but rather support for an all-encompassing ecological prosperity spanning the past, present, and future. It is a bond that is intergenerational and is tied to the spiritual, intellectual, and physical well-being of both the Māori and the environment. Furthermore, according to traditional Māori philosophy and worldviews, the gods and spirits imbue the natural world and inhabit the land, animals, and plants. People, as Kaitiaki caretakers of these environments and living beings, are their kin, as the Waitangi Tribunal articulated:

> Often translated as 'kinship', whanaungatanga does not refer only to family ties between living people, but rather to a much broader web of relationships between people (living and dead), land, water, flora and fauna, and the spiritual world of atua (gods) – all bound together through whakapapa [genealogy].[9]

Such a worldview is one of the reasons why *iwi*, or tribes, 'refer to mountains, rivers, and lakes in the same way as they refer to other humans, and why elders feel comfortable speaking directly to them'.[10] Kaitiakitanga is thus a

[7] ibid 224, 226, 228.

[8] The word Kaitiakitanga has been borrowed into English, is now an English word in the common law, and is no longer 'foreign'. We therefore do not italicize it except in quoting texts seminal to the eventual linguistic borrowing. We treat it as a proper noun, capitalizing it.

[9] Waitangi Tribunal, 'Ko Aotearoa Tēnei: A Report into Claims Concerning New Zealand Law and Policy Affecting Māori Culture and Identity, Te Taumata Tuarua – Volume 1' (Legislation Direct, 2011) 237.

[10] ibid.

community-based concept which is not the obligation of an individual but of an entire collective tribal community.[11] As articulated by Tūrama Hawira of the Māori tribe Ngāti Rangi in the 2004 Environment Court decision *Ngāti Rangi Trust v Manawatu-Wanganui Regional Council*: 'They [the environment and its resources] do not belong to us – we belong to them.'[12]

This form of kinship aligns with many of the world's Indigenous cosmogony origin stories that tell how Indigenous Peoples descend from, are part of, and are genealogically related to the natural world. The concepts of healthy individual spirituality and collective community well-being are directly connected to and dependent on a robust natural ecosystem. As such, the traditional Indigenous worldviews see the relationship of people to the natural world as one that must be based on respect and reciprocity, which better represents the *kaitiaki* stewardship model than Western property-based concepts of dominion, exploitation, and maximization of profit.[13]

11.3 AFFIRMING THE MĀORI PHILOSOPHY OF RELATIONSHIPS IN NEW ZEALAND LAW

As articulated by Professor Iorns Magallanes, 'New Zealand law has been recognising and taking account of Māori cosmology and cultural interests mainly since the 1980s',[14] which contrasts its previous Victorian-era laws and approaches to environmental practices, that discounted and ignored the Māori philosophy of being in kinship with nature.[15] Recent changes to New Zealand law have taken strides to incorporate the *kaitiaki* Māori philosophy of stewardship of nature into law by recognizing 'Māori relationships with the natural world and the concomitant responsibilities to care for it *as kin*', and protecting this relationship through its laws.[16] It asserts that in implementing this new legal, political, and economic order, New Zealand can better uphold human rights. In particular, the specific human rights of the Indigenous Māori as 'part of the settlement of Maori grievances stemming from the

[11] ibid.

[12] *Ngāti Rangi Trust v Manawatu-Wanganui Regional Council* A67/2004 [2004] NZEnvC 172 (18 May 2004) [106].

[13] Rebecca Tsosie, 'Climate Change and Indigenous Peoples: Comparative Models of Sovereignty' (2013) 26 Tulane Environmental Law Journal 239, 244–245.

[14] Catherine J Iorns Magallanes, 'Nature as an Ancestor: Two Examples of Legal Personality for Nature in New Zealand' (2020) 10(16) VUWLRP 1, 16.

[15] Andrew Geddis and Jacinta Ruru, 'Places as Persons: Creating a New Framework for Māori-Crown Relations' in Jason NE Varuhas and Shona Wilson Stark (eds) *The Frontiers of Public Law* (Hart 2020) 263–265.

[16] Iorns Magallanes (n 14) 16 (emphasis added).

colonisation of New Zealand and the subsequent loss of Maori control over their lands, waters and their treasured natural resources'.[17] In addition, through implementing specific legislation to affirm this new order and the favourable interpretation of relevant treaties, the upholding of Māori human rights benefits humanity and the environment.[18] In so doing, New Zealand has produced a model of co-governance structures and legislation that can guide our world in addressing catastrophic environmental problems and deep socio-economic injustice. As detailed in two case studies below, these co-governance structures may serve as a model for other States' relationships with their Indigenous Peoples, particularly as means to advance the UNDRIP's Articles 25–27, on legal recognition of rights to land, maintaining their spiritual connection to Indigenous Peoples, and fair, impartial, and independent adjudication of Indigenous land rights, and 29 on conservation of the environment; likewise, the chapter details how these approaches also advance the SDGs, particularly SDGs 6.6 on protecting and restoring water-related ecosystems, 11.4 on safeguarding the world's cultural and natural heritages, 15 on the preservation of terrestrial ecosystems, and 16.7 on inclusive decision-making.

The changes to New Zealand law that recognized Māori philosophy and cosmology can be best seen through the *Te Urewera Act 2014*,[19] and the *Te Awa Tupua (Whanganui River Claims Settlement) Act 2017*.[20] These laws will be examined through the Māori tribe Ngāi Tuhoe and the Te Urewera National Park land negotiations, and the legal personhood of the Whanganui River case studies, respectively. However, it is first necessary to explore the treaty that enabled these reforms to prevail – the Treaty of Waitangi 1840.

11.3.1 *The Roots of New Zealand's Environmental Achievement: The Treaty of Waitangi 1840*

The Treaty of Waitangi 1840 (the Treaty) implicitly references the *Whanganui* Māori tribes and their relationship with a significant riverway, the *Whanganui* River, as well as the relationship of the *Ngāi Tuhoe* Māori People with the *Te Urewera* region. It is the first step, taken nearly two centuries ago by the British Crown on behalf of the recently arrived British

[17] ibid 15.
[18] ibid 2.
[19] Te Urewera Act 2014 (New Zealand).
[20] Te Awa Tupua (Whanganui River Claims Settlement) Act 2017 (New Zealand).

settlers, toward understanding and acknowledging the philosophy and practice of the Māori relationship to the land. Along the way, the New Zealand Government came to understand the value of Indigenous TK to the ecosystem and the necessity of building an economy as self-sustaining as the environmental system itself.[21]

The Treaty is the one and only treaty signed between the Māori of Aotearoa New Zealand and the British Crown, on 6 February 1840. In comparison, the United States signed 368 treaties with various Native American tribes,[22] and the British Crown in Canada signed 70 treaties.[23] Concluded between Crown representatives and some Māori kinship groups, the Treaty is widely regarded as New Zealand's founding document. It sets the parameters of the relationship between the Māori and the Government of New Zealand through recommendations issued by the Waitangi Tribunal.[24]

A unique characteristic of the Treaty is its duality: it was negotiated, drafted, and signed as a document in two languages (English and Māori). Each of the two language versions is forever fixed and is of equal importance to the meaning of the treaty.[25] The Treaty was drafted in English by Henry

[21] Paul Dalziel, Caroline Saunders, and Catherine Savage, 'Culture, Wellbeing, and the Living Standards Framework: A Perspective' (Discussion Paper 19/02, Manatū Taonga Ministry for Culture and Heritage and Treasury, 2019) 21.

[22] Kevin Gover, 'Nation to Nation: Treaties between the United States and American Indian Nations' (2014) 15 National Museum of the American Indian 37, 37.

[23] The seventy historic treaties between Indigenous Peoples of Canada span a time period between 1701 to 1923 and include the Treaties of Peace and Neutrality (1701–1760); Peace and Friendship Treaties (1725–1779); Upper Canada Land Surrenders and the Williams Treaties (1764–1862/1923); Robertson Treaties and Douglas Treaties (1850–1854); and the Numbers Treaties (1871–1921). 'Treaties and Agreements' (Government of Canada, Crown-Indigenous Relations and Northern Affairs Canada, 2023) <www.rcaanc-cirnac.gc.ca/eng/1100100028574/1529354437231> accessed 7 March 2025. For a discussion of treaties in Canada and New Zealand, see John Borrows, 'Ground-Rules: Indigenous Treaties in Canada and New Zealand' (2006) 22 New Zealand Universities Law Review 188; see also Andrew Erueti, 'Reparations for Indigenous Peoples in Canada, New Zealand and Australia' in Damien Short and Corinne Lennox (eds), *Handbook of Indigenous Peoples' Rights* (Routledge 2016).

[24] New Zealand Ministry of Foreign Affairs and Trade, 'Digital Economy Partnership Agreement (DEPA) Non-Paper from New Zealand: *The Treaty of Waitangi*' (Government of New Zealand, 2019) <www.mfat.govt.nz/assets/Trade-agreements/DEPA/DEPA-Treaty-of-Waitangi-New-Zealand-August-2019.pdf> accessed 22 February 2024.

[25] It would be inaccurate to call the Treaty a 'bilingual text', since the term 'bilingual' implies a fluency in both languages on the part of a single authorial mind. The Treaty of Waitangi is better described as a 'bi-text'; the two parts of which are equal and parallel in meaning, distinguishable only in form (language) and constitute a single, 'laminated' whole. While one of the two parts of the bi-text may come into existence as a translation of the other, it is drafted at approximately the same time (either simultaneously or in close sequence). The 'translated' half, unlike most translations, is fixed, and not re-translatable, any more than the 'original' is

Williams, an English missionary fluent in the Māori language, and his teenage son Edward. This version was rejected after it was presented to some 500 assembled Māori chiefs at the village of Waitangi on 5 February 1840. The next day, after a full explanation of the contents of the draft, only 40 Māori chiefs agreed to sign the English draft. It was then re-drafted in Māori by Eruera Pare Hongi, Williams' assistant, who had corresponding fluency in English, with Williams as co-drafter.[26] Copies of the two treaty drafts were circulated around the country and many more chiefs subsequently signed, with most signing the Māori-language version only.[27] The Māori-language version of the signed Treaty, to which most Māori signatories assented, expresses the promise of sovereignty using the term *te tino rangatiratanga*, which corresponds to the unqualified exercise of chieftainship over their lands, villages, and all their treasures.[28] In contrast, the English portion of

re-writable: if it were to be re-written or re-translated, it would be a different text. The two parts of a bi-text are thus 'fused'. Bi-texts and translated texts do not come under the same kind of copyright. Whereas a translated text exists separately, with a separate copyright from that of the original, a bi-text is a single text with a single copyright. So, for instance, while there are many English translations of the French novel *Madame Bovary*, the Māori-language half of the Waitangi Treaty will never be updated, modified, or otherwise re-written or re-translated. Alan K Melby, Arle Lommel, and Lucía Morales Vàzquez, 'Bitext: History of Bitext (26)' in Sin-Wai Chan (ed), *Routledge Encyclopedia of Translation Technology* (2nd edn, Routledge 2015) 409.

26 Eruera Pare Hongi was a young Māori man fluent in the Māori language and a holder of Māori Traditional Knowledge and culture. Hongi had been educated in English and was knowledgeable of British culture. His people chose Hongi to represent the concerns of the Māori in the drafting of the Treaty. Eruera Pare Hongi had worked with James Busby, the Crown-appointed British Resident in New Zealand, to co-write *He Whakaputanga*, the declaration of Māori sovereignty over the land (signed by fifty-two chiefs) in alliance with the British King in 1835. James Busby was also to have a hand in drafting the Treaty of Waitangi in 1840. It is possible that Eruera Pare Hongi's translation of the English version of the unsigned draft Treaty made full use of his grasp of the Māori cultural understanding to render the text not merely literally (as a transposition without regard for the sensibility of the 'target') but 'transparently', so that its phrasing and conveyance of concepts seemed to have been drafted in and for Māori, with implicitly Māori-centric intelligibility. The success of the resulting Māori language portion of the Treaty is seen in its endorsement by the Māori chiefs, not to mention the fact that no subsequent treaty was ever negotiated or signed. For more on the history of the signed *Treaty of Waitangi* see Alison Jones and Kuni Kaa Jenkins, *He Korero: Words between Us. First Māori-Pākehā Conversations on Paper* (Huia Publishers 2011) 188. For the concept of 'transparent' or 'domesticating' translation versus 'foreignizing' translation, see Lawrence Venuti, 'Translation, Philosophy, Materialism' (1996) 79 Radical Philosophy 24.

27 Claudia Orange, 'Te Tiriti o Waitangi – The Treaty of Waitangi' (Te Ara: The Encyclopaedia of New Zealand, Government of New Zealand, 2023) <https://teara.govt.nz/en/te-tiriti-o-waitangi-the-treaty-of-waitangi> accessed 7 March 2025.

28 Katherine Sanders, '"Beyond Human Ownership"? Property, Power, and Legal Personality for Nature in Aotearoa New Zealand' (2018) 30 Journal of Environmental Law 207, 214; Sir Hugh Kāwharu, 'English Translation of the Maori Language Version of the Treaty of Waitangi' (Government of New Zealand, 2023) <https://nzhistory.govt.nz/files/documents/

the Treaty instead transferred sovereignty from the Māori to the British, recognizing only the Māori retention of 'full exclusive and undisturbed possession to their Lands and Estates Forests Fisheries and other properties which they may collectively or individually possess'.[29] The New Zealand constitutional framework subsequently denied the ongoing sovereign powers of the Māori Tribes, despite the version of the text that most Māori signatories accepted.[30]

From the moment they signed the Treaty until the mid twentieth century, jurists and scholars explain, the Government of New Zealand repeatedly ignored the specific Treaty of Waitangi Māori rights and claims despite sustained dissent from the Māori. During this period, the New Zealand Government laid claim to land and resources expressly set aside for the Māori in the Treaty. After prolonged and intense political action by the Māori, the Waitangi Tribunal (Tribunal) was established in 1975 as a standing commission of inquiry into Māori claims that laws, policies, acts, or omissions of the Crown are, or were, inconsistent with the principles, as opposed to the text of the Treaty.

In addition, the Tribunal is also authorized to make non-binding recommendations for redress in cases where the Government of New Zealand has breached its Treaty obligations.[31] When the Tribunal recommends redress, negotiations sometimes ensue between the New Zealand Government and Māori tribes at kinship levels known as *iwi* and *hapū*, which are Indigenous Māori descent groups.[32] The findings of Treaty breaches made by the Tribunal later became the starting point for Māori claims to Te Urewera National Park and the Whanganui River, which allowed for the exercise of customary authority over the land and river in accordance with tikanga Māori and the Treaty principles of *te tino rangatiratanga*.[33] This chapter now turns to a brief exploration of the Te Urewera National Park lands and the Whanganui River legal personality case studies.

treaty-kawharu-footnotes.pdf> accessed 7 March 2025. Note that, being a translation of a text that itself was written as a translation, what is supplied is actually a 'back translation' – useful mainly for gist, although for language professionals, it is a common technique of translation quality assessment (Treaty of Waitangi).

29 Treaty of Waitangi (n 28) 2.

30 ibid.

31 Treaty of Waitangi Act 1975, s 5(1).

32 A *hapū* being roughly a sub-tribe or clan, and an *iwi* a larger-scale descent group, such as a tribal community. Rāwiri Taonui, 'Tribal Organisation – The Significance of iwi and hapū' (Te Ara: The Encyclopaedia of New Zealand, Government of New Zealand, 2005) <https://teara.govt.nz/en/tribal-organisation/page-1> accessed 7 March 2025.

33 Sanders (n 28); Kāwharu (n 28).

11.3.2 *Case Study 1: Te Urewera Land Legislation*

In 2017, the Tribunal members issued their Te Urewera Report which found that the Ngāi Tūhoe Māori Tribe had rights to land that encompassed the Te Urewera National Park, rights which the Government of New Zealand had ignored.[34] The recommendations from the report instigated negotiations for reconciliation, with the Ngāi Tūhoe Māori, who were not signatories to the Treaty to retain control of their lands, seeking the return of their lands, which had been caged within the conservation estate.[35] However, despite not signing the Treaty, the Tūhoe were forcibly made subject to the New Zealand Government confiscating most of their lands and removing their tino rangatiratanga authority to control or manage their own affairs, which restricted their customary use of the Te Urewera lands. When Te Urewera National Park was created in 1954, the Tūhoe Māori were not consulted, nor were they recognized as having any special interest in the park or its governance.[36] Consequently, the Ngāi Tuhoe tribe sought redress for alleged breaches of the Treaty of Waitangi, including in the Waitangi Tribunal.

The Crown argued that the lands within the conservation estate were not available for return to Ngāi Tūhoe*iwi* or *hapū* ownership. It also asserted ownership of the beds of navigable rivers within the Te Urewera National Park under the *Coal Mines Act Amendment Act* 1903, arguing that no one owns water at common law. The Crown, moreover, claimed the ability to allocate rights to freshwater under the *Resource Management Act* 1991.[37] After robust direct negotiations between Ngāi Tūhoe and the Government of New Zealand, the Crown instead offered the Tūhoe Māori legal personality for the Te Urewera National Park, whereby no one owns the park. Rather, the park owns itself. The lands would remain protected, with public use, akin to national parkland. The park – the natural entity – however, would maintain its own separate identity and be governed with significant Tūhoe Māori input while respecting the Māori philosophy of a cosmological relationship with the lands.[38] As scholars underline, recognizing the legal personality of the land ultimately broke the deadlock between the Crown and some *iwi*.[39] The grant of legal personality aims to facilitate the acknowledgement of historic Treaty breaches and wrongs done to Māori Tribes. It is likewise a tool for developing

[34] Te Urewera, 'Waitangi Tribunal Report 2017' (Legislation Direct, 2017).
[35] Geddis and Ruru (n 15) 9.
[36] Iorns Magallanes (n 14).
[37] Sanders (n 28) 214–215.
[38] Iorns Magallanes (n 14).
[39] Geddis and Ruru (n 15) 9.

a compromise wherein the Crown gives up title to the lands without vesting sovereignty in the Māori since there is no transfer of land ownership.[40]

The negotiated Agreement pushed the Government of New Zealand to pass the *Te Urewera Act* 2014,[41] formalizing the deal to remove the National Park status and grant legal status of the Te Urewera region to itself, to be stewarded by the Ngāi Tūhoe Māori Tribes. The Act declared the land that had comprised Te Urewera National Park a legal entity with 'an identity in and of itself, inspiring people to commit to its care'.[42] It serves as a reflection of the negotiations and cultural understandings of the Tuhoe Māori in the context of their ongoing relationship with the region,[43] and sets out the principles governing its implementation, most importantly in relation to the environment and public education.[44] Most importantly, as outlined in Section 11, 'Te Urewera Declared to be Legal Entity', the *Te Urewera Act* 2014 details the central compromise between the Ngāi Tūhoe Māori Tribes and the New Zealand Government, declaring Te Urewera to be its own legal entity, with 'all the rights, powers, duties, and liabilities of a legal person'.[45] Such legal personality highlights the relationship between *Tūhoetanga* (Ngāi Tūhoe identity and culture) and 'the Crown's responsibility under the Treaty of Waitangi'.[46] It is a reminder of the fiduciary duty found at the core of the spirit and intent of the original relationship between Tuhoe Māori and the Government of New Zealand Agreement.[47] Thus, Te Urewera will 'hold title to its own land (i.e., title to itself), where that land is inalienable'.[48]

As for managing the lands, the *Te Kawa o te Urewera*,[49] or the Te Urewera Management Plan, 'is about the management of people for the benefit of the land – it is not about land management'.[50] The Te Urewera Management Plan is reinforced by the Te Urewera Act 2014, which encapsulates and brings into common law the kinship relationship between humanity and the land and forest by having at its core the governing concept of *tikanga*

40 Sanders (n 28) 210.
41 Te Urewera Act (n 19).
42 ibid s 3(3).
43 ibid s 4.
44 ibid s 5.
45 ibid s 11(1).
46 Iorns Magallanes (n 14) [38].
47 In effect, this means that the Māori words used to express the concepts in the legislation have been borrowed wholesale into English, and that they are now English lexical items and part of potential diction in the common law.
48 Iorns Magallanes (n 14) [36].
49 'Te Kawa o Te Urewera, the Te Urewera Management Plan' (Tūhoe, 2023) <www.ngaituhoe.iwi.nz/te-kawa-o-te-urewera> accessed 7 March 2025.
50 Sanders (n 28) 213.

Māori.[51] The legislation shows that people are considered part of forest management, and 'while a forest may have intrinsic value, worthy of respect, it is also a place that people inhabit; its plants and animals are not off-limits as a resource if used truly sustainably'.[52]

Ultimately, the granting of legal personality to Te Urewera National Park is an example of a compromise between a State and an Indigenous group, each of which claims political authority in these spaces. In such contemporary settlements, legal personality and the application of the concept of non-ownership facilitate relationships between the Crown and the Indigenous group, recognizing their competing claims to exercise authority over the geographic area.[53] Such a development helps to regulate human relationships relating to the land, forests, lakes, and rivers without de-naturing the natural entity. The example of Te Urewera National Park furthermore aligns with UNDRIP's Articles 25–26, on rights and spiritual connections to land, and 29 on conservation of the environment. The role of the Tribunal furthermore aligns with the UNDRIP commitment to fair, impartial, and independent adjudication of Indigenous land rights. The legal recognition of personality for the Te Urewera National Park also aligns with SDGs, particularly 11.4 on safeguarding the world's cultural and natural heritages, 15 on the preservation of terrestrial ecosystems, and 16.7 on inclusive decision-making.

11.3.3 *Case Study 2: Whanganui River Legislation*

As with the case of Te Urewera National Park, granting legal personality facilitated reconciliation and the acknowledgement of Treaty of Waitangi wrongs done to *Whanganui* Māori in relation to the Whanganui River.[54] It found that 'the Treaty of *Waitangi* had guaranteed *Whanganui Iwi* the rights to ownership, management, and control of the river, which *Whanganui Iwi* had never freely and willingly relinquished'.[55] In a similar manner to *Ngāi Tuhoe*, in 1999, the Tribunal in their *Whanganui* River Report[56] validated

[51] ibid 209.

[52] Iorns Magallanes (n 14) 44.

[53] Sanders (n 28) 208.

[54] ibid 210. For a recent analysis of the *kaitiaki* co-governance of the Te Urewera National Park, see J Mika, Tuhoe Self-Governance: Te Mana o Motuhake o Tuhoe,' and C Iorns Magallanes, 'Māori Co-governance and/or Co-management of Nature and Environmental Resources' both in Joseph and Benton (n 3) chs 9 and 11, respectively.

[55] Geddis and Ruru (n 15) 12.

[56] Waitangi Tribunal, 'The Whanganui River Report 1999' (GP Print, 1999).

and confirmed the Whanganui Māori claim to the Whanganui River which was a strong catalyst for a negotiated agreement between the Crown and Whanganui Māori Parties. The resulting *Tutohu Whakatupua Agreement* in 2012 was of special significance, because it statutorily recognized the River: 'Te Awa Tupua [s] a legal entity with standing in its own right'.[57] The Agreement expressly reflects 'the Whanganui Iwi [tribes' world] view that the River is a living entity in its own right and is incapable of being "owned" in an absolute sense'.[58] Water bodies are crucial to tribal identity, so much so that it is sometimes said not only that 'the river belongs to the people and the people belong to the river' but also more fundamentally, as in the Whanganui *whakatauki* (local proverb or aphorism), 'Ko au te awa, ko te awa ko au: I am the river, the river is me.'

The Agreement was subsequently legislated in the *Te Awa Tupua (Whanganui River Claims Settlement) Act* 2017. The legislation removed State ownership, conferring legal status and giving ownership of the riverbed to the Whanganui River itself under the name Te Awa Tupua, while making the Whanganui Māori, and a government representative, the voice and steward (*kaitiaki*) of Te Awa Tupua.[59] The Act further established a legal framework recognizing Te Awa Tupua as 'an indivisible and living whole, comprising the Whanganui River from the mountains to the sea, incorporating all its physical and metaphysical elements'.[60] The core of this groundbreaking legislation is found in Section 14, 'Te Awa Tupua declared to be legal person', wherein the central compromise between the Whanganui Māori and the New Zealand Government comes into focus. This compromise allows for the Whanganui Māori worldview of the Whanganui River as an ancestor and declares it to be its own legal entity.[61] An official *Kaitiaki* (guardian), called Te Pou Tupua, then upholds and protects the interests of the river and will 'act and speak on behalf of Te Awa Tupua'[62] to 'promote and protect the health and wellbeing of Te Awa Tupua',[63] The title to the riverbed is then passed from the Crown to Te Awa Tupua, so that Te Pou Tupua may act on the River's behalf.[64] Additionally, the Te Pou

[57] Tutohu Whakatupua (Whanganui Iwi–The Crown) (adopted 31 August 2012) Clause 2.1.2.
[58] ibid Clauses 2.1.2 and 2.7.
[59] Te Awa Tupua (n 20) s 20(9).
[60] ibid s 12.
[61] ibid s 14.
[62] ibid s 19(1) 9a.
[63] ibid s 19(1) 9c.
[64] De Vries-Stotijn, Van Ham, and Bastmeijer (n 2) 745.

Tupua will have representatives: a Māori representative and a representative of the Crown.[65]

Although it did not allow for Indigenous sovereign title, the Crown agreed to a cultural process that respects tikanga Māori and worldviews, beliefs, and values, and the Māori understanding of humanity's equality with, rather than superiority to, nature. The Act has, furthermore, been a major step in acknowledging the 'property claims' of the Whanganui Iwi. Although these claims may seem at odds with the Māori relationship with nature, conflicts over property rights are pervasive in Western legal systems. Ownership can, therefore, serve as a way for Māori to regain control over the conservation of the River. In such a sense, ownership of the river was said to be 'the heart, the core, and the pith' of the Whanganui Iwi claim.[66] However, Professor Iorns Magallanes caveats that the vesting of the riverbed is a Western European concept that in itself runs contrary to traditional Māori philosophy, in which one cannot own the land; one can only be in a relationship with the land and nature. He details that 'the vesting of fee simple title does not reflect traditional Māori concepts of responsibility and control … because Whanganui tribes did not view the river as property in a Western sense'.[67] Much like with the Te Urewera lands, the transfer of ownership to the riverbed is in essence a compromise between two Parties fighting over ownership. To make this agreement work, the Crown had to give up title to the riverbed, while the Māori could not take the sovereign title for themselves.

In the case of both the *Te Awa Tupua Act* 2014 and the Te Awa Tupua (Whanganui River Claims Settlement) Act 2017, the model of legal personality for nature presents constitutional significance given it shifts the Crown-Indigenous relationship from one of hierarchy, with the Crown on top, to one of a common goal of resources stewardship or *Kaitiakitanga*. This new model presents the Māori as subject-matter experts who lead in applying the Indigenous principles and laws of *tikanga Māori*. Such a rebalanced relationship also allows for reframing dialogue, not in terms of Western capitalism, resource extraction, or profit over resources, but instead in terms of perpetual stewardship on behalf of the interests of the Whanganui River and Te Urewera lands themselves. In other words, it brings the healthy sustainability of the natural entity into legal thought, where it is desperately needed. Additionally, this innovative solution provided a forum for dialogue and negotiation

65 Te Awa Tupua (n 20) s 20.

66 De Vries-Stotijn, Van Ham, and Bastmeijer (n 2) 745 citing Waitangi Tribunal (n 56) 332.

67 Iorns Magallanes (n 14) 26. For a more recent analysis of the *kaitiaki* co-governance of the Te Awa Tupua (Whanganui River) legal personality, see J Ruru, 'Māori Governance of Water: Innovation in Reconciliation Agreements' in Joseph and Benton (n 3) ch 13.

between the Indigenous Peoples and the descendants of the settlers on their lands. Though the vesting of legal personality in a natural entity was an unintended consequence of the negotiations, it still provides a model for breaking future Crown-Indigenous impasses over the Crown's refusal to vest Indigenous Peoples with a form of sovereignty.[68]

In any event, the role of the Tribunal and recognition for the Whanganui river's legal personality aligns with UNDRIP's Articles 25–26, on recognition of rights and spiritual connections to land, and 29 on conservation of the environment. This case study furthermore aligns with the UNDRIP commitment to fair, impartial, and independent adjudication of Indigenous land rights; likewise, these legal recognitions advance the SDGs, particularly SDGs 6.6 on protecting and restoring water-related ecosystems, 11.4 on safeguarding the world's cultural and natural heritages, and 16.7 on inclusive decision-making.

This chapter briefly analysed the Indigenous Māori worldview and tikanga Māori legal concepts such as *kaitiakitanga* (guardianship), *whakapapa* (genealogy), and *whanaungatanga* (acknowledging that everything is related) that place people within an intergenerational stewardship relationship with, not above, nature. It also explored the two case studies of the Te Urewera National Park and the Whanganui River within this *kaitiaki* co-governance worldview and the relational granting of legal personhood to these natural resources through specific legislation.

The next section explores these Māori worldviews and tikanga Māori *kaitiaki* concepts within the context of sustainable development for Māori trade, and through a recent innovative tikanga Māori policy metric for measuring Gross Domestic Product (GDP) for Aotearoa New Zealand that includes the well-being and protection of the environment.

11.4 SUSTAINABLE DEVELOPMENT AND MĀORI INDIGENOUS TRADITIONAL KNOWLEDGE

Accordingly, New Zealand's best practices in environment and treaty interpretation begin to emerge as a synthesis of Indigenous TK in philosophy and in New Zealand common law. This has global implications for the ambitious objectives of sustainable development, particularly concerning climate change and socio-economic developments in the timeframe of the UN's global Sustainable Development Goals (SDGs), and can help create a

68 Sanders (n 28) 211.

coherent, integrated approach to healthy ecosystems.[69] Specifically, many Indigenous and other experts and elders emphasize, the long-term sustainability of people and environments requires pervasive legal recognition of the substantive right of natural entities,[70] which includes representation in parliaments, boardrooms, and if need be, courtrooms. These lessons drawn from Indigenous philosophies are key for environmental management and conducting sustainable trade. For instance, many First Nations in Canada apply the time-honoured teachings of eco-systemic stewardship, watershed resource management, and sustainable harvesting. Indigenous Nations worldwide can and should be empowered to lead by example to show the world how to operate sustainably in a just economy. Such developments bring us to the topic of modern sustainable development advances that result from Māori knowledge and tikanga law. Featured in this section are key examples of how Indigenous TK can provide vital solutions to the current world environmental crisis, as implemented for Indigenous trade and for inter-Tribal trade and new substitutes for Gross Domestic Product (GDP). Such measures are furthermore shown to align with and advance the UNDRIP's commitment in Article 36 to developing economic and social cooperation with other Indigenous Peoples across borders, and SDGs 17.10 on equitable trade and 17.16 on enhancing global partnerships for sustainable development.

11.4.1 *Sustainable Development through Māori Trade*

For global Indigenous trade, the Māori are setting examples.[71] The first trade agreement to have specific Indigenous trade opportunities in the text was between New Zealand and the Republic of Taiwan. The *Agreement between New Zealand and the Separate Customs Territory of Taiwan, Penghu, Kinmen, and Matsu on Economic Cooperation* (ANZTEC), was signed on 10 July 2013, in Wellington, New Zealand, and is the first where Indigenous economic rights to international inter-tribal trade, that is, trade among the Indigenous Nations of the world, was recognized in a binding international trade agreement.

[69] Susanne Wuijts and others, 'An Ecological Perspective on a River's Rights: A Recipe for More Effective Water Quality Governance?' 44(6–7) Water International 647.

[70] De Vries-Stotijn, Van Ham, and Bastmeijer (n 2) 736–751.

[71] Likewise, New Zealand is also setting a global example for Indigenous trade alongside Indigenous Canadians, Taiwanese, and Australians through the Indigenous Peoples Economic and Trade Cooperation Arrangement (IPETCA). The IPETCA will be discussed in greater detail as a unique advancement for Indigenous trade in Chapter 14, Innovative Approaches to UNDRIP Principles in Indigenous Trade Agreements.

One of the factors in the success of the ANZTEC, which was also the first major trade agreement signed by the Republic of Taiwan, was the depth of Indigenous global connections and ancient ties. The Māori can trace their Polynesian seafaring and trading origins back to the Indigenous Peoples of Taiwan. Evidence suggests the Māori, who refer to New Zealand as Aotearoa, meaning 'land of the long white cloud', arrived from the Taiwan region roughly around the early 1300s as Polynesian seafaring traders.[72] This historic whakapapa (genealogical) and cultural connection solidified a strong cultural bond between the two separate and relatively distant geographic regions. While there exist express cultural exchange opportunities between the Indigenous Taiwanese and Māori of Aotearoa, there was an additional emphasis on economic collaboration. Chapter 19 of ANZTEC, 'Cooperation on Indigenous Issues', specifically speaks to how the two regions can 'expand and facilitate trade and economic relations between the Indigenous Peoples in the Separate Customs Territory of Taiwan, Penghu, Kinmen and Matsu and New Zealand's Māori'.[73] The development of meaningful trade ties between the Māori and the Indigenous Taiwanese continues with incremental inter-Tribal trade progress based on Indigenous Māori and Indigenous Taiwanese whakapapa and whanaungatanga – relationships. Under tikanga Māori, relationships are key, not business. Partners must establish mutual trust first for business to then follow. Moreover, this historic cultural connection enables the two Indigenous economies to be amplified, thus supporting Indigenous knowledge-based economies and communities that can continue to apply this knowledge for sustainable development. ANZTEC, accordingly, brings the Indigenous Peoples of New Zealand and Taiwan closer culturally, socially, and economically, in alignment with UNDRIP Article 36 and SDGs 17.10 on equitable trade and 17.16 on enhancing global partnerships for sustainable development.

In addition, underscoring New Zealand's trade approach as a possible model for other States, the 2013 ANZTEC trade agreement made a positive impression on the Australian Government, which is geographically situated

[72] Cultural Survival, 'Genetic Link Brings Indigenous Taiwanese and Maori Together' (Cultural Survival, 9 July 2004) <www.culturalsurvival.org/news/genetic-link-brings-Indigenous-taiwanese-and-Maori-together> accessed 7 March 2025; Taiwan Today, 'Maori tribespeople visit Taiwan to explore cultural ancestry' (Taiwan Today, 24 August 2018) <https://taiwantoday.tw/news.php?unit=2,6,10,15,18&post=140330> accessed 7 March 2025.

[73] Agreement between New Zealand and the Separate Customs Territory of Taiwan, Penghu, Kinmen, and Matsu on Economic Cooperation (ANZTEC) (New Zealand–Separate Customs Territory of Taiwan, Penghu, Kinmen, and Matsu) (adopted 10 July 2013) ch 19, art 1 (b), 199, <https://investmentpolicy.unctad.org/international-investment-agreements/treaty-files/3080/download> accessed 7 March 2025.

between New Zealand and Taiwan. The Government of Australia expressed interest in initiating similar negotiations for a trade framework to assist in Indigenous economic development. This resulted in the *New Zealand-Australian Indigenous Collaboration Arrangement* (Arrangement), with the initial scoping document signed in February 2020 and which contains promising sections for Māori and Indigenous Australian economic development through trade.[74] The Arrangement aims to serve as a general exploratory document that will empower representatives from both settler governments of New Zealand and Australia, as well as Indigenous representatives from Aotearoa and Indigenous Australia, to explore the economic opportunities which will mostly be interwoven in and influenced by Indigenous culture, well-being, and agency. However, the official information relayed for this Arrangement indicates an approach that may be less ambitious with regard to economic cooperation than that in ANZET, stating its purpose as one that can '[d]eepen cultural and people-to-people relationships among Aboriginal, Torres Strait Islander and Māori communities, businesses and organizations; [p]rovide a mechanism for collaboration and consultation on areas of mutual interest; and [e]nable sharing of information between governments and Indigenous [P]eoples to inform the development of policies that affect Indigenous [P]eoples'.[75] Given the progress made by New Zealand on Indigenous trade issues with Taiwan and Australia, there will likely be further advances for Indigenous trade through the Pacific Trade Alliance, where New Zealand and other countries like Canada are in mid-negotiation.[76] Such advances are crucial for supporting Indigenous economies and knowledge systems that can enable the flourishing of both the people and environments that benefit from these trade agreements, and like ANZTEC would furthermore align with UNDRIP Article 36 and SDGs 17.10, on equitable trade, and 17.16 on enhancing sustainable development partnerships globally.

11.4.2 *A New Measure of GDP: Well-Being and Protection of the Environment*

Aotearoa New Zealand stepped further to the forefront of the planet's socio-political landscape with the realization that something more than the basic

[74] New Zealand–Australian Indigenous Collaboration Arrangement (New Zealand–Australia) (adopted 28 February 2020) <www.niaa.gov.au/sites/default/files/publications/Indigenous-collaboration-arrangement.pdf> accessed 7 March 2025.

[75] ibid.

[76] 'Canada and the Pacific Alliance' (Government of Canada, 25 May 2022) <www.international.gc.ca/world-monde/international_relations-relations_internationales/pacific_alliance-alliance_pacifique/index.aspx?lang=eng> accessed 7 March 2025.

economic balance sheet of a State needed to be relied upon if the relatively small country wanted to thrive in the long term. To preserve its citizens' environment, the Government of New Zealand began assessing its economic system as more than just a set of commodities, jobs, and corporate extraction of raw materials. As discussed in this chapter, and related scholarship, New Zealand's relationship with the natural environment is now transitioning to one that accepts protecting value for the natural world is equivalent to conserving the long-term value for the well-being of humanity. This approach may hold promise for advancing the UNDRIP's Article 25 on upholding Indigenous responsibilities to future generations, and SDG 12 on sustainable consumption and production patterns.

This new approach to measuring value was developed when the New Zealand Treasury (Kaitohutohu Kaupapa Rawa) set out to replace the outdated GDP measure, which remains in use by most major economies and the OECD. GDP as it stands today is the monetary market value of all goods and services produced in a country in a given year.[77] Such an indicator is generally used to judge the strength of an economy of a country over time, or relative to that of other countries. Often, it is associated with social welfare and standard of living. However, for over half a century, GDP has been severely criticized for not adequately capturing human welfare and progress, especially as most economists, businesses, and governments call for unconditional GDP growth even if this paradoxically necessitates exploitation and destruction of the environment.[78] The challenge posed for Kaitohutohu Kaupapa Rawa was to enlarge the narrow measures of what constitutes economic worth and to capture the negative externalities that unsustainable growth inevitably creates. As such, the central objective of the New Zealand Treasury was to value, qualify, and include 'well-being' as part of a new and improved GDP for New Zealand.[79]

With this premise, the New Zealand Treasury in 2015 released the Living Standards Framework (LSF), an overarching policy model with four central 'capitals': natural capital, financial and physical capital, social capital, and human capital. The New Zealand LSF 'is based on the OECD's well-being framework, which puts people (individuals and households) at the center of the assessment'.[80] Additionally, the Māori endorsement is front and centre, as

[77] Jeroen CJM van den Bergh, 'The GDP Paradox' (2009) 30(2) Journal of Economic Psychology 117–135.

[78] ibid 118.

[79] Dalziel, Saunders, and Savage (n 21) 1.

[80] ibid 8.

articulated by the Minister for Māori Development – Te Puni Kokiri, who opined:

> The move by the Treasury to explore ways to view national wellbeing as representing more than the traditional Gross Domestic Product (GDP)-based measures is a welcome shift. However, to understand the collective impact of policies on the intergenerational well-being of all New Zealanders, the Living Standards Framework (LSF) cannot be blind to the things that drive us as a society: it must reflect who we are, what we value and how we can grow a shared sense of prosperity. [...] A new way of thinking about well-being has potential to benefit all New Zealanders. [...] Wellbeing considered from an [I]ndigenous perspective moves the public policy discourse beyond Western constructs of wellbeing and enables an improved lived experience of wellbeing for everyone.[81]

This new discourse is reflected throughout the four central capitals. For example, the new natural capital component contrasts the old GDP formula which measured natural capital strictly in terms of its potential to enhance corporate growth through harvest futures and forward contracts. The new GDP needed to quantify and value more factors to express degrees of human well-being and not just corporate viability. For the people of New Zealand, well-being could also be measured in terms of the environmental sustainability of the State, for example, in terms of security of access to clean water, breathable air, uncontaminated soil, and thriving ecosystems. New Zealand wanted to see these factors in its modified GDP LSF.

In developing the new GDP, the Government of New Zealand again found it helpful to consult and learn from the Māori worldviews, philosophies, and *kaitiaki* laws prescribing relationships with nature to best see natural capital through a non-corporate lens. The executive summary of the Treasury's exploratory publication, 'He Ara Waiora/A Path Toward Wellbeing: Exploring Te Ao Māori Perspectives on the Living Standards Framework for the Tax Working Group', notes:

> The Treasury has always recognized that there are many possible ways to understand intergenerational wellbeing. The Treasury indicated earlier this year that the Crown–Māori relationship is integral to all four capitals in our

81 Te Puni Kokiri and Ministry of Māori Development and Kaitohutohu Kaupapa Rawa and The Treasury, 'An Indigenous Approach to the Living Standards Framework, Treasury Discussion Paper 19/01' (New Zealand, 2019) <www.treasury.govt.nz/sites/default/files/2019-01/dp19-01.pdf> accessed 7 March 2025.

Living Standards Framework (LSF), and that the Treasury would be further exploring how this might be reflected in the framework.[82]

A series of discussion papers explored in detail the Māori approach to effective sustainable development and environmental stewardship, incorporating this approach into a well-being formula for a modified GDP. The Māori approach augments the New Zealand government's LSF by applying *tikanga Māori*. At the centre of this hybrid model is *waiora*, or well-being, which is grounded in water as the source of all life. Furthermore, each of the four LSF capitals is supported and augmented through Māori worldviews and *tikanga*. For natural capital, there is the added component of intergenerational sustainability which is expressed as *kaitiakitanga*, or stewardship of all resources. For human capital, there is a consideration for care and responsibility which is seen through *manaakitanga*, or care for others. For financial capital, there is prosperity, or *ōhanga*. Finally, for social capital, there is connectedness as expressed through *whanaungatanga*, or the connections between us.[83] Additionally, within the sphere of natural capital, the Māori and the Government of New Zealand model for measuring well-being looks at the land, which is seen 'not [...] just for its economic potential, but through familial and spiritual connections defined by cultural concepts such as *whakapapa* (genealogy) and *kaitiakitanga* (stewardship)'.[84] The emphasis is on how 'all aspects of the natural environment needed to support life and human activity include [...] natural places being managed or conserved to maintain their high cultural value'.[85] In short, the Māori/New Zealand Government model measures well-being regarding sustainable growth and distribution of the four Capitals, interlinked with and inter-dependent on intergenerational sustainability, care for one another, mutual prosperity, and connectedness of fellow citizens.[86] These four capitals, taken as an approach to measuring economic value, help provide a novel and increasingly necessary understanding of the fragility on which typical GDP measures and their assumptions rest. They also, if suitably implemented, advance the UNDRIP's Article 25 on responsibilities to future generations, and SDG 12 on sustainable consumption and production patterns.

[82] Emily O'Connell and others, 'He Ara Waiora/ A Pathway Towards Wellbeing: Exploring Te Ao Māori Perspectives on the Living Standards Framework for the Tax Working Group, New Zealand Treasury Discussion Paper 18/11' (New Zealand, 2018) 2 <www.treasury.govt.nz/publications/dp/dp-18-11-html> accessed 7 March 2025.

[83] ibid; Dalziel, Saunders, and Savage (n 21) 8.

[84] Te Puni Kokiri (n 81) 3.

[85] Dalziel, Saunders, and Savage (n 21) 21.

[86] ibid.

Aotearoa New Zealand is also not the only country that has access to such a valuable bounty of Indigenous TK to support its legislation and economy. Canada and the United States also have the potential to work with their Indigenous Peoples to evaluate, or re-evaluate, antiquated economic and well-being metrics. Moreover, while the Organisation for Economic Co-operation and Development (OECD) is also re-evaluating the role of GDP to better account for well-being, the governments of Canada and the United States have yet to examine alternative concepts of GDP specifically. However, in November 2020, the British Columbia Assembly of First Nations of Canada (BCAFN) released a proposal for a Traditional Knowledge-enhanced GDP measure, entitled 'Centering First Nations Concepts of Wellbeing: Toward a GDP – Alternative Index in British Columbia'.[87] In this proposal, the BCAFN provides the results of an exhaustive inventory of States that are currently looking at or applying alternative means of measuring GDP. Though the study examines and grades States in their attempted application of Indigenous concepts of well-being for alternative forms of GDP measurement,[88] it gives New Zealand the highest marks based on their application of the Māori concepts of well-being.[89] Nonetheless, the BCAFN factors for reckoning 'a good life' or 'well-being' strongly resemble the tikanga Māori and worldview factors of well-being (waiora), stewardship (kaitiakitanga) of all our resources, care for others (mana-akitanga), prosperity (ōhanga), and connectedness (whakapapa). Both sets of standards entail the understanding that human beings live *in* Nature, not above or outside Nature, and that humanity's decisions must respect Nature as an equal living entity. At its heart, it reaffirms the notion that global combined Indigenous Traditional Knowledge constitutes a key body of knowledge for seeing, valuing, preserving, and propagating the natural world as an environment that can thrive and foster a robust and sustainable economic world.

11.5 CONCLUSION

Exploring sustainable development more broadly in Aotearoa New Zealand, as guided by treaties and specific legislative co-governance models, highlights

[87] British Columbia Assembly of First Nations, 'Centering First Nations Concepts of Wellbeing: Toward a GDP – Alternative Index in British Columbia' (British Columbia Assembly of First Nations, 2020). For more on the OECD's reevaluation of GDP, see Organisation for Economic Co-operation and Development (OECD), 'Well-Being and beyond GDP' <www.oecd.org/well-being-and-beyond-gdp/> accessed 7 March 2025.

[88] Nations such as Ecuador, Bolivia, and the State of Washington; the study also makes mention of Scotland and Iceland as having identified factors that align with an Indigenous philosophy of 'wellbeing'.ibid.

[89] ibid 49.

the profound influence of Indigenous philosophies, laws, and TK on shaping governance, trade, and economies. As scholars note, Indigenous Peoples' deep-rooted connection to the environment, characterized by a reciprocal relationship of harvesting and giving back, provides a valuable perspective that challenges the prevailing paradigm of nature as a commodity to be exploited. By recognizing the role of human guardians, or *kaitiaki*, as representatives of nature's best interests, jurists highlight, the experience of Aotearoa New Zealand exemplifies an alternative, unique, and viable approach to environmental protection that transcends the human-centric ownership models prevalent in many colonial legal systems. Chapter 11 has provided an overview of Aotearoa New Zealand's remarkable journey towards cutting-edge sustainable development practices. By delving into Māori culture, practices, laws, and TK, insights emerge from the Māori philosophy of *whanaungatanga* (kinship) with nature and the application of *tikanga Māori* governance in trade and nature stewardship. Moreover, the evolution of treaty interpretation, specifically focusing on the Treaty of Waitangi 1840, has advanced Māori rights and responsibilities, providing a foundation for transformative policy and legislation, and possibly, sustainable development outcomes for the holistic well-being of people and the environment.

Looking ahead, Chapter 12 examines how Indigenous peace agreements in the Andes foster sustainable development. By analysing the unique approaches taken by Indigenous communities in the Andean region to promote harmony, justice, and ecological balance, valuable insights and lessons can be uncovered that are applicable to sustainable development efforts worldwide.

12

Indigenous Treaties for Sustainable Development in the Andes

12.1 INTRODUCTION

Alongside sustained conflicts over land and demands for social, environmental, political, and economic rights, Indigenous Peoples worldwide, and especially across the Americas, have also engaged in many ways with governments to advance reconciliation.[1] Both domestic and international reforms have been attempted in the Andes region, taking into account key principles and rights recognized in the International Labor Organization Convention 169 (ILO 169)[2] and the United Nations Declaration on the Rights of Indigenous Peoples (UNDRIP),[3] as well as in the UN International Covenant on Economic, Social and Cultural Rights (ICESCR).[4] While the 169 targets

1 Angus MacInnes, Marcus Colchester, and Andrew Whitmore, 'Free, Prior and Informed Consent: How to Rectify the Devastating Consequences of Harmful Mining for Indigenous Peoples' (2017) 15 Perspectives in Ecology and Conservation 152. The authors are grateful to Dr Cecilia Campero for her insights and key contributions, which share thoughts with her research in Cecelia Campero, Nathan Andrews, and Tracy Smith-Carrier, 'Mining, the Sustainable Development Goals and Impact Assessments: A Review of Governance and Local Impacts' (2024) 42(5) Impact Assessment and Project Appraisal 423; Cecilia Campero and others, 'De-politicising Seawater Desalination: Environmental Impact Assessments in the Atacama Mining Region, Chile' (2021) 120 Environment Science and Policy 187; and Cecilia Campero and M Leila Harris, 'The Legal Geographies of Water Claims: Seawater Desalination in Mining Regions in Chile' (2019) 11(5) Water (Basel) 886, also to Adv Smriti Pokhrel for her insights and research assistance in this chapter.

2 Convention Concerning Indigenous and Tribal Peoples in Independent Countries (adopted 27 June 1989, entered into force 5 September 1991) 1660 UNTS 383 (ILO No 169).

3 UNGA, 'United Nations Declaration on the Rights of Indigenous Peoples' (13 September 2007) UN Doc A/RES/61/295 (UNDRIP).

4 International Covenant on Economic, Social and Cultural Rights (adopted 16 December 1966, entered in force 3 January 1976) 993 UNTS 3.

under the seventeen Sustainable Development Goals (SDGs) are not in themselves binding international law, as has been noted in previous chapters, the priorities and aspirations agreed by the UN in the SDGs align with many international accords and commitments, and are also the subject of many domestic laws and policies including key provisions of legal agreements with Indigenous Peoples, as well as important aspects of Indigenous legal systems.[5] In this chapter, it is argued that Indigenous agreements in the Andes often reference and even prioritize important SDG targets, seeking for instance to end poverty, to fight hunger, to secure health, education, clean water and energy, to protect life on land and life below water, to ensure more sustainable communities, to promote peace, justice, and strong institutions, and much more. Unfortunately, it is also noted, such aspirations alone may not be enough to address current injustices and power imbalances in the Andes – specifically in Chile and Bolivia – for Indigenous Peoples.

Indigenous and non-Indigenous legal and public policy scholars, as well as critical legal geographers and others, have analysed Indigenous laws and agreements to better understand how socio-environmental and socio-economic (in)justices and dispossessions are addressed through diverse legal discourses and the multiple overlapping legal frameworks of Indigenous Peoples, taking into consideration gaps, ambiguities, and the pluralistic character of law.[6] Their findings explore the ways in which law, territories, and coloniality shape each other, and the sustainable development opportunities affected by ecosystems, livelihoods, and governance systems. The chapter

5 Mandy Li-Ming Yap and Krushil Watene, 'The Sustainable Development Goals (SDGs) and Indigenous Peoples: Another Missed Opportunity?' (2019) 20 Journal of Human Development and Capabilities 451. See also John Borrows, 'Indigenous Legal Traditions in Canada' (2005) 19 Washington University Journal of Law and Policy 167; John Borrows, Larry Chartrand, and Oonagh E Fitzgerald, *Braiding Legal Orders: Implementing the United Nations Declaration on the Rights of Indigenous Peoples* (McGill-Queen's University Press 2023); S James Anaya, *Indigenous Peoples in International Law* (2nd edn, Oxford University Press 2004); Tara Dawn Atleo, 'Local Indigenous Planning Instruments for Intergenerational Equity in Ahousaht Traditional Territories of Canada' in Marie-Claire Cordonier Segger, Marcel Szabó, and Alexandra R Harrington (eds), *Intergenerational Justice in Sustainable Development Treaty Implementation: Advancing Future Generations Rights through National Institutions* (Cambridge University Press 2021) 528.

6 Christopher Turner, '"Overlap": Causes and Implications of Contested Indigenous Claims to Territory in the Context of the BC Treaty Process' (MA thesis, University of Northern British Columbia, 2011); Sean Robertson, 'Natives Making Space: The Softwood Lumber Dispute and the Legal Geographies of Indigenous Property Rights' (2015) 61 Geoforum 138 <www.sciencedirect.com/science/article/abs/pii/S0016718515000652?via%3Dihub> accessed 10 March 2025. For further understanding see Campero, Andrews, and Smith-Carrier (n 1); Campero and others (n 1); Campero and Harris (n 1); Li-Ming Yap and Watene (n 5); Borrows (n 5); Borrows, Chartrand, and Fitzgerald (n 5); Anaya (n 5).

focuses on two peace agreements as illustrative examples. First, the 2018 Agreement for Development and Peace in La Araucanía, Chile is considered, and second the 2010 Agreement between the Bolivian Government and the Confederation of Indigenous Peoples from the East, Chaco, and Amazonia is reviewed. This analysis offers insights into the role of peace agreement negotiations and agreements in the Andean region of the Americas in constructing new relationships between States and Indigenous Peoples, including in relation to national and international responses to urgent sustainability challenges, and to key targets adopted in the seventeen SDGs.

In what follows, a theoretical framework employing critical literature on law, public policy, Indigenous rights, and legal geography is advanced, drawing on the works of leading scholars from the region and guided by insights of Dr Cecilia Campero among other experts. In the next section, the domestic and international legal framework for Indigenous Peoples in Chile and Bolivia are briefly introduced. The chapter then considers how peace agreements with Indigenous Peoples address, or fail to address, key sustainable development priorities reflected in the SDGs. In the final remarks, it is suggested that the Indigenous agreements surveyed present a strong alignment with key targets that the UN has prioritized under certain SDGs, such as SDG 2: Zero Hunger, even as they touch less on others. It is also noted that such agreements recognize and respond to the principles and rights recognized in the UN Declaration on the Rights of Indigenous Peoples (UNDRIP).

12.2 LEGAL RELATIONS OF INDIGENOUS PEOPLES IN THE ANDES

According to Indigenous legal scholars and geographers, Indigenous languages and legal relationships can be reviewed on differing spatial scales and perspectives, each reflecting a specific geographical context or as one scholar describes: 'space is law's mirror'.[7] The relationship is dynamic, comprised of processes of making, un-making, and re-making between law, space, place and society.[8] As is especially clear in the Andes mountains, these processes involve societal and political constructs which can offer changing

7 Andreas Philippopoulos-Mihalopoulos, 'Law's Spatial Turn: Geography, Justice and a Certain Fear of Space' (2010) 6 Law, Culture and the Humanities 10 <https://journals.sagepub.com/doi/10.1177/1743872109355578> accessed 10 March 2025; Lindsay Keegitah Borrows, *Otter's Journey through Indigenous Language and Law* (UBC Press 2018).

8 Nicholas Blomley, *Law, Space and the Geographies of Power* (The Guilford Press 1994); Chris Butler, 'Critical Legal Studies and the Politics of Space' (2009) 18 Social & Legal Studies 313; David Delaney, *The Spatial, the Legal and the Pragmatics of World-Making: Nomospheric*

views on, and positions vis-a-vis the relevant spaces and territories, shaping possession or dispossession, power or powerlessness, security or insecurity.[9]

It is possible to focus on (in)justice and how these dynamics can shape territory and law – taking into account power relations.[10] Different academic approaches have been adopted over the last twenty years, from certain scholars' analysis of property rights in land[11] to other's contested legal geographies of water claims.[12] Such analyses hold important insights into the way power and resistance shape access to legal recourse and influence decision-making. In addition, some scholars examine human but also non-human dimensions of law, arguing that current legal instruments are often not well adapted to nature-society dynamics, including some scholars analysis of rivers' rights to legal standing in court,[13] or others' water requirements for non-humans (animal and plants).[14] Yet, there has been relatively little work applying this lens to Indigenous geographies.[15] Moreover, attention to Indigenous Peoples' laws and experiences in the Andes has been scarce.[16]

Investigations (Routledge 2010); Campero, Andrews, and Smith-Carrier (n 1); Campero and others (n 1); Campero and Harris (n 1).

9 Timothy MacNeill, *Indigenous Cultures and Sustainable Development in Latin America* (Palgrave Macmillan 2020); Robert Andoliina, Nina Laurie, and Sarah A Radcliffe, *Indigenous Development in the Andes: Culture, Power, and Transnationalism* (Duke University Press 2009). For more see Campero, Andrews, and Smith-Carrier (n 1); Campero and others (n 1); Campero and Harris (n 1).

10 David Delaney, 'Legal Geography I: Constitutivities, Complexities, and Contingencies' (2015) 39 Progress in Human Geography 96.

11 Nicholas Blomley, 'Law, Property, and the Geography of Violence: The Frontier, the Survey, and the Grid' (2003) 93 Annals of the Association of American Geographers 121; Nicholas Blomley, 'Property and the Landscapes of Gentrification' in Nicholas Blomley (ed), *Unsettling the City: Urban and the Politics of Property* (Routledge 2004).

12 Wendy Jepson, 'Claiming Water: Contested Legal Geographies of Water in South Texas' (2012) 102 Annals of the Association of American Geographers 614.

13 Lidia Cano Pecharroman, 'Rights of Nature: Rivers That Can Stand in Court' (2018) 7 Resources 13, 13. Meg Parsons, Karen Fisher, and Roa Petra Crease, 'Legal and Ontological Pluralism: Recognising Rivers as More-than-Human Entities' in *Decolonising Blue Spaces in the Anthropocene* (Palgrave Macmillan 2021); Erin O'Donnell, *Legal Rights for Rivers: Competition, Collaboration and Water Governance* (Routledge 2018); Anaya (n 5).

14 Jamie McEvoy and others, 'Ecological Drought: Accounting for the Non-Human Impacts of Water Shortage in the Upper Missouri Headwaters Basin, Montana, USA' (2018) 7 Resources 14.

15 Joel E Correia, 'Indigenous Rights at a Crossroads: Territorial Struggles, the Inter-American Court of Human Rights, and Legal Geographies of Liminality' (2018) 97 Geoforum 73. For more see O'Donnell (n 13); Elizabeth Jane Macpherson (ed), *Indigenous Water Rights in Law and Regulation: Lessons from Comparative Experience* (Cambridge University Press 2019); Zoe Todd, 'Legal and Ontological Pluralism: Recognising Rivers as More-Than-Human Entities' in Karen O'Brien, Nicole Schafenacker, and Siri Eriksen (eds), *Indigenous Environmental Justice* (Springer 2021).

16 Correia (n 15).

Indigenous peace agreements are important to consider in an exploration of how the principles of UNDRIP and the SDGs are being reflected in treaty law, including accords from Bolivia and Chile. According to the law of many Indigenous Peoples, territories must be understood as dynamic and alive, watersheds where humans and non-human ancestors, current and future generations interact.[17] Scholars have examined the co-existence of Indigenous law alongside colonial ideas of Indigenous customs, demonstrating how asymmetrical power relations are (re)produced by Western forms of property in treaty making, for instance in studies of British Columbia, Canada.[18] Along this line, as Harm, Koschade, and Peter outline, Indigenous ontologies, based on cultural and spiritual experiences, confront different legal conceptions of jurisdiction and territory.[19] Some argue that recognition of Indigenous jurisdiction can help to address violence while supporting self-determination in Canada.[20] Key experts call for a greater attention to be paid to jurisdiction beyond the limits of scale, to allow analysis of Indigenous legal systems, governance, and stakeholder relationships.[21]

17 Robertson (n 6). For more see Laura Westra, *Environmental Justice and the Rights of Indigenous Peoples: International and Domestic Legal Perspectives* (Routledge 2008); Macpherson (n 15); Jacinta Ruru, 'Indigenous Ancestors' in Sumudu Atapattu, Carmen G Gonzalez, and Sara L Seck (eds), *The Cambridge Handbook of Environmental Justice and Sustainable Development* (Cambridge University Press 2021) 183.

18 Brian Egan and Jessica Place, 'Minding the Gaps: Property, Geography, and Indigenous Peoples in Canada' (2013) 44 Geoforum 129; Brian Egan, 'Towards Shared Ownership: Property, Geography, and Treaty Making in British Columbia' (2013) 95 Geografiska Annaler: Series B, Human Geography 33 <www.jstor.org/stable/43299137> accessed 10 March 2025. Alan Hanna, 'Spaces for Sharing: Searching for Indigenous Law on the Canadian Legal Landscape' (2018) 51(1) University of British Columbia Law Review 105.

19 Melinda Harm, 'Mining Sacred Space: Law's Enactment of Competing Ontologies in the American West' (2012) 44 Environment and Planning 1443; Bettina Koschade and Evelyn Peters, 'Algonquin Notions of Jurisdiction: Inserting Indigenous Voices into Legal Spaces' (2006) 88 Geografiska Annaler: Series B, Human Geography 299 <www.jstor.org/stable/3878375> accessed 10 March 2025. For more see Kathleen Birrell, *Indigeneity: Before and Beyond the Law* (Routledge 2016); Amar Bhatia and others (eds), *Decolonizing Law: Indigenous, Third World and Settler Perspectives* (Routledge 2021), Cathal Doyle, *Indigenous Peoples, Title to Territory, Rights and Resources* (Routledge 2015).

20 Sarah Hunt, 'Witnessing the Colonialscape: Lighting the Intimate Fires of Indigenous Legal Pluralism' (PhD thesis, Simon Fraser University, 2014). For more see Catherine Bell & Val Napoleon (eds), *First Nations' Legal Involvement in Canadian Legal Education* (University of Saskatchewan Press 2008); Leah Gazan, *Restructuring Relations: Indigenous Self-Determination, Governance, and Gender* (SAGE 2021); Val Napoleon, 'Thinking About Indigenous Legal Orders' (2012) 1(1) Indigenous Policy Journal; Borrows (n 5).

21 John Borrows, *Law's Indigenous Ethics* (University of Toronto Press 2019); Borrows (n 5); John Borrows, 'Indigenous-Municipal Legal Relationships: Moving beyond the Duty to Consult' in Patricia M Barkaskas and Renisa Mawani (eds), *The Colonial Problem: An Indigenous Perspective on Crime and Injustice in Canada* (UBC Press 2019). See also Mariana Valverde,

Peace treaties of Indigenous peoples with governments occur in a context, and in the Americas this can include parameters set by the Inter-American Court of Human Rights, despite the challenges of implementing international rulings in domestic law to provide redress for socio-environmental injustice and human rights violations, as has been explored by Correia and others in Paraguay.[22] Similarly, as Robinson and others have considered, agreements may be shaped by the legal implementation of the *Nagoya Protocol on Access to Genetic Resources and the Fair and Equitable Sharing of Benefits Arising from Their Utilization* at local scales, particularly regarding patent activity and benefit-sharing obligations, as well as respect and protections for Indigenous knowledge.[23] From these experiences, it has been argued that there are overlaps and often contradictions, given multiple judicial constructions relating to jurisdiction and rights – particularly in postcolonial States where recognition of customary law and governance is occurring.[24]

It is possible to further explore these interacting regimes by focusing on how peace agreements align with the priorities highlighted in the global SDGs, taking UNDRIP principles into account. While legal agreements may be reflecting the SDGs, it can be suggested, and this may be beneficial for many at local, national, and international scales, much more work is needed to advance reconciliation.

'Jurisdiction and Scales: Legal "Technicalities" as Resources for Theory' (2009) 18 Social & Legal Studies 139 <https://journals.sagepub.com/doi/10.1177/0964663909103622> accessed 10 March 2025.

22 ibid. See also Correia (n 15).

23 Daniel Robinson and others, 'Legal Geographies of Kava, Kastom and Indigenous Knowledge: Next Steps under the Nagoya Protocol' (2021) 118 Geoforum 169; Nagoya Protocol on Access to Genetic Resources and the Fair and Equitable Sharing of Benefits Arising from Their Utilization to the Convention on Biological Diversity (adopted 29 October 2010, entered into force 12 October 2014) UN Doc UNEP/CBD/COP/DEC/X/1; Convention on Biological Diversity (adopted 5 June 1992, entered into force 29 December 1993) 1760 UNTS 79 (CBD), preamble, arts 8(j), 17. See also CBD, 'Kunming-Montreal Global Biodiversity Framework' (19 December 2022) UN Doc CBD/COP/DEC/15/4.

24 Franz von Benda-Beckmann, Keebet von Benda-Beckmann, and Anne Griffiths, 'Space and Legal Pluralism: An Introduction' in Franz von Benda-Beckmann, Keebet von Benda-Beckmann and Anne Griffiths (eds), *Spatializing Law: An Anthropological Geography of Law in Society* (Routledge 2009). See also Jessie Hohmann and Marc Weller (eds), *The UN Declaration on the Rights of Indigenous Peoples: A Commentary* (Oxford University Press 2018); Marie-Claire Cordonier Segger and Wayne Garnons-Williams (eds), *Indigenous Peoples Inspiring Sustainable Development: Implementing UNDRIP through International Law and Covenants* (Cambridge University Press 2025 forthcoming); Claire Charters and Rodolfo Stavenhagen (eds), *The UN Declaration on the Rights of Indigenous Peoples: A Contemporary Evaluation* (Routledge 2021).

12.3 LEGAL FRAMEWORKS IN RELATION TO INDIGENOUS PEOPLES

ILO 169 and UNDRIP represent important achievements in the vindication of Indigenous rights: the ILO 169 Convention was ratified by several Latin American countries in the early 1990s, and UNDRIP agreed in the same spirit, extending the reach of important Indigenous Peoples rights and principles. Countries of the Andes, including Bolivia, Paraguay, Perú, and Colombia are among those States which adopted UNDRIP and ILO 169 early,[25] while other countries in the Americas, such as Chile, delayed approval for over a decade, despite pressure from Indigenous organizations. ILO 169 was adopted into law in Chile in 2008, through the enactment of Regulation 236 (2008) during the first term of President Michelle Bachelet's government.[26] Chile and Bolivia have also given their official support to the UNDRIP.

Governments from different countries are constitutionally required to apply international agreements and norms in diverse ways, at the domestic level. As scholars emphasize, several countries have modified their constitutions and adapted institutions to comply with key principles reflected in the UNDRIP, such as Article 10, Article 19, and Article 26 which are also obligations enshrined in ILO 169 at Article 6, Article 15, and Article 16.[27] For instance, constitutional reforms were processed in Ecuador in 2008 and in Bolivia in 2009 to incorporate the right to consultation according to ILO 169, which guarantees free prior and informed consent (FPIC) in important instances.[28] Other countries, such as Chile, have adopted a different approach by enacting Regulation 124/2009, which was later further modified by Regulation 66/2014. The latter's purpose was to establish the procedure for consultation and participation of Indigenous Peoples in relation to the Indigenous Law 19253/1993, which recognized Indigenous rights to participate in decision-making, but in a less binding and action-oriented manner. The Government of Bolivia, under President Evo Morales, also enacted Law 73/2010 guaranteeing the self-determination of Indigenous Peoples and recognizing Indigenous jurisdiction to administer justice according to their own systems. Along these lines,

[25] ILO No 169 (n 2).

[26] Jorge Contesse, 'Consulta y pueblos indígenas: el caso de Chile' (2010) 14 (3) Revista de la Fundación para el Debido Proceso Legal 32.

[27] ILO No 169 (n 2) art 6, art 15, and art 16; UNDRIP (n 3) art 10, art 19 and art 26.

[28] Constitution of the Republic of Ecuador, art 57 (*Political Database of the Americas*, 31 January 2012, English) <https://pdba.georgetown.edu/Constitutions/Ecuador/english08.html> accessed 10 March 2025; 'Article 30.II of Bolivia (Plurinational State of) 2009' (*Constitute* [English]) <www.constituteproject.org/constitution/Bolivia_2009> accessed 10 March 2025.

Law 341/2013 was also enacted in Bolivia seeking to recognize the right to participation and social control in different areas.[29]

As several scholars have observed, internal regulations accompanying the recognition of Indigenous law appear to be affected by public policies which can constrain application, including restrictive processes and scarce resources for the correct application of the law.[30] For instance, while Chilean Regulation 66/2013 has the goal of regulating the consultation process in relation to the rights enshrined in ILO 169, the law has been criticized for limiting the rights of Indigenous Peoples. For example, the consultation process can be affected if there is unclear engagement of Indigenous representative institutions, or obligations can be constrained to instances in which an Indigenous community or group can demonstrate that they are 'susceptible to direct impact' (an unclear concept).[31] Similarly, Regulation 40/2012, which included Indigenous consent and participation in the Environmental Impact Assessment (EIA) process, has been questioned for not including Indigenous cooperation or consultation before an assessment begins in the EIA and for omitting social and economic dimensions during the mitigation and compensation process, which only considers the environment.[32] Hence, it can be argued that the principles of engagement and consultation of the UNDRIP and ILO 169 still require further resources domestically in key countries.

[29] Bolivia, Law No. 073 of 29 December 2010, 'Jurisdictional Delimitation Law', *Legislative Assembly of the Plurinational State of Bolivia* (2010); Bolivia, Law No. 341 of 5 February 2013, 'Law of Participation and Social Control', *Legislative Assembly of the Plurinational State of Bolivia* (2013).

[30] Raquel Yrigoyen, 'De la tutela indígena a la libre determinación del desarrollo, la participación, la consulta y el consentimiento' (2009) 40 El otro derecho 11;Susan Bass and Environmental Law Institute, *Prior Informed Consent and Mining: Promoting the Sustainable Development of Local Communities* (Environmental Law Institute 2004) <www.eli.org/research-report/prior-informed-consent-and-mining-promoting-sustainable-development-local-communitie> accessed 10 March 2025. For more see Janna Promislow, 'Public Law in Indigenous Contexts, Indigenous Law in the Contexts of Public Law' in Jason NE Varuhas and Shona Wilson Stark (eds), *Researching Public Law in Common Law Systems* (Edward Elgar 2023); George K Foster, 'Indigenous Participation in Resource Development: The Promise and Limitations of International Safeguards' in Dwight Newman (ed), *Research Handbook on the International Law of Indigenous Rights* (Edward Elgar 2022); Cathal Doyle, 'Challenges for Indigenous Peoples' Rights to Lands, Territories and Resources' in *State of the World's Indigenous Peoples: Rights to Lands, Territories and Resources* (United Nations 2021).

[31] Isabel Aninat, 'Los desafíos pendientes del Convenio 169' (2014) 369 Centros de Estudios Publicos <www.cepchile.cl/cep/site/docs/20160304/20160304100553/pder369_IAninat.pdf> accessed 10 March 2025.

[32] ibid.

12.4 INDIGENOUS AGREEMENTS IN THE ANDES: THE CASE OF CHILE AND BOLIVIA

12.4.1 2018 *National Agreement for Development and Peace in La Araucanía, Chile*

Tensions between the Chilean Government and the Mapuche Peoples in La Araucanía date back before the nineteenth century, when the Government dispossessed Indigenous People from their lands and forced them to adopt colonial rules while dismissing their language, ways of knowing, traditions, and worldviews.[33] In 1989 the New Imperial Agreement, an attempt at reconciliation with the Mapuche movement was signed resulting in the creation of important laws and institutions such as *Establishing Standards for the Protection, Promotion and Development of Indigenous Peoples, and Creating the National Corporation for Indigenous Development* 1993 (Indigenous Law 1993),[34] establishing the National Corporation for Indigenous Development (CONADI). However, after more than thirty years, social, political, and economic inequalities still persist for the Mapuche Peoples, fuelling important conflicts in La Araucanía.

In 2018, the Chilean Government, led by President Sebastian Pinera, promoted the 'National Agreement for Development and Peace in La Araucanía' in an attempt to reconcile and address injustices in the Araucanía Region that were being faced by the Mapuche People.[35] Critical accounts of this agreement suggest that negotiations were characterized by lack of plurality, transversality, and broad participatory debate, with Mapuche voices and needs not fully reflected, while other scholars express cautious optimism with respect to the treaty process.[36] Some scholars critique the

[33] Ministerio de Desarrollo Social, Gobierno de Chile 'Acuerdo Nacional por el Desarrollo y la Paz en La Araucanía' (2018).

[34] Chile, Ministry of Planning and Cooperation, Law 19253, 'Establishing Standards for the Protection, Promotion and Development of Indigenous Peoples, and Creating the National Corporation for Indigenous Development' (1993).

[35] Corporación Nacional de Desarrollo Indígena (CONADI), *Public Policies without a Rights-based Approach: National Agreement for the Development and Peace in La Araucanía (Chile)* (Universidad Nacional de Colombia 2020) https://biblioteca-repositorio.clacso.edu.ar/handle/CLACSO/102588 accessed 10 March 2025.

[36] Gabriel Mora-Galleguillos, 'Políticas sin enfoque de derechos: Acuerdo Nacional por el Desarrollo y la Paz de La Araucanía' (2022) 21 Forum: Revista Departamento de Ciencia Política 228; Germán Bidegain, 'From Cooperation to Confrontation: The Mapuche Movement and Its Political Impact, 1990–2014' in Jennifer L McKinnon and Anne L Grossman (eds), *Latin American Politics and Society* (University of Chicago Press 2017). But see René Hurtado, 'Análisis de Clase del Acuerdo Nacional por el Desarrollo y la Paz en la

underlying notions of jurisdiction and territory which, while taking into account UNDRIP principles such as the right to 'maintain and strengthen their distinctive spiritual relationship with their traditionally owned or otherwise occupied and used lands, territories, waters and coastal seas and other resources' (UNDRIP, art 25), are not seen as being sensitive enough to Mapuche worldviews,[37] and the Indigenous law which governs stewardship of the Araucanía,[38] while others consider the agreement to demonstrate signs of progress in the evolving relationships, even as debates and resistance continues.[39]

Three principles guide this agreement: (1) willingness for dialogue, agreement and peace finding, (2) recognition and appreciation of diversity, and (3) comprehensive and inclusive development for the region – *Impulso Araucanía 2018-2026* (Araucanía Impulse Plan 2018–2026).[40] As part of the latter, several initiatives have been adopted which align with key SDGs, including SDG 3: Good Health and Wellbeing, particularly target 3.8, which seeks to 'achieve universal health coverage, including access to quality essential health-care services'; SDG 4: Quality Education, specifically target 4.5, which aims to 'ensure equal access to all levels of education and vocational training for the vulnerable, including Indigenous peoples'; SDG 6: Clean

Araucanía' (*Red Digital*, 2019); Comunicaciones OC, 'El "Acuerdo Nacional por el Desarrollo y la Paz en La Araucanía": Análisis crítico desde la perspectiva de derechos humanos' (Observatorio Ciudadano, 27 September 2018).

37 Galleguillos (n 36); Bidegain (n 36). But see Harm (n 19); Koschade and Peters (n 19).

38 Kelly Bauer, 'Negotiating Autonomy: Mapuche Territorial Demands and Chilean Land Policy' in *Negotiating Autonomy: Mapuche Territorial Demands and Chilean Land Policy* (University of Pittsburgh Press 2022); Lincoyan Painecura Medina, 'Peace in Araucanía: Observations on Its Interpretation and Proposal' (2023) 6(3) Revista Chilena de Derecho y Ciencia Política; Galleguillos (n 36); Carla Alberti, Juan Pablo Luna, and Sergio Toro Maureira, 'Plan Araucanía: Los errores de la política pública en el conflicto mapuche' (CIPER, 26 November 2018) <www.ciperchile.cl/2018/11/26/plan-araucania-los-errores-de-la-politica-publica-en-el-conflicto-mapuche/> accessed 10 March 2025. For more, see S Sanhueza and others, 'Institutionalized Violence in Schools and Language Displacement: The Voices of Mapuche Speakers and Elders' (2025) 15 Frontiers in Psychology 1485569 <www.frontiersin.org/journals/psychology/articles/10.3389/fpsyg.2024.1485569/full> accessed 10 March 2025; Cristián Larroulet Vignau and Jean P Sepúlveda, 'The Economic Impact of Violence in Southern Chile' (2024) Applied Economics <www.tandfonline.com/doi/full/10.1080/00036846.2024.2409845> accessed 10 March 2025; R Maher and others, 'The Role of Multistakeholder Initiatives in the Radicalization of Resistance: The Forest Stewardship Council and the Mapuche Conflict in Chile' (2024) Journal of Management Studies <https://onlinelibrary.wiley.com/doi/full/10.1111/joms.13015 > accessed 10 March 2025.

39 ibid.

40 'Plan Impulso Araucanía (2018–2016)', Gobierno de Chile <https://planimpulso.cl/wp-content/uploads/2019/12/Plan_impulso_araucania.pdf> accessed 10 March 2025.

Water and Sanitation, notably target 6.1 and target 6.6, which call for 'universal and equitable access to safe and affordable drinking water' and the protection of 'water-related ecosystems'; SDG 11: Sustainable Cities and Communities, particularly with target 11.4 and target 11.1, which emphasize safeguarding 'cultural and natural heritage' and ensuring 'access to adequate, safe and affordable housing and basic services'; and SDG 15: Life on Land, specifically target 15.1 and target 15.6, which promote 'sustainable use of terrestrial ecosystems' and 'equitable sharing of the benefits arising from the utilization of genetic resources'.[41] For instance, three of the activities prioritized in the Araucanía Impulse Plan 2018–2026 focus on agricultural reconversion, renewable energies, and tourism. Both food security and goals are climate action goal are highlighted vis-à-vis recognition of the need to move to a better economic alternative from livestock and cereal plantations to fruit plantations.[42] A support programme is proposed for Indigenous communities, with the aim of increasing the area dedicated to fruit trees, vineyards, and vegetables. This initiative could be seen to support SDG 2: Zero Hunger including target 2.3 which seeks to 'double the agricultural productivity and incomes of small-scale food producers, in particular women, indigenous peoples, family farmers, pastoralists and fishers, including through secure and equal access to land, other productive resources and inputs, knowledge, financial services, markets and opportunities for value addition and non-farm employment', 2.4, which aims to 'ensure sustainable food production systems and implement resilient agricultural practices that increase productivity and production, that help maintain ecosystems, that strengthen capacity for adaptation to climate change, extreme weather, drought, flooding and other disasters and that progressively improve land and soil quality', and SDG 13: Climate Action, including target 13.2, which calls for the integration of 'climate change measures into national policies, strategies and planning'. To advance the objectives of the agricultural programme, capacity-strengthening efforts, new investment, technology transfer, and associated activities are proposed. While these elements of the agreement could be very positive, a great deal depends on the way that the programme is implemented. If UNDRIP principles are respected, in particular Article 23, which affirms that 'Indigenous peoples have the right to determine and develop priorities and strategies for the development or use of their lands or territories and other resources', Article 11(1), which recognizes that 'Indigenous peoples have the right to practise and revitalize their cultural traditions and customs', and

41 ibid. Also see Comunicaciones (n 36).
42 ibid.

Article 29(1), which states that 'Indigenous peoples have the right to the conservation and protection of the environment and the productive capacity of their lands or territories and resources', there is potential for important advances to help achieve crucial SDG targets under the collaboration occasioned by the agreement in a manner that respects Indigenous rights.[43]

Renewable energies, including hydroelectric, wind, and bioenergetic, for water supply are also prioritized in the plan under the agreement. Specifically, the plans call for efforts to: 'Prioritize renewable energies, focusing on Indigenous People, and energy access for intercultural educational establishments'.[44] In doing so and in accordance with UNDRIP article 32(1), which affirms that 'Indigenous peoples have the right to determine and develop priorities and strategies for the development or use of their lands or territories and other resources', the plan seeks to promote community generation initiatives via the development of energy projects partially owned by communities, in association with energy companies, committing to 'promote the contribution of indigenous and non-indigenous communities to energy projects through a new energy model, focused on the use of energy resources for local development, which is relevant and sustainable'.[45] As discussed earlier in this volume, such initiatives, taking into account the principles of UNDRIP such as Article 26(2) that affirms 'Indigenous peoples have the right to own, use, develop and control the lands, territories and resources that they possess by reason of traditional ownership or other traditional occupation or use', and Article 20(1) that says 'Indigenous peoples have the right to maintain and develop their political, economic and social systems or institutions', could contribute to advancing SDG 7: Affordable and Clean Energy through target 7.2, which seeks to 'increase substantially the share of renewable energy in the global energy mix by 2030', SDG 8: Decent Work and Economic Growth through target 8.3 which aims to 'promote development-oriented policies that support productive activities, decent job creation, entrepreneurship, creativity and innovation, and encourage the formalization and growth of micro-, small- and medium-sized enterprises, including through access to financial services',

[43] UNDRIP (n 3) art 23, art 11(1) and art 29(1). See also Timothy MacNeil, 'Andean Indigenous Sustainable Development' in *Indigenous Cultures and Sustainable Development in Latin America* (Palgrave Macmillan 2020); Verónica Figueroa Huencho, 'Implementation of Indigenous Public Policies and Tensions to Governance: Evidences from the Chilean Case' (2021) 15(2) Critical Policy Studies 209; Carla Alberti and Shannan Mattiace, 'State Responses to Autonomy Demands: Indigenous Movements and Regional Threats in Bolivia and Ecuador' (2023) Journal of Politics in Latin America <https://doi.org/10.1177/1866802X231183453>.

[44] Plan Impulso Araucanía (n 40) 33.

[45] ibid 34.

and SDG 17: Partnerships for the Goals which calls to 'encourage and promote effective public, public-private and civil society partnerships, building on the experience and resourcing strategies of partnerships'.[46] While the programme overall appears to be potentially a positive development, there is significant concern about challenges associated with efforts to install large-scale hydroelectric facilities which have been rejected by the community, and could – if UNDRIP Free, Prior, Informed Consent (FPIC) commitments are not respected – lead to harmful impacts.[47] In the alternative, if the agreement and Plan Impulso Araucanía opened opportunities for small scale hydropower or other renewable energy alternatives to be chosen and installed with the Indigenous community, as has been done elsewhere, there is potential for interesting advances.[48]

In the *Plan Impulso Araucanía* the parties also propose to advance rural and cultural tourism, enriched with the history and culture of Indigenous Peoples: 'The goal of the "Impulse Plan" in its Tourism axis is . . . to enrich this activity with Mapuche history and culture . . . We will enhance the region's cultural wealth with the development of new Mapuche tourism products through the "Indigenous Paradises" programme, with Mapuche entrepreneurs and/or businessmen'.[49] These initiatives would hold potential to contribute to efforts to advance SDG 2: Zero Hunger particularly target 2.3, which aims to 'double the agricultural productivity and incomes of small-scale food producers, in particular women, Indigenous peoples, family farmers, pastoralists and fishers, including through secure and equal access to land, other productive resources and inputs, knowledge, financial services, markets and opportunities for value addition and non-farm employment'; SDG 12: Responsible Consumption and Production through target 12.8 which seeks to 'ensure that people everywhere have the relevant information and awareness for sustainable development and lifestyles in harmony with nature' and SDG 8: Decent Work and Economic Growth through target 8.9 which calls to 'devise and

[46] United Nations, Transforming Our World: The 2030 Agenda for Sustainable Development (UNGA Res 70/1, 21 October 2015) UN Doc A/RES/70/1, target 7.2, target 8.3 and target 17.17 (SDGs).

[47] Manuel Prieto and Carl Bauer, 'Hydroelectric Power Generation in Chile: An Institutional Critique of the Neutrality of Market Mechanisms' (2012) 37(2) Water International 131 <www.tandfonline.com/doi/abs/10.1080/02508060.2012.662731> accessed 10 March 2025.

[48] K Bauer, 'Small Hydropower, Large Obstacle? Exploring land use conflict and Indigenous opposition to renewable energy in southern Chile' (2023) 96 Energy Research & Social Science 102973; SRJ Tsuji, DDP McCarthy, and S Quilley, 'Green Energy—Green for Whom? A Case Study of the Kabinakagami River Waterpower Project in Northern Canada' (2021) 13(16) Sustainability 9445.

[49] Plan Impulso Araucanía (n 40) 30.

implement policies to promote sustainable tourism that creates jobs and promotes local culture and products'.[50]

Finally, under the agreement the Plan Impulso Araucanía expresses a commitment to creating working plans that encourage Indigenous groups to participate in the administration of national parks, specifically the Nahuelbuta, Conguillío, and Huerquehue parks. 'They will be incorporated into the planning of tourism development so they can continue developing their commercial and tourist activities that have cultural significance'.[51] This initiative might contribute to efforts in Chile to advance SDG 1: No Poverty through target 1.4 which aims to 'ensure that all men and women, in particular the poor and the vulnerable, have equal rights to economic resources, as well as access to basic services, ownership and control over land and other forms of property, inheritance, natural resources, appropriate new technology and financial services, including microfinance', SDG 8: Decent Work and Economic Growth through target 8.9, which calls to 'devise and implement policies to promote sustainable tourism that creates jobs and promotes local culture and products', and SDG 15: Life on Land through target 15.1, which aims to 'ensure the conservation, restoration and sustainable use of terrestrial and inland freshwater ecosystems and their services, in particular forests, wetlands, mountains and drylands, in line with obligations under international agreements', and target 15.6, which seeks to 'promote fair and equitable sharing of the benefits arising from the utilization of genetic resources and promote appropriate access to such resources'.

As part of the institutional framework, the Plan proposed the creation of a Ministry and Council of Indigenous Peoples, and promoted greater political participation of Indigenous Peoples through minimum quotas of Indigenous candidates in elections.[52] While it may not sufficiently advance ILO 169 through, for instance, strengthening consultation rights and operationalizing obligations to ensure Free, Prior, Informed Consent (FPIC) in all respects, the agreement and the Plan appear to respect certain aspects of UNDRIP and ILO 169, and to hold potential to improve efforts to advance certain SDGs depending on how they are implemented.

[50] SDGs (n 46) target 2.3, target 12.8 and target 8.9.

[51] Plan Impulso Araucanía (n 40) 21.

[52] Ariel Becerra-Chávez and Mauricio Morales-Quiroga, 'Reserved Indigenous Seats and Electoral Turnout: Evidence from the Chilean Constitutional Convention' (2022) 28(4) Nationalism and Ethnic Politics 491; Pedro Cayul, 'Indigenous Representation and Participation: The Case of the Chilean Mapuche' (2024) 90 Electoral Studies 102818; Huencho (n 43).

12.4.2 2010 *Agreement between the Bolivian Government and the Confederation of Indigenous Peoples from the East, Chaco, and Amazonia*

After an intense conflict over the construction of a road which was crossing not only Indigenous lands but also the Isiboro Sécure Indigenous Territory and National Park (Tipnis), a protected area for the conservation of nature in the Amazonia region, the Government of Bolivia, under President Evo Morales, signed an agreement with the Confederation of Indigenous Peoples from the East, Chaco, and Amazonia in 2010.[53] The agreement, which many noted reflected many rights identified in the UNDRIP, was structured around eight main points: (1) land and territory, (2) Indigenous autonomy, (3) consultation rights, (4) productive development, (5) legislative development, (6) political participation and representation, (7) education, and (8) communication.[54] It is possible to analyse the agreement from the perspective of its respect for rights and principles enshrined in the UNDRIP and ILO Convention 169, and its contributions towards achieving key targets globally.

The Parties to the agreement underline a clear commitment to mobilizing national and international finance to achieve key objectives that align with important priorities identified in the global SDGs. For instance, the agreement guarantees funding for social and productive development projects led, co-managed, or approved by Indigenous groups, such as food security programmes. This initiative can help advance SDG 2: Zero Hunger targets in target 2.1 to 'End hunger and ensure access by all people, in particular the poor and people in vulnerable situations, including infants, to safe, nutritious and sufficient food all year round'; and in target 2.3 to 'Double the agricultural productivity and incomes of small-scale food producers, in particular women, Indigenous peoples, family farmers, pastoralists and fishers, including through secure and equal access to land, other productive resources and inputs'. And SDG 8: Decent Work and Economic Growth through target 8.3 that seeks to 'Promote development-oriented policies that support productive activities, decent job creation, entrepreneurship, creativity and innovation'; and through target 8.5 that aims to 'Achieve full and productive employment and decent work for all women and men, including for young people and persons with

[53] Ana Delgado, 'The TIPNIS Conflict in Bolivia' (2017) 39 Contexto Internacional <www.researchgate.net/publication/316867537_The_TIPNIS_Conflict_in_Bolivia> accessed 10 March 2025.

[54] ibid.

disabilities, and equal pay for work of equal value'.[55] The Government also guarantees funding for educational infrastructure for Indigenous People, which aligns well with efforts to advance SDG 4: Education including target 4.5 that aims to 'Eliminate gender disparities in education and ensure equal access to all levels of education and vocational training for the vulnerable, including Indigenous peoples'; and target 4.a that seeks to 'Build and upgrade education facilities that are child, disability and gender sensitive and provide safe, non-violent, inclusive and effective learning environments for all'; and towards the Indigenous programme for climate change which could support SDG 13: Bold Action on Climate Change, especially target 13.2 which promotes to 'Integrate climate change measures into national policies, strategies and planning'.[56]

The drafters did seek to promote Indigenous consultation and participation. For instance, the agreement appears to reflect UNDRIP Article 32(2), which provides that: 'States shall consult and cooperate in good faith with the Indigenous Peoples concerned through their own representative institutions in order to obtain their free and informed consent prior to the approval of any project affecting their lands or territories and other resources, particularly in connection with the development, utilization or exploitation of mineral, water or other resources'. In particular, in UNDRIP, the drafters recognize that infrastructure and natural resources development projects will require Indigenous consultation and participation when assessments begin: 'Before designing and executing infrastructure projects that can affect Indigenous territories, such as roads, hydroelectric and natural resources exploitation (such as hydrocarbons, mining, etc.) the Government will inform and consult Indigenous groups which will be affected or are susceptible to being affected'.[57] These provisions, while perhaps not clearly noting the need for free consent, do commit to prior and informed consent, and if successful, could contribute to efforts to achieve SDG 9 on Industry, Infrastructure, and Innovation, particularly target 9.1 that states 'Develop quality, reliable,

[55] SDGs (n 46) target 2.1, target 2.3, target 8.3, and target 8.5.

[56] ibid target 4.5, target 4.a, target 13.2. See also UNDRIP (n 3) art 14 and art 29. For further reference, Rodolfo Stavenhagen, 'Cultural Rights: A Social Science Perspective' in Claire Charters and Rodolfo Stavenhagen (eds), *Making the Declaration Work: The United Nations Declaration on the Rights of Indigenous Peoples* (International Work Group for Indigenous Affairs 2009) 267; Federico Lenzerini, 'Article 29: Right to Conservation and Protection of the Environment and the Productive Capacity of Indigenous Lands and Resources' in Hohmann and Weller (n 24) 792.

[57] Gobierno Plurinacional de Bolivia, 'Acta de concertación Ministerio de Autonomía, Ministerio de Desarrollo Rural y Tierras, Ministerio de Hidrocarburos y Energía – Confederación de Pueblos Indígenas del Oriente, Chacho y Amazonia' (2010).

sustainable and resilient infrastructure, including regional and transborder infrastructure, to support economic development and human well-being, with a focus on affordable and equitable access for all' and SDG 12 Sustainable Consumption and Production, notably target 12.2 that aims 'By 2030, achieve the sustainable management and efficient use of natural resources'.[58] Before passing a new law that might be of interest to Indigenous People, the Government also commits to attempt to integrate Indigenous perspectives by involving them in discussions in the Legislative Chamber and across governmental entities and ministries,[59] potentially supporting SDG 16: Peace, Justice and Strong Institutions through target 16.7 'Ensure responsive, inclusive, participatory and representative decision-making at all levels'. This content is also aligned with international norms in ILO Convention 169, specifically Articles 6 (1) (a), which commits 'Governments shall consult the [Peoples] concerned, through appropriate procedures and in particular through their representative institutions, whenever consideration is being given to legislative or administrative measures which may affect them directly' and 15 (1) that commits 'The rights of the [P]eoples concerned to the natural resources pertaining to their lands shall be specially safeguarded ... the [P]eoples concerned shall wherever possible participate in the benefits of such activities, and shall receive fair compensation for any damages which they may sustain as a result of such activities'.[60] Along these lines, the Government, in collaboration with Indigenous groups, commits to develop a regulation to ensure that proper consultation is carried out for projects in the hydrocarbon sector. Despite acknowledging consultation and participation rights, some commentators did critique the Government of President Evo Morales for 'double discourse' in the way that there is simultaneous promotion of participatory and consultation rights, while also restriction of such rights in the approval of extractive industry investment projects.[61]

58 SDGs (n 46) target 9.1, target 12.2, and target 16.7. For more see Winfried Huck, *Sustainable Development Goals: Article-by-Article Commentary* (Beck/Hart/Nomos 2022).

59 Gobierno Plurinacional (n 57); For more see Pål Wrange, 'SDG16: Promote Peaceful and Inclusive Societies for Sustainable Development, Provide Access to Justice for All and Build Effective, Accountable and Inclusive Institutions at All Levels' in Jonas Ebbesson and Ellen Hey (eds), *The Cambridge Handbook of the Sustainable Development Goals and International Law* (Cambridge University Press 2020); Liora Lazarus, 'Securitizing Sustainable Development? The Coercive Sting in SDG 16' in Markus Kaltenborn, Markus Krajewski, and Heike Kuhn (eds), *Sustainable Development Goals and Human Rights* (Springer 2020).

60 ILO No 169 (n 2) art 6 (1) (a) and art 15 (1).

61 Anthony Bebbington and Denise Humphreys Bebbington, 'An Andean Avatar: Post-Neoliberal and Neoliberal Strategies for Securing the Unobtainable' (2011) 16(1) New Political Economy 131 <www.tandfonline.com/doi/abs/10.1080/13563461003789803> accessed 10 March 2025.

As part of the agreement, the Government also agrees to recognize Indigenous lands and the distribution of public lands to Indigenous communities. The treaty specifically states that this process will be conducted with respect demonstrated for the rights and principles enshrined in ILO 169 and the UNDRIP.[62] Moreover, the Parties specify that mining and forestry laws will be modified following Indigenous consultation and participation. The Government also commits to respect the application of Indigenous customs in the acknowledgement of Indigenous autonomy.[63]

This agreement, as proposed, while explicitly considering Indigenous rights under ILO 169 and the UNDRIP, is not quite as advanced with respect to, for instance, efforts to promote gender equality which could support SDG 5 particularly target 5.c, that aims to 'Adopt and strengthen sound policies and enforceable legislation for the promotion of gender equality and the empowerment of all women and girls at all levels'.[64] Hence, policies reflect a 'one size fits all' approach to Indigenous decision-making. In principle, programmes, policies, services, and funding across government should be available, co-developed, and delivered in ways that reflect the distinct needs and governance structures of Indigenous peoples.

12.5 CONCLUSION

This chapter has explored how important Indigenous peace agreements in the Andes respect the rights and principles enshrined in UNDRIP and the ILO Convention 169, and could help to advance the global SDGs. Whether the agreement was signed prior to the elaboration and adoption of the SDGs, such as the Agreement between the Bolivian Government and the Confederation of Indigenous Peoples from the East, Chaco, and Amazonia, or after their adoption, under these agreements many of the key priorities identified in the SDGs are meant to receive support and even financial assistance. Treaty commitments especially align with key SDGs such as SDG 2: Zero Hunger, SDG 4 Education, SDG 6 and 7 Clean Water and Clean Energy, SDG 8 Decent Employment, SDG 9 Infrastructure, SDG 12 Sustainable

[62] ILO No 169 (n 2) art 6 and art 15; UNDRIP (n 3) art 18–19 and arts 32.

[63] Bebbington and Bebbington (n 61).

[64] Patricia Kameri-Mbote and Nkatha Kabira, 'SDG 5: Achieve Gender Equality and Empower All Women and Girls' in Ebbesson and Hey (n 59); Karen Morrow, 'Gender and the Sustainable Development Goals' in Duncan French and Louis J Kotzé (eds), *Sustainable Development Goals: Law, Theory and Implementation* (Edward Elgar 2020); Josephine A Odera and Judy Mulusa, 'SDGs, Gender Equality and Women's Empowerment: What Prospects for Delivery?' in Kaltenborn, Krajewski, and Kuhn (n 59).

Consumption and Production, SDG 13 Climate Action, and SDG 14 and 15, Life Below Water and Life on Land, as well as SDG 16 Justice. However, concerns remain that while the potential exists for these instruments to promote sustainable development, in a manner that respects UNDRIP, if implementation is not carefully calibrated they could be just as likely to perpetuate injustice and power imbalance. Concerns raised in the negotiation of the Chilean peace agreement included indications that Mapuche voices and needs were not properly taken into account, with political agendas being prioritized in their place.[65] It is possible that if the process had developed differently, further key priorities aligned with SDGs 3: Good Health and Wellbeing and 4: Quality Education, for instance, might have been better supported by the agreement. Some scholars and leaders have also expressed concern that the agreement did not do enough to strengthen the participation of Indigenous women, and promote gender equality (SDG 5).

Similar to other studies where Indigenous ontologies confront different legal concepts of jurisdiction,[66] the Chilean peace agreement in Araucanía suggests the need to critically understand conflicts and potential solutions as being not only defined by political scales but also by Indigenous perspectives, legal systems, and values. Additionally, while the agreement proposes to support and scale up political participation of Indigenous Peoples, it was seen by some as sidestepping important principles from ILO 169 such as strengthening Free Prior and Informed Consent (FPIC) consultation rights. Similarly, although ILO 169 and the UNDRIP are clearly reflected in the peace agreement in Bolivia, an analysis of the text reveals a troubling 'one size fits all' approach, which some scholars suggest gives less attention than warranted to key priorities such as SDG 5: Gender Equality.

These findings matter for the growing debates on Indigenous rights and law, in both academia and policy. In terms of public policy lessons, it is possible that such peace agreements are also opening spaces for dialogue and action to promote sustainable development in line with SDGs. It also highlights that attention should be paid to reflecting the distinct needs and governance structures of Indigenous Peoples. From a research perspective, analysis of the case study agreements also reveals distinct efforts – and resulting binding obligations on governments and the international community – to respect UNDRIP rights and principles, while advancing key SDG targets in the Andean region.

65 Hurtado (n 36); Comunicaciones (n 36).

66 Harm (n 19); Koschade and Peters (n 19).

13

Rights of Indigenous Peoples to Advance SDGs in Bangladesh and Mexico

13.1 INTRODUCTION

While the 2030 Sustainable Development Goals (SDGs) are considered to form an 'indivisible whole', some argue that their focus lies more with the agency and impacts of sustainable development on humans and the environment respectively, and less so with the inevitable and intertwined relationship between humans and the environment. This is where Indigenous ontologies and environmental stewardship stand out – Indigenous Peoples express cultural and spiritual ties to the ecosystems and lands of their locality that is fundamental to their role as environmental guardians.[1] As such, exploring the substantial intersections between global conservation values and the extent of influences of the Indigenous Peoples over the area inherited and controlled by them enables a closer understanding of the intersections of communities and the biosphere, and how to advance the SDGs.[2] Such an exploration is particularly evident in the treaties with Indigenous Peoples in Bangladesh and Mexico.

In both Bangladesh and Mexico, treaties between Indigenous Peoples and governments opened potential to safeguard the heritage and well-being of said Indigenous Peoples. Throughout the historical colonization of these two

[1] Stephen T Garnett and others, 'A Spatial Overview of the Global Importance of Indigenous Lands for Conservation' (2018) 1(7) Nature Sustainability 369–374. The authors are deeply grateful to Adv Hafij Khan and Dr. Odette Lara Morales for their insights, research and substantive contributions to this chapter.

[2] Jörn PW Scharlemann and others, 'Towards Understanding Interactions between Sustainable Development Goals: The Role of Environment–Human Linkages' (2020) 15(6) Sustainability Science 1573–1584.

regions, persistent turmoil and armed conflicts took place between the national authorities and Indigenous communities, much like other settled regions once safeguarded by Indigenous Peoples. Many of these conflicts revolved around establishing land rights between the historical guardians of the land and the colonizers or settlers,[3] with at least two of these conflicts occurring in Bangladesh and Mexico. These struggles, many at the end of the twentieth century, resulted in peace accords between the Indigenous Peoples and the opposing Bangladeshi and Mexican authorities. Specifically, the Zapatista movement of Mexico resulted in the San Andrés Accords of 1996 (San Andrés Accords), which focused on securing land and freedom.[4] Later, the Chittagong Hill Tracts conflict in Bangladesh was resolved through the Chittagong Hill Tracts Treaty of 1997 (Hill Tracts Treaty), which emphasized the need for protecting the region in the face of resource exploration and development.[5] Parties to both the San Andrés Accords and the Hill Tracts Treaty (together, the Peace Accords), generally, aimed to bring peace in the areas inhabited by the Indigenous Peoples of these countries, and feature innovative legal and governance approaches to promote the rights of the Indigenous Peoples. For the Indigenous communities of both Mexico and Bangladesh, freedom to achieve development by way of protecting land management practices is crucial to ensuring cultural integrity and survival, most pertinently through issues such as local food security and ecological stewardship.

Against this backdrop, this chapter discusses the Peace Accords to examine their compatibility with the sustainable development of localities in Bangladesh and Mexico particularly their potential to promote the environmental, economic and social sustainability and local food security of these regions. This chapter specifically identifies the relevant provisions of the San Andrés Accords and the Chittagong Hill Tracts Treaty concerning their compatibility with SDGs 2 and 13, which address food security and

[3] Raja Devasish Roy and Simon William M'Viboudoulou, 'Study on Best Practices and Examples in Respect of Resolving Land Disputes and Land Claims, Including Consideration of the National Commission on Indigenous Peoples (Philippines) and the Chittagong Hill Tracts Land Dispute Resolution Commission (Bangladesh) and the Working Group on Indigenous Populations/Communities of the African Commission on Human and Peoples' Rights' (2014) UN Doc E/C.19/2014/4, Permanent Forum on Indigenous Issues, United Nations Economic and Social.

[4] Richard Stahler-Sholk, 'The Zapatista Social Movement: Innovation and Sustainability' (2010) 35(3) Alternatives 269–290.

[5] SM Monjurul Ahsan, 'Conflicting Issues and Challenges Related to Common Property Management and Customary Rights of the Indigenous People of Chittagong Hill Tracts in Bangladesh' (Master's thesis, Oñati International Institute for the Sociology of Law, 2011).

environmental protection. It further examines the effectiveness of the relevant provisions of the Peace Accords in promoting the rights of Indigenous Peoples in relation to these SDGs. The chapter concludes that stronger implementation measures are required from the respective governmental authorities to fully achieve the potential of the Peace Accords.

13.2 GLOBAL LEGAL AND POLICY FRAMEWORKS FOR SUSTAINABLE DEVELOPMENT OF INDIGENOUS PEOPLES

The 2030 Agenda for Sustainable Development addresses five critical areas of policy: people, planet, prosperity, peace, and partnership. For instance, SDG 2 seeks to end hunger, achieve food security, improve nutrition, and promote sustainable agriculture, while SDG 13 seeks to take urgent action to combat climate change and its impacts.[6] Reaffirming the principles of the Rio Declaration on Environment, specifically Article 12, the drafters of the SDGs took into account the twenty-first Conference of the Parties (COP 21) that would be held in Paris a few months later with a profound hope for a universal and ambitious climate agreement. It sought to create a global response to climate change and implement its agenda for all stakeholders, including all countries of the world.[7]

The Paris Agreement that was ultimately adopted at COP 21 emphasized the intrinsic relationship between the eradication of poverty, climate change responses, and sustainable development. Its Parties also acknowledged the rights of local communities and Indigenous People.[8] Many scholars and Indigenous leaders have called for a global response to climate change with the spirit of taking a holistic approach to, striving to eradicate poverty and secure more sustainable development while promoting environmental integrity.[9] To do so, the Parties to the Paris Agreement recognized the significance of holistic, balanced, and integrated non-market approaches which must be available to the Parties for implementing the relevant measures to address these sustainable development goals.[10] Though it is mainly concerned with urgent actions to combat of climate change, the treaty recognizes progress is closely connected to ending hunger and ensuring food security, focusing on

[6] United Nations General Assembly, 'Transforming Our World: The 2030 Agenda for Sustainable Development' (25 September 2015) A/Res/70/1.

[7] ibid preamble, arts 32, 59.

[8] Paris Agreement (adopted 12 December 2015, entered into force 4 November 2016) Decision 1/CP.21, Annex, UN Doc FCCC/CP/2015/10/Add.1, 55 UNTS 61, preamble.

[9] ibid arts 2, 4.1, 6.1–6.2, 6.4.

[10] ibid.

human well-being, including through the eradication of poverty and hunger, that is indispensable to security and environmental integrity. It is against this backdrop that both Bangladesh and Mexico ratified to the Paris Agreement.[11]

Additionally, Mexico alongside 143 other countries adopted the United Nations Declaration on the Rights of Indigenous Peoples (UNDRIP).[12] Bangladesh, however, abstained from voting.[13] The UNDRIP recognizes the urgency of respect for and promotion of the rights inherent to Indigenous Peoples, specifically in relation to their rights to resources and territories. Many jurists and leaders argue that control over the development of lands and resources is vital to Indigenous self-determination. The UNDRIP also imposes additional duties such as preventing, in Article 8, the dispossession and forced removal of Indigenous Peoples and affirming, in Article 20, their rights to develop systems or institutions that enable their own means of development.[14]

It is within the goals and requirements set by these international conventions that we find the potential to achieve the SDGs as specific targets. This specifically relates to achieving food security and combatting climate change, goals that can be fostered through the San Andrés Accords and the Hill Tracts Treaty, which include provisions that directly help promote SDGs 2 on food security, 13 on combatting climate change, and 16 on peace, justice, and strong institutions.

13.3 THE SAN ANDRÉS ACCORDS: IMPLEMENTING TREATY FOR LAND AUTONOMY

Beginning with the San Andrés Accords, this section discusses the historical background that led to the creation of the Accords, analysing the Accords themselves, and the consequences of the Accords for sustainable development and the Indigenous peoples implicated within these regimes.

[11] UNTC, 'Status of the Paris Agreement' <https://treaties.un.org/Pages/ViewDetails.aspx?src=TREATY&mtdsg_no=XXVII-7-d&chapter=27&clang=_en> accessed 11 March 2025.

[12] UN Res 61/295, 'United Nations Declaration on the Rights of Indigenous Peoples' (2007) UN Doc A/RES/61/295.

[13] United Nations, 'Adoption of the United Nations Declaration on the Rights of Indigenous Peoples: 14 Years Later' (Department of Economic and Social Affairs Indigenous Peoples, 13 September 2021) <www.un.org/development/desa/indigenouspeoples/news/2021/09/adoption-of-the-united-nations-declaration-on-the-rights-of-indigenous-peoples-14-years-later/> accessed 11 March 2025.

[14] See also Chapter 2, for more on the UNDRIP.

13.3.1 *Historical Background of the San Andrés Accords*

As jurists and historians explain, the 1996 San Andrés Accords came as a result of a mass displacement of Indigenous Peoples in the Mexican state of Chiapas. A shift in land management and access resulting from Mexico's implementation of the North American Free Trade Agreement (NAFTA), despite a nearly century-long history of prioritizing people-centric land management, led to deep concern and reactions. Initially, as a result of the Mexican Revolution in 1917, a new clause, Article 27 or more commonly known as the 'agrarian reform article', was included in the Mexican Constitution. Article 27 incorporated a declaration for the rights of the people over the land and natural resources of Mexico. In achieving this goal, Article 27 enabled the Government of Mexico to seize these lands from landlords that held expansive property, and prohibit subsequent ownership by landlords and corporations, for land to be redistributed to the people.[15] Article 27 of the Mexican Constitution thus created the *ejidatarios*, or collective landholders, collectively owning plots of land commonly known as *ejidos*. This system supported the poorest and enabled them to sustain themselves through access to land.[16] The *ejidatarios* had every liberty to utilize those lands for housing and farming purposes but not to transfer or to create any liabilities on those lands.[17]

However, this system faced significant challenges when Mexico amended Article 27 of its Constitution to facilitate NAFTA's terms and conditions. Specifically, the amendments to the Constitution did not recognize the *ejidatarios* form of land ownership. This led to a mass displacement of people from the *ejidos*, which largely impacted the Indigenous People in Chiapas, who were highly dependent on the *ejidos* for agriculture and livelihoods. The ensuing unrest caused by this displacement led to negotiations with the Government of Mexico, which ultimately resulted in the signing of the San Andrés Accords on 16 February 1996.[18]

15 *Political Constitution of the United Mexican States*, Official Gazette of the Federation (5 February 1917).

16 Cinthia Valenzula, 'Re-conceptualization of Economic Migrants: An Interpretative Research Study of NAFTA in Mexico' (Doctoral dissertation, Arizona State University, 2019) 21; James J Kelly Jr, 'Article 27 and Mexican Land Reform: The Legacy of Zapata's Dream' (1993) 25 Columbia Human Rights Law Review 541.<https://scholarship.law.nd.edu/cgi/viewcontent.cgi?article=1693&context=law_faculty_scholarship> accessed 11 March 2025.

17 Mitch Creekmore, 'Ejido Land vs. Private Property–What's the Difference?' (2000) 1 Arizona Journal of Real Estate and Business 1–2.

18 Courtney Jung, 'The Politics of Indigenous Identity: Neoliberalism, Cultural Rights, and the Mexican Zapatistas' (2003) 70(2) Social Research: An International Quarterly 433–461 <https://blogs.newschool.edu/janey-program/files/2011/10/Courtney_Jung.pdf> accessed 11 March 2025.

13.3.2 *Analysis of the San Andrés Accords*

The resulting San Andrés Accords consist of five separate documents signed between Mexican Government representatives and the Zapatista Army of National Liberation or *Ejército Zapatista de Liberación Nacional* (EZLN). These documents included (i) the *Joint Proposals that the Federal Government and the EZLN agree to remit to the National Debating and Decision-Making Bodies* (Joint Proposals); (ii) the *Joint Declaration that the Federal Government and the EZLN shall submit to National Debating and Decision-Making Bodies* (Joint Declaration); (iii) the *Commitments to Chiapas made by the State and Federal Governments and the EZLN* (Commitments); (iv) the *Actions and Measures for Chiapas Joint Commitments and Proposals from the State and Federal Governments* (Actions and Measures); and (v) the *Agreement Regarding the Joint Proposals between the Federal Government and the EZLN* (Agreement).[19] Each of the five documents sought to address the concerns of Indigenous People in Chiapas by ensuring their autonomy and affirming their rights. Some examples found within each of these documents are discussed here.

First, the Joint Proposals incorporate issues and principles which guide the future legal framework for Chiapas and direct the amendment and reformation of the Federal Constitution.[20] The Joint Proposals do this largely by accepting sustainability as one of the essential criteria to govern the relationship between the State, the Indigenous communities, and the rest of society.[21] Specifically, the Joint Proposals contain provisions, such as Article II.6(e), which describe 'collective access to the use and enjoyment of natural resources'.[22] Of relevance to SDG 2 on food security, the Joint Proposals additionally require that the State satisfy the basic needs of the Indigenous People by enabling them to take charge of their health, housing, and food.[23] The proposed constitutional amendments also sought to consider the territorial integrity that is integral to Indigenous communities. It suggested establishing preferential systems that benefit Indigenous communities first and

[19] UN Peacemaker, 'Peace Agreement Database of the United Nations Peacemaker: Mexico' <https://perma.cc/3Q59-77CS> accessed 10 March 2025.

[20] Government of Mexico and EZLN, 'Joint Proposals that the Federal Government and the EZLN Agree to Remit to the National Debating and Decision-Making Bodies in Accordance with Paragraph 1.4 of the Rules of Procedure' (adopted 16 February 1996) *Peace Agreement Database of the United Nations Peacemaker: Mexico* <https://perma.cc/K3LE-72EL> accessed 11 March 2025 (Joint Proposals of the San Andrés Accords).

[21] ibid art IV.3.

[22] ibid art II.6(e).

[23] ibid art III.5.

foremost, especially with regard to the use and extraction of natural resources.[24]

Second, the Joint Declaration promotes and recognizes the human rights of the Indigenous People.[25] It expressly stipulates a commitment to guarantee that basic needs of Indigenous Peoples are satisfied. This allows Indigenous Peoples to have access to better nutrition, health, and housing. This thus bolsters the Government of Mexico's ability to achieve sustainable progress for their people by ensuring continuity of the cultures and environments stewarded by the Indigenous People of Chiapas. Further, the commitments may advance SDG 3 on health and well-being, and SDG 11 on sustainable communities.[26]

Third, the Commitments hold the Government of Mexico accountable for ensuring the autonomy and other relevant rights for Chiapas.[27] Parties emphasized the recognition of Indigenous Peoples' '[r]ight to use and enjoy natural resources' that are on their territories. Of relevance to SDG 16 on peaceful and justice it also committed to promote their access to legal protection by incorporating their conflict resolution methods and practices into the relevant legal proceedings.[28] Also proposed were amendments to the statutes of the State of Chiapas, which included establishing conditions that are necessary to provide resources that facilitate the self-driven development of the land owned by the Indigenous People, agrarian nuclei, and communities.[29]

Fourth, the Parties to the Actions and Measures agreed to implement the Commitments by recognizing the local Indigenous culture.[30] These Actions and Measures included the 'promise to set up an agrarian table' which was accompanied by a commitment from all relevant authorities to conduct

24 ibid.

25 Government of Mexico and EZLN, 'Joint Declaration that the Federal Government and the EZLN Shall Submit to National Debating and Decision-Making Bodies, San Andrés Accords (Federal Government of Mexico' (adopted 16 February 1996) *Peace Agreement Database of the United Nations Peacemaker: Mexico* <https://perma.cc/Z43Q-KDLC> accessed 11 March 2025 (Joint Declaration of the San Andrés Accords).

26 ibid paras 3(6), 4(2).

27 Government of Mexico, Government of Chiapas, and EZLN, 'Commitments for Chiapas by the State and Federal Governments and the EZLN under Paragraph 1.3 of the Rules of Procedure,' (adopted 16 February 1996) *Peace Agreement Database of the United Nations Peacemaker: Mexico* <https://perma.cc/5MHC-LMKE> accessed 11 March 2025 (Commitments of the San Andrés Accords).

28 ibid art I.

29 ibid art II.

30 Government of Mexico, Government of Chiapas, and EZLN, 'Actions and Measures for Chiapas Joint Commitments and Proposals from the State and Federal Governments, and the EZLN' (adopted 16 February 1996) *Peace Agreement Database of the United Nations Peacemaker: Mexico* <https://perma.cc/8N4F-KUG4> accessed 11 March 2025 (Actions and Measures of the San Andrés Accords).

agrarian censuses to ascertain the status of land ownership within the state, requiring participation of the representatives from all the stakeholders.[31] Additionally, and of relevance to SDG 13, the Actions and Measures included the requirement that there be a '[r]espect for the environment'.[32] This requirement of respect is highlighted as an inescapable criteria and is required when drafting relevant policies and development programmes. Based on this requirement, any implementation of plans created by authorities, especially regarding the use or extraction of natural resources, must therefore aim to avoid any adverse impacts on Indigenous cultural and natural heritage. The consequences of any adverse effects or damages due to the exploitation of Indigenous natural resources by the State must also, of relevance to the UNDRIP Article 28 on redress for confiscated Indigenous lands, result in adequate compensation.[33]

Finally, the Agreement encompasses the first three documents, namely, the Joint Proposals, the Joint Declarations, and the Commitments, and requires the implementation of national agrarian reform to a greater extent by compensating Indigenous People for their displacement and protecting their rights.[34] This document in particular emphasizes the urgency of enacting a constitutional amendment by reflecting on the solutions proposed for the critical problems faced by agrarian stakeholders. Specifically, it summarizes the two basic demands made by Emiliano Zapata which address national agrarian issues – two demands which require freedom and land ownership.[35] It additionally considers it insufficient to simply pay compensation for damages which have already occurred; it instead pushes for developing policy that addresses sustainability at its core. This would thus enable the preservation of territories, lands, and natural resources, which is referred to as 'the social costs of development projects' in the documents.[36]

[31] ibid.

[32] ibid.

[33] ibid.

[34] Government of Mexico and EZLN, 'Agreement Regarding the Documents: "Joint Declaration that the Federal Government and the EZLN shall submit to National Debating and Decision-Making Bodies"; "Joint Proposals that the Federal Government and the EZLN agree to submit to National Debating and Decision-Making Bodies, in respect of Point 1.4 of the Rules of Procedure"; and "Commitment for Chiapas made by the State and Federal Governments and the EZLN, in respect of Point 1.3 of the Rules of Procedure"' (16 February 1996) *Peace Agreement Database of the United Nations Peacemaker: Mexico* (Joint Declaration regarding the Documents of the San Andrés Accords) <https://perma.cc/CP5R-95HH> accessed 11 March 2025.

[35] ibid art B.1.

[36] ibid art B.2.

13.3.3 *Consequences of the San Andrés Accords*

As jurists and scholars note, the San Andrés Accords included multiple provisions that sought to help secure a more sustainable future for the state of Chiapas, which by extension may promote SDG, 1 to end poverty, 2 on food security, 14 and 15 to protect life below water and life on land, and 16 on building inclusive and peaceful societies. Specifically, the drafters of the San Andrés Accords proposed legal and constitutional framework reform that can facilitate a new relationship between the Mexican State and Indigenous Peoples. Underlying these proposals, also, is the doctrine of equality in any reforms, which subsequently both enables and requires Mexico's federal government including the Congress of the Union and state legislatures to ensure Indigenous People are entitled to autonomy and self-determination, consistent with Articles 3–4 of the UNDRIP on Indigenous autonomy and self-determination.[37] The Mexican State, in abiding by the requirements set by the San Andrés Accords over the subsequent years, enacted specific constitutional amendments as proposed by the State of Chiapas, created the Commission for Municipal Reform and Redistribution in Chiapas to oversee the implementation of the changes, and settled the disputes between the federal government and the EZLN through consensus in subsequent meetings.[38]

Of the changes resulting from the San Andrés Accords, one holds significant weight for progressing toward sustainable development in Mexico. In 2001, a major constitutional amendment revised Article 2 of the Constitution to establish Indigenous environmental rights in Mexico's domestic law.[39] This provision protects and recognizes Indigenous Peoples' right to autonomy as a product of self-determination and enables them to maintain and improve the lands and environment that they own.[40] Additionally, Indigenous communities have 'preferential use of the natural resources' in their respective territories and can abide by customary forms of property

37 Joint Proposals of the San Andrés Accords (n 20); Joint Declaration of the San Andrés Accords (n 25).

38 Commitments of the San Andrés Accords (n 27); Actions and Measures of the San Andrés Accords (n 30); and Joint Declaration regarding the Documents of the San Andrés Accords (n 34).

39 César Nava Escudero, 'Indigenous Environmental Rights in Mexico: Was the 2001 Constitutional Reform Facilitated by International Law?' (2011) 4(2) Mexican Law Review <www.scielo.org.mx/scielo.php?script=sci_arttext&pid=S1870-05782012000100002> accessed 11 March 2025.

40 'Mexico's Constitution of 1917 with Amendments through 2015' arts 2.A, 2.A.V <www.constituteproject.org/constitution/Mexico_2015.pdf?lang=en> accessed 11 March 2025.

ownership in establishing their rights for possession over said lands.[41] The amendment to Article 2 also required that relevant authorities be obliged to facilitate food programmes to improve nutrition while simultaneously supporting community self-sufficiency to address food security problems through its core causes, of relevance to SDG 2.[42]

Implementing the measures agreed to through the San Andrés Accords has thus led to changes for Chiapas that enable food security while fostering environmental stewardship in Indigenous communities. In this sense, the San Andrés Accords have enabled Mexico to have established frameworks that help further SDGs 2, on food security, 13 on combatting climate change, and 16, in peace and justice. They also are consistent with the UNDRIP's Articles 3–4 on Indigenous autonomy and self-determination, 8 on preventing and 28 on redressing land appropriation, and 26–27 on land rights.

13.4 THE CHITTAGONG HILL TRACTS TREATY OF BANGLADESH: RESOLUTIONS FOR RESOURCE DEVELOPMENT

As with the San Andrés Accords of Mexico, this section discusses the historical background that led to the creation of the Chittagong Hill Tracts Treaty of Bangladesh, analyses the Hill Tracts Treaty itself, and considers the consequences of the Hill Tracts Treaty as it relates to how Indigenous stewardship can help foster sustainable development more broadly.

13.4.1 *Historical Background of the Chittagong Hill Tracts Treaty*

The Hill Tracts Treaty is another example of an accord signed between a country's national authorities and Indigenous Peoples. To understand the history of how this treaty became a necessary conflict resolution and sustainable development measure, a geopolitical understanding of the Chittagong Hill Tracts area is first required.

The Chittagong Hill Tracts is a hilly area situated in the southeast part of Bangladesh and contains three districts – Khagrachari, Rangamati, and Bandarban. This area is the home to the majority of the Bangladeshi Indigenous Peoples, which include Tribal groups of Chakma Raj, Bohmong Raj, and Mong Raj. The region has had a long history of communal land cultivation that is likewise communally, rather than privately, owned. British colonial powers historically maintained a non-interference policy for this region,

[41] ibid arts 2.A, 2.A.VI.

[42] ibid arts 2.B.III, 2.B.VII.

however, this policy gradually changed in the mid-1800s.[43] During this transition, Indigenous communities become concerned that extraction projects began exploiting the water and land, degrading the natural resources from the Chittagong Hill Tracts region. One such project was the construction of a hydroelectric power plant in 1962 which used the water from the Karnaphuli River. This dam created a significant reservoir, the Kaptai Lake, which engulfed large swathes of land and displaced many Indigenous Peoples from the area. In addition, their territory faced increased militarization under the guise of national security starting in the 1970s, and the forest began to be degraded through logging projects in the 1980s created by the Forest Department of the Government of Bangladesh for purely commercial gain. Developments like these caused the dispossession of many Indigenous Peoples from their land, ruining communities' plantations and farms in the process.

Despite having their cultural and economic lifestyles altered drastically, as scholars note, Indigenous Peoples did not have a separate identity under the Constitution of the People's Republic of Bangladesh. They could not advocate nor protect their unique rights within the Chittagong Hill Tracts region. Thus, the relationship between the State and the Indigenous communities deteriorated in 1972, and after more than two decades of insurgency and armed conflict, the two sides signed the Hill Tracts Treaty in 1997.[44]

13.4.2 *Analysis of the Chittagong Hill Tracts Treaty*

The overall objectives of the Hill Tracts Treaty were 'to elevate political, social, cultural, educational and financial rights and to expedite the socio-economic development process of all citizens in the Chittagong Hill Tracts'.[45] In the accords, Parties not only considered the Chittagong Hill Tracts region to be that of a Tribal population; Parties to the Treaty also recognized the need to protect

43 Mohammad Shahabuddin, 'The Myth of Colonial "Protection" of Indigenous Peoples: The Case of the Chittagong Hill Tracts under British Rule' (2018) 25(2) International Journal on Minority and Group Rights 210–235 <www.jstor.org/stable/26557892> accessed 11 March 2025.

44 M Emran Ali and Toshiyuki Tsuchia, 'Changes in Land Use Practices of Indigenous People in the Chittagong Hill Tracts of Bangladesh: An Analysis of Political-Economy Perspective' (2003) 9(1) Journal of Forest Planning 47–58 <www.jstage.jst.go.jp/article/jfp/9/1/9_KJ00007911262/_pdf> accessed 11 March 2025.

45 Chittagong Hill Tracts Treaty, 1997 (Government of the People's Republic of Bangladesh – Parbatya Chattagram Jana Sanghati Samity or PCJSS) (adopted 2 December 1997) preamble <www.satp.org/satporgtp/countries/bangladesh/document/actandordinances/cht1990.htm> accessed 11 March 2025.

its character as such.[46] The local Hill District Council gained the responsibility for land management, development, and preservation of the environment and jhum cultivation.[47] The Hill District Council would approve any transfer of land within the Chittagong Hill Tracts, with the exclusion of only a few government projects. The Treaty also gave priority to the original landowners in the Kaptai Lake region as a form of compensation for prior displacement during hydroelectric plant development.[48] In addition to the Hill District Council, the Hill Tracts Treaty also required the formation of the Chittagong Hill Tracts Regional Council, responsible for overseeing laws as well as social justice. It is also tasked with coordinating and supervising the development activities conducted under the Hill District Councils. The Hill Tracts Treaty additionally provided land surveys and, subject to the availability of land, two acres of land would be given to each landless family or any family owning less than two acres. Any remaining land disputes would be settled through a land commission.[49] A task force was also created to rehabilitate Tribal evacuees who were implicated in the government-led development projects.[50]

The Hill Tracts Treaty provided extensive guidance on the implementation of the provisions within its text. For instance, an Implementation Committee was formed to oversee the implementation of the Hill Tracts Treaty, which included subsequent amendments to various pieces of implicated legislation.[51] The Hill Tracts Treaty and its Advisory Council also ensured that the institutional frameworks governed by the Hill Tracts Treaty had representation from both Government and Tribal communities throughout the negotiation and implementation process, and included representatives from all three Chittagong Hill Tracts districts and Tribal groups. The Advisory Council was composed of representatives from non-Tribal residents of the three Hill Districts.[52] Accordingly, by combining the necessary restorative provisions, the

46 ibid art A.1.

47 Jhum cultivation is a traditional shifting cultivation farming technique practiced by Indigenous communities in the Chittagong Hill Tracts and in certain parts of Northeast India. It involves clearing land of trees and vegetation then using burning every set number of years to stimulate growth. 'Robust Yield of Jhum in the Hill Tracts' *Bangladesh Pratidin* (10 August 2014).

48 Chittagong Hill Tracts Treaty, 1997 (n 45) arts B.2, B.34, B.26(1), and B.26(4).

49 ibid arts C.2–C.4, C.9(e).

50 ibid art D.1.

51 The implicated legislation, which required modifications, additions, amendments, and repealing provision, included the Hill District Local Government Council Acts, 1989, the Rangamati Hill District Local Government Council Act, 1989, the Khagrachari Hill District Local Government Council Act, 1989 and the Bandarban Hill District, Local Government Council Act, 1989. The modifications were required pursuant to ibid art B.

52 The implicated legislation, which required modifications, additions, amendments, and repealing provision, included the Hill District Local Government Council Acts, 1989, the

Chittagong Hill Tracts Treaty sought to resolve the unrest in a more democratic manner by including all the Chittagong Hill Tracts stakeholders in the regional decision-making processes.

13.4.3 *Consequences of the Chittagong Hill Tracts Treaty*

In many respects, scholars suggest, the Hill Tracts Treaty appears to pay more regard to institutional establishments than legal reforms. The Treaty includes implementation provisions that help continue to promote SDG 2 on food security, and also SDGs 14 and 15 on protecting life below water and on land throughout its lifespan, alongside SDG 16 on peaceful and justice, while aligning also with the UNDRIP Articles 8 against land dispossession, 26–27 on Indigenous rights to land and institutional redress mechanisms, 30 against militarization, and 32 on land and resource development. Namely, the implementation of the Hill Tracts Treaty enabled three different pieces of legislation to come into force.

First, the Chittagong Hill Tracts Local Council Act 1998 established the Chittagong Hill Tracts Local Council for monitoring and coordinating the development activities conducted under the supervision of all the relevant bodies including the Hill District Council.[53] Scholar argue this enabled increased accountability for the initiatives developed under the Hill District Council. Second, the Chittagong Hill Tracts Land-dispute Resolution Commission Act 2001 established a commission for quickly addressing land-related disputes in the Chittagong Hill Tracts.[54] This may enable claimants to access a forum appropriate for settling these land disputes in a timely and effective manner, aligning with the UNDRIP's Article 27. Finally, the Chittagong Hill Tracts Development Board Act 2014 empowered the Chittagong Hill Tracts Development Board to prepare development projects and schemes for the region and allow for land acquisition only as necessary.[55] This can be contrasted with the previous version of this same act from 1976, which enabled the Chittagong Hill Tracts Development Board to force land

Rangamati Hill District Local Government Counci1 Act, 1989, the Khagrachari Hill District Local Government Council Act, 1989 and the Bandarban Hill District, Local Government Council Act, 1989. The modifications were required pursuant to art B in ibid art D.19.

[53] The Chittagong Hill Tracts Local Council Act, 1998 (Act No 12 of 1998) <http://bdlaws.minlaw.gov.bd/act-822.html> accessed 11 March 2025.

[54] The Chittagong Hill Tracts Land-dispute Resolution Commission Act, 2001 (Act No 53 of 2001) <http://bdlaws.minlaw.gov.bd/act-877.html> accessed 11 March 2025.

[55] The Chittagong Hill Tracts Development Board Act, 2014 (Act No. 8 of 2014) ss 9, 15 <http://bdlaws.minlaw.gov.bd/act-1150.html> accessed 11 March 2025.

acquisition and granted indemnity for anyone involved with the Board 'for anything done or intended to be done in good faith'.[56] The new 2014 enactment thus avoided the unquestionable nature of the steps taken by the Board and curtailed this arbitrary power, furthering the UNDRIP Articles 8 against dispossession and 26 affirming Indigenous land rights.

Together, these pieces of legislation each help to strengthen local autonomy and enhance general oversight for the development and land acquisition projects in the Chittagong Hill Tracts region. Though these enactments do not directly set out environmental or food security measures for Indigenous Peoples of this region, the established commissions and councils nonetheless help resolve critical land disputes, in harmony with the UNDRIP's Articles 26–27 and SDG 16 on promoting peaceful societies, and facilitate initiatives that help foster the well-being of the region and communities overall. Indirectly, the Hill Tracts Treaty enabled a more equitable future for the people in this region and enabled a healthier environment and strengthened food security as a result.

13.5 COMPARING AND IMPLEMENTING TREATIES BETWEEN INDIGENOUS PEOPLE AND GOVERNMENTS

Both the San Andrés Accords of Mexico and the Hill Tracts Treaty of Bangladesh take distinct legal approaches to resolving conflicts for the respective region's peoples. Nonetheless, these approaches converge and produce similar outcomes to advancing sustainable development, specifically in that they both prioritize land management and implementation to advance the well-being of their respective regions. In particular, they appear to align with the UNDRIP Articles 8 on the prevention of land dispossession, Article 10 against the forcible removal from lands or territories, Article 26 on the right to lands and resources traditionally owned, used, or occupied, and Article 27 on the adjudication of land rights.

In relation to land management, both Peace Accords concern the settlement of disputes arising out of land ownership and displacement, in furtherance of the UNDRIP Article 27. They both seek to establish mechanisms to return land ownership to the impacted or displaced Indigenous People. Many emphasize that such a focus on land is vital to resolving conflict long term because land is fundamentally inseparable from food security and environmental conservation. Land in such a sense provides the power for the

[56] The Chittagong Hill Tracts Development Board Ordinance, 1976 (Ordinance No LXXVII of 1976) s 16 <http://bdlaws.minlaw.gov.bd/act-533.html> accessed 11 March 2025.

people to govern the use of the land, and in order for Indigenous Peoples to cultivate food staples that provide the necessary nutrients for their communities' survival. Through such a lens, the San Andrés Accords appear to directly address the management, preservation, and right to use natural resources, in alignment with the UNDRIP Articles 23 on Indigenous development priorities and Article 26, particularly paragraphs 26(1)–(2) on development of Indigenous lands and resources, while highlighting the need to prioritize basic necessities like food, health, and nutrition.[57] This San Andrés Accords seek to prioritize autonomy for the Indigenous People of Chiapas and focus on ensuring protection of the human and environmental rights of Indigenous communities. The Hill Tracts Treaty provides for the allotment of land, and environmental protection, which specifically highlights the rights to land for jhum cultivation and rubber plantations which is an additional form of economic security in addition to general food security and environmental well-being.[58] These provisions likewise align with the UNDRIP paragraphs 26(1)–(2), and Article 32 on the development and use of lands and resources. The Hill Tracts Treaty also prioritized institutional representation to enable Indigenous Peoples to have a say in land governance, which resembles, partially, the UNDRIP Article 23's provision on Indigenous rights to exercise economic priorities, though such institutional representation is not quite the same as an Indigenous institution-administered programme, as contemplated by Article 23.

Implementation additionally is central to both Peace Accords. In general, peace agreements tend to help form new relationships between conflicting Parties, but these agreements often lack sufficient implementation measures to monitor and fulfil the treaty obligations at all levels of government.[59] Though both the San Andrés Accords and the Hill Tracts Treaty created implementation steps following their ratification, specifically in relation to proposals for and enactment of constitutional amendments in Mexico and establishing councils and commissions in Bangladesh, both countries' governments nonetheless did not fulfil the full breadth of the terms and conditions stipulated in the respective treaties.[60] By extension, the shortfalls

57 UN Peacemaker (n 19) arts II.6(e) and III.5.

58 Chittagong Hill Tracts Treaty, 1997 (n 45) art B.34.

59 Jérémie Gilbert, 'Indigenous Peoples and Peace Agreements: Transforming Relationships or Empty Rhetoric?' (Rethinking Transitions: Equality and Social Justice in Societies Emerging from Conflict, 2011) <www.researchgate.net/publication/347647251_Indigenous_Peoples_and_Peace_Agreements_Transforming_Relationships_or_Empty_Rhetoric> accessed 11 March 2025.

60 María Inclán, *The Zapatista Movement and Mexico's Democratic Transition: Mobilization, Success, and Survival* (Oxford University Press 2018); Pranab Kumar Panday and Ishtiaq Jamil,

in implementation also mean that the potential for sustainable development found in the Peace Accords are not fully realized until implementation is realized.

In the case of Mexico's agreement, many note that the constitutional amendments stipulated in the San Andrés Accords were not implemented in full, with the 2001 constitutional reform establishing a series of provisions that did not equip the Indigenous Peoples and communities with the capacity to exercise their environmental rights in full. Concerns have also been raised that the accords failed to recognize the Indigenous communities as legal entities that would enable them to have the legal capacity to exercise their ownership rights. Many of the commitments set forth by the San Andrés Accords nonetheless remained within the purview of this constitutional amendment and thus the government authority left their duties and responsibilities under the agreement unfulfilled.[61]

In Bangladesh, jurists and Indigenous leaders argue that the Hill Tracts Treaty also remained largely unimplemented by the government due to the government's non-compliance with the duties and responsibilities set forth by the agreement. Contrary to the UNDRIP Article 30, militarization of the Chittagong Hill Tracts continued, which resulted in deep mistrust and confusion for the Indigenous Peoples towards the government authorities. Armed conflicts between the Indigenous communities and non-Indigenous settlers of the Chittagong Hill Tracts have not yet come to an end. Violence between the government security forces and the insurgent communities of the Chittagong Hill Tracts continues as well.[62] Contrary to the UNDRIP's Article 26, many also raise concerns that land acquisition is also pervasive, while no land rights are given to the Indigenous communities to enable the environmental conservation and food security rights that could have been enabled by the Hill Tracts Treaty.[63]

Moving forward, scholars and others argue that it is necessary to implement and respect the treaties signed between the Indigenous Peoples and governments for the full benefits of the Peace Accords to be achieved. To accomplish this, they note, governments in Mexico must establish institutional frameworks to resolve the disputes over Indigenous rights and implement the commitments as recognized by the San Andrés Accords. As recognized in UNDRIP, Indigenous communities have the right to participate in leadership

'Conflict in the Chittagong Hill Tracts of Bangladesh: An Unimplemented Accord and Continued Violence' (2009) 49(6) Asian Survey 1052–1070.

61 Escudero (n 39).

62 Panday and Jamil (n 60).

63 The Chittagong Hill Tracts Development Board Act, 2014 (n 55).

and decision-making for their communities.[64] Many also argue that governments in Bangladesh need to likewise implement and respect the institutional requirements stipulated in the Hill Tracts Treaty. They should in this view also provide legal recognition of the inherent rights of Indigenous communities including their land rights, rights for sustainable development, and right to achieve food security. This can be accomplished with policy that aligns with local practices.[65] Both countries additionally need to implement and respect principles laid out in the UNDRIP, particularly the above-described Articles 8, 23, 26–27, 30, and 32. They should also entrench the rights of Indigenous People in their respective constitutions.[66] Only in these ways can the full potential of these treaties for sustainable development be realized.

13.6 CONCLUSION

Land rights are crucial for ensuring environmental sustainability and food security for communities. The conflicts arising out of Mexico and Bangladesh are no exceptions to this, as struggles to ensure land rights for Indigenous People created the very accords that recognize and protect these rights, especially when Indigenous collective ownership traditions stand in sharp contrast to the private ownership regimes in most global legal systems. The constitutional reforms arising from the San Andrés Accords and the institutional restructuring necessitated by the Hill Tracts Treaty show that substantive support is crucial for ensuring the equitable protection of traditional land ownership. Thus, fully implementing these treaties can help foster sustainable development, especially in relation to SDGs 2 and 13 to end hunger and fight the impacts of climate change. Only in this way can development truly leave no one behind and build up a better future for the generations yet to come.

[64] Stahler-Sholk (n 4).
[65] Emran Ali and Tsuchia (n 44).
[66] Escudero (n 39).

PART V

Conclusions and Lessons for Treaty Reform

14

UNDRIP Principles and Sustainability Innovations in Indigenous Trade Rules

14.1 INTRODUCTION

The Indigenous Peoples Economic and Trade Cooperation Arrangement (IPETCA)[1] is the first modern comprehensive international Indigenous trade arrangement in history,[2] hailed by many as revolutionary for its content and philosophy and for the international Indigenous inclusiveness in its negotiations and its eventual implementation and governance. This arrangement is cooperative, voluntary, and flexible. It serves as a significant step in protecting

[1] Co-author Wayne Garnons-Williams, the founding President of the International Inter-tribal Trade and Investment Organization (IITIO), was Canada's Indigenous lead for negotiating IPETCA and presents up-to-date, as of publication of this article, information regarding this arrangement through the following section. See also 'Indigenous Peoples Economic and Trade Cooperation Agreement', Final Version (New Zealand, Canada, Australia, and Taiwan, February 2022) (IPETCA) <https://mfatgovtnz2020.cwp.govt.nz/assets/Trade-General/Trade-policy/Indigenous-Peoples-Economic-and-Trade-Cooperation-Arrangement-IPETCA-FINAL-VERSION.pdf> accessed 17 March 2025.

[2] The origins of Canada's Indigenous participation in modern international trade through IPETCA began with the North American Free Trade Agreement (NAFTA) renegotiations of 2016, for which the IITIO made a formal submission to Global Affairs Canada on the topic of the re-opened NAFTA negotiations. Of the 2,500 submissions to the Government of Canada on NAFTA issues for re-negotiation, IITIO's was the only submission to be devoted to the specific topic of Indigenous trade. The IITIO submission of July 2017 was a catalyst that started the collaborative development of Canada Indigenous trade policy. Although it was not fully implemented in the Canada United States Mexico Agreement (CUSMA, also referred to as USMCA) as a result of the policies of the Trump administration, the IITIO submission's concepts for Indigenous trade were successfully applied in the subsequent trade agreements of Mercosur, the Inclusive Trade Action Group, and, which became, IPETCA. See International Inter-tribal Trade and Investment Organization, 'NAFTA Submission to Global Affairs Canada from IITIO' (16 July 2017).

Indigenous rights and the environment.[3] It brings to the forefront the nexus of Indigenous philosophy, economics, trade, and environmental stewardship and addresses four key hopes: first, for Indigenous partnership and inclusiveness in the development and administration of the arrangement; second, for respect for Indigenous worldviews, cultures, and ways-of-life; third, for environmental concerns becoming integrated Indigenous business; and fourth, for the exercise of tangible international Indigenous opportunities for sustainable development through trade.

As a text that is primarily inspired and informed by the United Nations Declaration on the Rights of Indigenous Peoples (UNDRIP) and that seeks to advance many of the United Nations Sustainable Development Goals (SDGs), in the IPETCA participants to the arrangement acknowledge the importance of significant international environmental agreements, bringing sustainability and Indigenous rights to the core tenets of international Indigenous trade.[4] The four participants that became directly involved in IPETCA' specifically New Zealand, Canada, Australia, and Taiwan,[5] were also encouraged to collaborate with Indigenous Peoples during the negotiations. As such, each of the four principal participants confirmed internal consultation mechanisms that opened the doors for a new level of confidential domestic interaction among and with their designated Indigenous representatives.

This chapter discusses the origins, legal framework, and future of the IPETCA as an innovation in collaboration for inter-Tribal and international Indigenous trade. To better understand why the IPETCA is viewed by some jurists and experts as innovative, impactful, and inspirational, this chapter will first examine the origins of how IPETCA came into existence, from the cultural connections that grew the momentum for negotiations to the organizations and institutions that facilitated its negotiation. The chapter then examines the impact of IPETCA in terms of various international instruments, including the SDGs, UNDRIP, and other international and Indigenous trade treaties. Finally, implementation of the IPETCA is reviewed including the working mechanisms involved for IPETCA to flourish and the viability for others, specifically the United States, to join the arrangement.

3 See 'Overview: The Indigenous Peoples Economic and Trade Cooperation Arrangement' (Global Affairs Canada, 8 November 2023) <www.international.gc.ca/trade-commerce/indigenous_peoples-peuples_autochtones/ipetca_overview-aceepa_apercu.aspx?lang=eng> accessed 15 March 2025.

4 These instruments include but are not limited to the UN SDGs, UN Financing for Development Addis Ababa Action Agenda, the UN Framework Convention on Climate Change and the UN Convention on Biological Diversity. See IPETCA (n 1) para 3(e).

5 Observer States to IPETCA include the United States, Peru, and Chile.

14.2 ORIGINS OF IPETCA

The origins of the IPETCA stem from the Government of New Zealand's initiative during its 2021 leadership within the Asia-Pacific Economic Cooperation (APEC). Taiwan joined the discussions subsequently and became a founding member upon the arrangement's conclusion in December 2021.

Also featuring prominently in IPETCA's origin is the story of the Māori People and their quest to rediscover their ancestral home.[6] According to the elders, scholars, and leaders, the Māori's ancestors, highly skilled Polynesian ocean explorers and traders, located hospitable, uninhabited islands in the South Pacific in a constant and natural migration of successive generations, ultimately settling in Aotearoa, modern-day New Zealand, around the fourteenth century A.D.[7] Polynesian seafaring ancestors' cultural and economic influence is found across the vast expanse of South Pacific islands they discovered. Though Māori origin stories were passed down from generation to generation, it was noted that the exact location of their ancestral homeland, Hawaiki, was eventually lost. A collective cultural yearning remained to understand who they were and where they came from before the ancestors set foot on the 'long white cloud' they now named Aotearoa, and to reconnect with their ancestral family line. Since the 1970s, linguistics experts have drawn a connection between the language roots of the Indigenous Māori and those of other Polynesians, which traced their ancestry and migration back north into Asia. This connection was underlined in 2005 when genetic testing and analysis of Taiwan's nine Indigenous Tribes, which currently makes up approximately 2 per cent of the island's population, presented a high match ratio with the DNA of the Polynesian Māori of Aotearoa.[8] The

[6] The Asia-Pacific Economic Cooperation (APEC) is a regional economic forum established in 1989 to leverage the growing inter-dependence of the Asia-Pacific. APEC's twenty-one members aim to create greater prosperity for the region's people by promoting balanced, inclusive, sustainable, innovative, and secure growth and accelerating regional economic integration.

[7] Richard Walter and others, 'Mass Migration and the Polynesian Settlement of New Zealand' (2017) 30 Journal of World Prehistory 351.

[8] Adam Dudding, 'New Zealand's Long-Lost Taiwanese Cuzzies' (Stuff News, March 2015) <www.stuff.co.nz/travel/destinations/asia/67390585/new-zealands-long-lost-taiwanese-cuzzies> accessed 15 March 2025; Cultural Survival, 'Genetic Link Brings Indigenous Taiwanese and Maori Together' <www.culturalsurvival.org/news/genetic-link-brings-indigenous-taiwanese-and-maori-together> accessed 15 March 2025; Trejaut and others, 'Mitochondrial DNA Provides a Link between Polynesians and Indigenous Taiwanese' (2005) 3(8) PLoS Biology e281; Jean A Trejaut and others, 'Traces of Archaic Mitochondrial Lineages Persist in Austronesian-Speaking Formosan Populations' (2005) 3(10) PLoS Biology e376. <https://doi.org/10.1371/journal.pbio.0030281> accessed 15 March 2025.

recognition that the Māori are culturally and ancestrally linked to Indigenous Peoples in Taiwan led to closer political, cultural, and economic activity between these two groups.[9]

Through the establishment of the 'Indigenous Taiwan Aotearoa New Zealand Business Council for the benefit of Indigenous Peoples of Taiwan and Māori of New Zealand, a new joint Indigenous business council, a platform was developed to foster long-term economic and trade relations between Indigenous Taiwanese and Māori.[10] It operates trade connections and implementing a hosting service for enquiries in relation to the sale or purchase of goods and services from either Taiwan or New Zealand provided that the enquiries include an Indigenous Taiwanese or Māori component, facilitating cooperation to enable the Māori to access Taiwan markets and vice versa while forming business relationships, and sharing trade and investment-enabling information that includes an Indigenous component.[11] This joint Indigenous business council paved the way for both governments to cooperate in developing a meaningful international framework for Indigenous trade, creating an opportunity for Aoteoroa-New Zealand to include Taiwan in the APEC and the IPETCA trade discussions purposely.

Additionally, in 2019, the New Zealand Ministry of Foreign Affairs and Trade (MFAT) signed a consultation and engagement Memorandum of Understanding (MOU) with Te Taumata. This organization serves as a key Māori partner for dialogue with the New Zealand government on trade-related issues. It represents the interests of Māori businesses and exporters during Indigenous trade discussions with both MFAT and countries from around the world. It is intended to be independent and accountable to Māori for meaningful results to protect and improve Māori trade interests.[12] Te Taumata also assists the Ministry in better understanding and connecting with Māori and Iwi trade-related interest groups.

Te Taumata crucially sought to address the growing concerns among many Māori about increasing volatility and uncertainty for agricultural traders in the global marketplace. This is especially important since Aoteoroa-New Zealand is a relatively small player in the global economy and the Māori portion of the

9 Central News Agency, 'New Zealand Office showcases indigenous connections with Taiwan' (Taiwan News, 17 July 2020) <www.taiwannews.com.tw/en/news/3968349> accessed 15 March 2025.

10 Taiwan Aotearoa New Zealand Business Council, 'About' <https://itanzbc.com> (ITANZ) accessed 15 March 2025.

11 ibid arts 1–4.

12 Te Taumata <www.tetaumata.com/> accessed 17 March 2025.

New Zealand trade economy is an even smaller subset, centred mainly around forestry, ocean fisheries, and lamb, beef, sheep, dairy, and kiwi production.[13] There are also concerns about the fast-moving pace of change and the number of negotiations made by businesses and governments that can impact the interest of the Māori.[14] In this respect, Te Taumata activities seek to address these concerns by commissioning research to improve the understanding of complex Free Trade Agreement (FTA) issues where there is a strong Māori interest, providing a Māori lens and analysis on key FTA developments through social media, and facilitating opportunities for engagement with regional and local Māori issues impacting trade.[15] These Māori-specific market reports, trade reports, and statistical analyses also apply cultural sensitivity and traditional environmental values to economic issues in such a way as to positively impact not just the Māori economy but all of New Zealand.[16] These reports and contributions have been instrumental in shaping trade policy and negotiations to be conscious of Māori concerns and interests. In the case of the IPETCA, Te Taumata's contributions and leadership, in conjunction with the forum created through the joint business council, enabled New Zealand's 2021 leadership of APEC, with participation from Taiwan, to recognize and foster the need to develop an inclusive international Indigenous trade framework.[17]

In addition to New Zealand and Taiwan's participation in the IPETCA, Canada's Indigenous representatives likewise contributed to the negotiations and agreements. As discussed in Chapter 9, Canadian Indigenous representatives, through the International Inter-tribal Trade and Investment Organization (IITIO), made a formal submission to Global Affairs Canada regarding the re-opened North American Free Trade Agreement (NAFTA) negotiations.[18] Their submission, devoted to Indigenous trade, created a catalyst that started the collaborative development of Canada's Indigenous

[13] New Zealand Foreign Affairs and Trade, 'The Māori Economy – A Fact Sheet' (2018) <www.mfat.govt.nz/assets/Trade-agreements/UK-NZ-FTA/The-Maori-Economy_2.pdf> accessed 17 March 2025.

[14] Te Taumata (n 12).

[15] ibid.

[16] ibid. See also Chapter 12 on Māori philosophies and worldviews that are used to inform both environmental management as well as trade and treaty negotiations.

[17] Adventure Magazine, 'Maori and Taiwan – Cousins with an Ancient History' (14 September 2022) <https://adventuremagazine.co.nz/maori-and-taiwan-cousins-with-an-ancient-history/#:~:text=One%20standout%20clue%20to%20the,skin%20colour%20and%20physical%20features> accessed 17 March 2025; Cultural Survival (n 8).

[18] 'NAFTA Submission to Global Affairs Canada from IITIO' (July 2017) <http://iitio.org/nafta/>.

trade policy. Though the submission was not fully implemented in the updated FTA, known as the Canada-United States-Mexico Agreement (CUSMA),[19] IITIO's concepts were later integrated into the Inclusive Trade Action Group,[20] which formed modest international Indigenous trade provisions that helped build momentum and groundwork for New Zealand to take a larger step in the development of an exclusive Indigenous international trade instrument.[21]

Four of the members of APEC ultimately became directly involved in the development and negotiations of the IPETCA. Throughout 2021, New Zealand chaired the discussions, with Canada, Australia, and Taiwan participating and Mexico, Peru, Chile, and Papua New Guinea serving as observers. Each of the four participants, jurists note, additionally worked collaboratively with their own domestic Indigenous Peoples during the negotiations by confirming internal consultation mechanisms that allowed confidential domestic interactions with and among their designated Indigenous representatives.

14.2.1 *The IPETCA's Trade Negotiations*

Typically FTA negotiations involve some form of consultation with industry representatives about their economic concerns and ideal outcomes for the trade agreement, which can include greater market access, reduced tariffs into

[19] Though the IITIO submission was not implemented in full, Indigenous trade and economic prosperity was still incorporated into the final CUSMA agreement. For more information, see Agreement between the United States of America, the United Mexican States, and Canada (United States-Mexico-Canada Agreement) (signed 30 November 2018, entered into force 1 July 2020), art 32.1. See also Chapter 9.

[20] A joint declaration signed by New Zealand, Canada, and Chile on developing the Inclusive Trade Action Group made various promising vision statements regarding Indigenous trade agreements. This included the statement that '[they] commit to working together to deliver on our expectations that trade can contribute to the achievement of sustainable development and solutions for global issues of concern including with regard to gender equality, Indigenous Peoples, domestic regional economic development, Small and Medium Enterprises (SMEs), labour rights, environment and climate change.' New Zealand Foreign Affairs & Trade, 'Inclusive Trade Action Group' <www.mfat.govt.nz/en/trade/nz-trade-policy/inclusive-trade-action-group/> accessed 15 March 2025.

[21] The NAFTA negotiations and newly developed inclusive trade policies also contributed to developing the Global Affairs Indigenous Working Group on International Trade (IWG). This group is an open body where representatives from various federal government departments with a vested interest in international Indigenous trade can discuss with representatives from any and all interested Indigenous organizations or governments. Indigenous member organizations included the major national Indigenous political organizations, specifically the Assembly of First Nations, Inuit Tapiriit Kanatami, Native Council of Canada, and the Métis Federation. Global Affairs, Government of Canada, 'International Trade Agreements and Indigenous Peoples' <www.international.gc.ca/trade-commerce/indigenous_peoples-peuples_autochtones/approach-approche.aspx?lang=eng> accessed 17 March 2025.

foreign markets, and measures addressing foreign competitors in the domestic market. These consultations are often common-sense for government representatives to confirm that the specific domestic industry's concerns, interests, and objectives are being elicited. These industries, however, do not have inherent rights nor do the governments have fiduciary duties to protect their interests.[22] Indigenous trade negotiations, on the other hand, have a marked difference – specifically, Indigenous Peoples have inherent rights to be protected during trade negotiations. These rights can, for example, are recognized in courts due to treaty or constitutional protection, as is the case in Canada.[23]

To fulfill these obligations, IPETCA participants each had a body of Indigenous experts from academia, business, NGOs, and tribal government sectors which allowed each participant to prepare initial domestic Indigenous trade positions for the negotiations adequately. However, only New Zealand in its funding of Te Taumata provided additional financial support for their contributions, as denoted through their 2019 MOU. The governments of Canada, Australia, and Taiwan did not provide any supplemental funding to their Indigenous trade representatives participating in negotiations, though the Government of Taiwan did provide organizational logistics, translation facilities, technology, and meeting facilities.

The actual process for each round of negotiations started with a gathering to discuss general principles of aspirations for each participant. Furthermore, New Zealand provided an initial draft of the IPETCA text that was developed in consultation with the Māori, which other participant representatives brought to their respective domestic Indigenous working groups for debate and discussion. In Canada, for example, the Global Affairs representative shared this draft with the Global Affairs Indigenous Working Group on Indigenous Trade (IWG), which they then broke down into various components to accept, reject, or modify based on consensus and informed by Canadian law, Indigenous legal and philosophical principles, including the

[22] *McKinney v University of Guelph* [1990] 3 SCR 229, 26; *R.W.D.S.U. v Dolphin Delivery Ltd.* [1986] 2 SCR 573; *Vriend v Alberta* [1998] 1 SCR 493, paras 65–66; *R. v Buhay* [2003] 1 SCR 631, para 31; *Highwood Congregation of Jehovah's Witnesses (Judicial Committee) v Wall* [2018] 1 SCR 750, para 39.

[23] See s 35 of the *Constitution Act, 1982* which states that 'existing aboriginal and treaty rights are [...] recognized and affirmed'. These rights include the Aboriginal economic right to both national and international inter-Tribal trade, stifled by the *Indian Act* and affirmed through *R. v Van der Peet* [1996] 2 SCR 507. Note that the Government of Canada is in express agreement that the Indigenous membership and representation on the IWG is not fulfilling its Crown duty to provide full and frank consultation in accordance with the existing judicial standards. The consultation obligation of the federal government to Indigenous Peoples is a separate and distinct process.

seventh-generation principle, international conventions, business principles, and public policy. Additionally, the dialogue surrounding the IPETCA draft sought to ensure that the arrangement would not erode or reduce the Aboriginal and treaty rights nor the inherent Indigenous economic right of inter-Tribal trade. However, as with many negotiated draft texts, the Canadian negotiators sought clarifications regarding rationale and wording from the New Zealand drafters before issuing a formal response. This resulted in a 'telephone tag', where the New Zealand negotiator had to relay the information to the Government of Canada negotiator, who in turn had to attempt to relay the explanation back to the Canadian IWG, an issue seen in each of the other negotiating participants.

To alleviate the resulting frustration about access to clarifications and information, the Indigenous leads from the four countries formed an international Indigenous IPETCA committee, led by Māori hosts but excluding government representatives.[24] The IPETCA Indigenous meetings sought to provide resolution to passages that could not be adequately explained or resolved by the regular State trade representatives. This facilitated direct dialogue among the various contributing Indigenous representatives by innovating on traditional lines of multilateral information sharing and negotiation. The international Indigenous IPETCA committee met in three rounds, commencing with the New Zealand Round, followed by a Canada Round, and closing with a clean-up round of remaining small outstanding issues, with additional offline meetings with subject matter experts to expedite the deliberation process. The committee proceeded through each group analysing clauses and posing questions regarding various passages while also raising possible solutions to the drafting issues before a broader meeting between the four participants. The final clean-up round resolved minor changes to create the resulting IPETCA document, which was finished during New Zealand's 2021 term as APEC Chair.

14.3 SUSTAINABLE DEVELOPMENT THROUGH THE IPETCA

As jurists, Indigenous leaders and scholars noted, the IPETCA is innovative in its creation, formalization, and implementation of an Indigenous rights and sustainable development-forward arrangement that sets an example for future ambitious collaborations between and amongst Indigenous Nations and

[24] The Indigenous leads for the IPETCA negotiations were as follows: New Zealand – Traci Houpapa; Australia – Darren Godwell; Chinese Taipei – Liu Da-Wei; Canada – Wayne Garnons-Williams.

States. In drafting the IPETCA, the negotiators were deliberate in carefully crafting references to and incorporating various international instruments, including the SDGs, UNDRIP, and other international and Indigenous trade, environment, human rights, and sustainable development treaties. The principles behind and articles agreed in the IPETCA regarding UNDRIP and the SDGs, Indigenous trade and investment, Traditional Knowledge and cultural expressions, and areas of cooperation can provide a legal and textual analysis of the innovations that enable the IPETCA to be an ambitious tool for sustainable development.

Firstly, the IPETCA includes extensive work on protecting human rights through UNDRIP, and environmental protection through numerous international instruments. These priorities are placed front and center – they are expressly laid out in the articles of the IPETCA and are not applied in isolation. Article 3, entitled 'International Instruments', details key concepts related to these priorities when applied to conducting international Indigenous trade. The preamble and the first subsection of Article 3 reinforce the interconnectedness of the IPETCA to human rights and environmental protection, stating particularly that 'existing international human rights obligations are interrelated, interdependent and mutually reinforcing, and should be considered alongside each other when advancing the rights of Indigenous [P]eoples and their participation in international trade'.[25] In the arrangement, participants also also recognize the 'need to strengthen the knowledge, technologies, practices and efforts of Indigenous Peoples related to the protection of endangered species, biodiversity loss, and climate change in these international agreements'.[26] In Article 3, Clauses (d) and (e), a clear and direct relationship with the various international agreements including but not limited to UNDRIP, the SDGs, the UN Financing for Development Addis Ababa Action Agenda, the *United Nations Framework Convention on Climate Change*, the *Paris Agreement*, the *Convention on Biological Diversity* (CBD) and its protocols and international obligations, the *United Nations Convention to Combat Desertification* (UNCCD), and the *Convention on the International Trade in Endangered Species* (CITES) is outlined.[27]

Specifically in relation to UNDRIP, the IPETCA furthermore outlines that participants which have signed UNDRIP are expected to carry out their fiduciary obligations in relation to domestic Indigenous Peoples and trade to support traditional Indigenous philosophies. The Preamble's paragraph 1(a)

[25] IPETCA (n 1) arts 1, 3.
[26] ibid paras 3(d)–(e).
[27] ibid.

(xiii) in particular underscores that 'the United Nations Declaration [UNDRIP] expressly places the responsibility on States to take, in conjunction with Indigenous [P]eoples, effective measures to recognize and protect the exercise of Indigenous [P]eoples' right to maintain, control, protect, and develop their cultural heritage, Traditional Knowledge, and traditional cultural expressions, as well as the manifestations of their sciences, technologies, and cultures'.[28] The last paragraph of the preamble additionally reinforces this message and addresses private sector participation to implement these values, stating that their standard of conduct expected needs to be 'carried out ethically and responsibly and consistent with Indigenous [P]eoples' rights, values and cultural traditions, and customs'.[29] In Table 14.1, additional articles in the IPETCA and the corresponding SDGs they address are provided. For example, Article 1(a)(xiv) of the IPETCA directly addresses SDGs 3, 10, and 16 through the measures and protections afforded to advance cultural heritage, Traditional Knowledge, and traditional cultural expressions, as well as the manifestations of their sciences, technologies, and cultures. However, for the IPETCA to realize its potential, its participants may need to go beyond developing meaningful trade arrangements amongst themselves with respect to each of the individual IPETCA articles they can also vigorously apply the spirit and intent of the document to actuate the empowerment of Indigenous Peoples to apply their own Indigenous philosophies for the use of land, water, and resources.

Concerning the SDGs, many targets and underlying aspirations are embedded in the cultural philosophies of each of the Indigenous Peoples in all the IPETCA participating economies. The Indigenous representatives found that they have the shared understanding that there is a causal connection between the role of steward and guardian to the ecosystem and the benefit that international Indigenous trade will bring. This is especially crucial, since for Indigenous Peoples, business and economic growth are inextricably linked to maintaining balance and protecting the environment, and differ largely from the other economic models of maximizing profit through unsustainable exploitation.[30] Incorporating these measures to advance SDGs and implement related international accords for sustainable development may be essential for a trade and policy climate where disregard for negative social and environmental

28 IPETCA (n 1) art 3, para 1(a)(xiii).

29 ibid art 3, para 1(a)(xxii).

30 See generally John Maynard Keynes, *The General Theory of Employment, Interest, and Money* (Palgrave Macmillan 1936) and Adam Smith, *The Wealth of Nations* (W. Strahan and T. Cadell 1776).

TABLE 14.1 *Cross-reference chart connecting relevant articles of the IPETCA with UNDRIP and UN SDGs*

IPETCA article	UNDRIP articles	UN SDGs
Article 1(a)(iii) *Free from discrimination*	Article 2	Goals 16, 5, 10
Article 1(a)(vii) *FPIC*	Article 19	Goals 16, 12
Article 1(a)(v) *Right to own economic systems and institutions*	Article 3	Goals 8, 9, 10
Article 1(a)(ix) *Traditional knowledge*	Article 31	Goals 4, 12
Article 1(a)(xii) *Right to lands territories and resources and traditional use of lands and waters*	Articles 26, 32	Goals 6, 13, 14, 15
Article 1(a)(xiv) *Right to maintain/control cultural heritage and Traditional Knowledge*	Articles 2, 31	Goals 3, 10, 16
Article 1(a)(xv) *Right of self-determination over decision making*	Article 3, 4	Goals 16, 17
Article 1(a)(xvi) *Disproportionate inequality & marginalization of SDG's*		Goals 5, 16, 8
Article 1(a)(xvii) *Addis Ababa Agenda on financing for development*		Goals 8, 9
Article 3(d) *SDG's and Addis Ababa Action Agenda on financing for development & protection of lands and waters*	Articles 20(1), 23	Goals 6, 13, 14, 15
Article 3(e) *International environmental agreements*	Article 29(1)	Goals 6, 7, 8, 9, 12, 13, 14, 15, 16
Article 4(a)(ii) *Engage freely with their traditional and other economies*	Articles 20(1), 23	Goals 1, 2, 3, 4, 5, 8, 9, 10, 12
Article 4(a)(iv) *Promote Indigenous world view of sustainable management of natural resources*	Article 29(1)	Goals 6, 7, 8, 9, 12, 13, 14, 15, 16
Article 7(a) *Holistic Traditional Knowledge*	Article 31	Goals 7, 8, 9, 10, 13, 14, 15, 16
Article 7(b)(c)(d)(e) *Protection of cultural heritage*	Articles 8(1), 11, 15(1), 31	Goals 3, 4, 5, 8, 10, 16

impacts that fall disproportionately on the most vulnerable is no longer realistic.[31] However, the preamble also recognizes that historically concerns have been raised that Indigenous engagement may have been downplayed by certain States in larger international environmental agreements.[32] Article 3, 'International Instruments' reaffirms that applying SDGs and international environmental accords to the arrangement remains important; it does so for the sake of clarity and to avoid a possible argument that the statements found in the preamble have little impact on application.[33] As in the case of the SDGs, additional articles in the IPETCA that address specific articles in UNDRIP in Table 14.1 are likewise summarized. Most notably, Article 1(a)(viii) provides an example of the IPETCA's implementation of free, prior, and informed consent (FPIC) which encapsulates Article 19 of UNDRIP.

Anchoring these international instruments in the central sections of the IPETCA thus secures a clear and unmistakable symmetry between Indigenous culture, philosophy and way of life, and Indigenous trade and commerce. The sections serve as guideposts and central pillars for how the IPETCA should be applied in the field of Indigenous international trade and mirror the philosophy of respect for Mother Earth and for a take-only-what-you-need approach. The IPETCA makes it clear that both business and government have a crucial role to play when working with Indigenous Nations on trade by applying not merely the letter of the law but also the spirit and intent of the arrangement.

Secondly, for the first time in international trade negotiations, States and their respective Indigenous representatives have agreed on a definition for the phrase *Indigenous Trade and Investment*. Section 2 of the IPETCA defines this as 'forms of trade and investment with, between, and among, Indigenous [P]eoples from the participating economies'.[34] This can include trade and investment to build long-term exchange networks; Indigenous laws and values including reciprocity, care, trust, respect, and generosity, operating within an intergenerational framework; and the responsibility of Indigenous Peoples to

[31] See Marie-Claire Cordonier Segger, *Crafting Trade and Investment Accords for Sustainable Development Athena's Treaties* (Oxford University Press 2021) 101.

[32] The preamble text states specifically that 'the participating economies: Acknowledge the disproportionate inequality and marginalisation of Indigenous Peoples on key indicators of the Sustainable Development Goals (SDG's) and the contribution that enhanced Indigenous trade and investment can make to addressing those realities'. Furthermore, the text states that the member states, '[a]cknowledge that the Addis Ababa Action Agenda on Financing for Development, which supports implementation of the SDG's, acknowledges that Indigenous Peoples continue to be excluded from participating fully in the economy'. See IPETCA (n 1) paras 1(a)(xvi)–(xvii), note 160.

[33] See ibid para 3(i), note 160.

[34] IPETCA (n 1) para 2(a).

protect their lands, resources, and the spiritual interrelationship of the human and natural world. This would be done in conjunction with enabling Indigenous Peoples to develop their economic and social systems.[35] Additionally, the inclusion of 'Indigenous laws and values' in Article 2(a)(ii) encapsulates the need to move beyond conventional bilateral rules when addressing Indigenous trade. Specifically, some jurists note, this speaks to including Indigenous Peoples' consent in harvesting and extractive industries.[36] This perspective presupposes that Indigenous laws should be enforced throughout the resource harvesting process right through to the primary and secondary manufacturing processes, including packaging, shipping, and distribution to reduce the environmental footprint derived from economic sustainability.

Thirdly, with respect to cultural heritage, Traditional Knowledge, and traditional cultural expressions, the dominant theme of the IPETCA has been to maximize the opportunities to empower Indigenous Peoples to protect their lands, culture, and way of life by incorporating Indigenous culture and philosophy into environmentally responsible trade practices. Article 7 states the value of such Traditional Knowledge in advancing 'innovation, sustainable development, and ecologically sound management of the environment'.[37] This provides the context for the rest of the Article, which encapsulates how this knowledge should be used by the participating economies.[38]

Finally, Article 8 provides an understanding of the areas of cooperation, that is, the 'nuts and bolts' of the Indigenous trade arrangement in terms of the twenty-two possible Indigenous trade issues to implement.[39] Within this list of issues is referenced the collaboration inherent in working on environmental and business issues and the resulting opportunities. It notes that the participating economies will cooperate domestically, regionally, and internationally to support policies and programmes related to exchanging best practices on promoting and expanding market opportunities, supporting Indigenous Peoples in responding to the adverse effects of climate change, considering ways to advance and promote Responsible Business Conduct (including the principle of equality of opportunity), and sharing methods and best practices

[35] ibid paras 2(a)(i)–(iv).

[36] ibid para 2(a)(ii).

[37] ibid para (7)(a).

[38] ibid paras (7)(b)–(e).

[39] ibid para 8(d) covers twenty-two suggested business and trade activities including access to capital markets, global investing, e-commerce, training, business networks and collaboration, Indigenous women and youth entrepreneur support, Indigenous goods authentication and tracing, foreign trade zone use, trade financing, Indigenous SMEs, supplier diversity mandates, and responsible business conduct. It is to be noted that article eight, while extensive, is not mandatory or exhaustive.

for monitoring and assessing, with reference to UNDRIP, SDGs, and other relevant indicators.[40] The four sections are broad and general enough to encompass a wide assortment of activities that can be equally applicable between trade with Tribal Nations in different participating economies. This cooperative approach to environmental standards allows for some degree of flexibility over the environmental standards imposed within Indigenous jurisdiction.

These sustainable development components found throughout the IPETCA demonstrate the ambitious nature of the arrangement to secure a sustainable and just future for the Indigenous Peoples involved and their partners. Of course, it can be underlined, eventual implementation and enforcement of these measures may require participants to act not only in the legal textual context of the arrangement but also to strive to implement the spirit and intent of the articles in the IPETCA. In this regard, and with an understanding of how the IPETCA was negotiated and the clauses incorporated into the arrangement, we look now at how the IPETCA should be implemented based on its design.

14.4 WORKING MECHANISM AND IMPLEMENTATION

Many international trade instruments include operating mechanisms that enables the printed word to come to life through implementation. Traditionally, such mechanisms could be limited to government dialogue at the State level. Obligations typically include providing explanatory notes, supplemental regulations, guidelines, and policies related to the trade instrument. In the case of the IPETCA, Indigenous People are intended to play a significant part in the day-to-day operation and implementation of the IPETCA, which has necessitated specific implementation mechanisms. The responsibilities of the States are broadened to include the Indigenous counterparts, thus requiring implementation measures that innovate on the old to ensure just, equitable, and accountable results for this arrangement. In this section, we will discuss how the IPETCA is being implemented, including the working mechanisms involved for the IPETCA to flourish through its Partnership Council and the Informal APEC Caucus on Indigenous Trade and Investment (Informal Caucus). Additionally, we will look at the viability of other States, specifically the United States, to join the arrangement.

14.4.1 *IPETCA Partnership Council and the Informal APEC Caucus*

Through the IPETCA Partnership Council, the participating economy representatives and Indigenous representatives share the administration of the

[40] ibid paras 8(d)(x)–(xi), (xvi), (xxi).

arrangement with the Informal Caucus for extra assurance that the Indigenous spirit and intent of the text are carried through to action. Article 9 of the IPETCA outlines the Partnership Council responsible for operating the arrangement.[41] The Council is authorized to have up to two government and up to two Indigenous Peoples' representatives from each participating economy.[42] An interim body is stipulated in Article 9(e) that operates during the selection period for the four eventual Council representatives.[43] Once the Partnership Council is fully operational in accordance with Article 9(b), the Council serves the function of approving the work programme to facilitate activities, deciding priorities with its available budget, encouraging 'multilateral and regional organizations' for projects that 'enable Indigenous business' 'to export goods and services', and inviting 'experts, leaders, elders, knowledge keepers or organizations to the Partnership council meetings' for knowledge sharing and decision-making to the benefit of Indigenous Peoples and businesses.[44] The Partnership Council additionally has the discretion to perform additional functions should they be considered relevant to the implementation and operation of the IPETCA.[45]

The IPETCA references the above-described Informal Caucus in Article 10. It is a body working outside the formal scope of the IPETCA and mandated to work alongside the annual APEC meetings to raise awareness of Indigenous trade issues at the larger APEC forums.[46] Article 10 was included in response to the concern that the IPETCA and its work could be isolated and ignored by the mainstream trading mechanisms that occur annually. The Informal Caucus was, jurists explain, seen as the best way to attract the attention of the APEC members to educate, influence, and encourage members to both join the IPETCA and engage on Indigenous trade concerns. There is no formal reporting relationship between the two bodies; nonetheless, it can be reasonably inferred that, while the Partnership Council operates the IPETCA, the external representation to the outside world of Indigenous trade issues is the responsibility of the Informal Caucus.

41 ibid art 9.

42 ibid para 9(c) defines 'Indigenous People's Representative' in such a way as to ensure that the nomination and selection of the two representatives will be carried out by Indigenous Peoples, for Indigenous Peoples. Should the Indigenous Peoples of the membership economy prove unable to select their Indigenous representatives, a secondary process will kick in, empowering the participating economy to seek the advice of Indigenous experts, elders, knowledge keepers and Indigenous organizations to help select the Indigenous representatives for the IPETCA Partnership Council.

43 ibid para 9(e).

44 ibid para 9(b).

45 ibid paras 9(f)(v)–(vi).

46 ibid art 10.

14.4.2 *The Viability of Joining IPETCA for APEC Members and Others*

Article 16 of IPETCA, 'New Participants', deliberately anticipates welcoming new members to join the arrangement. New membership is developed through a tiered approach to participation: initial observation status on the APEC Caucus on Indigenous Trade and Investment, subsequent participation in the APEC Caucus, and, once the participating economy is ready, an invitation to participate as a full member on the IPETCA Partnership Council.[47] Article 16(c) additionally empowers the IPETCA Partnership Council to entertain applications for membership in the Council. These applications for membership are, however, not exclusive to APEC economies:

> After the IPETCA Partnership Council has been fully established under paragraph 9, it will consider expressions of interest from any APEC Member Economy, WTO Member, or other economy made through the relevant entity of that economy . . .[48]

Thus, any economy can make an application, so long as they meet the procedural criteria,[49] and a 'positive decision'[50] is made by the Partnership Council for the applicant's inclusion in the Council. For example, on 17 October 2023 Canada and Ukraine signed a free trade agreement in force as of 1 January 2024,[51] that includes an extensive and supportive Indigenous Trade Chapter.[52] Ukraine, not being an APEC member, but being supportive of its Ukrainian Indigenous population, is well positioned to make a favourable application to join the IPETCA Partnership Council and become a full participating economy, thereby 'jumping the line' and avoiding the gradual tiered approach to membership.

Most States with Indigenous Peoples may choose the cautious, gradual, tiered approach to their involvement with IPETCA. Each of these States may

47 One mechanism outside art 16 that expressly empowers the Informal APEC Council to recruit new members is art 10(b)(iv) entitled 'Informal APEC Caucus on Indigenous Trade and Investment', which allows the caucus to 'Invite other APEC member economies or members of other APEC bodies to attend its meetings as observers. . .'. This marketing tool is a powerful and explicit means of enticing interest and gradual participation from other APEC member economies and their Indigenous Peoples.

48 IPETCA (n 1) para 16(c).

49 ibid.

50 ibid.

51 Canada-Ukraine Free Trade Agreement (signed 22 September 2023, Ottawa), ch 25 'Trade and Indigenous Peoples', which came into force on July 1, 2024 *Canada-Ukraine Free Trade Agreement Implementation Act*, 2023, SC 2024, c 3 (royal assent March 19, 2024). For more details on the Indigenous chapter in this agreement, see Chapter 5.

52 ibid ch 25, Trade and Indigenous Peoples.

undertake an internal domestic process of self-examination with regards to their constitutional makeup and laws in relation to their Indigenous Peoples. Such a self-examination would have to be carried out prior to developing a full application for participation in the IPETA Partnership Council. The necessary steps preceding an application for participation in IPETCA on the part of the United States of America can provide an excellent illustration.

Original pre-European Indigenous trade in the United States was complete with ceremonies, trade languages, and trade routes conveying a robust array of goods for trade. This independent Tribal sovereignty for trade and beyond was, however, shifted to a domestic dependent Nation status with the advent of colonization and the development of the colonies into States.[53] This domestic dependent Nation designation reduced but also secured elements of Tribal sovereignty, enabling the agreements and covenants that protected and formalized Indigenous trade to evolve.[54] Based on these unique legal evolutions, modern US Tribal Nation-to-State relations contain, within the federal trade system, untapped international inter-Tribal trade opportunities. Specifically, the Tribal Nations have the potential to build a healthy inter-Tribal and international Indigenous trading system, but developing such a system would require a range of improvements at both the domestic and international levels. Amongst the requirements for these ambitions would be to embrace and respect good Tribal governance and Traditional Knowledge by States and international corporations alike. Experts have noted, however, that Tribal Nations have yet to fully capitalize on the US trade system, and the US government has yet to fully appreciate the opportunities available to help Tribal Nations realize trade opportunities under current international laws.

Additionally, the IPETCA offers four core enhancements for both US Tribal sovereignty and federal authority over international trade and commerce among Tribal Nations. These enhancements include:

1. Enable Indigenous partnership and inclusiveness in the development and administration of the IPETCA;
2. Demonstrate active respect for Indigenous worldviews, cultures, and ways of life;
3. Bolster environmental stewardship and sustainability as embraced as part and parcel of Indigenous business; and
4. Promote and support the exercise of tangible international Indigenous trade opportunities.

[53] For more information about the designation of domestic dependent nation status for US Tribes, refer to Chapter 10.

[54] *Cherokee Nation v Georgia*, 30 US (5 Pet) 1 (1831) 30.

It has been suggested that the IPETCA endorsement falls in line with the US federal power to authorize US Tribes to conduct international inter-Tribal trade.[55] This federal jurisdiction is exclusive, with Professors John Nowak and Ronald Rotunda stating that '... the Court, historically, has not had any significant difficulties in upholding a plenary federal power over all forms of commercial regulations of foreign commerce and dealings with American Indians. That is because ... those powers do not really interfere with state powers ... The Court has always recognized a plenary power in Congress to deal with matters touching upon foreign relations or foreign trade.'[56] Such exclusivity is reaffirmed through Article 1, Section 10 of the US Constitution which clarifies the prohibition of state activity in international trade matters.[57]

In this light, it may be markedly easier for some governments to endorse an international economic arrangement, like the IPETCA, rather than a treaty. The US Constitution lays out a distinct difference in the required authority for endorsing treaties and treaty-level agreements, while it remains silent on the required authority for endorsing all other documents that are less than a treaty. The IPETCA falls under this latter category. For the sake of consistency, anything less than a full treaty will be called an 'executive agreement'. Executive agreements may be considered politically binding in contrast to treaties which are legally binding. In the same vein, select international instruments can be endorsed by the President in the form of an executive

55 Constitution of the United States of America, art 1, s 8 Commerce clause which states that the United States Congress shall have power '[t]o regulate Commerce with foreign Nations, and among the several States, and with the Indian Tribes' <www.law.cornell.edu/constitution/articlei> accessed 15 March 2025.

56 John E Nowak and Ronald D Rotunda, *Constitutional Law* (8th edn, West Academic Publishing 2010) 159, 160.

57 United States Constitution, art I, § 10 states in part:

> No State shall enter into any Treaty, Alliance, or Confederation...
> No State shall, without the Consent of Congress lay any Imports or Duties on Imports or Exports...
> No State shall, without the Consent of Congress, lay any Duty of Tonnage, ... enter into any Agreement of Compact with another State, or with a foreign Power, ...

However, this does not speak to any corresponding prohibition toward Indian Tribes. Here, Nowak and Rotunda point to the US Constitution's reservation of exclusive powers over trade to the federal government, stating that '... one of the prime areas of commercial problems that the Constitution solved was the imposition of restrictions on imports and exports by the states. The Constitution specifically prohibits state governments from imposing such duties without the consent of the national government. The art I s 10 listing of activities that are prohibited to the states primarily focuses upon matters touching upon their foreign trade or relations with foreign countries. Thus, there is no constitutional recognition of any "reserved powers" of the states to act in these areas.' See ibid 160.

agreement without congressional approval.[58] Executive agreements thus serve as a common and expedient tool in the United States that save significant time and effort through executive endorsement.[59]

Because the IPETCA is an economic arrangement undertaken by the participants for the benefit of their Indigenous Peoples, it may be non-binding; it does not qualify as an international treaty. As such, it is executable by the President of the United States as a sole executive agreement. Such administrative convenience was part of the appeal for structuring the IPETCA as an arrangement; doing so also allowed Taiwan to join in its capacity as 'Chinese Taipei', its title within APEC.[60]

As such, there is thus a strong argument for the US federal government to endorse the IPETCA, as this economic arrangement relates to the political classification of Tribal membership, supports Indigenous international trade, and is established in long-standing legal and constitutional paradigms that remain relatively impervious to state objections and Senate powers. As of 2025, the United States has yet to endorse the IPETCA formally; however, the door remains open to greater US involvement in this arrangement and others in the future, particularly in light of its observer status with IPETCA's Partnership Council granted in April 2024.[61]

14.5 CONCLUSION

For the IPETCA to truly succeed, its participating economies must go beyond developing meaningful trade arrangements amongst themselves and vigorously apply the spirit and intent of the IPETCA to allow Indigenous Peoples to apply their own philosophies to the sustainable use and harvesting of land, water, and resources. Particularly, the freedom to apply the spirit and intent of the IPETCA is to protect Indigenous cultures and their ecosystems while allowing reasonable commercial harvest for resources. In this way, the environmental agreements, protocols, and tools that have been expressly and

[58] *States v Belmont*, 301 US 324 (1937) 331.

[59] Oona A Hathaway, 'Presidential Power over International Law: Restoring the Balance' (2009) 119 Yale Law Journal 140, 150–152.

[60] Had the IPETCA been concluded as a formal international trade treaty, it may have required Taiwan to, as it did with ANZTEC, sign in its capacity as a WTO member; specifically the: 'Separate Customs Territory of Taiwan, Penghu, Kinmen and Matsu'.

[61] Office of the United States Trade Representative, 'United States Granted Observer Status in the Indigenous Peoples Economic and Trade Cooperation Arrangement (IPETCA)' <https://ustr.gov/about-us/policy-offices/press-office/press-releases/2024/april/united-states-granted-observer-status-indigenous-peoples-economic-and-trade-cooperation-arrangement> accessed 13 March 2025.

intentionally incorporated into the IPETCA can be applied to their fullest to assist Indigenous nations in their quest to protect their Indigenous cultures and uphold their Indigenous laws and values. Through the promises of the IPETCA, we can collectively respect Mother Earth by taking only what is needed and ensuring that the seventh generation's future is looked after by stewarding the planet's ecosystems and watersheds for those future generations.

15

New Directions for Treaties Advancing Sustainable Development in the Context of the Rights of Indigenous Peoples

As the chapters and lessons of this volume make clear, the implications of treaties adopted for, or implicating, Indigenous Peoples represent a legal approach that can advance the implicit and entrenched relationship between human rights and sustainable development. With this in mind, research for this volume has underlined that Indigenous treaties can be understood and implemented as sustainability-advancing instruments, allowing their full potential to be realized.

This volume has focused on the legal aspects of Indigenous treaties to achieve the seventeen United Nations Sustainable Development Goals (SDGs). The chapters provide a serious contribution to the current academic scholarly debates on the implications of Indigenous law for augmenting domestic and international regimes to achieve sustainable development effectively and equitably. In this context, it was crucial to carefully document the historical and modern injustices that persist to hinder the full realization of the benefits sought in the treaties, largely due to failures in implementing the treaty promisesand related legal and policy reforms.

The volume was structured into five parts, each discussing different aspects of understanding and implementing various international, multi-national, and Nation-to-Nation covenants that affirm Indigenous knowledge and sustainable development. Part I, and the corresponding introductory chapter, established the foundations for analysis by presenting the Indigenous worldview that frames this volume. It presented the reasoning behind Indigenous ontologies, which focused on the collective and on the inseparable relationships between humans and nature, and argued that they are central to reforming current biases which have been so damaging to ecological and personal well-being.

Following this introductory note, Part II laid the foundations for the rest of the volume by exploring several relevant international conventions and declarations enshrining key principles of international Indigenous Law. This part defined and provided the theoretical background underpinning the principle of leveraging treaty and international law for sustainable development and its implications. Specifically, Chapter 2 provided a comprehensive analysis of the international legal framework governing Indigenous Peoples' rights, focusing on the Indigenous and Tribal Peoples Convention, 1989 (ILO 169) and the United Nations Declaration on the Rights of Indigenous Peoples (UNDRIP), as well as the fundamental principle of free, prior, and informed consent (FPIC). These serve as crucial instruments later required to analyse treaties themselves for sustainable development. This chapter also emphasized the significance of consent as a cornerstone of Indigenous rights and sustainable development. The chapter concluded by acknowledging the complexities involved in its practical application. By delving into substantive and procedural aspects of international law, this chapter established an understanding of the role of international legal norms in promoting Indigenous rights and facilitating sustainable development.

Chapter 3 then explored the implementation of sustainable development through the lens of the seventeen SDGs. It presented foundational insights and related instruments which guide sustainable development as seen through the history and motivation behind adopting a global set of goals and targets to achieve and measurable sustainable development advances by 2030. The chapter then focused on how these SDGs intersect with the interests and contributions of Indigenous Peoples, specifically by highlighting the historical disparities faced by these communities and how treaties and other covenants have the potential to foster or frustrate the achievement of these goals. It then delved into guidelines for sustainable resource management and Indigenous development within the SDG framework, emphasizing inclusive approaches and participatory decision-making. By bridging principles with practical strategies, this chapter underscored the importance of integrating Indigenous knowledge, fostering partnerships, and implementing the SDGs to achieve sustainable development while respecting Indigenous rights and aspirations.

Chapter 4 then transitioned into presenting an understanding of the vital role of Indigenous trade and investment in promoting sustainable development. It emphasized Nation-building approaches centred on the significance of robust Tribal infrastructure. The chapter then addressed important barriers hindering Indigenous inter-Tribal trade, including poor Tribal governance, state, or provincial interference in Tribal jurisdiction, the limits facing Indigenous foreign trade zones, the exclusion of Indigenous Traditional Knowledge (TK) from intellectual property (IP) regimes, and historical challenges in trade financing. Additionally, the chapter explored Indigenous trade and commerce engagements with non-Indigenous enterprises, both with and without federal permission, highlighting the implications, challenges, and opportunities involved. By examining these aspects, the chapter advocated for empowering Indigenous Nations through trade and investment, fostering economic opportunities while preserving cultural heritage, and working towards sustainable development by creating a strong economic baseline.

Part III then examined how treaty implementation can address sustainable economic development by targeting key sectors and bodies of legal discourse. Chapter 5 explored the complex relationship between Traditional Knowledge (TK) and intellectual property (IP) concerning genetic resources. It began by examining the challenges of distinguishing TK from IP, highlighting the Munzer Model as a potential compromise for addressing TK within the IP framework. The chapter then delved into national efforts to protect and recognize TK, focusing on US and Canadian cases. Furthermore, it detailed the evolving landscape of TK in international trade agreements, highlighting its increasing recognition and integration as a 'new norm'. By analysing these historic and current developments in TK recognition, this chapter emphasized the need for a balanced approach that respects the unique nature of TK while navigating the complexities of IP frameworks. It underscored the importance of preserving and utilizing TK and genetic resources for the benefit of Indigenous communities and for advancing sustainable development.

Chapter 6 then brought in the complexities of the intersection between renewable resources, sustainable development, and Indigenous treaty law. It began by examining international guidance for renewable energy sources and their role in achieving sustainability objectives. This chapter then delved into the principles and rules governing sustainable forestry practices, fisheries management, and energy development. It highlighted the importance of international agreements, protocols, and treaties in promoting responsible resource management, conservation, and the recognition of Indigenous rights and knowledge. By considering these principles and rules within the context of Indigenous treaty law, it highlighted the need for harmonious and inclusive approaches to renewable resource use in the age of sustainable development. It underlined the significance of collaboration, respect for Indigenous knowledge, and the integration of sustainability principles to ensure a balanced and equitable relationship between renewable resources, Indigenous rights, and sustainable development.

Subsequently, Chapter 7 sought to capture the intricate relationship inherent between Indigenous cultural heritage and Indigenous rights, not only for advancing sustainable development but also for enabling the well-being of

Indigenous communities. It began by analysing the guidance provided by the UNDRIP and ILO 169 regarding the preservation and protection of cultural heritage, particularly in the context of the triple planetary crisis. Additionally, it emphasized the importance of resilient and vibrant cultural heritage for achieving sustainable development. The chapter highlighted the challenges posed by climate change, biodiversity loss, and environmental degradation to Indigenous cultural heritage and emphasized the need for resilience and safeguarding measures. It further examined the treatment of cultural heritage in Indigenous treaties, delving into legal and historical perspectives in the US jurisprudence and political landscape, and then addressed the ability of Canadian modern treaties to foster or frustrate the ability to safeguard cultural heritage. By considering these aspects, the chapter underscored the significance of recognizing and preserving Indigenous cultural heritage, advocating for enhanced legal frameworks, collaborative approaches, and the integration of Indigenous rights and knowledge to ensure the continuity and vitality of cultural heritage for present and future generations.

Chapter 8 concluded Part III by exploring the complex relationship between extractive industries, sustainable development, and Indigenous treaty law. It began by examining the international law guidance available for extractive industries, analysing frameworks and principles that promote responsible and sustainable practices in resource extraction while considering the social, economic, and environmental dimensions. This chapter then focused on the specific challenges of oil and gas exploration, highlighting the impacts on Indigenous communities and emphasizing the importance of meaningful consultation, consent, and fair benefit-sharing in alignment with Indigenous treaty rights. Furthermore, it explored the mining sector's implications for sustainable development, considering the social, economic, and environmental aspects and emphasizing the role of Indigenous treaty law in ensuring responsible practices, equitable resource distribution, and the protection of Indigenous rights and lands. In conclusion, the chapter emphasized the need for a balanced approach that respects Indigenous rights, integrates Indigenous perspectives and consent, and promotes sustainable practices to foster collaboration and achieve sustainable development goals while enabling the well-being and self-determination of Indigenous Peoples.

Part IV then presented case studies of treaty drafting and implementation to identify various solutions that have been used to address the complex problem of advancing sustainable development and Indigenous rights through treaties, while recognising the many remaining challenges. It provided comparative insights from different domestic experiences and traditions, identifying areas of commonality and difference in efforts to activate domestic institutions in the interest of intergenerational equity. Firstly, Chapter 9 presented a case study from Canada, examining the intricate relationship between Indigenous Peoples and the developments related to British, then Canadian, governance. It began by exploring the historical and legal context within which Indigenous Peoples exist in Canada, tracing the impact of colonization and the recognition of Indigenous rights. The chapter then investigated the potential for affirming these rights through treaties and trade agreements, highlighting the role of treaties in recognizing and protecting Indigenous rights and the opportunities and challenges presented by trade agreements for Indigenous economic development and self-determination. It further analysed the Canadian government's efforts to domestically enforce the UNDRIP and the intersection of Canadian treaties with trade agreements. This chapter emphasized the importance of ongoing dialogue, collaboration, and the implementation of measures aligned with the UNDRIP's Articles 20, 26, and 28 as well as SDG 14 on life below water, 16.7 on inclusive decision-making, 17.10 on equitable trade, 17.16–17 on multi-stakeholder partnerships, and 10.2 on promoting social, economic, and political inclusion, to foster the recognition, empowerment, and well-being of Indigenous Peoples within the Canadian context.

Chapter 10 delved into the US's treatment of Indigenous Peoples, with a specific focus on Indigenous sovereignty and economic rights. It began by introducing the topic and setting the context for the discussion by providing a history of the treatment of Indigenous Peoples in the US legal framework, with an emphasis on the series of cases dubbed the Marshall Trilogy. This included the struggles and advancements in recognizing Tribal Nation sovereignty and economic rights. It examined the recognition and affirmation of Tribal Nation sovereignty within the United States, including legal developments and court decisions that have shaped Indigenous self-governance. This chapter analysed the landmark case of *McGirt v Oklahoma*, emphasizing its role in addressing past legal injustices, establishing Tribal reservation boundaries, and strengthening Tribal jurisdiction. It also investigated US Tribal sovereignty in the context of international Indigenous trade, showcasing how Indigenous communities engage in economic activities and exercise their sovereignty on the global stage. The chapter noted how ensuring restitution or recognition of Indigenous rights would align with SDG 10.2, fostering social, economic, and political inclusion, 10.3 and 16b on non-discriminatory laws and policies, and SDG 16.7 on responsive, inclusive, participatory, and representative decision-making at all levels, in addition to the provisions in the UNDRIP Articles 8, 11, and 26–28. This chapter emphasized the importance of recognizing and upholding the treaty right to economic sovereignty to protect and promote Indigenous economic rights within the United States.

Chapter 11 presented the New Zealand case study, examining the paradigm of giving nature legal standing within the country's judicial and legislative framework. It began with an introduction that sets the stage for the discussion. This chapter then explored the Māori philosophy of a relationship with nature, emphasizing the profound connection and inherent value Māori place on the environment. It delved into the ways in which New Zealand law has affirmed this philosophy, particularly through the roots of the country's environmental achievements as anchored in the Treaty of Waitangi. The chapter then presented two case studies – the Te Urewera Land Legislation and the Whanganui River Legislation – showcasing the innovative approaches taken to grant legal personhood to natural entities. It further explored the incorporation of Māori Indigenous Traditional Knowledge in sustainable development practices, highlighting Māori trade and the introduction of new measures of well-being and environmental protection. The chapter also examined how these case studies interface with the UNDRIP, particularly Articles 25–26, rights to land and maintaining spiritual ties, 29 on conservation and protection of the environment, and 36 on the development of contacts with other Indigenous Peoples across borders; likewise, the chapter detailed how these approaches advance the SDGs, particularly SDGs 6.6 on water-related ecosystems, 11.4 on the world's cultural and natural heritages, 15 on the preservation of terrestrial ecosystems, 16.7 on inclusive decision-making, and 17.16 on enhancing global partnerships for sustainable development. The chapter concluded by emphasizing the significance of giving nature legal standing and the implications for both Māori and New Zealand's approach to sustainable development.

Chapter 12 presented case studies of Indigenous peace agreements in the Andes region. It began with an introduction highlighting the significance of understanding legal geography and its relevance to Indigenous Peoples. It then explored the legal frameworks that protect Indigenous rights, focusing on international instruments such as declarations and conventions. It then examined specific agreements in the Andes that enact these legal frameworks, with a spotlight on the National Agreement for Development and Peace in La Araucanía, 2018, in Chile, and the Agreement Between the Bolivian Government and the Confederation of Indigenous Peoples from the East, Chaco, and Amazonia in 2010. These case studies showcased the intersection of legal, social, and political dynamics in promoting Indigenous rights and fostering peace. By analysing the legal geographies of these agreements, the chapter contributed to a deeper understanding of the complex challenges and opportunities Indigenous communities face in achieving sustainable development and peace in the Andes region.

Finally, for Part IV, Chapter 13 presented agreements between Indigenous Peoples and governments, specifically peace accords in Bangladesh and Mexico that focus on promoting sustainable development. The introduction sets the stage for subsequent discussions by emphasizing the importance of global legal and policy frameworks in shaping these agreements, with the UNDRIP and the SDGs. The two case studies from Bangladesh and Mexico were analysed, shedding light on the unique characteristics, provisions, and outcomes of agreements between Indigenous Peoples and governments in these contexts. A comparative analysis presented commonalities, differences, and lessons learned from these case studies. This analysis found that these case studies align with SDGs 2 on food security, 13 on combating climate change, and 16 on peaceful and inclusive societies, while also holding potential to advance the UNDRIP's articles 8 against land dispossession, 26–27 on land and institutional redress mechanisms, 30 against militarization, and 32 on land and resource development. Ultimately, the chapter concluded by highlighting the significance of ongoing dialogue, collaboration, and respect for Indigenous rights in achieving sustainable development goals globally. It underscored the importance of incorporating Indigenous perspectives and aspirations into the design and implementation of such agreements.

The last section, Part V, scoped future directions and options, distilling lessons learned from current practices, for the reform of political and legal institutions at the national, regional, and global levels by drawing on a new treaty that provides solutions and innovations that address the complex problems presented throughout this volume. Chapter 14 closed off the volume by exploring the innovative approaches to incorporating the principles of the UNDRIP and sustainable development in a newly negotiated Indigenous trade arrangement. The chapter detailed the origins of the Indigenous Peoples Economic Trade and Cultural Arrangement (IPETCA), focusing on its innovations that enabled trade negotiations that amplified Indigenous views and values while enabled by the participating economies of New Zealand, Taiwan, Australia, and Canada. The chapter then delved into the sustainable development aspects of IPETCA, showcasing how it references, in para 1(a)(xiii), the principles of UNDRIP and fosters economic growth while respecting Indigenous rights; similarly, the chapter demonstrated how IPETCA's drafters recognize, in Article 3, the obligations found in other multilateral instruments, reaffirming SDGs including 3, 10, and 16. Table 14.1 in Chapter 14 further provides an overview of IPETCA articles which engage or reference articles from the UNDRIP and goals from the SDGs.

The chapter illuminated IPETCA's working mechanism and implementation, highlighting the role of the IPETCA Partnership Council and the

Informal APEC Caucus in facilitating dialogue and collaboration. Finally, the chapter contemplated the viability of other countries such as the United States joining IPETCA and the potential benefits this could bring. In conclusion, the chapter underscored the importance of innovative approaches like IPETCA in advancing Indigenous trade agreements that prioritize sustainable development and uphold the principles of UNDRIP.

In summary, this volume has reviewed the current contributions of law toward the implementation of treaties that advance the rights of Indigenous People while simultaneously fostering the SDGs. Specifically, it emphasized the critical importance of integrating Indigenous knowledge and treaties into the framework of sustainable development. The key findings from the book identify elements of the future international law and governance research agenda and offer tentative conclusions on the state of international efforts to secure and strengthen the implementation of treaties that impact Indigenous Peoples. Thus, the invaluable wisdom and practices of Indigenous Peoples to promote respect, reciprocity, and harmony with the natural world can champion a convergence of Indigenous knowledge with global sustainable development agendas. The hope is that respectful engagement and carefully crafted legal challenges may contribute to a more balanced and resilient future. As the world faces unprecedented challenges such as natural disasters, resource scarcity, and human rights violations, the harmonization of worldviews may secure a safer and healthier and more sustainable path forward for those – inspired by covenant – who are willing to walk together.

Table of Cases and Court Decisions

(in alphabetical order)

Akins v United States, 407 F. Supp. 748 (1978) (United States).

Calder et al v Attorney-General of British Columbia [1973] S.C.R. 313 (Canada).

Campbell et al v AG BC/AG Cda & Nisga'a Nation et al, 2000 B.C.S.C. 1123 (Canada).

Canada (Human Rights Commission) v Canada (Attorney General) 2012 F.C. 445 (Canada).

Certain Activities carried out by Nicaragua in the Border Area (Costa Rica v Nicaragua) [2015] I.C.J 78.

Cherokee Nation v Georgia, 30 US (5 Pet.) 1 (1831) (United States).

Churchill Falls (Labrador) Corp. v Hydro-Québec [2018] 3 S.C.R. 101 (Canada).

Coldwater First Nation v Canada (Attorney General) [2020] FCA 34 (Federal Court of Appeal).

Cowichan Tribes, 'Cowichan Sweaters and the 2010 Olympics' (Cowichan Tribes, 2010).

Delgamuukw v British Columbia [1997] 3 S.C.R. 1010 (Canada).

Grand River Enterprises Six Nations Ltd v United States (Award, UNCITRAL, 12 January 2011) (NAFTA Ch 11 Arbitration).

Haida Nation v British Columbia (Minister of Forests) [2004] 3 S.C.R. 511 (Canada).

Hupacasath First Nation v Canada (Minister of Foreign Affairs), 2015 F.C.A. 4, 379 D.L.R. (4th) 737 (Canada).

Inter-American Court of Human Rights (IACtHR) Jurisprudence on Indigenous Rights (e.g., *Saramaka People v Suriname* [2007] IACtHR Series C No 172).

Johnson v M'Intosh 21 US (8 Wheat) 543 (1823) (United States).
Karnuth v U.S., 279 US 231 (1929) 240–241 (United States).
Lone Wolf v Hitchcock, 187 US 553 (1903) (United States).
McCandless v US ex rel. Diabo, 25 F.2d 71 (1928) (United States).
McGirt v Oklahoma, 591 US ___ (2020) (United States).
Minnesota v Mille Lacs Band of Chippewa Indians, 526 US 172 (1999) (United States).
Morton v Mancari, 417 US 535 (1974) (United States).
Nebraska v Parker, 577 US ___ (2016) (United States).
Ngati Rangi Trust v Manawatu-Wanganui Regional Council [2019] NZEnvC 197 (New Zealand Environment Court).
Northwest Atlantic Fisheries Organization (NAFO) v Foreign Fishing Operators (1986) 19 Dumping at Sea Tribunal Reports 1.
Nunatsiavut v Canada (Attorney General), 2015 F.C. 492 (Canada).
Quebec (Attorney General) v Moses [2010] 1 S.C.R. 557 (Canada).
R. v Marshall [1999] 3 S.C.R. 456 (Canada).
R. v Mitchell [2001] 1 S.C.R. 911 (Canada).
R. v Sioui [1990] 1 S.C.R. 1025 (Canada).
R. v Sparrow [1990] 1 S.C.R. 1075 (Canada).
R. v Van der Peet [1996] 2 S.C.R. 507 (Canada).
Smith v The Queen [1960] S.C.R. 776 (Canada).
Solem v Bartlett 465 US 463 (1984) (United States).
Taku River Tlingit First Nation v British Columbia (Project Assessment Director) [2004] 3 S.C.R. 550 (Canada).
Thomas and Saik'uz First Nation v Rio Tinto Alcan Inc [2022] B.C.S.C. 15 (Canada).
Tsilhqot'in Nation v British Columbia [2014] 2 S.C.R. 257 (Canada).
United States v Dion, 476 US 734 (1986) (United States).
United States v Kagama, 118 US 375 (1886) (United States).
United States v Sandoval, 231 US 28 (1913) (United States).
United States v Wheeler, 435 US 313 (1978) (United States).
United States v Winans, 198 US 371 (1905) (United States).
Wangan and Jagalingou Family Council v National Native Title Tribunal [2017] FCA 116 (Federal Court of Australia).
Washington State Department of Licensing v Cougar Den Inc, 586 US ___ (2019) (United States).
Williams Lake Indian Band v Canada, 2018 S.C.C. 4 (Canada).
Worcester v Georgia, 31 US (6 Pet.) 515 (1832) (United States).

Table of Domestic Acts and Regulations

(in alphabetical order)

Agreement between the Bolivian Government and CIDOB (Confederation of Indigenous Peoples of the East, Chaco, and Amazonia) (2010).

An Act Approving the Agreement Concerning James Bay and Northern Québec, SQ 1976, c 46, RSQ c C-67 (Canada).

Bill S-16, An Act Respecting the Recognition of the Haida Nation and the Council of the Haida Nation, SC 2024.

British North America Act 1867 (United Kingdom).

Canadian Energy Regulator Act (CERA), SC 2019, c 28, s 10 (Canada).

Canadian Energy Regulator Act 2019 (Canada).

Canadian Environmental Assessment Act S.C. 1992, c 37 (Canada).

Chittagong Hill Tracts Development Board Act (2014) (Bangladesh).

Chittagong Hill Tracts Land-dispute Resolution Commission Act (2001) (Bangladesh).

Chittagong Hill Tracts Local Council Act (1998) (Bangladesh).

Chittagong Hill Tracts Peace Accord (1997) (Bangladesh).

Coal Mines Act Amendment Act 1903 (New Zealand).

Constitution Act 1982, Canadian Charter of Rights and Freedoms (Canada).

Curtis Act of 1898, 30 Stat 495 (United States).

Declaration on the Rights of Indigenous Peoples Act, S.B.C. 2019, c 44 (Canada).

First Nations Land Management Act SC 1999, c 24 (Canada).

Fisheries Act RSC 1985, c F-14 (Canada).

General Allotment Act (Dawes Act) of 1887, 24 Stat 388 (United States).

Immigration and Nationality Act of the United States 1952 (amended 1965).

Impact Assessment Act, SC 2019, c 28 (Canada).
Indian Act, RSC 1985, c I-5 (Canada).
Indian Oil and Gas Act, RSC 1985, c I-7 (Canada).
Indian Oil and Gas Regulations, 2019, SOR/2019-196 (Canada).
Indian Removal Act of 1830, 4 Stat 411 (United States).
Indian Reorganization Act of 1934, 48 Stat 984 (United States).
Indigenous Law No 19.253 (1993) (Chile).
James Bay and Northern Québec Native Claims Settlement Act, SC 1976–77, c 32, RS c J-03 (Canada).
Kativik Act, RSQ, c C-11.1 (Canada).
Law No 341 (2013) (Bolivia) (Indigenous participation and social control).
Law No 73 (2010) (Bolivia) (Indigenous self-determination and jurisdiction).
Mexican Constitution (1917, amended 2001), art 2 (Indigenous rights and autonomy) (Mexico).
National Agreement for Development and Peace in La Araucanía (2018) (Chile).
Native American Business Development, Trade Promotion, and Tourism Act of 2000, 25 USC §§ 4301–4304 (United States).
Native Title Act 1993 (Cth) (Australia).
Regulation No 40 (2012) (Chile) (Environmental Impact Assessment system).
Regulation No 66 (2014) (Chile) (consultation procedures under ILO 169).
Resource Management Act 1991 (New Zealand).
San Andrés Accords (1996) (Agreement between Mexican Government and EZLN) (Mexico).
Te Awa Tupua (Whanganui River Claims Settlement) Act 2017 (New Zealand).
Te Urewera Act 2014 (New Zealand).
The Indian Arts and Crafts Act of 1990 (P.L. 101-644) (United States).
US Code §1151 (United Kingdom).
United Nations Declaration on the Rights of Indigenous Peoples Act, S.C. 2021, c 14 (Canada).
United States Constitution.

Table of Multilateral and Indigenous Treaties and Declarations

(in order of appearance)

Tåîchô Land Claims and Self-Government Agreement (Tåîchô—Government of Canada–Government of the Northwest Territories) (adopted 25 August 2003, entered into force 4 August 2005).

Agreement between New Zealand and the Separate Customs Territory of Taiwan, Penghu, Kinmen, and Matsu on Economic Cooperation (ANZTEC) (signed 10 July 2013).

Agreement between the Bolivian Government and the Confederation of Indigenous Peoples from the East, Chaco, and Amazonia (signed 2010).

Arrangement on Indigenous Peoples' Economic and Trade Cooperation (signed 17 June 2022) (IPETCA).

Canada—Ukraine Free Trade Agreement (signed 22 September 2023, Ottawa).

Canada—United States-Mexico Agreement (Mexico–Canada–United States) (adopted 30 November 2018, entered into force 1 July 2020).

Champagne and Aishihik First Nations Final Agreement (Champagne and Aishihik First Nations–Government of Canada–Government of the Yukon) (adopted 19 June 1992).

Chiixuujin / Chaaw Kaawgaa 'Big Tide (Low Water)' Haida Title Lands Agreement (Canada and Haida Nation, 2025).

Convention on Access to Information, Public Participation in Decision-Making and Access to Justice in Environmental Matters (adopted 25 June 1998, entered into force 30 October 2001) 2161 UNTS 447.

Convention on Biological Diversity (adopted 5 June 1992, entered into force 29 December 1993) 1760 UNTS 79.

Convention on International Trade in Endangered Species (adopted 3 March 1973, entered into force 1 July 1975) 993 UNTS 243.

Doig River First Nation Treaty 8 Agreement (Canada and Doig River First Nation, 2022).

Food and Agriculture Organization of the United Nations (FAO), International Plan of Action to Prevent, Deter and Eliminate Illegal, Unreported and Unregulated Fishing (FAO, 2001).

Free Trade Agreement between the European Union and New Zealand (signed 9 July 2023, not yet in force) COM(2023) 375 final.

Free Trade Agreement between the United Kingdom of Great Britain and Northern Ireland and New Zealand (signed 28 February 2022, entered into force 31 May 2023) CP 736.

Gaayhllxid / Gíihlagalgang 'Rising Tide' Haida Title Lands Agreement (Canada and Haida Nation, 2024).

Gwich'in Comprehensive Land Claim Agreement (Gwich'in Tribal Council–Government of Canada–Government of the Northwest Territories) (adopted 13 July 1991, entered into force 10 April 1992).

ILO, 'C107 – Indigenous and Tribal Populations Convention, 1957' (26 June 1957) Geneva, 40th ILC session (ILO C107).

ILO, 'International Labour Organization Convention 169 Concerning Indigenous and Tribal Peoples in Independent Countries' (27 June 1989) 28 ILM 1382 (entered into force 5 September 1991) (ILO C169)

International Convention on the Elimination of All Forms of Racial Discrimination (adopted 21 December 1965, entered into force 4 January 1969) 660 UNTS 195 (CERD).

International Covenant on Economic, Social and Cultural Rights (adopted 16 December 1966, entered into force 3 January 1976) 993 UNTS 3.

James Bay and Northern Québec Agreement and Complementary Agreements (Cree Nation of Eeyou Istchee–Inuit of Nunavik–Government of Canada–Government of Quebec–Hydro-Quebec) (adopted 11 November 1975).

Kluane First Nation Final Agreement (Kluane First Nation–Government of Canada–Government of the Yukon) (adopted 18 October 2003) (KFNA).

Kwanlin Dun First Nation Final Agreement (Kwanlin Dun First Nation–Government of Canada–Government of the Yukon) (adopted 19 February 2005).

Labrador Inuit Land Claims Agreement (Inuit of Labrador–Government of Newfoundland and Labrador–Government of Canada) (adopted 22 January 2005) (LILCA).

Little Salmon/Carmacks First Nation Final Agreement (Little Salmon/Carmacks First Nation–Government of Canada–Government of the Yukon) (adopted 21 July 1997).

Nang K'uula / Nang K'úulaas Recognition Agreement (Canada, Haida Nation, and British Columbia, 2023).

National Agreement for Development and Peace in La Araucanía (signed 24 November 2017).

New Zealand-Australia Indigenous Collaboration Arrangement (signed February 2020).

Nisga'a of British Columbia Final Agreement (Nisga'a Nation–Government of Canada–Government of British Columbia) (adopted 27 April 1999, entered into force 11 May 2000).

North American Free Trade Agreement (NAFTA) (signed 17 December 1992, entered into force 1 January 1994) 32 ILM 289.

Paris Agreement (adopted 12 December 2015, entered into force 4 November 2016) UN Doc FCCC/CP/2015/L.9/Rev.1, 55 ILM 743.

Stockholm Declaration (Declaration of the UN Conference on the Human Environment, 16 June 1972) UN Doc A/CONF.48/14/Rev.1.

The Carcross/Tagish First Nation Final Agreement (Khà Shâde Héni of the Carcross/Tagish First Nation–Government of Canada– Government of the Yukon) (adopted 22 October 2005).

The Hague Agreement Concerning the International Registration of Industrial Designs, Geneva Act (adopted 2 July 1999, entered into force 23 December 2003) WIPO TRT/HAGUE/006 (1999 Geneva Act).

The Umbrella Final Agreement (Council for Yukon Indians–Government of Canada–Government of the Yukon) (adopted 29 May 1993).

Treaty of Amity, Commerce, and Navigation (His Britannic Majesty–United States of America) (adopted 24 June 1795, entered into force 29 February 1796) (Jay Treaty).

Treaty of Fort Laramie (United States-Sioux, Cheyenne, Arapaho, et al, signed 17 September 1851) 11 Stat 749.

Treaty of Ghent (His Britannic Majesty–United States of America) (adopted 16 February 1815, entered into force 17 February 1815).

Treaty of New Echota (United States-Cherokee Nation, signed 29 December 1835, ratified 23 May 1836) 7 Stat 478.

Treaty of Waitangi (United Kingdom-Māori, signed 6 February 1840).

Treaty with the Yakama Nation (United States-Yakama Nation, signed 9 June 1855) 12 Stat 951.

Tsawwassen First Nation Final Agreement (Tsawwassen First Nation–Government of Canada–Government of British Columbia) (adopted 6 December 2007).

UN Biodiversity Conference (COP15), Kunming-Montreal Global Biodiversity Framework (adopted 19 December 2022) CBD/COP/DEC/15/4.

UN General Assembly Res 70/1, 'Transforming Our World: The 2030 Agenda for Sustainable Development' (21 October 2015) UN Doc A/RES/70/1 (SDGs).

UNESCO, Convention for the Safeguarding of the Intangible Cultural Heritage (adopted 17 October 2003, entered into force 20 April 2006) 2368 UNTS 3.

UNGA, Transforming Our World: The 2030 Agenda for Sustainable Development, Res 70/1 (2015) A/RES/70/1.

United Nations Agreement on Straddling and Highly Migratory Fish Stocks (UN Fish Stocks Agreement or UNSFA) (adopted 4 August 1995, entered into force 11 December 2001) 2167 UNTS 3.

United Nations Convention on the Law of the Sea (UNCLOS) (adopted 10 December 1982, entered into force 16 November 1994) 1833 UNTS 3.

United Nations Convention to Combat Desertification (adopted 17 June 1994, entered into force 26 December 1996) 1954 UNTS 3.

United Nations Fish Stocks Agreement (adopted 4 August 1995, entered into force 11 December 2001) 2167 UNTS 3.

United Nations Framework Convention on Climate Change (adopted 9 May 1992, entered into force 21 March 1994) 1771 UNTS 107.

United Nations Human Rights Office of the High Commissioner, 'Report of the Special Rapporteur on Extreme Poverty and Human Rights: Climate Change and Poverty' (17 July 2019) UN Doc A/HRC/41/39 (17 July 2019).

United Nations Res 61/295, 'United Nations Declaration on the Rights of Indigenous Peoples' (2007) UN Doc A/RES/61/295 (UNDRIP).

United Nations, UN Treaty Collection, 'Nagoya Protocol on Access to Genetic Resources and the Fair and Equitable Sharing of Benefits Arising from their Utilization to the Convention on Biological Diversity' (29 October 2010) UNEP/CBD/COP/DEC/X/1.

WIPO Treaty on Intellectual Property, Genetic Resources and Associated Traditional Knowledge (adopted May 2024, not yet in force).

World Intellectual Property Organization (WIPO) Performances and Phonograms Treaty (adopted 20 December 1996, entered into force 20 May 2002).

Table of Recommended Resources

(in alphabetical order)

Aird, K and G Fox, *Indigenous Living Heritage in Canada* (Canadian Commission for UNESCO's IdeaLab with the First Peoples' Cultural Council 2020).

Aitken, Janice, 'The Trust Doctrine in Federal Indian Law' (1997) 18 Northern Illinois University Law Review 115.

Aktürk, Gül and Martha Lerski, 'Intangible Cultural Heritage: A Benefit to Climate-Displaced and Host Communities' (2021) 11 Journal of Environmental Studies and Sciences 305.

Ali, M Emran and Toshiyuki Tsuchia, 'Changes in Land Use Practices of Indigenous People in the Chittagong Hill Tracts of Bangladesh' (2003) 9(1) Journal of Forest Planning 47–58.

Anaya, James, 'Indigenous Peoples' Participatory Rights in Relation to Natural Resource Extraction' (2005) 22 Arizona Journal of International and Comparative Law 7.

Statement upon Conclusion of the Visit to Canada by the United Nations Special Rapporteur on the Rights of Indigenous Peoples, James Anaya (United Nations Human Rights Office of the High Commissioner 2013).

Anderson, Robert, Sarah Krakoff and Bethany Berger, *American Indian Law: Cases and Commentary* (4th edn, West Academic Publishing 2020).

Archibald, DW, R McIver and R Rangeley, 'The Implementation Gap in Canadian Fishery Policy: Fisheries Rebuilding and Sustainability at Risk' (2021) 129 Marine Policy.

Arnaquq-Baril, Alethea, 'Angry Inuk' (National Film Board, 2016) <www.nfb.ca/film/angry_inuk/>.

Arsenault, Rachel, 'Water Insecurity in Ontario First Nations: An Exploratory Study on Past Interventions and the Need for Indigenous Water Governance' (2021) 13(5) Water 717.

Baird, W David and Danney Goble, *The Story of Oklahoma* (2nd edn, University of Oklahoma Press 2013).

Barelli, Mauro, 'The Role of Soft Law in the International Legal System' (2009) 58 International and Comparative Law Quarterly 958.

Baugh, Daniel, *The Global Seven Years War 1754–1763* (Routledge 2014).
Bell, Catherine and Robert Patterson (eds), *Protection of First Nations' Cultural Heritage: Laws, Policy and Reform* (University of British Columbia Press 2009).
Blomley, Nicholas, *Law, Space and the Geographies of Power* (Guilford Press 1994).
'Property and the Landscapes of Gentrification' in *Unsettling the City* (Routledge 2004).
Boldt, Meno, *Surviving as Indians: The Challenge of Self-Government* (University of Toronto Press 1993).
Borrows, John, *Braiding Legal Orders* (McGill-Queen's University Press 2023).
Canada's Indigenous Constitution (University of Toronto Press 2010).
Borrows, John and others, 'Braiding Legal Orders: Implementing the United Nations Declaration on the Rights of Indigenous Peoples' (Centre for International Governance Innovation, 2019) 70.
Boutilier, Sasha, 'Free, Prior, and Informed Consent and Reconciliation in Canada: Proposals to Implement Articles 19 and 32 of the UN Declaration on the Rights of Indigenous Peoples' (2017) 7 The University of Western Ontario Journal of Legal Studies.
Brascoupé, Simon and Karin Endemann, 'Intellectual Property and Aboriginal People: A Working Paper' (Minister of Indian Affairs and Northern Development, 1999) No R32–204/19991E <http://publications.gc.ca/collections/Collection/R32–204-1999E.pdf>.
Brugnach, Marcela, Marc Craps and Art Dewulf, 'Including Indigenous Peoples in Climate Change Mitigation: Addressing Issues of Scale, Knowledge and Power' (2014) 140(1) Climatic Change 19.
Calder, Ryan S and others, 'Future Impacts of Hydroelectric Power Development on Methylmercury Exposures of Canadian Indigenous Communities' (2016) 50(23) Environmental Science & Technology.
Cameron, L and others, 'The Turtle Lodge: Sustainable Self-Determination in Practice' (2019) 15(1) AlterNative: An International Journal of Indigenous Peoples 13.
Canby, William C, *American Indian Law in a Nutshell* (6th edn, West Academic Publishing 2015).
Casebeer, Kenneth M, 'Subaltern Voices in the Trail of Tears' (2014) 4 University of Miami Race & Social Justice Law Review 1.
Castellano, Marlene Brant, 'Ethics of Aboriginal Research' (2004) 1(1) Journal of Aboriginal Health 104.
Chang, David A, 'Enclosures of Land and Sovereignty' (2011) 109 Radical History Review 108.
Chircop, Aldo, Timo Koivurova and Krittika Singh, 'Is There a Relationship between UNDRIP and UNCLOS?' (2019) 33 Ocean Yearbook 1.
Cohen, Felix S, *Handbook of Federal Indian Law* (US Govt Printing Office 1945).
Committee on the Role of International Law in Sustainable Natural Resources Management for Development International Law Association, 'The Role of International Law in Sustainable Natural Resources Management for Development' in *International Law Association Final Report of the 79th Biennial Conference* (International Law Association 2020) <www.ila-hq.org/images/ILA/docs/kyoto/Draft%20Resolution%204%20&%...>.

Cordonier Segger, Marie-Claire, *Athena's Treaties: Crafting Trade and Investment Accords for Sustainable Development* (Oxford University Press 2021).

'Exploring the Role of International Law in Sustainable Natural Resources Management for Development' (Lauterpacht Centre for International Law, 2021) 6 <www.lcil.cam.ac.uk/blog/exploring-role-international-law-sustainable-natural-resources-management-development-prof>.

Cordonier Segger, Marie-Claire and J Caceres Bustamante, 'Sustainable Development and Climate Change Mitigation in International Trade and Investment Law' (2023) 15(1) Trade, Law and Development 1.

Cordonier Segger, Marie-Claire, I Espa and N Schrijver (eds), *Sustainable Development in International Law on Natural Resources* (Wolters Kluwer 2025).

Cordonier Segger, Marie-Claire and W Garnons-Williams, *UN Declaration on the Rights of Indigenous Peoples, ILO Convention 169 and Sustainable Development through Indigenous Treaties* (Cambridge University Press 2025).

Cordonier Segger, Marie-Claire, W Garnons-Williams and E Wu, 'Indigenous Treaties with Canada: Obstacles or Opportunities to Realizing the SDGs' (2022) 3(1) McGill InterGentes Journal on International Law & Legal Pluralism 1013.

Cordonier Segger, Marie-Claire and Markus Gehring (eds), *Sustainable Development in World Investment Law* (Kluwer Law International 2010).

Cordonier Segger, Marie-Claire, Markus Gehring and M Tokas, 'Trade and Sustainability in EU-Americas Trade Relations' (2023) 50(3) Legal Issues of Economic Integration 227 1.

Cordonier Segger, Marie-Claire and Alexandra Harrington, 'Environment and Sustainable Development' in Simon Chesterman, David M Malone and Santiago Villalpando (eds), *The Oxford Handbook of United Nations Treaties* (Oxford University Press 2019).

Cordonier Segger, Marie-Claire, Alexandra Harrington and C Voigt (eds), *Courage, Contributions & Compliance: The Routledge Handbook of Climate Law and Governance* (Routledge 2024) 1.

Cordonier Segger, Marie-Claire and Sébastien Jodoin (eds), *Sustainable Development, International Criminal Justice, and Treaty Implementation* (Cambridge University Press 2013).

Cordonier Segger, Marie-Claire and Ashfaq Khalfan, *Sustainable Development Law: Principles, Practice and Prospects* (Oxford University Press 2004).

Cordonier Segger, Marie-Claire and Nico J Schrijver, 'ILA Guidelines for Sustainable Natural Resources Management for Development' (2021) 68 Netherlands International Law Review 317.

Cordonier Segger, Marie-Claire and S Stephenson (eds), *Research Handbook on Investment Law and Sustainable Development* (Edward Elgar 2024).

Cordonier Segger, Marie-Claire and Marcel Szabo (eds), *Intergenerational Justice in Sustainable Development Treaty Implementation* (Cambridge University Press 2020).

Cordonier Segger, Marie-Claire, Marcel Szabo and Alexandra Harrington, *Implementing International Law through Domestic Institutions for Inter-Generational Justice* (Cambridge University Press 2020).

Cordonier Segger, Marie-Claire with HE CJ Weeramantry (eds), *Sustainable Development in International Courts and Tribunals* (Routledge 2017).

Cordonier Segger, Marie-Claire and L Young, 'Contributions or Complications: CETA, Climate Change and Sustainability in Canada' (2023) 50(3) Legal Issues of Economic Integration 323.

Cornell, Stephen and Joseph Kalt, 'Two Approaches to Economic Development on American Indian Reservations: One Works, the Other Doesn't' in Miriam Jorgensen (ed), *Rebuilding Native Nations: Strategies for Governance and Development* (University of Arizona Press 2006).

Cornell, Steven, 'What Makes First Nations Enterprises Successful? Lessons from the Harvard Project' (Harvard Project on American Indian Economic Development, Native Nations Institute for Leadership, Management, and Policy, 2006) JOPNA No 2006-01.

Correia, Joel, 'Indigenous Rights at a Crossroads' (2018) 97 Geoforum 73.

De Vries-Stotijn, Anne, Ilon Van Ham and Kees Bastmeijer, 'Protection through Property: From Private to River Held Rights' (2019) 44 Water International 736.

Delaney, David, *The Spatial, the Legal and the Pragmatics of World-Making: Nomospheric Investigations* (Routledge 2010).

Diaz-Sarachaga, Jose Manuel, Daniel Jato-Espino and Daniel Castro-Fresno, 'Is the Sustainable Development Goals (SDG) Index an Adequate Framework to Measure the Progress of the 2030 Agenda?' (2018) 26(6) Sustainable Development 663.

Dudding, Adam, 'New Zealand's Long-Lost Taiwanese Cuzzies' (Stuff News, March 2015).

Dutfield, Graham, 'TRIPS-Related Aspects of Traditional Knowledge' (2001) 33(2) Case Western Reserve 240.

Dyck, The Honourable Lillian Dyck, 'Border Crossing Issues and the Jay Treaty Report' (Standing Committee on Aboriginal Peoples, Senate of Canada, 2016) <https://sencanada.ca/content/sen/committee/421/APPA/Reports/APPA-JayTreatyReport_e.pdf>.

Egan, Brian and Jessica Place, 'Minding the Gaps' (2013) 44 Geoforum 129.

Escudero, César Nava, 'Indigenous Environmental Rights in Mexico: Was the 2001 Constitutional Reform Facilitated by International Law?' (2011) 4(2) Mexican Law Review.

Evans, Denise, 'Superimposed Nations: The Jay Treaty and Aboriginal Rights' (1995) 4 Dalhousie Journal of Legal Studies.

Feehan, James P and Melvin Baker, 'The Origins of a Coming Crisis: Renewal of the Churchill Falls Contract' (2007) 30(1) Dalhousie Law Journal 209.

Ferris, Elizabeth and Jane McAdam, 'Planned Relocations in the Context of Climate Change: Unpacking the Legal and Conceptual Issues' (2015) 4 Cambridge Journal of International and Comparative Law 137.

Flowers, Bill, 'Inadequate Consultation on the Muskrat Falls Project' (Institut de recherche en politiques publiques, 13 December 2016) <https://policyoptions.irpp.org/fr/magazines/decembre-2016/inadequate-consultation-on-the-muskrat-falls-project/>.

Ford, James and others, 'Adaptation and Indigenous Peoples in the United Nations Framework Convention on Climate Change' (2016) 139(3–4) Climatic Change 429.

Fraser-Kruck, Heidi, *Canada's Failure to Support the United Nations Declaration on the Rights of Indigenous Peoples: An Intersectional Analysis of the Repercussions as*

Seen through the Inter-woven Lenses of Women's Rights, Environmental Rights, and Poverty Alleviation (University of Ottawa 2009).
Frideres, James S, *Native People in Canada: Contemporary Conflicts (Prentice-Hall Canada Inc., 1983)* 14; *Royal Commission on Aboriginal Peoples, 'Volume 1 – Looking Forward Looking Back'* (1996).
Fumoleau, René and Arctic Institute of North America, *As Long as This Land Shall Last: A History of Treaty 8 and Treaty 11, 1870–1939* (University of Calgary Press 2004).
Gadamus, Lily and others, 'Building an Indigenous Evidence-Base for Tribally-Led Habitat Conservation Policies' (2015) 62 Marine Policy 116.
Garnett, Stephen T and others, 'A Spatial Overview of the Global Importance of Indigenous Lands for Conservation' (2018) 1(7) Nature Sustainability 369–374.
Getches, David and others, *Cases and Materials on Federal Indian Law* (7th edn, West Academic Publishing 2017).
Gilbert, Jérémie and Corinne Lennox, 'Towards New Development Paradigms: The United Nations Declaration on the Rights of Indigenous Peoples as a Tool to Support Self-determined Development' (2019) 23(1–2) The International Journal of Human Rights.
Global Affairs Canada, *Canada's Implementation of the 2030 Agenda for Sustainable Development – Voluntary National Review* (Government of Canada 2018).
Grinlinton, David and Prue Taylor (eds), *Property Rights and Sustainability: The Evolution of Property Rights to Meet Ecological Challenges* (Brill 2011).
Hansen, John G and Rose Antsanen, 'What Can Traditional Indigenous Knowledge Teach Us About Changing Our Approach to Human Activity and Environmental Stewardship in Order to Reduce the Severity of Climate Change?' (2018) 9(3) International Indigenous Policy Journal.
Hardin, Garrett, 'The Tragedy of the Commons' (1968) 162 Science.
Harm, Melinda, 'Mining Sacred Space' (2012) 44 Environment and Planning 1443.
Harvard Project on American Indian Economic Development, 'Determinants of Development Success in the Native Nations of the United States' (Harvard University, University of Arizona, 2008).
Higgins, Noelle, 'Changing Climate; Changing Life – Climate Change and Indigenous Intangible Cultural Heritage" (2022) 11(3) Laws 47.
HM Treasury, 'The Economics of Biodiversity: The Dasgupta Review – Abridged Version' (2021) London: HM Treasury.
Hohmann, Jessie and Marc Weller (eds), *The UN Declaration on the Rights of Indigenous Peoples: A Commentary* (Oxford University Press 2018).
Hosonuma, Noriko and others, 'An Assessment of Deforestation and Forest Degradation Drivers in Developing Countries' (2012) 7(4) Environmental Research Letters.
Inclán, María, *The Zapatista Movement and Mexico's Democratic Transition* (Oxford University Press 2018).
'Inclusive Trade Action Group, Work Program 2020–2022' (Government of New Zealand, 2020) <www.mfat.govt.nz/assets/Trade-General/Trade-policy/ITAG-Inclusive-Trade-Action-Group/ITAG-work-programme-2020-2022.pdf>.

'Indigenous Peoples and the Nature They Protect' (UN Environment Programme, 2020) <www.unep.org/news-and-stories/story/indigenous-peoples-and-nature-they-protect>.

International Law Association, 'The Role of International Law in Sustainable Natural Resources Management for Development' (2020) Kyoto Conference Resolution No 4/2020.

International Renewable Energy Agency (IRENA), 'World Energy Transitions Outlook: 1.5°C Pathway' (2022).

Iorns Magallanes, Catherine J, 'Nature as an Ancestor: Two Examples of Legal Personality for Nature in New Zealand' (2020) 10(16) VUWLRP 1.

Jai, Julie, 'Bargains Made in Bad Times' in John Borrows and Michael Coyle (eds), *The Right Relationship: Reimagining the Implementation of Historical Treaties* (University of Toronto Press 2017).

Janda, Richard, 'Why Does Form Matter – The Hybrid Governance Structure of Makivik Corporation' (2006) 30(3) Vermont Law Review 788.

Jones, Alison and Kuni Kaa Jenkins, *He Korero: Words between Us – First Māori-Pākehā Conversations on Paper* (Huia Publishers 2011).

Jorgensen, Miriam and Jonathon Taylor, 'What Determines Indian Economic Success? Evidence from Tribal and Individual Indian Enterprises' (Harvard Project on American Indian Economic Development, 2000) PRS 00-3 4-5.

Jung, Courtney, 'The Politics of Indigenous Identity: Neoliberalism, Cultural Rights, and the Mexican Zapatistas' (2003) 70(2) Social Research 433–461.

Kedar, Alexandre, Ahmad Amara and Oren Yiftachel (eds), *Emptied Lands: A Legal Geography of Bedouin Rights in the Negev* (Stanford University Press 2018).

Kelly Jr, James J, 'Article 27 and Mexican Land Reform: The Legacy of Zapata's Dream' (1993) 25 Columbia Human Rights Law Review 541.

Kelly-Scott, Karen and Kristina Smith, 'Aboriginal Peoples Fact Sheet for Canada' (Statistics Canada, 2015).

Kemp, René and Pim Martens, 'Sustainable Development: How to Manage Something That Is Subjective and Never Can Be Achieved?' (2007) 3(2) Sustainability: Science, Practice and Policy 5.

Kintner, Earl W and Jack L Lahr, *An Intellectual Property Law Primer: A Survey of the Law of Patents, Trade Secrets, Trademarks, Franchises, Copyrights, and Personality and Entertainment Rights* (C. Boardman Company 1982).

Kuruk, Paul, 'Protecting Folklore under Modern Intellectual Property Regimes: A Reappraisal of the Tensions between Individual and Communal Rights in Africa and the United States' (1999) 48(4) American University Law Review.

Laughlin, Jacob, 'Foreign-Trade Zones in Indian County: Is a Foreign-Trade Zone Right for Your Tribe?' (2017) 42(1) American Indian Law Review.

LeBlanc, The Honourable Richard D, 'Muskrat Falls: A Misguided Project – Volume 1: Executive Summary, Key Findings and Recommendations' (Commission of Inquiry Respecting the Muskrat Falls Project, Queen's Printer for Newfoundland and Labrador, 2020) <www.gov.nl.ca/iet/files/Volume-1-Executive-Summary-Key-Findings-and-Recommendations.pdf>.

Leopold, Aldo, *A Sand County Almanac with Essays on Conservation from Round River* (Oxford University Press 1966).

Lofts, Katherine and others, 'Feature – Brief on Sustainable Development Goal 13 on Taking Action on Climate Change and Its Impacts: Contributions of International Law, Policy and Governance' (2017) 13(1) JSDLP 183.
Loukacheva, Natalia, 'Indigenous Inuit Law, "Western" Law and Northern Issues' (2012) 3(2) Arctic Review on Law and Politics 200.
Macdonald, David and Daniel Wilson, *Shameful Neglect: Indigenous Child Poverty in Canada* (Canadian Centre for Policy Alternatives 2016) 24.
MacInnes, Angus and others, 'FPIC: Rectifying Mining Impacts' (2017) 15 Perspectives in Ecology and Conservation 152.
Maigua, Yolanda Terán and Cathy Gutierrez-Gomez, 'Responding to Cultural Loss: Providing an Integral Indigenous Perspective of a "Kichwa Child"' (2015) 92(1) Childhood Education.
Martinez Cobo, José R, 'Study of the Problem of Discrimination against Indigenous Populations' (30 July 1981) UN Doc E/CN.4/Sub.2/476.
Mason, Fred, 'The Newfoundland Cod Stock Collapse: A Review and Analysis of Social Factors' (2002) 1(17) UCLA Electronic Green Journal.
Mattias, Åhrén, 'The Provisions on Lands, Territories and Natural Resources in the UN Declaration' in Claire Charters and Rodolfo Stavenhagen (eds), *Making the Declaration Work* (IWGIA 2009) 212.
McGuire, Michaela M, 'We Can Do Our Own Thing Here on Haida Gwaii' (2023) 14(3) The International Indigenous Policy Journal 1–25.
Meier, Benjamin Mason and Lawrence O Gostin (eds), *Human Rights in Global Health: Rights-Based Governance for a Globalizing World* (Oxford University Press 2018).
Meuleman, Louis and Ingeborg Niestroy, 'Common But Differentiated Governance: A Metagovernance Approach to Make the SDGs Work' (2015) 7(9) Sustainability 12295.
Mia'iingan, Wapshkaa (Aaron Mills), 'Aki, Anishinaabek, kaye tahsh Crown' (2010) 9(1) Indigenous Law Journal 120–123.
Millennium Ecosystem Assessment, *Ecosystems and Human Well-being* (Millennium Ecosystem Assessment 2005).
Miller, George Tyler and Scott Spoolman, *Living in the Environment* (19th edn, Brooks/Cole Cengage Learning 2018).
Miller, Jim, *Compact, Contract, Covenant: Aboriginal Treaty-Making in Canada* (University of Toronto Press 2009).
Mitchell, Terry, 'UNDRIP and the 2009 Bolivian Constitution: Lessons for Canada' (Centre for International Governance Innovation, 2014).
Morin, Jean-Frédéric and Mathilde Gauquelin, 'Trade Agreements as Vectors for the Nagoya Protocol's Implementation, CIGI Papers No.115' (CIGI, 2016) <www.cigionline.org/sites/default/files/documents/Paper%20no.115.pdf>.
Moyse, Pierre-Emmanuel, 'Report of the Workshop on Indigenous Traditional Knowledge, Traditional Cultural Expressions, and Intellectual Property – ISED/CIPP Practical Workshop on Indigenous Knowledge and Cultural Expressions and Intellectual Property' (Centre for Intellectual Property Policy, 2020).
Munzer, Stephen R and Kal Raustiala, 'The Uneasy Case for Intellectual Property Rights in Traditional Knowledge' (2009) 27 Cardozo Arts and Entertainment Law Journal 37–97.

National Inquiry into Missing and Murdered Indigenous Women and Girls, 'Calls for Justice' (3 June 2019).
Nowlin, Christopher, 'Indigenous Capitalism and Resource Development in an Age of Climate Change: A Timely Dance with the Devil?' (2020) 17(1) JSDLP 71.
O'Sullivan, Dominic, *Sharing the Sovereign: Indigenous Peoples, Recognition, Treaties and the State* (Palgrave Macmillan 2021).
Olsen, Sylvia, *Working with Wool: A Coast Salish Legacy and the Cowichan Sweater* (Sono Nis Press 2010) 8.
Oosten, Jarich, Frederic Laugrand and Willem Rasing, *Inuit Laws – Tirigusuusiit, Piqujait, and Maligait* (2nd edn, Nunavut Arctic College 2017).
Otis, Delos Sacket, *The Dawes Act and the Allotment of Indian Lands* (University of Oklahoma Press 1973).
Otis, Ghislain, 'Constitutional Recognition of Aboriginal and Treaty Rights: A New Framework for Managing Legal Pluralism in Canada?' (2014) 46(3) The Journal of Legal Pluralism and Unofficial Law 320.
Panday, Pranab Kumar and Ishtiaq Jamil, 'Conflict in the Chittagong Hill Tracts of Bangladesh' (2009) 49(6) Asian Survey 1052–1070.
Pearson, Jasmine, Guy Jackson and Karen E McNamara, 'Climate-Driven Losses to Indigenous and Local Knowledge and Cultural Heritage' (2021) 1 The Anthropocene Review 1.
Penney, Jessica and Patricia Johnson-Castle, 'Not So Grand Plans: The Continued Erasure of Indigenous Rights in Newfoundland and Labrador's Hydroelectric "Development"' (Yellowhead Institute, 2021) <https://yellowheadinstitute.org/2021/06/10/not-so-grand-plans-hydro/>.
Philippopoulos-Mihalopoulos, Andreas, 'Law's Spatial Turn' (2010) 6 Law, Culture and Humanities 10.
Posey, Darrell A and Graham Dutfield, *Beyond Intellectual Property: Toward Traditional Resource Rights for Indigenous Peoples and Local Communities* (International Development Research Centre 1996).
Prott, Lyndel V and Patrick J O'Keefe, '"Cultural Heritage" or "Cultural Property"' (1992) 1(2) International Journal of Cultural Property 310.
Prucha, Paul Francis, *The Great Father: The US Government and American Indians* (University of Nebraska Press 1988).
Purvin, Diane M, 'Weaving a Tangled Safety Net: The Intergenerational Legacy of Domestic Violence and Poverty' (2003) 9 Violence against Women.
Ramos-Castillo, Ameyali, Edwin J Castellanos and Kirsty Galloway McLean, 'Indigenous Peoples, Local Communities and Climate Change Mitigation' (2017) 140(1) Climatic Change 1.
Reo, Nicholas J and others, 'Invasive Species, Indigenous Stewards, and Vulnerability Discourse' (2017) 41(3) American Indian Quarterly.
'Report 2 – Sustaining Canada's Major Fish Stocks – Fisheries and Oceans Canada' in *2016 Fall Reports of the Commissioner of the Environment and Sustainable Development* (Office of the Auditor General of Canada, 2016).
Robertson, Lindsay, *Conquest by Law: How the Discovery of America Dispossessed Indigenous Peoples of Their Lands* (Oxford University Press 2007).
Robertson, Sean, 'Natives Making Space' (2015) 61 Geoforum 138.

Roy, Raja Devasish and Simon William M'Viboudoulou, 'Study on Best Practices and Examples in Respect of Resolving Land Disputes and Land Claims' (2014) UN Doc E/C.19/2014/4.

Royal Commission on Aboriginal Peoples, 'Volume 2 – Restructuring the Relationship' (1996) 454.

Royster, Judith, Michael Blumm and Elizabeth Kronk, *Native American Natural Resources Law* (3rd edn, Carolina Academic Press 2002).

Sanders, Katherine, '"Beyond Human Ownership"? Property, Power, and Legal Personality for Nature in Aotearoa New Zealand' (2018) 30 Journal of Environmental Law 207.

Scharlemann, Jörn PW and others, 'Towards Understanding Interactions between Sustainable Development Goals: The Role of Environment–Human Linkages' (2020) 15(6) Sustainability Science 1573–1584.

Scholtz, Christa and Maryna Polataiko, 'Transgressing the Division of Powers: The Case of the James Bay and Northern Quebec Agreement' (2019) 34(3) Canadian Journal of Law and Society 393.

Schrijver, Nico, 'Advancements in the Principles of International Law on Sustainable Development' in Marie-Claire Cordonier Segger and Christopher Weeramantry (eds), *Sustainable Development Principles in the Decisions of International Courts and Tribunals* 1992–2012 (Routledge 2017).

Schutling, Gerard, 'ILO Convention 169: Can It Help?' (1997) 10 Abya Yala News 4, 10.

Seck, Sara L, 'Business, Human Rights, & the Triple Planetary Crisis: Confronting Overconsumption', Paper prepared for UConn Business & Human Rights Workshop (10 March 2022).

Seeland, Klaus, *Nature Is Culture: Indigenous Knowledge and Social-Cultural Aspects of Trees and Forests in Non-European Cultures* (Studies in Indigenous Knowledge 1997).

Sethi, S Prakash and others, 'Freeport-McMoRan Copper & Gold, Inc.: An Innovative Voluntary Code of Conduct to Protect Human Rights, Create Employment Opportunities, and Economic Development of the Indigenous People' (2011) 103(1) Journal of Business Ethics.

Shahabuddin, Mohammad, 'The Myth of Colonial "Protection" of Indigenous Peoples: The Case of the Chittagong Hill Tracts under British Rule' (2018) 25 (2) International Journal on Minority and Group Rights 210–235.

Short, Damien, Corinne Lennox, Julian Burger and Jessie Hohmann (eds), *The United Nations Declaration on the Rights of Indigenous Peoples: A Contemporary Evaluation* (Routledge 2021).

Simeone, Tonina, 'Indigenous Traditional Knowledge and Intellectual Property Rights' (Library of Parliament of Canada, 2004) No PRB 03-38E 5.

Simkin, Jodi, *Creating a New Reality: Repatriation, Reconciliation and Moving Forward* (Canadian Commission for UNESCO's IdeaLab 2020).

Stahler-Sholk, Richard, 'The Zapatista Social Movement: Innovation and Sustainability' (2010) 35(3) Alternatives 269–290.

Stinson, James and Elizabeth Lunstrom, *Biocultural Nation Making: Biopolitics, Cultural-Territorial Belonging, and National Protected Areas* (Sage 2021).

Stopp, Marianne P, 'The Coast Salish Knitters and the Cowichan Sweater – An Event of National Historic Significance' (2012) 76 Material Culture Review.

Swepston, Lee, 'A New Step in the International Law on Indigenous and Tribal Peoples' (1990) 15 Oklahoma City University Law Review 677.

Takeda, Louise, *Islands' Spirit Rising: Reclaiming the Forests of Haida Gwaii* (UBC Press 2015).

'TFN Development Corporation of the Tsawwassen First Nation' (TFN Economic Development Corporation, 2023) <https://tfnedc.com/>.

Thornton, Thomas F and Claudia Comberti, 'Synergies and Trade-offs between Adaptation, Mitigation and Development' (2013) 140(1) Climatic Change 5.

Tiefenbrun, Susan, 'U.S. Foreign Trade Zones of the United States, Free Trade Zones of the World, and Their Impact on the Economy' (2013) 12(2) Journal of International Business and Law.

Tribal Economic Development Principles-at-Glance Series, 'Native American Foreign Trade Zones' (U.S. Department of the Interior, 2020).

Truth and Reconciliation Commission of Canada, 'Honouring the Truth, Reconciling for the Future – Summary of the Final Report of the Truth and Reconciliation Commission of Canada' (2015).

Tsosie, Rebecca, 'Climate Change and Indigenous Peoples: Comparative Models of Sovereignty' (2013) 26 Tulane Environmental Law Journal 239.

Tully, James, 'Sustainable Democratic Constitutionalism and Climate Crisis' (2020) 65 McGill Law Journal 545.

Turner, Nancy J, *The Earth's Blanket: Traditional Teachings for Sustainable Living* (University of Washington Press 2005).

UN, 'International Workshop of Free, Prior and Informed Consent and Indigenous Peoples' (17–19 January 2005) PFII/2005/WS.2/4.

United Nations Sustainable Development, 'United Nations Conference on Environment and Development Rio de Janeiro, Brazil – Agenda 21' (3–14 June 1992).

Unterhalter, Elaine and Amy North, *Education, Poverty and Global Goals for Gender Equality: How People Make Policy Happen* (Routledge 2018).

Vié, Jean-Christophe, Craig Hilton-Taylor and Simon N Stuart (eds), *Wildlife in a Changing World – An Analysis of the 2008 IUCN Red List of Threatened Species* (IUCN Red List of Threatened Species 2008).

Visbeck, Martin and others, 'A Sustainable Development Goal for the Ocean and Coasts: Global Ocean Challenges Benefit from Regional Initiatives Supporting Globally Coordinated Solutions' (2014) 49 Marine Policy 88.

von Benda-Beckmann, Franz and others (eds), *Spatializing Law: An Anthropological Geography of Law in Society* (Routledge 2009).

von Schorlemer, Sabine, Sylvia Maus and Felix Schmermer (eds), *UNESCO World Heritage and the SDGs – Interdisciplinary Perspectives* (UNESCO-Lehrstuhl 2020).

Waldron, Ingrid, *Environmental Racism in Canada* (Canadian Commission for UNESCO's IdeaLab, 2020).

Walz, Yvonne and others, 'Disaster-Related Losses of Ecosystems and Their Services. Why and How Do Losses Matter for Disaster Risk Reduction?' (2021) 63 International Journal of Disaster Risk Reduction 7.

Ward, Tara, 'The Right to Free, Prior, and Informed Consent: Indigenous Peoples' Participation Rights within International Law' (2011) 10 Northwestern Journal of Human Rights 54.

WIPO, 'Background Brief No. 3, Developing a National Strategy on Intellectual Property, Traditional Knowledge and Traditional Cultural Expression' (WIPO, 2016) <www.wipo.int/edocs/pubdocs/en/wipo_pub_tk_3.pdf>.

'Intellectual Property Needs and Expectations of Traditional Knowledge Holders: Report on Fact-finding Missions on Intellectual Property and Traditional Knowledge 1998–1999' (WIPO, 2001).

Wood, Mary Christina, 'Indian Land and the Promise of Native Sovereignty' (1994) 4 Utah Law Review 1471.

'World Leaders, Corporations at COP26, Take Major Step to Restore and Protect Forests' (United Nations, 2021) <https://news.un.org/en/story/2021/11/1104642>.

Wuijts, Susanne and others, 'An Ecological Perspective on a River's Rights: A Recipe for More Effective Water Quality Governance?' (2019) 44 Water International 647.

Yap, Mandy and Krushil Watene, 'SDGs and Indigenous Peoples' (2019) 20 Journal of Human Development and Capabilities 451.

Young, Frankie, 'A Trojan Horse: Can Indian Self-Government Be Promoted through the Indian Act?' (2019) 97(3) Canadian Bar Review 699.

For EU product safety concerns, contact us at Calle de José Abascal, 56–1°,
28003 Madrid, Spain or eugpsr@cambridge.org.

www.ingramcontent.com/pod-product-compliance
Lightning Source LLC
LaVergne TN
LVHW011528200926
848484LV00001B/194

* 9 7 8 1 1 0 8 4 2 8 9 6 5 *